MARIHUANA
The First
Twelve Thousand Years

Ernest L. Abel

PLENUM PRESS · NEW YORK AND LONDON

Library of Congress Cataloging in Publication Data

Abel, Ernest L   1943-
Marihuana, the first twelve thousand years.

Bibliography: p.
Includes index.
1. Marihuana—History. 2. Marihuana. I. Title.
[DNLM: 1. Cannabis. 2. Drug abuse—History.
QV77.7 Al39m]
BF209.C3A23   615'.7827   80-15606
ISBN 0-306-40496-6

© 1980 Plenum Press, New York
A Division of Plenum Publishing Corporation
227 West 17th Street, New York, N.Y. 10011

To the Buckley clan:
BOB, GLAD, BARB, JOYCE,
MAUREEN, VIC, PHIL,
SUE, JASON,
and
BECKY

Contents

Introduction

Of all the plants men have ever grown, none has been praised and denounced as often as marihuana (*Cannabis sativa*). Throughout the ages, marihuana has been extolled as one of man's greatest benefactors— and cursed as one of his greatest scourges. Marihuana is undoubtedly a herb that has been many things to many people. Armies and navies have used it to make war, men and women to make love. Hunters and fishermen have snared the most ferocious creatures, from the tiger to the shark, in its herculean weave. Fashion designers have dressed the most elegant women in its supple knit. Hangmen have snapped the necks of thieves and murderers with its fiber. Obstetricians have eased the pain of childbirth with its leaves. Farmers have crushed its seeds and used the oil within to light their lamps. Mourners have thrown its seeds into blazing fires and have had their sorrow transformed into blissful ecstasy by the fumes that filled the air.

Marihuana has been known by many names: hemp, hashish, dagga, bhang, loco weed, grass—the list is endless. Formally christened *Cannabis sativa* in 1753 by Carl Linnaeus, marihuana is one of nature's hardiest specimens. It needs little care to thrive. One need not talk to it, sing to it, or play soothing tranquil Brahms lullabies to coax it to grow. It is as vigorous as a weed. It is ubiquitous. It flourishes under nearly every possible climatic condition.

It sprouts from the earth not meekly, not cautiously in suspense of where it is and what it may find, but defiantly, arrogantly, confident that whatever the conditions it has the stamina to survive.

It is not a magnanimous herb. Plants unfortunate enough to fall in the shade of its serrated leaflets will find that marihuana does not share its sunlight. It wants it all. Marihuana also does not like to share its territory. It encroaches on its neighbors. Its roots gobble up all the nutrients in the soil, and like a vampire it sucks the life blood from the earth.

Marihuana is a very rapidly growing plant, attaining a usual height of three to twenty feet at maturity. Five hundred years ago, the French author Rabelais wrote that it was "sown at the first coming of the swallows and pulled out of the ground when the cicadies began to get hoarse."

Marihuana is dioecious, which means that there are sexually distinct male and female plants. At one time, farmers believed that only the females produced the intoxicating hashish resin. Now it is known that both sexes produce this gummy secretion. The male, however, manufactures less resin and produces flowers earlier than the female. To prevent a pollinating marriage, cannabis growers destroy these males as soon as they are detected. Had he known of this age-old custom, Freud might have written an insightful treatise on the symbolism of this bit of agricultural castration.

The intoxicating resin is secreted by glandular hairs located around the flowers and to a certain extent in the lower portions of the plant. The actual substance in the resin responsible for the plant's inebriating effects is a chemical called delta-9-tetrahydrocannabinol (Δ^9-THC). In very hot climates, as in India and North Africa, so much resin is produced that the plant appears to be covered with a sticky dew even as it bakes under the parching rays of the hot sun. This resin serves as a protective shield preventing loss of water from the plant to the dry air. And of course, the more resin, the more Δ^9-THC likely to be present.

Cannabis seeds are brownish and rather hard. When pressed, they yield a yellowish-green oil once used to make soap, lamp oil, paint, and varnish. Bird fanciers claim that hemp seed stimulates birds to develop superior plumage. While the seeds contain far less Δ^9-THC than the leaves or flowers, the chemical is still present. Although there are no reports of any birds flying into trees or houses after feasting on a meal of cannabis seeds, it was by burning these seeds and inhaling the fumes given off that some ancient societies first experienced cannabis's intoxicating powers.

The stem of the plant is square and hollow and covered with strong fibers. The first step in removing these fibers is called retting and involves soaking the stems so that partial decomposition occurs. This disengages the nonfibrous tissue. The stem is then bent so that the fibers can separate. Once separated, they can be stripped away and spun into thread or twisted into cordage and rope.

Cannabis will grow under most conditions that will support life. It is inherently indestructible. Long after other species of plants have disappeared because of drought, infestation, or climatic changes, cannabis will still exist. Cannabis is one of nature's best examples of survival of the fittest.

Depending on the conditions under which it grows, cannabis will either produce more resin or more fiber. When raised in hot, dry climates, resin is produced in great quantities and fiber quality is poor. In countries with mild, humid weather, less resin is produced and the fiber is stronger and more durable.

It is because of these climate-related characteristics that most Europeans knew very little of the intoxicating properties of the cannabis plant until the nineteenth century when hashish was imported from India and the Arab countries. Prior to this time, cannabis was merely a valuable source of fiber and seed oil to most Europeans, nothing more.

In India, Persia, and the Arab countries, the main value of the plant resided in its inebriating resin. People in these countries were also among the first to use cannabis fiber to make nets and ropes. But the sticky covering on the plant was what they valued most, especially where alcohol was proscribed by religious doctrine.

Depending on his personal interests, the cannabis farmer could increase his yield of fiber or resin by various measures. To produce a plant with a better fiber, he grew his plants very close to one another. This reduced the amount of sunlight falling on individual plants and promoted the growth of long stems and fibers. To obtain more resin, he sowed his seeds farther apart. This gave each plant more sunlight and forced the plant to secrete more resin in order to keep itself from drying out. But regardless of whether he was after the fiber or the resin, male plants were always destroyed before they could court the females, since the production of seeds by the female invariably reduced the quality of fiber and resin.

Cannabis was harvested by various methods. If the fiber were primarily of interest, the stems would be cut fairly close to the ground with a specially designed sickle with the blade set at right angles to the handle.

Harvesting the resin was a different matter. People who grew cannabis for personal pleasure simply snipped some leaves whenever the desire moved them. In countries such as Nepal where cannabis became part of the agricultural economy, the resin was gathered more systematically but in a less sanitary fashion: after the female plants were ripe with their sticky coverings, workers were hired to run naked through the cannabis fields. As they brushed against the plants, a certain amount of resin would adhere to their bodies. At the end of each run they would scrape the sticky resin from their bodies and start again. Since cannabis resin and water do not mix very well, the perspiration from their sweating bodies did not find its way into these scrapings. (The same cannot be said for whatever else was on their bodies.) After the harvesting was through, the scrapings were shaped into bricks and readied for market. Buyers were rarely finicky about anything other than how pleasureable was the intoxication they felt when they consumed their purchases.

I

THE EARLY YEARS

1

Cannabis in the Ancient World

Millions of years ago, humanoid creatures descended from the trees in Africa. These first men stood erect, their eyes peering into the beyond, their hands grasping rudimentary weapons and tools, ready to bend nature to their will.

The descendants of these first men wandered into almost every corner of the earth and evolved into four main racial groups: the Negroids, Australoids, Mongoloids, and Caucasoids. Each race, living under different climatic conditions and in virtual isolation from one another, developed special physical characteristics to enable them to survive in their particular part of the world. Along with these physical traits there emerged rudimentary cultures as distinct as the colors of their skins. Some communities relied primarily on hunting for survival, refining their skills and weapons through the ages to capture prey and eventually to conquer and enslave rival communities. Others subsequently discovered that the seeds and leaves of certain plants would appease hunger and sustain life. Once they became farmers, men gave up their spears and knives for plowshares and permanent settlements came into being.

The earliest civilizations sprouted along the banks of great rivers —the Hwang-Ho in China, the Indus in India, the Tigris and Euphrates in Mesopotamia (where biblical scholars have sought in vain for traces of the Garden of Eden), and the Nile in Egypt. The soil along these riverbanks was particularly suited for agriculture, being rich and deep and invigorated annually by new deposits of fertile silt.

Whether they remained hunters or became farmers, the people who lived long before the written word was invented, discovered through trial and error the best materials for shaping, molding, bending, twisting, and sharpening objects into tools. In each civilization these discoveries were much the same; the only differences were the materials at hand.

On the basis of artifacts and the history of China in its later years, archaeologists now assure us that hemp has been a familiar agricultural crop in China from the remote beginnings of settlement in that part of the world down to our own time. When the Chinese went about testing materials in their environment for suitability as tools, they most certainly would have looked into the possibility of using hemp whenever they required some kind of fiber.

Cannabis in China

The earliest record of man's use of cannabis comes from the island of Taiwan located off the cost of mainland China. In this densely populated part of the world, archaeologists have unearthed an ancient village site dating back over 10,000 years to the Stone Age.

Scattered among the trash and debris from this prehistoric community were some broken pieces of pottery the sides of which had been decorated by pressing strips of cord into the wet clay before it hardened. Also dispersed among the pottery fragments were some elongated rod-shaped tools, very similar in appearance to those later used to loosen cannabis fibers from their stems.[1] These simple pots, with their patterns of twisted fiber embedded in their sides, suggest that men have been using the marihuana plant in some manner since the dawn of history.

The discovery that twisted strands of fiber were much stronger than individual strands was followed by developments in the arts of spinning and weaving fibers into fabric—innovations that ended man's reliance on animal skins for clothing. Here, too, it was hemp fiber that the Chinese chose for their first homespun garments. So important a place did hemp fiber occupy in ancient Chinese culture that the *Book of Rites* (second century B.C.) ordained that out of respect for the dead, mourners should wear clothes made from hemp fabric, a custom followed down to modern times.[2]

While traces of early Chinese fabrics have all but disappeared, in 1972 an ancient burial site dating back to the Chou dynasty (1122–249 B.C.) was discovered. In it were fragments of cloth, some bronze containers, weapons, and pieces of jade. Inspection of the cloth showed it to

---

[1]K. Chang, *The Archeology of Ancient China* (New Haven: Yale University Press, 1968), pp. 111–12; C. T. Kung, *Archeology in China* (Toronto: University of Toronto Press, 1959), 1: 131.

[2]H. Li, "The Origin and Use of Cannabis in Eastern Asia: Their Linguistic Cultural Implications," in *Cannabis and Culture,* ed. V. Rubin (The Hague: Mouton, 1975), p. 54.

be made of hemp, making this the oldest preserved specimen of hemp in existence.[3]

The ancient Chinese not only wove their clothes from hemp, they also used the sturdy fiber to manufacture shoes. In fact, hemp was so highly regarded by the Chinese that they called their country the "land of mulberry and hemp."

The mulberry plant was venerated because it was the food upon which silkworms fed, and silk was one of China's most important products. But silk was very expensive and only the very wealthy could afford silken fabric. For the vast millions of less fortunate, cheaper material had to be found. Such material was typically hemp.

Ancient Chinese manuscripts are filled with passages urging the people to plant hemp so that they will have clothes.[4] A book of ancient poetry mentions the spinning of hempen threads by a young girl.[5] The *Shu King*, a book which dates back to about 2350 B.C., says that in the province of Shantung the soil was "whitish and rich . . . with silk, hemp, lead, pine trees and strange stones . . ." and that hemp was among the articles of tribute extorted from inhabitants of the valley of the Honan.[6]

During the ninth century B.C., "female man-barbarians," an Amazon-like dynasty of female warriors from Indochina, offered the Chinese emperor a "luminous sunset-clouds brocade" fashioned from hemp, as tribute. According to the court transcriber, it was "shining and radiant, infecting men with its sweet smelling aroma. With this, and the intermingling of the five colors in it, it was more ravishingly beautiful than the brocades of our central states."[7]

Ma, the Chinese word for hemp, is composed of two symbols which are meant to depict hemp:

The part beneath and to the right of the straight lines represent hemp fibers dangling from a rack. The horizontal and vertical lines represent the home in which they were drying.

[3]H. Li, "An Archeological and Historical Account of Cannabis in China," *Economic Botany* 28 (1974); 437–48.

[4]M. D. Merlin, *Man and Marihuana* (Rutherford, N.J.: Fairleigh Dickenson University Press, 1968), p. 80.

[5]Merlin, *Man and Marihuana*, p. 81.

[6]*Ibid.*

[7]Quoted in E. H. Schafer, *The Golden Peaches of Samarkand* (Berkeley: University of California Press, 1963), p. 195.

As they became more familiar with the plant, the Chinese discovered that it was dioecious. Male plants were then clearly distinguished from females by name (*hsi* for the male, *chu* for the female). The Chinese also recognized that the male plants produced a better fiber than the female, whereas the female produced the better seeds.[8] (Although hemp seed was a major grain crop in ancient China until the sixth century A.D.,[9] it was not as important a food grain as rice or millet.[10])

Hemp fiber was also once a factor in the wars waged by Chinese land barons. Initially, Chinese archers fashioned their bowstrings from bamboo fibers. When hemp's greater strength and durability were discovered, bamboo strings were replaced with those made from hemp. Equipped with these superior bowstrings, archers could send their arrows farther and with greater force. Enemy archers, whose weapons were made from inferior bamboo, were at a considerable disadvantage. With ineffectual archers, armies were vulnerable to attack at distances from which they could not effectively return the hail of deadly missiles that rained upon them. So important was the hemp bowstring that Chinese monarchs of old set aside large portions of land exclusively for hemp, the first agricultural war crop.[11]

In fact, every canton in ancient China grew hemp. Typically, each canton tried to be self-sufficient and grow everything it needed to supply its own needs. When it couldn't raise something itself, it grew crops or manufactured materials that it could trade for essential goods. Accordingly, crops were planted around homes not only because of the suitability of the land, but also because of their commercial value. The closer to the home, the greater a crop's value.

Because food was essential, millet and rice were grown wherever land and water were available. Next came the vegetable gardens and orchards, and beyond them the textile plants, chiefly hemp.[12] Next came the cereals and vegetables.

After the hemp was harvested by the men, the women, who were the weavers, manufactured clothes from the fibers for the family. After the family's needs were satisfied, other garments were produced for sale. To support their families, weaving began in autumn and lasted all winter.[13]

[8]Li, "Origin and Use," p. 54.
[9]*Ibid.*, p. 56.
[10]K. C. Chang, *Food in Chinese Culture* (New Haven: Yale University Press, 1977), pp. 72–3.
[11]W. Eberland, *The Local Cultures of South and East China* (Leiden: E. J. Brill, 1968), p. 102.
[12]M. Granet, *Chinese Civilization* (London: Kegan Paul, Trench, Trubner and Co., 1930), p. 143.
[13]*Ibid.*, p. 145.

The Invention of Paper

Among the many important inventions credited to the Chinese, paper must surely rank at the very top. Without paper, the progress of civilization would have advanced at a snail's pace. Mass production of newspapers, magazines, books, notepaper, etc, would all be impossible. Business and industry would come to a standstill without paper to record transactions, keep track of inventories, and make payments of large sums of money. Nearly every activity we now take for granted would be a monumental undertaking were it not for paper.

According to Chinese legend, the paper-making process was invented by a minor court official, Ts'ai Lun, in A.D. 105. Prior to that time, the Chinese carved their writings onto bamboo slips and wooden tablets. Before the invention of paper, Chinese scholars had to be physically fit if they wished to devote their lives to learning. When philosopher Me Ti moved around the country, for example, he took a minimum of three cartloads of books with him. Emperor Ts'in Shih Huagn, a particularly conscientious ruler, waded through 120 pounds of state documents a day in looking after his administrative duties![14] Without some less weighty writing medium, Chinese scholars and statesmen could look forward to at least one hernia if they were any good at their jobs.

As a first alternative to these cumbersome tablets, the Chinese painted their words on silk fabric with brushes. But silk was very expensive. A thousand silkworms working day in and day out were needed to produce the silk for a simple "thank you" note.

Ts'ai Lun had a better idea. Why not make a tablet out of fiber? But how? Producing writing tablets the way clothes were manufactured, by patiently intermingling individual fibers was not practical. There had to be some other way to get fibers to mix with one another in a lattice structure that would be sturdy enough not to fall apart.

No one knows how Ts'ai Lun finally discovered the secret of manufacturing paper from fiber. Perhaps it was a case of trial and error. However, the method he finally devised involved crushing hemp fibers and mulberry tree bark into a pulp and placing the mixture in a tank of water. Eventually, the fibers rose to the top all tangled together. Portions of this flotsam were then removed and placed in a mold. When dried in such molds, the fibers formed into sheets which could then be written on.

When Ts'ai Lun first presented his invention to China's arm-weary

---

[14]T. F. Carter, *The Invention of Paper in China* (New Haven: Yale University Press, 1968), p. 3.

bureaucrats, he thought they would react to it with great enthusiasm. Instead, he was jeered out of court. Since no one at court was willing to recognize the importance of paper, Ts'ai Lun decided that the only way to convince people of its value was through trickery. He would use paper, he told all who would listen, to bring back the dead!

With the help of some friends, Ts'ai Lun feigned death and had himself buried alive in a coffin. Unknown to most of those who witnessed the interment, the coffin contained a small hold; through it, a hollow bamboo shoot had been inserted, to provide the trickster an air supply.

While his family and friends mourned his death, Ts'ai Lun patiently rested in his coffin below the earth. Then, some time later, his conspirators announced that if some of the paper invented by the dead man were burned, he would rise from the dead and once again take his place among the living. Although highly skeptical, the mourners wished to give the departed every chance, so they set a sizable quantity of paper ablaze. When the conspirators felt that they had generated enough suspense, they exhumed the coffin and ripped off the cover. To the shock and amazement of all present, Ts'ai Lun sat up and thanked them for their devotion to him and their faith in his invention.

The resurrection was regarded as a miracle, the power of which was attributed to the magic of paper. So great an impression did the Houdini-like escape create that shortly thereafter the Chinese adopted the custom, which they still follow to this day, of burning paper over the graves of the dead.

Ts'ai Lun himself became an overnight celebrity. His invention was accorded the recognition it deserved and the inventor was appointed to an important position at court. But his fame was his undoing. As the new darling at court, rival factions sought to win him over to their side in the never-ending squabbles of life among the rich and powerful. Without meaning to, Ts'ai Lun became embroiled in a power battle between the empress and the emperor's grandmother. Court intrigue was simply too much for the inventor, and when he was subsequently summoned to give an account of himself, instead of appearing before his inquisitors, his biographer states that he went home, took a bath, combed his hair, put on his best robes, and drank poison."[15]

Although entertaining, the story of Ts'ai Lun's invention is apocryphal. The discovery of fragments of paper containing hemp fiber in a grave in China dating back to the first century B.C., puts the invention long before the time of Ts'ai Lun. Why Ts'ai Lun was given credit for the invention, however, is still a mystery.

The Chinese kept the secret of paper hidden for many centuries, but

[15]*Ibid.*

eventually it became known to the Japanese. In a small book entitled *A Handy Guide to Papermaking*, dating back to the fifth century A.D., the author states that "hemp and mulberry . . . have long been used in worshipping the gods. The business of paper making therefore, is no ignoble calling."[16]

It was not until the ninth century A.D. that the Arabs, and through them the rest of the world, learned how to manufacture paper. The events that led to the disclosure of the paper-making process are somewhat uncertain, but apparently the secret was pried from some Chinese prisoners captured by the Arabs during the Battle of Samarkand (in present-day Russia).

Once the Arabs learned the secret, they began producing their own paper. By the twelfth century A.D., paper mills were operating in the Moorish cities of Valencia, Toledo, and Xativa, in Spain. After the ouster of the Arabs from Spain, the art became known to the rest of Europe, and it was not long before paper mills were flourishing not only in Spain, but in France, Italy, Germany, and England, all of them using the ancient Chinese system "invented" by Ts'ai Lun.

MAGICAL MARIHUANA

During the course of its long history in China, hemp found its way into almost every nook and cranny of Chinese life. It clothed the Chinese from their heads to their feet, it gave them material to write on, and it became a symbol of power over evil.

Like the practice of medicine around the world, early Chinese doctoring was based on the concept of demons. If a person were ill, it was because some demon had invaded his body. The only way to cure him was to drive the demon out. The early priest-doctors resorted to all kinds of tricks, some of which were rather sophisticated, like drug therapy, which we will examine shortly. Other methods involved outright magic. By means of charms, amulets, spells, incantations, exhortations, sacrifices, etc., the priest-doctor did his utmost to find some way of getting the upper hand over the malevolent demon believed responsible for an illness.

Among the weapons to come out of the magical kit bag of the ancient Chinese conjurers were cannabis stalks into which snake-like figures were carved. Armed with these war hammers, they went to do battle with the unseen enemy on his home ground—the sickbed. Standing over the body of the stricken patient, his cannabis stalk poised to

---

[16]K. Chohoki, *A Handy Guide to Papermaking* (Berkeley: University of California Press, 1948), p. 2.

strike, the priest pounded the bed and commanded the demon to be gone. If the illness were psychosomatic and the patient had faith in the conjurer, he occasionally recovered. If his problem were organic, he rarely improved.

Whatever the outcome, the rite itself is intriguing. Although there is no way of knowing for sure how it came about, the Chinese tell a story about one of their emperors named Liu Chi-nu that may explain the connection between cannabis, snakes, and illness. One day Liu was out in the fields cutting down some hemp, when he saw a snake. Taking no chances that it might bite him, he shot the serpent with an arrow. The next day he returned to the place and heard the sound of a mortar and pestle. Tracking down the noise, he found two boys grinding marihuana leaves. When he asked them what they were doing, the boys told him they were preparing a medicine to give to their master who had been wounded by an arrow shot by Liu Chi-nu. Liu Chi-nu then asked what the boys would do to Liu Chi-nu if they ever found him. Surprisingly, the boys answered that they could not take revenge on him because Liu Chi-nu was destined to become the emperor of China. Liu berated the boys for their foolishness and they ran away, leaving behind the medicine. Some time later Liu himself was injured and he applied the crushed marihuana leaves to his wound. The medicine healed him and Liu subsequently announced his discovery to the people of China and they began using it for their injuries.

Another story tells of a farmer who saw a snake carrying some marihuana leaves to place on the wound of another snake. The next day the wounded snake was healed. Intrigued, the farmer tested the plant on his own wound and was cured.[17]

Whether these stories had anything to do with the idea that marihuana had magical power or not, the fact is that despite the progress of Chinese medicine far beyond the age of superstition, the practice of striking beds with stalks made from marihuana stems continued to be followed until the Middle Ages.[18]

MEDICINAL MARIHUANA

Although the Chinese continued to rely on magic in the fight against disease, they also gradually developed an appreciation and knowledge of the curative powers of medicines. The person who is generally credited with teaching the Chinese about medicines and their

[17]K. C. Wong, and W. Lien-Teh, *History of Chinese Medicine* (Shanghai: National Quarantine Service, 1936), p. 4.

[18]J. Doolittle, *Social Life of the Chinese* (New York: Harper and Bros., 1865), 1: 309.

actions is a legendary emperor, Shen-Nung, who lived around the twenty-eighth century B.C.

Concerned that his subjects were suffering from illness despite the magical rites of the priests, Shen-Nung determined to find an alternate means of relieving the sick. Since he was also an expert farmer and had a thorough familiarity with plants, he decided to explore the curative powers of China's plant life first. In this search for compounds that might help his people, Shen-Nung used himself as a guinea-pig. The emperor could not have chosen a better subject since he was said to possess the remarkable ability of being able to see through his abdominal wall into his stomach! Such transparency enabled him to observe at firsthand the workings of a particular drug on that part of the body.

According to the stories told about him, Shen-Nung ingested as many as seventy different poisons in a single day and discovered the antidotes for each of them. After he finished these experiments, he wrote the Pen Ts'ao, a kind of herbal or Materia Medica as it later became known, which listed hundreds of drugs derived from vegetable, animal, and mineral sources.

Although there may originally have been an ancient Pen Ts'ao attributed to the emperor, no original text exists. The oldest Pen Ts'ao dates back to the first century A.D. and was compiled by an unknown author who claimed that he had incorporated the original herbal into his own compendium. Regardless of whether such an earlier compendium did or did not exist, the important fact about this first-century herbal is that it contains a reference to ma, the Chinese word for cannabis.

Ma was a very peculiar drug, the text notes, since it possessed both yin and yang. The concepts of yin and yang that pervade early Chinese medicine are attributed to another legendary emperor, Fu Hsi (ca, 2900 B.C.) whom the Chinese credit with bringing civilization to the "land of mulberry and hemp." Before Fu Hsi, so the legends say, the Chinese lived like animals. They had no laws, no customs, and no traditions. There was no family life. Men and women came together instinctively, like salmon seeking their breeding ground; they mated, and then went off on their separate ways.

The first thing Fu Hsi did to produce order out of chaos was to establish matrimony on a permanent basis. The second thing was to separate all living things into the male and female principle—the male incorporating all that was positive, the female embodying all that was negative. From this dualistic principle arose the concept of two opposing forces, the yin and the yang.

Yin symbolized the weak, passive, and negative feminine influence in nature, whereas yang represented the strong, active, and positive masculine force. When these forces were in balance, the body was healthy. When one force dominated the other, the body was in an unhealthy condition. Marihuana was thus a very difficult drug to contend with because it contained both the feminine *yin* and the masculine *yang*. Shen-Nung's solution to the problem was to advise that *yin*, the female plant, be the only sex cultivated in China since it produced much more of the medicinal principle than *yang*, the male plant. Marihuana containing *yin* was then to be given in cases involving a loss of *yin* from the body such as occurred in female weakness (menstrual fatigue), gout, rheumatism, malaria, beri-beri, constipation, and absentmindedness.

The *Pen Ts'ao* eventually became the standard manual on drugs in China, and so highly regarded was its author that Shen-Nung was accorded the singular honor of deification and the title of Father of Chinese Medicine. Not too long ago China's drug guilds still paid homage to the memory of Shen-Nung. On the first and fifteenth of each month, many drugstores offered a 10 percent discount on medicines in honor of the legendary patron of the healing arts.

PAINLESS SURGERY

As physicians became more and more familiar with the properties of drugs, *ma* continued to increase in importance as a therapeutic agent. In the second century A.D., a new use was found for the drug. This discovery was credited to the famous Chinese surgeon Hua T'o, who is said to have performed extremely complicated surgical procedures without causing pain. Among the amazing operations he performed are organ grafts, resectioning of intestines, laparotomies (incisions into the loin), and thoracotomies (incisions into the chest). All of these difficult surgical procedures were said to have been rendered painless by means of *ma-yo*, an anesthetic made from cannabis resin and wine. The following passage, taken from his biography, describes his use of cannabis in these operations:

> But if the malady resided in the parts on which the needle [acupuncture], cautery, or medicinal liquids were incapable of acting, for example, in the bones, in the stomach or in the intestine, he administered a preparation of hemp [*ma-yo*] and, in the course of several minutes, an insensibility developed as if one had been plunged into drunkenness or deprived of life. Then, according to the case, he performed the opening, the incision or the amputation and relieved the cause of the malady; then he apposed the tissues by sutures and applied linaments. After a certain number of days the patient finds he has recovered without having experienced the slightest pain during the operation.[19]

---

[19]Quoted in M. S. Julien, "Chirurgie Chinoise—Substance anesthétique employée en Chine, dans le commencement du IIIᵉ siecle de notre ere, pour paralyser momentanement la sensibilite," *Comptes Rendus de l'Académie de Sciences*, 28 (1894); 195–8.

Although modern research has borne out marihuana's anesthetic properties and has shown that alcohol does indeed augment many of marihuana's actions, it is unlikely that Hua T'o could have produced total insensibility to pain by the combination of these drugs unless he administered so much of them that his patients lost consciousness.

While *ma*'s stature as a medicinal agent began to decline around the fifth century A.D., it still had its advocates long into the Middle Ages. In the tenth century A.D., for example, some Chinese physicians claimed that the drug was useful in the treatment of "waste diseases and injuries," adding that it "clears blood and cools temperature, it relieves fluxes; it undoes rheumatism; it discharges pus."[20]

AN EARLY PSYCHEDELIC

Since the Chinese are the first people on record to use the marihuana plant for their clothes, their writing materials, their confrontation with evil spirits, and in their treatment of pain and disease, it is not surprising that they are also the first people on record to experience marihuana's peculiar psychoactive effects.

As so many other testimonials to marihuana's multifaceted past have been found interred deep within the bowels of the earth, so too was the proof of China's early flirtation with marihuana's intoxicating chemistry found buried away in an ancient tomb. Rather than any piece of cloth or handful of seeds, however, the evidence takes the form of an inscription containing the symbol for marihuana, along with the adjective or connotation meaning "negative."[21]

Unfortunately, we will never know what the gravediggers had in mind when they were chiseling these words in granite. Was it just a mindless piece of graffiti? Even if it were, it indicates that the Chinese were well aware of marihuana's unusual properties from very ancient times, whether they approved of them or not.

Many did not approve. Due to the growing spirit of Taoism which began to permeate China around 600 B.C., marihuana intoxication was viewed with special disdain. Taoism was essentially a "back to nature" philosophy which sought ways of extending life. Anything that contained *yin*, such as marihuana, was therefore regarded with contempt since it enfeebled the body when eaten. Only substances filled with *yang*, the invigorating principle in nature, were looked upon favorably.

Some Chinese denounced marihuana as the "liberator of sin."[22] A

---

[20]Li, "Origin and Use," p. 56.
[21]Li, "Archeological and Historical Account," p. 441.
[22]N. Taylor, *Narcotics: Nature's Dangerour Gifts* (New York: 1966), p. 20. All references to this quotation, as far as I can determine, are derived from Taylor's *Narcotics*, which cites no original source for it.

late edition of the *Pen Ts'ao* asserted that if too many marihuana seeds were eaten, they would cause one to "see demons." But if taken over a long time, "one can communicate with the spirits."[23]

However, by the first century A.D., Taoists became interested in magic and alchemy,[24] and were recommending addition of cannabis seeds to their incense burners. The hallucinations thus produced were highly valued as a means to achieving immortality.[25]

For some people, seeing spirits was the main reason for using cannabis. Meng Shen, a seventh-century physician, adds, however, that if anyone wanted to see spirits in this way, he would have to eat cannabis seeds for at least a hundred days.[26]

The Chinese have always been a highly reserved people, a nation rarely given to excesses. Temperance and restraint are cherished virtues of their society. But these are ideal traits, not always easy to live up to. And on more than on occasion, the waywardness of segments of the Chinese population was denounced by the authorities.

In a book attributed to Shen-Nung's successor, the "yellow emperor," for example, the author felt that alcoholism had truly gotten out of hand:

> Nowadays people use wine as a beverage and they adopt recklessness as usual behavior. They enter the chamber of love in an intoxicated condition; their passions exhaust their vital forces; their cravings dissipate their essence; they do not know how to find contentment with themselves; they are not skilled in the control of their spirits. They devote all their attention to the amusement of their minds, thus cutting themselves off from the joys of long life. Their rising and retiring is without regularity. For these reasons they reach only one half of the hundred years and then they degenerate.[27]

Alcohol, in fact, was a much more serious problem in China than marihuana, and opium overshadowed both in the attention it later received. The Chinese experiment with marihuana as a psychoactive agent was really more of a flirtation than an orgy. Those among the Chinese who hailed it as the "giver of delight" never amounted to more than a small segment of the population.

[23]Li, "Origin and Use," p. 56.
[24]J. A. MacCulloch (ed.), *The Mythology of All Races* (Boston: Marshall Jones Co., 1928), 8: 13.
[25]J. Needham, *Science and Civilization in China* (Cambridge: Cambridge University Press, 1974), 5 (pt. 2): 150.
[26]H. Li, "Hallucinogenic Plants in Chinese Herbals," *Journal of Psychedlic Drugs* 10 (1978): 17–26
[17]I. Veith, ed., *The Yellow Emperor's Classic on Internal Medicine* (Baltimore: Williams and Wilkins, 1949), pp. 97–8.

Japan

As in China, hemp fiber was highly regarded among the Japanese and figured prominently in their everyday lives and legends.

Hemp (*asa*) was the primary material in Japanese clothes, bedding, mats, and nets. Clothes made of hemp fiber were especially worn during formal and religious ceremonies because of hemp's traditional association with purity in Japan.[28] So fundamental was hemp in Japanese life that it was often mentioned in legends explaining the origins of everyday things, such as how the Japanese earthworm came to have white rings around its neck.

According to Japanese legend, there were once two women who were both weavers of hemp fiber. One woman made fine hemp fabric but was a very slow worker. Her neighbor was just the opposite—she made coarse fabric but worked quickly. During market days, which were held only periodically, it was customary for Japanese women to dress in their best clothes, and as the day approached, the two women began to weave new dresses for the occasion. The woman who worked quickly had her dress ready on time, but it was not very fashionable. Her neighbor, who worked slowly, only managed to get the unbleached white strands ready, and when market day came, she didn't have her dress ready. Since she had to go to market, she persuaded her husband to carry her in a large jar on his back so that only her neck, with the white undyed hemp strands around it would be visible. In this way, everyone would think she was clothed instead of being naked inside the jar. On the way to the market, the woman in the jar saw her neighbor and started making fun of her coarse dress. The neighbor shot back that at least she was clothed. "Break the jar", she told everyone who could hear, "and you will find a naked woman." The husband became so mortified that he dropped the jar, which broke, revealing his naked wife, clothed only in hemp strands around her neck. The woman was so ashamed as she stood naked before everyone that she buried herself in the earth so she would not be seen and she turned into an earthworm. And that, according to the Japanese, is why the earthworm has white rings around its neck.[29]

Hemp fiber also played a part in love and marital life in Japan. Another ancient Japanese legend tells of a soldier who had been romancing a young girl and was about to bid her farewell without giving her so much as his name, rank, or regiment. But the girl was not about to be jilted by this handsome and charming paramour. Unbeknownst to her

[28]M. Joya, *Things Japanese* (Tokyo: Tokyo News Service, 1963), pp. 23–4.
[29]*Ibid.*, pp. 196–7.

mysterious lover, she fastened the end of a huge ball of hemp rope to his clothing as he kissed her farewell. By following the thread, she eventually came to the temple of the god Miva, and discovered that her suitor had been none other than the god himself.[30]

Besides its role in such legends, hemp strands were an integral part of Japanese love and marriage. Hemp strands were often hung on trees as charms to bind lovers[31] (as in the legend), gifts of hemp were sent as wedding gifts by the man's family to the prospective bride's family as a sign that they were accepting the girl,[32] and hemp strands were prominently displayed during wedding ceremonies to symbolize the traditional obedience of Japanese wives to their husbands.[33] The basis of the latter tradition was the ease with which hemp could be dyed. Just as hemp could be dyed to any color, so too, according to an ancient Japanese saying, must wives be willing to be "dyed in any color their husbands may choose."[34]

Yet another use of hemp in Japan was in ceremonial purification rites for driving away evil spirts. As already mentioned, in China evil spirits were banished from the bodies of the sick by banging rods made from hemp against the head of the sickbed. In Japan, Shinto priests performed a similar rite with a *gohei*, a short stick with undyed hemp fibers (for purity) attached to one end. According to Shinto beliefs, evil and impurity cannot exist alongside one another, and so by waving the *gohei* (purity) above someone's head the evil spirit inside him would be driven away.[35]

INDIA: THE FIRST MARIHUANA-ORIENTED CULTURE

India has known little peace. Invaded from both land and sea, it has seen many conquerors and has witnessed many empires come and go. Cyrus and Darius of Persia sent their armies there. On the heels of the Persians came Alexander the Great. After Alexander came more Greeks, then Parthians from Iran, Kushans from beyond the mountains in the north, then Arabs, followed by the Europeans. Unlike China, which remained remote and isolated from the rest of the world for much of its history, India was known to all the great nations of the ancient world.

Although the inhabitants of India are descended from a people known as the Aryans or "noble ones," the Aryans were not the original natives of the Indian subcontinent but instead invaded it from north of

[30]G. Schafer, "Hemp," *CIBA Review* 49 (1945): 1780.
[31]MacCulloch, *Mythology*, 8:380, note 7.
[32]Joya, *Things Japanese*, p. 361.
[33]*Ibid.*, p 24.
[34]*Ibid.*
[35]*Ibid.*

the Himalayas around 2000 B.C. Before the Aryans, who were light-skinned and blue-eyed, a dark-skinned and dark-eyed people, Australoid in origin, inhabited India. When the Aryans entered the country, they found a complex civilization, including well-designed housing, adjoining toilet facilities, and advanced drainage systems. The early inhabitants worked with gold and silver, and they also knew how to fashion tools and ornaments from copper and iron.

When the Aryans first settled in India they were predominantly a nomadic people. During the centuries that followed their invasion, they intermarried with the original inhabitants, became farmers, and invented Sanskrit, one of man's earliest written languages.

A collection of four holy books, called the *Vedas*, tells of their daring exploits, their chariot battles, conquests, subjugation of enemy armies, eventual settlement in the land of the Indus, and even how their god Siva brought the marihuana plant down from the Himalayas for their use and enjoyment.

According to one of their legends, Siva became enraged over some family squabble and went off by himself in the fields. There, the cool shade of a tall marihuana plant brought him a comforting refuge from the torrid rays of the blazing sun. Curious about this plant that sheltered him from the heat of the day, he ate some of its leaves and felt so refreshed that he adopted it as his favorite food, hence his title, the Lord of Bhang.

Bhang does not always refer to the plant itself but rather to a mild liquid refreshment made with its leaves, and somewhat similar in potency to the marihuana used in America.

Among the ingredients and proportions of them that went into a formula for bhang around the turn of the century were:

Cannabis	220 grains
Poppy seed	120 grains
Pepper	120 grains
Ginger	40 grains
Caraway seed	10 grains
Cloves	10 grains
Cardamom	10 grains
Cinnamon	10 grains
Cucumber seed	120 grains
Almonds	120 grains
Nutmeg	10 grains
Rosebuds	60 grains
Sugar	4 ounces
Milk	20 ounces

Boiled together[36]

---

[36]M. V. Ball, "The Effects of Haschisch Not Due to Cannabis Indica," *Therapeutic Gazette*, 34 (1910): 777–80.

Two other concoctions made from cannabis in India are ganja and charas. Ganja is prepared from the flowers and upper leaves and is more potent than bhang. Charas, the most potent of the three preparations, is made from the flowers in the height of their bloom. Charas contains a relatively large amount of resin and is roughly similar in strength to hashish.

Bhang was and still is to India what alcohol is to the West. Many social and religious gatherings in ancient times, as well as present, were simply incomplete unless bhang was part of the occasion. It is said that those who speak derisively of bhang are doomed to suffer the torments of hell as long as the sun shines in the heavens.

Without bhang at special festivities like a wedding, evil spirits were believed to hover over the bride and groom, waiting for an opportune moment to wreak havoc on the newlyweds. Any father who failed to send or bring bhang to the ceremonies would be reviled and cursed as if he had deliberately invoked the evil eye on his son and daughter.

Bhang was also a symbol of hospitality. A host would offer a cup of bhang to a guest as casually as we would offer someone in our home a glass of beer. A host who failed to make such a gesture was despised as being miserly and misanthropic.

War as another occasion in which bhang and more potent preparations like ganja were often resorted to. Indian folksongs dating back to the twelfth century A.D. mention ganja as a drink of warriors. Just as soldiers sometimes take a swig of whiskey before going into battle in modern warfare, during the Middle Ages in India, warriors routinely drank a small amount of bhang or ganja to assuage any feelings of panic, a custom that earned bhang the cognomen of *vijaya*, "victorious" or "unconquerable."[37]

A story is told of a guru named Gobind Singh, the founder of the Sikh religion, which alludes to bhang's usage in battle. During a critical skirmish in which he was leading his troops, Gobind Singh's soldiers were suddenly thrown into a panic at the sight of an elephant bearing down on them with a sword in its trunk. As the beast slashed its way through Gobind Singh's lines, his men appeared on the verge of breaking rank. Something had to be done to prevent a disastrous rout. A volunteer was needed, a man willing to risk certain death to accomplish the impossible task of slaying the elephant. There was no shortage of men to step forward. Gobind Singh did not take time to pick and choose. To the man closest to him he gave some bhang and a little opium, and then watched as the man went out to kill the elephant.

[37]I. C. Chopra and R. N. Chopra, "The Present Position of Hemp Drug Addiction in India," *Indian Medical Research Memoirs* 31 (1929): 2.

Fortified by the drug, the loyal soldier rushed headlong into the thick of battle and charged the sword-wielding elephant. Deftly evading the slashing blows that could easily have severed his body in two, he managed to slip under the elephant and with all his strength he plunged his own weapon into the unprotected belly of the beast. When Gobind Singh's men saw the elephant lying dead in the field, they rallied and soon overpowered the enemy. From that time forth, the Sikhs commemorated the anniversary of that great battle by drinking bhang.

"To the Hindu the Hemp Plant Is Holy"

The earliest allusion to bhang's mind-altering influence is contained in the fourth book of the *Vedas*, the *Atharvaveda* ("Science of Charms"). Written some time between 2000 and 1400 b.c., the *Atharvaveda* (12:6.15) calls bhang one of the "five kingdoms of herbs . . . which release us from anxiety." But it is not until much later in India's history that bhang became a part of everyday life. By the tenth century a.d., for example, it was just beginning to be extolled as *indracanna*, the "food of the gods." A fifteenth-century document refers to it as "light-hearted," "joyful," and "rejoices," and claims that among its virtues are "astringency," "heat," "speech-giving," "inspiration of mental powers," "excitability," and the capacity to "remove wind and phlegm."[38]

By the sixteenth century a.d., it found its way into India's popular literature. The *Dhurtasamagama*, or "Rogue's Congress," a light farce written to amuse audiences, has two beggars come before an unscrupulous judge asking for a decision on a quarrel concerning a maiden at the bazaar. Before he will render his decision, however, the judge demands payment for his arbitration. In response to this demand, one of the beggars offers some bhang. The judge readily accepts and, tasting it, declares that "it produces a healthy appetite, sharpens the wits, and acts as an aphrodisiac."[39]

In the *Rajvallabha*, a seventeenth-century text dealing with drugs used in India, bhang is described as follows:

> India's food is acid, produces infatuation, and destroys leprosy. It creates vital energy, increases mental powers and internal heat, corrects irregularities of the phlegmatic humor, and is an *elixir vitae*. It was originally produced like nectar from the ocean by churning it with Mount Mandara. Inasmuch as it is believed to give victory in the three worlds and to bring delight to the king of gods (Siva), it was called *vijaya* (victorious). This

---

[38]G. A. Grierson, "On References to the Hemp Plant Occurring in Sanskrit and Hindi Literature," in *Indian Hemp Drugs Commission Report* (Simla, India: 1893–4), 3: 247–8.
[39]*Ibid.*, p. 248.

desire-fulfilling drug was believed to have been obtained by men on earth for the welfare of all people. To those who use it regularly, it begets joy and diminishes anxiety.[40]

Yet it was not as a medicinal aid or as a social lubricant that bhang was preeminent among the people of India. Rather, it was and still is because of its association with the religious life of the country that bhang is so extolled and glorified. The stupefaction produced by the plant's resin is greatly valued by the fakirs and ascetics, the holy men of India, because they believe that communication with their deities is greatly facilitated during intoxication with bhang. (According to one legend, the Buddha subsisted on a daily ration of one cannabis seed, and nothing else, during his six years of asceticism.[41]) Taken in early morning, the drug is believed to cleanse the body of sin. Like the communion of Christianity, the devotee who partakes of bhang partakes of the god Siva.

Cannabis also held a preeminent place in the Tantric religion which evolved in Tibet in the seventh century A.D. out of an amalgam of Buddhism and local religion.[42] The priests of this religion were wizards known as lamas ("superiors"). The high priest was called the Dalai Lama ("mighty superior").

Tantrism, a word that means "that which is woven together," was a religion based on fear of demons. To combat the demonic threat to the world, the people sought protection in the spells, incantations, formulas (mantras), and exorcisms of their lamas, and in plants such as cannabis which were set afire to overcome evil forces.

Cannabis was also an important part of Tantric religious yoga sex acts consecrated to the goddess Kali. During the ritual, about an hour and a half prior to intercourse the devotee placed a bowl of bhang before him and uttered the mantra: "Om hrim, O ambrosia-formed goddess [Kali] who has arisen from ambrosia, who showers ambrosia, bring me ambrosia again and again, bestow occult power [*siddhi*] and bring my chosen deity to my power."[43] Then, after uttering several other mantras, he drank the potion. The delay between drinking the bhang and the sex act was to allow the drug time to act so that it would heighten the senses and thereby increase the feeling of oneness with the goddess.[44]

At the turn of the twentieth century, the Indian Hemp Drugs Com-

[40]*Ibid.*
[41]S. Beal, *Fo-Sho-Hing-Tsan-King* (Oxford: Clarendon Press, 1882), p. 143.
[42]See M. R. Aldrich, "Tantric Cannabis Use in India" *Journal of Psychedelic Drugs* 9 (1977): 227–33.
[43]Cf. Agehananda Bharati, *The Tantric Tradition* (London: Rider and Co., 1965), p. 251; A. Avalon, *Tantra of the Great Liberation* (New York: Dover, 1972), p. 73.
[44]Bharati, *Tantric Tradition*, p. 251.

mission, which had been summoned in the 1890s to investigate the use of cannabis in India, concluded that the plant was so much an integral part of the culture and religion of that country that to curtail its usage would certainly lead to unhappiness, resentment, and suffering. Their conclusions:

> To the Hindu the hemp plant is holy. A guardian lives in the bhang leaf.... To see in a dream the leaves, plant, or water of bhang is lucky.... No good thing can come to the man who treads underfoot the holy bhang leaf. A longing for bhang foretells happiness.
> ... Besides as a cure for fever, bhang has many medicinal virtues.... It cures dysentery and sunstroke, clears phlegm, quickens digestion, sharpens appetite, makes the tongue of the lisper plain, freshens the intellect, and gives alertness to the body and gaiety to the mind. Such are the useful and needful ends for which in his goodness the Almighty made bhang.... It is inevitable that temperments should be found to whom the quickening spirit of bhang is the spirit of freedom and knowledge. In the ecstasy of bhang the spark of the Eternal in man turns into light the murkiness of matter.... Bhang is the Joygiver, the Skyflier, the Heavenly-guide, the Poor Man's Heaven, the Soother of Grief.... No god or man is as good as the religious drinker of bhang.... The supporting power of bhang has brought many a Hindu family safe through the miseries of famine. To forbid or even seriously to restrict the use of so holy and gracious an herb as the hemp would cause widespread suffering and annoyance and to large bands of worshipped ascetics, deep-seated anger. It would rob the people of a solace in discomfort, of a cure in sickness, of a guardian whose gracious protection saves them from the attacks of evil influences.... So grand a result, so tiny a sin![45]

PERSIA

India was not the only country to be invaded by the Aryans. By 1500 B.C., Persia, Asia Minor, and Greece had been overrun and the Aryans were establishing permanent settlements as far west as France and Germany. Although the people who settled in these countries eventually developed into different nationalities, with different customs and traditions, their common Aryan ancestry can still be traced in their languages which collectively are called Indo-European. For example, the linquistic root *an*, which is found in various *can*nabis-related words, can be found in French in the word ch*an*vre and in German as h*an*f. Our own word cannabis is taken directly from the Greek, which in turn is taken from *canna*, an early Sanskrit term.

When the Aryans first settled in Persia (modern-day Iran, "the land of the Aryans"), they separated into two kingdoms—Medea and Parsa

[45]J. M. Campbell, "On the Religion of Hemp," in *Indian Hemp Drugs Commission Report* (Simla, India: 1892–4), 3: 250–2.

(Persia). Four centuries later, Cyrus the Great, the ruler of Parsa, unified the country, and with the combined forces of the Medes and Parsa behind him, he led his armies eastward and westward. By 546 B.C., the Persian or Achaemenid Empire as it was called (from Achaemenes, Cyrus' ancestor), reached from Palestine to India. Twenty years later, the Persians defeated Egypt and extended their control over that great kingdom as well.

It was not until 331 B.C. that the Persian empire finally collapsed; its nemesis—the Greeks and their brilliant leader—Alexander the Great.

The Aryans who settled in Persia came from the same area in central Russia as their cousins who invaded India, so it is hardly surprising that the Persian word *bhanga* is almost identical to the Indian term *bhang*.

The *Zend-Avesta* is the Persian counterpart to the *Vedas*. However, unlike the *Vedas*, many of the books that were once a part of the *Zend-Avesta* have disappeared. The book itself was said to have been written by the Persian prophet Zoroaster, around the seventh century B.C., and reputedly was transcribed on no fewer than 1200 cowhides containing approximately two million verses!

Professor Mirceau Eliade, perhaps the world's foremost authority on the history of religions, has suggested that Zoroaster himself may have been a user of bhanga and may have relied on its intoxication to bridge the metaphysical gap between heaven and earth.[46] One of the few surviving books of the *Zend-Avesta*, called the *Vendidad*, "The Law Against Demons," in fact calls bhanga Zoroaster's "good narcotic,"[47] and tells of two mortals who were transported in soul to the heavens where, upon drinking from a cup of bhanga, they had the highest mysteries revealed to them.

The *Vendidad* also contains a cryptic reference to bhanga's being used to induce abortions, but this seems not to have been an accepted usage of the drug in ancient Persia since the abortionist is called an old hag, not a doctor.[48]

The Cult of the Dead

Around the seventh century B.C., yet another swarm of Aryan warriors came out of central Siberia looking for new lands upon which to graze their animals. This time they claimed a vast territory stretching from northern Greece and beyond the Black Sea to the Altai Mountains in central Siberia as their new homeland.

Known as the Scythians, these conquerors, like their Aryan ances-

---

[46]M. Eliade, *Shamanism* (New York: Pantheon Books, 1964), pp 399–400.
[47]J. Darmester, ed., *The Zend-Avesta* (London: Oxford University Press, 1882), pp. 267–8.
[48]*Ibid.*, p. 309.

tors before them, were skilled in warfare and renowned for their horse-manship. And also like their ancestors who settled in India and Persia, the Scythians were no strangers to the intoxicating effects of marihuana. According to Herodotus, a Greek historian who lived in the fifth century B.C., marihuana was an integral part of the Scythian cult of the dead wherein homage was paid to the memory of their departed leaders.

Herodotus' passion for detail and devotion to fact has often provided scholars with their only contact with long-forgotten people and their customs. Nowhere was this more true than in the case of the Scythians. Were it not for Herodotus' description of the funerary customs of the Scythians, for example, one of the best known instances of the use of marihuana in the ancient world would never have been recorded.

The funereal practice alluded to by Herodotus took place among the Scythians living northeast of Macedonia on the first anniversary of the death of one of their chiefs. The ceremony that commemorated that passing was a rather grisly affair, not one for the faint of heart, but of course the Scythians could hardly have been accused of being faint-hearted. First, it called for the death of fifty of the chief's former body-guards, along with their horses. The bodies of these men were then opened, their intestines and inner organs were removed, various herbs were placed in the open cavities, and the bodies were then stitched back together. Meanwhile, their horses, each fully bridled, were killed and impaled on stakes arranged in a circle around the chief's tomb. The dead bodies of the chief's erstwhile protectors were then lifted onto the horses and were left to rot as they stood their last watch over the tomb of their former leader.

Following this sobering rite, all those who had assisted in the burial cleansed themselves in a unique purification ritual. First, they washed their bodies thoroughly with cleansing oil. Then they erected small tents, into which they placed metal censors containing red-hot stones. Next, the men crawled into the tents and dumped marihuana seeds onto the hot stones. The seeds soon began to smolder and throw off vapors, which in the words of Herodotus, caused the Scythians to "howl with joy."[49] Seemingly, the purification was the Scythian counterpart to the hard-drinking frazzled Irish wake, with marihuana instead of alcohol as the ceremonial intoxicant.

Even though Herodotus' accuracy in recording history has often been borne out by other historical documents, scholars found this bizarre burial custom including the marihuana-induced intoxication too incredible to be true.

[49]Herodotus, *Histories* 5.72–5.

But in 1929 a Russian archaeologist, Professor S. I. Rudenko, made a fantastic discovery in the Pazyryk Valley of central Siberia. Digging into some ancient ruins near the Altai Mountains on the border between Siberia and Outer Mongolia, Rudenko found a trench about 160 feet square and about 20 feet deep. On the perimeter of the trench were the skeletons of a number of horses. Inside the trench was the embalmed body of a man and a bronze cauldron filled with burnt marihuana seeds![50] Clearing the site further, Rudenko also found some shirts woven from hemp fiber and some metal censors designed for inhaling marihuana smoke which did not appear to be connected with any religious rite. To Rudenko, the evidence suggested that inhalation of smoldering marihuana seeds occurred not only in a religious context, but also as an everyday activity, one in which Scythian women participated alongside the men.

Although he does not identify them, Herodotus had also heard of another tribe of nomads who used marihuana for recreational purposes. Speaking of these unidentified people, Herodotus states that when they "have parties and sit around a fire, they throw some of it into the flames. As it burns, it smokes like incense, and the smell of it makes them drunk, just as wine does us. As more fruit is thrown on, they get more and more intoxicated until finally they jump up and start dancing and singing."[51]

The Scythians eventually disappeared as a distinct national entity, but their descendants spread through Eastern Europe. While remembrances of their ancestors were lost, memories of ancestral customs were still retained, although, of course, these were modified down through the centuries. It is in this regard that anthropologist Sula Benet's comment that "hemp never lost its connection with the cult of the dead"[52] takes on added significance since she has traced the influence of the Scythians and their hemp funerary customs down to the modern era in Eastern Europe and Russia.

On Christmas eve, for instance, Benet notes that the people of Poland and Lithuania serve *semieniatka*, a soup made from hemp seeds. The Poles and Lithuanians believe that on the night before Christmas the spirits of the dead visit their families and the soup is for the souls of the dead. A similar ritual takes place in Latvia and in the Ukraine on

---

[50]S. I. Rudenko, *Frozen Tombs of Siberia* (Berkeley: University of California Press, 1970), p. 285. See also, T. T. Rice, *The Scythians* (New York: Praeger, 1970), p. 90; M. I. Artamanov, "Frozen Tombs of the Scythians," *Scientific American* 212 (1965): 101–9.
[51]Herodotus, *Histories* 1.202.
[52]S. Benet, "Early Diffusion and Folk Uses of Hemp," in *Cannabis and Culture*, ed. V. Rubin (The Hague: Mouton, 1975), p. 43.

Three Kings Day. Yet another custom carried out in deference to the dead in Western Europe was the throwing of hemp seeds onto a blazing fire during harvest time as an offering to the dead—a custom that originated with the Scythians and has seemingly been passed on from generation to generation for over 2500 years.

BABYLONIA, PALESTINE, AND EGYPT

The farthest west marihuana fibers have ever been found in the ancient world is in Turkey. Sifting through artifacts dating back to the time of the Phrygians, a tribe of Aryans who invaded that country around 1000 B.C., archaeologists unearthed pieces of fabric containing hemp fibers in the debris around Gordion, an ancient city located near present-day Ankara.[53]

Although the Scythians had contacts with the people of Babylonia, who lived to the west of the Phyrgians, no hemp fiber or definite mention of hemp (*Cannabis sativa*) to the west of Turkey can be found until the time of the Greeks.[54] There are some vague references, however, which may or may not be cannabis. In a letter written around 680 B.C. by an unknown woman to the mother of the Assyrian king Esarhaddon, for example, mention is made of a substanced called *qu-nu-bu*[55] which could be cannabis.

There is also very little evidence that the Egyptians ever cultivated the plant during the time of the Pharaohs. Papyrus documents from

---

[53]L. Bellinger, "Textiles from Gordion," *Bulletin of the Needle and Bobbin Club* 46 (1962): 5-33.

[54]In his *Dictionary of Assyrian Botany* (p. 220), Campbell identified the Sumerian term *a·zal·la* and the Akkadian term *azallu* as cannabis on the basis of their similarities to the Syrian *azal*, meaning "to spin." Campbell also took the Assyrian work *gurgurangu* as another reference to cannabis because of its similarity to *garganinj*, the Persian word for cannabis. Building on these similarities, Campbell then identified the Sumerian drug *gan·zi-gun·na* as hashish [literally, a robber (gan) who spins away (gun·nu) the soul (zi)]. Campbell also felt that the similarity between *gan·zi* and the Hindu word *qanjha* also support his arguments. However, in a later discussion of this issue (p. 229), he acknowledges the possibility that the Sumerian and Akkadian words he tentatively identified as hashish could just as likely be words denoting narcotics in general and opium specifically.

A letter written around 680 B.C. by an unknown woman to the mother of the Assyrian king, Esarhaddon, mentions a substance called *qu-nu-bu* which also may have been cannabis, but again there is no certainty for this identification. Cf. L. Waterman, *Royal Correspondence of the Assyrian Empire* (Ann Arbor: University of Michigan Press, 1930), letter 368.

[55]L. Waterman, *Royal Correspondence of the Assyrian Empire* (Ann Arbor: University of Michigan Press, 1930), Letter 368.

ancient Egypt list the names of hundreds of drugs and their plant
sources, but there is no unequivocal mention of marihuana in any of its
forms.[56] While some scholars have contended that the drug *smsm t*,
mentioned in the Berlin and Ebers papyri, is cannabis,[57] this opinion is
conjecture. No mummy has ever been discovered wrapped in fabric
made from cannabis. In the ruins of El Amarna, the city of Akhenaton
(the Pharaoh who tried to introduce monotheism to ancient Egypt),
archaeologists found a "three ply hemp cord" in the hole of a stone and
a large mat bound with "hemp cords,"[58] but unfortunately they did not
specify the type of hemp. Many different bast fibers were called hemp
and no one can be certain that the fibers at El Amarna are cannabis,
especially since Deccan hemp (*Hibiscus cannabinus*) grows in Egypt.[59]

The earliest unmistakable reference to cannabis in Egypt does not
occur until the third century A.D., when the Roman emperor Aurelian
imposed a tax on Egyptian cannabis.[60] Even then, however, there was
very little of the fiber in Egypt.

There is no evidence that the ancient Israelites ever knew of the
plant, although several attempts have been made to prove that they did.
Because the Arabs sometimes referred to hashish as grass, some writers
have argued that the "grass" eaten by Nebuchadrezzar was actually
hashish. Another contention is that the phantasmagoria of composite
creatures and brilliant colors seen by Ezekiel are unintelligible except
from the standpoint of hashish intoxication.

In the most recent attempt to infuse marihuana with biblical antiquity, the Old Testament has been tickled, teased, and twisted into
surrendering secret references to marihuana that it never contained.
From the fact that the Scythians had made contact with the people of
Palestine during the seventh century B.C., it has been suggested that
knowledge and usage of the plant was passed on to the Israelites

[56]*E.g.*, H. von Deines and H. Grapow, *Grundriss der Medizin der alten Aeypten* (Berlin: Verlag, 1959).
   There is also no reference to cannabis in any of the hieroglyphic writings on historical documents during the time of the pharaohs. The earliest reference to hashish in
Egypt occurs in the twelfth century A.D. (Ayyubid dynasty). Not long thereafter, the
drug became a controversial issue in Egyptian society and laws were passed to outlaw
its usage (see Chapter 2).
[57]*Ibid.*, 6: 493.
[58]T. E. Peet and C. L. Woolley, *City of Akhenaton* (Boston: Egypt Exploration Society, 1923), 1: 81.
[59]A. Lucas, *Ancient Egyptian Materials and Industries* (London: Edward Arnold, 1962), p. 149.
[60]A. C. Johnson, "Roman Egypt," in *Economic Survey of Ancient Rome*, ed. T. Frank (Patter-son, N.J.: Pageant Books, 1959), 2: 3.

through some kind of cultural exchange. Linguistic arguments are then advanced to prove that the Israelites were users of marihuana.

For example, because the Hebrew adjective *bosm* (Aramaic *busma*), meaning "aromatic" or "sweet smelling," is found in connection with the word q^e *neh* (which can also be written as *kaneh* or *keneb*) and because of the similarity between *kaneh* and *bosm*, and the Scythian word *kannabis*, it is argued that they are one and the same.[61]

However, the word *kaneh* or q^e *neh* is a very vague term[62] that has disconcerted more than a few distinguished biblical scholars. A reference to q^e *neh* in Isaiah 43:24 refers not to a "sweet-smelling" but a "sweet-tasting" plant. Few people would ever say that marihuana leaves taste sweet. Because of this reference to a sweet-tasting plant, some biblical scholars and botanists believe that the q^e *neh* is probably sugarcane.

Although the *Bible* states that q^e *neh* came from a "far country" (Jeremiah 6:20), sugar grew in India, which is in keeping with the passage from Jeremiah. The reference to q^e *neh* as a spice in Exodus 30:23 also suggests sugar rather than cannabis.[63]

The earliest reference to cannabis among the Jews actually does not occur until the early Middle Ages when the first unmistakable mention of it is found in the *Talmud.*

The Jews of Talmudic times were particularly concerned about certain precepts which prohibited the mingling of heterogeneous substances, and on at least one occasion the sages argued over whether hemp seeds could be sown in a vineyard. The majority opinion was that such intermingling was permissible, indicating that they recognized a certain similarity between cannabis and the grape. This similarity could not have been due to the appearance of the two plants and must have centered around the intoxication produced by each.

A similar question likewise arose concerning the purification of wicker mats which were placed over grapes during wine pressing to keep them from scattering. The decision rendered by the rabbis was that if the baskets were made of hemp they could be used, provided they were thoroughly cleaned.[64] However, if they were made of some other material, the rabbis ruled that they could not be employed in wine pressing until twelve months had elapsed since the time they were last used.

[61]Benet, "Early Diffusion," pp. 39–49.
[62]*E.g.,* Exodus 30:23; Isaiah 43:24; Jeremiah 6:20; Ezekiel 27:19; Song of Songs 4:14.
[63]Cf. H. N. Moldenke and A. L. Moldenke, *Plants of the Bible* (Waltham, Mass.: Chronica Botanica Co., 1952), pp. 39–41; R. H. Harrison, *Healing Herbs of the Bible* (Leiden: E. J. Brill, 1966), p. 42.
[64]*Abodah Zarah* 74b.

The Birthplace of Democracy

Greece: land of myth and beauty, home to some of the greatest minds the world has ever known—Socrates, Plato, Aristotle—birthplace of democracy; Greece was all of these and more. It gave the world its first great art, literature, theater, political institutions, sporting events, scientific and medical discoveries—the list is endless.

Yet despite these monumental achievements, Greece was a turbulent country and war was no stranger to its inhabitants. When they were not fighting among themselves, the Greeks faced the threat of invasion from empires like that of Darius and Xerxes. When Alexander the Great came to power, the Greeks in turn became world conquerors.

Alexander's was not the first campaign outside the Greek mainland. The Trojan war (ca. 1200 B.C.) saw Greek armies encamped on the shores of the Dardanelles in Asia Minor almost ten centuries before Alexander.

According to the Greek poet Homer (ca. 850 B.C.), who described the events of that war in the *Iliad*, the war was fought over a woman, the most beautiful mortal in the world—Helen, daughter of the great god Zeus and his human paramour. The *Iliad* tells of the great battles that took place before the walls of Troy, and the great heroes who fought them. It ends, however, not with the fall of Troy, but with the death of Hector, the Trojan prince, at the hands of the great Achilles. The actual conquest of Troy and the homeward journey of the Greeks is chronicled in Homer's other great epic, the *Odyssey*. Although it is primarily the story of the events that befell the great hero Odysseus as he tries to return to his island-home of Ithaca, the story contains a brief scene in which some readers believe they have come across one of the earliest references to cannabis in Greek literature.

The Mysterious Nepenthe

On their way back from Troy, Helen, who had been reunited with her husband, Menelaus, stopped off in Egypt for a brief layover. While Menelaus took on new supplies, his wife went about exploring what was even in those times an ancient civilization. During this brief visit to the land of the Pharaohs, Helen paid a visit to a woman by the name of Polydamna. Polydamna was a dealer in drugs.

Many years later, during a magnificent party thrown by Menelaus in his palace in Sparta, the conversation naturally turned to the recent war in Troy. Someone remarked how sad it was that Odysseus, who had been a great friend of Menelaus' as well as of many of the guests at the party, had not been heard of since his departure from Troy. The mention of Odysseus cast a shadow over the festivities and everyone started to become morose. The more the guests spoke of the lost hero, the sadder they became. The party was turning into a wake.

As spirits plummeted, Helen herself started feeling remorseful, not because of any grief she felt over the missing Odysseus, but because all this sadness and melancholy were spoiling her party. If she did not do something quickly, the party would die, the guests would go home, and, sooner than she cared for, she would have to return to the boring life of being a woman in an age when women were seen, made love to, but rarely heard or spoken to.

The situation called for emergency measures and Helen met the situation head on. Reaching into her bag of tricks, she came up with a drug given her by Polydamna. Secretly, she placed the compound into the wine of her guests. The drug, which Homer only identifies as *nepenthe* ("against sorrow"), was a compound with the power to suppress despair. Whoever drank this mixture, Homer wrote, would be incapable of sadness, even if his mother and father lay dead, or his son were slain before his very eyes.[65]

The drug was an instant success. The guests forgot their sorrow and regained their spirits. Although the conversation still revolved around Odysseus, it no longer evoked any grief. Helen even told the guests how she and Odysseus had once spent some compromising moments together. All the while her husband listened to the news that he had been cuckholded by his best friend, he remained calm and indifferent, so great was the power of Polydamna's drug.

What was this soporific, this stupefying drug that restrained even the deepest sense of grief and sorrow? No one really knows. There is no reason for Homer not to have identified it if he had had some specific drug in mind.

To add even more mystery to this enigma, the Greek historian Diodorus of Sicily, who visited Egypt in the first century B.C., also refers to a "nepenthic" drug from that country which brought forgetfulness of all sorrows.[66] Like Homer, he too never gives this drug a name.

Conjecture always lurks in the shadow of uncertainty, and throughout the ages many have tried to identify Homer's elusive nepenthe. One of the more interesting guesses is that the drug was cannabis.

For example, when poet Samuel Taylor Coleridge invited a friend to come for a visit, he coaxed him to bring along some drugs "and I will give a fair trial to opium, henbane, and nepenthe. By the bye," he added, "I have always considered Homer's account of *nepenthe* as a

[65]*Odyssey* 4: 219–32.
[66]Diodorus, *Histories* 1.97.7.

banging lie."[67] At the time that he wrote this letter in 1803, Coleridge was one of the few Europeans who were acquainted with the Indian beverage bhang. His pun indicates that, as far as he was concerned, nepenthe and bhang were one and the same.

E.W. Lane, editor of *The Thousand and One Nights*, was similarly convinced: " 'Benj,' the plural of which in Coptic is 'nibendji,' is without doubt the same plant as the 'nepenth,' which has so much perplexed the commentators of Homer. Helen evidently brought the nepenthe from Egypt, and benj is there still reported to possess all the wonderful qualities which Homer attributes to it."[68]

Not everyone agreed. Thomas De Quincey, author of *Confessions of an Opium Eater*, rejected cannabis as the sorrow-killing agent mentioned by Homer preferring his own favorite, opium, which he regarded as a "panacea, a pharmakon nepenthes" for all woes.[69]

While no one will ever know what drug Homer had in mind, it is certain that it was not cannabis since cannabis was not known in Egypt until more than a thousand years after Homer wrote his stirring epics. On the other hand, opium is mentioned in ancient Egyptian writings, and of all the possibilities that have been suggested it still remains the most likely.

While the ancient Greeks remained ignorant of the intoxicating properties of the cannabis plant, they were not slow to appreciate the durability and strength of its fiber. As early as the sixth century B.C., Greek merchants whose Milesian colonies served as a middle station between mainland Greece and the eastern coast of Asia Minor, had been carrying on a lucrative business transporting cannabis fiber to the ports along the Aegean.[70]

The Thracians, a Greek-speaking people living in the Balkans who were probably more closely related to the Scythians than to the Greeks, were especially adept at working hemp. Writing aroung 450 B.C., Herodotus says of their clothes that they "were so like linen that none but a very experienced person could tell whether they were of hemp or flax; one who had never seen hemp would certainly suppose them to be linen.[71]

Herodotus does not say whether the Thracians used any of the other parts of the plant, but Plutarch (46–127 B.C.), writing some 400 years later, mentions that after their meals, it was not uncommon for the

[67]Quoted in D. Ebin, *The Drug Experience* (New York: Grove Press, 1965), p. 103.
[68]E. W. Lane, ed., *The Thousand and One Nights*, (London: Routledge, 1889), CXI, n. 76.
[69]T. DeQuincey, *Confessions of an Opium Eater* (New York: American Library, 1966), p. 94.
[70]A. J. Warden, *The Linen Trade* (New York: A. M. Kelley, 1968), p. 43.
[71]Herodotus, *Histories* 4.74., ed. A. D. Rubin (London: W. Heinemann, 1921).

Thracians to throw the tops of a plant which looked like oregano into the fire. Inhaling the fumes of this plant, the people became drunk and then so tired they finally fell asleep.[72]

However, Thrace was far from the center of Greek culture and most Greeks remained ignorant of cannabis's intoxicating properties. Theophrastus, the famous Greek botanist (372–287 B.C.), does not list cannabis among the native plants of Greece and nowhere is there any reference to it in the Greek myths, although various drugs such as *datura* (Jimson weed), *mandragora* (mandrake), and *hyoscyanus* (henbane) are described as consciousness-modifying drugs in use at ancient Greek shrines and oracles.[73]

In the third century B.C., Hiero II (270–15 B.C.), ruler of the Greek city-state of Syracuse, did not send his envoys to the Black Sea city of Colchis which supplied many Greek cities with hemp, but to the far-off Rhone Valley in France.[74] So sophisticated about the various characteristics of hemp fiber was he that only the most superior varieties were to be used to make the ropes for his proposed armada. (This incident is the earliest reference to cannabis in Western Europe known to historians.)

Since the Greeks had become so knowledgeable about the kinds of fibers produced by cannabis growing in different geographical regions, they would no doubt also have mentioned the intoxicating properties of the plant had these been known. Although there are references to cannabis both as a delicacy and a remedy for backache in Greek literature dating back to the fourth century B.C.,[75] no notice of the plant as an intoxicant occurs until the nineteenth century.[76]

ROME

The Roman Empire was the last and greatest colossus of the ancient world. At the summit of its glory, it extended from England in the west to Russia in the east. No fewer than a 100 million people lived within its frontiers.

[72]Plutarch, "Of the Names of Rivers and Mountains, And of Such Things as Are To Be Found Therein," in id. *Essays and Miscellanies*, ed. (London: Simplin, Marshall, Hamilton Kent and Co., n.d.), vol. 5.
[73]C. Stefanis, C. Ballas, and D. Madianou, "Sociocultural and Epidemiological Aspects of Hashish Use in Greece," in *Cannabis and Culture*, ed. V. Rubin (The Hague: Mouton, 1975), p. 307.
[74]*Athenaeus* 5.205f.
[75]See T. F. Bruner, "Marihuana in Ancient Greece and Rome? The Literary Evidence," *Bulletin of the History of Medicine*, 47 (1973): 344–55.
[76]Stefanis *et al.*, "Sociocultural and Epidemiological Aspects," p. 307.

It was an empire primarily governed by a small elite aristocracy in Rome whose commands were dutifully administered by a well-oiled bureaucracy which could call upon a highly trained and devoted army whenever force was necessary.

Most of the everyday chores in the city were performed by slaves. About one-half million lived in Rome. A middle-class businessman might own about 10; the emperor owned about 25,000.

Wealthy Romans spent most of their time eating, bathing, gambling, and whoring. But some also had a taste for the arts. Since the Romans did not excel very greatly in the latter, prominent men would bring Greek writers, painters, philosophers, and scientists to Rome to work for them and to converse with whenever the feeling moved them. Of this Graecophilia, the Roman poet Horace observed: "Captive Greece has taken captive her rude conqueror."

Among the eminent Greek scientists who found employment among the Romans was Pedacius Dioscorides. Born in Asia Minor in the early part of the first century A.D., he became a physician and spent much of his early career in the Roman army tending the needs of the soldiers as they traveled the world conquering new lands to add to the empire. During these campaigns, Dioscorides collected and studied the various plants he encountered in different parts of the world and eventually he put what he had learned into a herbal.

The first copy of this book was published in A.D. 70. Dioscorides called it a *materia medica* and it became to the Western world what the *Pen Ts'ao* was to the Chinese. It identified each of the plants listed according to its native habitat and the names by which it was known. Peculiar features were then noted, and finally, symptoms and conditions for which the plant had proven beneficial were described.

The book became an instant success and was subsequently translated into nearly all of the languages of the ancient and medieval world. For the next fifteen centuries it remained an important reference for physicians, and no medical library was considered complete unless it housed at least one copy of this herbal.

Among the more than 600 entries appearing in the book was cannabis. This plant, Dioscorides wrote, was not only very useful for manufacturing strong ropes, but the juice of its seeds was also very beneficial in treating earaches and in diminishing sexual desires.[77]

Although this is all Dioscorides had to say on the subject, it was the first time cannabis had been described as a medical remedy in a Western medical text. And since Dioscorides' herbal continued to be one of the

[77]Dioscorides, *Materia Medica* 3.165.

most important books in medicine for the next 1500 years, cannabis became a common household remedy for treating earaches throughout Europe during the Middle Ages.

Another prominent physician whose work was to influence the course of medical science for the next fifteen centuries was Claudius Galen (A.D. 130–200). Born in Pergamum, a country located in modern-day Turkey, Galen was the son of a wealthy and ambitious landowner who dreamed one night that his son would become the most famous physician in the world. The lavish praise and attention bestowed upon him by his father made Galen an insufferable egotist. "Whoever seeks fame need only become familiar with all that I have achieved," he once told his pupils.[78]

Such a statement may seem conceited, but it was true. Galen was to become the most famous physician of the ancient and Middle Ages, and a thorough study of his writings was mandatory for any aspiring doctor.

To prepare his son for the future, Galen's father sent him to the best medical schools of the day. By the time he was thirty, Galen had completed his formal training and had been made surgeon to the gladiators. From the cuts and wounds he was called upon to treat, he was able to learn a great deal about the anatomy of the body. Such experience proved invaluable since Roman law did not permit dissection of the human body. Only skeletons picked clean by scavengers were available to the would-be anatomist.

During his own lifetime, Galen was recognized as the leading authority on anatomy and physiology. He was a prolific writer, his medical pronouncements were never challenged, and his writings became the standard references of the medical profession. These writings, along with Dioscorides' herbal, were the most influential books in Western medicine for centuries.

Like Dioscorides, Galen had little to say about cannabis, but he does state that the Romans, at least those with money, used to top off their banquets with a marihuana-seed desert, a confectionary treat which left guests with a warm and pleasurable sensation. To be avoided, however, was an overindulgence in this confection, for among the adverse aftereffects of too many seeds were dehydration and impotence. Other properties Galen mentions are antiflatulence and analgesia. "If consumed in large amounts," he says, it "affects the head by sending to it a warm and toxic vapor."[79]

---

[78]Galen, quoted in F. Marti-Ibanez, *The Epic of Medicine* (New York: Clarkson Potter, 1960), p. 92.
[79]Galen, *De Facultatibus Alimentorum* 100.49.

Following Galen, Oribasius, court physician to the emperor Julian (fourth century A.D.), wrote that cannabis seed "harms the head," had antiflatulent effects, produced a "warm feeling," and caused weight-reduction.[80]

Most Romans, however, had little familiarity with cannabis seed. Very little hemp was raised in Italy.[81] If anything, the Romans were interested in the plant because of its fiber, for with good strong fiber Rome could outfit its expanding navy and keep it at sea longer.

Most of Rome's hemp came from Babylonia.[82] The city of Sura was particularly renowned for its hempen ropes.[83] Other cities such as Colchis, Cyzicus, Alabanda, Mylasa, and Ephesus, which had been leading producers during the Greek empire, continued to produce and export hemp as their chief product under the Romans.

The only other Roman author to give cannabis more than just a passing reference was the indefatigable encyclopedist of the ancient world, Caius Plinius Secundus (A.D. 23–79), otherwise known as Pliny the Elder. One of the best known members of the Roman establishment, Pliny preferred reading and writing to the more usual pastimes of the aristocracy. At the time of his death in A.D. 79, he left behind 160 manuscripts, many of which unfortunately have long since disappeared.

His most famous work, copies of which have been preserved down through the ages, was called the *Natural History*. These volumes are a collection of fact and fantasy which Pliny copied from other books or which he transcribed from conversations with various people throughout the empire. Most of the factual material was taken from Aristotle's books. The fantasy included anything and everything. Nothing was too incredible to be recorded. Pliny records that there are some men without mouths who inhale the fragrance of flowers instead of eating food, that horses will commit suicide if they discover that they have engaged in an incestual relationship with a close relative, etc. Exotic animals such as the unicorn and the winged horse are also given their due.

But like his contemporaries, Pliny had very little to record about cannabis. The fibers of the plant, he noted, made superb rope. The juice of the cannabis seed was also useful for extracting "worms from the ears, or any insect which may have entered them." While the seeds

[80]Oribasius, quoted by Bruner, "Marihuana," p. 351.
[81]Bruner, "Marihuana," p. 351. While Roman farmers as a rule did not raise much hemp, some writers did advise how best to sow hemp seeds for a good crop, e.g., Columella, *Res Rustica* 2.7.1, 2.12.21, 11.275; cf. Pliny, *Natural History* 19.57.
[82]T. Frank, *An Economic Survey of Ancient Rome* (Patterson, N.J.: Pageant Books, 1959), 4:131.
[83]*Ibid.*, pp. 616, 823–4.

could also render men impotent, they were beneficial in alleviating gout and similar maladies.[84]

Wherever the people of the ancient world roamed, they carried with them the seeds of the precious cannabis plant. From China in the east to the Rhone Valley in the west, the seeds were spread. Cold weather, hot weather, wet or dry, fertile soil or barren, the seeds were not to be denied.

Except in India and China, most of the ancient world was completely ignorant of the intoxicating properties of the plant. Ancient European legends and herbals had little to say regarding its peculiar psychological effects.

If Europeans saw any magic in cannabis, it was its fibers, not its intoxicating power, that aroused their awe and admiration. Farther to the south, however, cannabis eventually inspired sentiments of a different kind in a people who challenged Europe for world domination.

[84]Pliny, *Natural History* 20.97.

2

Hashish and the Arabs

The Arab countries are hot. Hot and dusty. But mainly hot. It is only in recent times that a privileged few have found some respite from the heat through the miracle of air conditioning. The rest of the people are not so fortunate. Like their forefathers, they must endure temperatures that often soar to over 100°F. The excessive heat dictates that the people work only in the mornings and the evenings ("Only mad dogs and Englishmen go out in the noonday sun").

The sun also dictates the kinds of animals and plants that will survive. The camel has adapted in a way that allows it to go without water for days. Not only can it store large quantities of water in its body, but the camel also does not sweat. By a similar adaptation, plants are able to survive by being able to retain their water. It is because of this capacity to minimize evaporation that plants such as cannabis are able to live in the parching Arabian heat.

The means by which cannabis accomplishes this amazing feat is by producing a thick, sticky resin that coats its leaves and flowers. This protective canopy prevents life-sustaining moisture from disappearing into the dry air.

But this thick sticky resin is not an ordinary goo. It is the stuff that dreams are made of, the stuff that holds time suspended in limbo, the stuff that makes men forgetful, makes them both sad and deleriously happy, makes them ravenously hungry or completely disinterested in food. It is a god to some and a devil to others. It is all of these things and more. This resin, this shield against the sun, this sticky goo is . . . hashish.

The Discovery of Hashish

Little is known of the first Arab who discovered the marvelous properties of hashish. There is no shortage of legends, however, to fill in the dark, long-forgotten memories of that eventful moment. One of the most colorful of these stories tells how Haydar, the Persian founder of a religious order of Sufis, discovered hashish in A.D. 1155.[1]

According to the legend, Haydar was an ascetic monk who lived a life of rigid privation and self-chastisement in a monastery which he built in the mountains of Persia. For ten years he lived in this distant retreat, never leaving it for even a brief moment, seeing no one except his disciples.

One hot summer day, however, Haydar fell into a state of depression and, contrary to his custom of never venturing out of his monastery, he wantered off into the fields to be alone. When he returned, his disciples, who had become alarmed at his unusual absence, noted a strange air of happiness and whimsy in his demeanor. Not only that, the hitherto reclusive monk even allowed them to enter his personal chambers, something he had never done before.

Astounded by this dramatic change in their master's character, his disciples eagerly questioned the monk about what it was that had put him into this frame of mind. Haydar responded to their curiosity with amusement and proceeded to tell them how he had been wandering in the fields and had noticed that of all the plants near the monastery, only one had not been standing motionless in the oppressive heat of the day. Unlike its torpid and inanimate neighbors, this unusual plant seemed to dance joyfully in the sun's warmth. Overwhelmed by curiosity, Haydar picked a few of its leaves and ate them to see what they would taste like. The result was the euphoric state his disciples now observed in him.

Upon hearing of this wonderful plant and desirous of sharing their master's pleasure, Haydar's pupils entreated him to show them this strange plant so that they too could partake of its marvelous virtues. Haydar agreed, but not before he made them promise under oath that they would not reveal the secret of the plant to anyone but the Sufis (the poor). So it was, according to the legend, that the Sufis came to know the pleasures and contentment of hashish.

After his discovery, Haydar lived another ten years, allegedly subsisting on cannabis leaves. Shortly before his death in A.D. 1221, he asked that cannabis seeds be sown around his tomb so that his spirit might walk in the shade of the plant that had given him such pleasure during his lifetime.

Such is the legend of Haydar and his discovery of the powers of hashish. It is a simple story, amusing and entertaining, and of course, apocryphal.

[1]F. Rosenthal, *The Herb* (Leiden: E. J. Brill, 1971), pp. 49–50. Cf. also W. B. O'Shaughnessy, "On the Preparations of the Indian Hemp, or Gunjah," *Transactions of the Medical and Physical Society of Bombay*, 8 (1842): 421–61.

THE SMELL OF DEATH

Although sometimes called the "wine of Haydar," hashish was known to the Arabs long before its alleged discovery by the ascetic monk. In the tenth century A.D., an Arab physician, Ibn Wahshiyah, wrote of it in his book *On Poisons*, claiming that the odor of hashish was lethal:

> If it reaches the nose, a violent tickle occurs in the nose, then in the face. The face and eyes are affected by an extreme and intense burning; one does not see anything and cannot say what one wishes. One swoons, then recovers, then swoons again and recovers again. One goes on this way until he dies. A violent anxiety and fainting occurs until one succumbs, after a day, a day and a half, or more. If it is protracted, it may take two days. For these aromatics, there is no remedy. But if God wills to save him, he may be spared from death by the continuance of vomiting or by another natural reaction.[2]

While Ibn Wahshiyah was more ignorant than knowledgeable of the properties of hashish, he was at least superficially familiar with some of its effects. In general, however, Arab physicians before and after Ibn Wahshiyah had very little to say about the medicinal virtues of cannabis and most of what they did say was taken from Galen.

THE HIPPIES OF THE ARAB WORLD

The apocryphal oath by which Haydar entrusted his disciples not to reveal the secret of hashish to anyone but the Sufis underlies the close association between the drug and the Sufi movement in the Arab community.

The origin of the name Sufi is connected with the wearing of undyed garments made from wool (*suf*) rather than cotton. Such clothing was originally worn as a symbol of personal penitence, but was condemned by religious leaders because it suggested that such people were dressing in imitation of Jesus rather than Mohammed, who wore cotton.

The Sufis were the hippies of the Arab world. Their origins were in Persia where they began as a group of ascetics who banded together to discuss religious topics and to recite the *Koran* aloud. Some of these bands eventually formed fraternities and established monasteries such as that founded by Haydar.

Although the original leaders of the movement were orthodox in their religious principles, their successors and the new members who were drawn to the movement adopted a more mystical approach toward

[2]Quoted in M. Levey, "Mediaeval Arabic Toxicology," *Transactions of the Philosophical Society* 56 (1966): 43.

religion which was contrary to Islamic orthodoxy. Furthermore, since most of the new devotees came from the lower and middle classes, the sociopolitical attitudes of this new sect were increasingly regarded with distrust and suspicion by the upper classes and by the authorities.

Religious leaders were unfavorably inclined toward them because the mystical philosophy of the Sufis taught that divine truth and communion with God cannot be imparted to others. Instead, it had to be experienced directly. To the Sufis, the mind was simply incapable of articulating such understanding; it had to be acquired by oneself through experience.

One of the ways the Sufis encouraged the attainment of these spiritual insights was through the arousal of ecstatic states. There were several different ways of achieving this condition, but the one most commonly resorted to was through intoxication by means of drugs such as hashish. It was because of their frequent usage of hashish that the Sufis were credited both with the dissemination of the drug and with the downfall of Islamic society. For the Sufis, however, hashish was merely a means of stimulating mystical consciousness and appreciation of the nature of Allah. To the Sufi, a Moslem critic wrote, eating hashish is "an act of worship."

Sufism was much more than a heretical religious movement. It represented a counterculture within the Arab community in the same way that the hippies of the 1960's represented an ideological and behavioral counterculture within American society. Both were peopled by "dropouts" who rejected the dominant economic system in favor of communal living and sharing of material goods. Both had their symbols. For the hippies, it was long hair and beads; for the Sufi, garments made of wool.

Since neither the hippie nor the Sufi had any interest in advancing himself in society or in economic gain, both were looked down upon by the Establishment in their respective eras as being lazy and worthless. In many cases, their behavior was attributed to the effect of drugs.

More than intriguing, the dominant drug in both countercultures was made from cannabis. For the hippie, it was marihuana; for the Sufi, hashish.

Since the drugs were similar, it is not surprising that many of the accusations leveled at cannabis have a familiar ring. Both marihuana and hashish were accused of sapping the user's energy, thereby robbing him of his willingness to work. This "amotivational syndrome," as it is presently called, was regarded as a threat to the dominant culture since it undermined the work eithic.

Insanity was another evil attributed to chronic use of these drugs. Hashish drove men to madness, its Arab critics declared, by drying up the moistures in the lower parts of the body. This resulted in vapors'

rising to the brain, thereby causing the mind to weaken and be destroyed. Many critics contended that hashish produced physical dependence. As a result of this dependence, the hashish addict spent all of his
time and efforts looking for more hashish.[3]

A second feature common to both the hippies and the Sufis was
their physical withdrawal from the dominant culture. The country
commune of the hippie and the remote monastery started by Haydar
were both created to remove each group from the hostility of the Establishment. In these retreats, the devotees could follow their own way of
life without incurring the wrath of those who disagreed with their ideas.
These communes were also similar in their devotion to spiritual leaders
who were looked up to as fountainheads of enlightenment. Timothy
Leary and Haydar both enjoyed the respect and admiration of their
followers. Both also recommended drugs as a means of expanding consciousness. They were heroes to the counterculture, false prophets to
nonbelievers.

The hippie and Sufi movements were also similar in their attitudes
toward family and contemporary sexual morality. Both went to extremes, but in this case they went to opposite extremes. The hippies
were accused of being promiscuous; the Sufis, of being effeminate and
homosexual. In both cases, however, cannabis was blamed for their
sexual deviations. Marihuana, the critics of the twentieth century declared, caused hippies to become sex-crazed. Hashish, on the other
hand, was accused of diminishing the libido, causing men to turn from
women to other men.

Further parallels between the hippies and the Sufis could be drawn,
the point being that despite the 1000-year gulf between them, the two
movements resembled one another in more ways than they differed. But
perhaps the most interesting parallel of all is the answers the Sufis and
the hippies gave in response to those who criticized their use of cannabis.

Both ardently maintained that cannabis gave them otherwise unattainable insights into themselves. It allowed them to see new and different meanings in what appeared to be otherwise trivial experiences. It
made them feel more witty and gave them deeper understanding. It
caused them to see beautiful colors and designs in what seemed commonplace to others. It increased their pleasure in music. It gave happiness, and reduced anxiety and worry.[4]

The one comparison that breaks the link between the Sufis and the
Hippies is social background. In contrast to the hippies, many of whom

[3]See Rosenthal, *Herb*, p. 97–8.
[4]*Ibid.*, p. 97.

came from well-to-do middle-class families, most Sufis were from the lower classes. One of the main reasons the Sufis chose hashish over other intoxicants like alcohol was that hashish was cheap. Although proscribed in the *Koran*, wine was always available to those who could afford it. But wine was a luxury, the intoxicant of the rich; hashish was all the poor could afford.

Their heretical religious stance and their refusal to conform to the standards of Arab society combined to make the Sufis pariahs in the Arab world. And because hashish was so much a part of the Sufi's everyday life, it came to be looked upon as the cause of their unholy, contemptible, and disgusting behavior. By eliminating hashish, the Arab world felt it could rid itself of a loathsome drug habit that encouraged defiance, insubordination, and a general disregard for the status quo. While the efforts to eliminate hashish were often quite dramatic, all attempts ultimately proved futile. Every society seems to have evolved its own escape route from reality. For the Sufis, that escape route took the form of hashish.

THE GARDENS OF CAFOUR

Although hashish was well known in the eastern Arab countries by the eleventh century A.D., it was not until the middle of the thirteenth century that it was introduced into Egypt. For this information, we are indebted to a Moslem botanist named Ibn al-Baytar (d. A.D. 1248).

Ibn al-Baytar was born in Malaga in Spain, apparently the son of wealthy parents for he was able to afford to travel to far-off lands. Generally, the early sightseers in the Arab world left home to make the honored pilgrimage to the holy cities of Mecca and Medina. This was a religious duty required of every Moslem, but the farther away from these holy shrines, the more difficult was such an undertaking. For those who could afford the pilgrimage, however, the trip offered a wonderful opportunity to visit other countries and meet new people.

In the course of his journey, Ibn al-Baytar passed through Egypt where for the first time he observed hashish being eaten. The main users of the drug, he noted, were the Sufis.

According to Ibn al-Baytar, the Sufis had a special way of preparing their hashish. First, they baked the leaves until they were dry. Then, they rubbed them between their hands to form a paste, rolled it into a ball, and swallowed it like a pill. Others dried the leaves only slightly, toasted and husked them, mixed them with sesame and sugar, and chewed them like gum.

The sight of these people and their unconventional clothes and behavior unsettled Ibn al-Baytar, and he voiced his opinion in his diary. "People [i.e., the Sufis] who use it [hashish] habitually have proved its pernicious effect," he writes, for "it enfeebles their minds by carrying to them maniac affections, sometimes it even causes death." Ibn al-Baytar then adds: "I recall having seen a time when men of the vilest class alone dared to eat it, still they did not like the name takers of hashish applied to them."[5] This latter comment reflects the attitude of the upper-class Moslem's opinion of the Sufis and their use of hashish. It also shows, however, that by the twelfth century, the label "hashish user" had become so derogatory that even the Sufis were upset at being so taunted.

One of the favorite gathering places for hashish users in Egypt was the "gardens" of Cafour in Cairo. "The green plant which grows in the garden of Cafour replaces in our hearts the effects of old and noble wine," states a poem written in tribute to the renowned gathering place of hashish connoisseurs. Another poem coos: "Give me this green plant from the garden of Cafour, this plant which surpasses wine itself in the number of people it enslaves."

The authorities felt differently. Unwilling to tolerate the rabble collecting in the city's garden spot, the governor of Cairo ordered out the troops. In A.D. 1253, all the cannabis plants growing in the area were chopped, gathered, and hurled onto a massive pyre the flames of which could be seen for miles around. "A just punishment of God," was the pronouncement of the more pious citizens of Cairo, as they watched the fire destroy the plants.

With Cafour gone, hashish devotees had to go elsewhere to obtain their heady rations. Their inconvenience was only temporary. Seeing an opportunity to make some easy money, the farmers on the outskirts of Cairo began sowing cannabis seeds.

At first this was a legitimate enterprise, since these farmers paid a tax for the privilege. But in A.D. 1324, the new governor decided that the situation had once more gotten out of hand. Troops were summoned into action. Every day for an entire month, the army foraged into the countryside on search-and-destroy missions; the enemy—hashish plants.

After this show of force, the fields remained barren of cannabis for a few months. Cultivation then resumed as before. There was just too much money to be made to give up production permanently. To protect themselves from renewed interference, growers and merchants offered bribes and it was business as usual.

But in A.D. 1378 another order came down from the office of the governor to destroy the cannabis fields. This time the farmers decided to resist. Not one to back down, the governor dispatched Egypt's version

[5]*Ibid.*, p. 57; cf. also R. P. Walton, *Marihuana* (Philadelphia: J. B. Lippincott, 1938), p. 13.

of a S.W.A.T. team against the hashish farmers. But the farmers were determined to preserve their lucrative business, and eventually the troops backed off and instead of fighting, decided to place the area under seige, hoping to starve the farmers into submission.

The people held out for several months, but the outcome was never in doubt. When the soldiers finally broke through the defenses and poured into the valley there was no alternative but to capitulate. The resistance crushed, the soldiers placed the valley under martial law. Fields were set ablaze. Towns were either razed to the ground or placed under strict surveillance. Local cafes which had previously been known as centers for the hashish trade were closed. Proprietors of these businesses were hunted down and killed. Patrons of these shops who were known to the authorities had a different fate in store for them. All known hashish addicts were assembled in the town square, and in full view of all the townspeople, the soldiers wrenched out their teeth.[6]

By A.D. 1393, however, the hashish business was once again a thriving enterprise, a situation which prompted the Egyptian historian Maqrizi, who was a contemporary, to write: "as a consequence [of hashish use], general corruption of sentiments and manners ensued, modesty disappeared, every base and evil passion was openly indulged in, and nobility of external form alone remained in these infatuated beings."[7] But deplore the situation though Maqrizi might, hashish had become too much a part of the Arab way of life for it to be forsaken, whatever the criticisms and pressures against it.

THE DIARY FROM PRISON

They came from all parts of Genoa in Italy to listen to these fantastic tales of far-off lands, of strange customs and wealth beyond the imagination. They came not to the theater, or the palace, but the dungeon.

From the damp, dimly lit underground prison, a Venetian merchant was dictating to a copyist the details of a fascinating journey he had just completed, a journey that had taken him from Venice to the court of the Kublai Khan, great emperor of China. He had been gone twenty-five years and had traveled thousands of miles. Now he could only travel the length of his cell.

At first the jailers and townspeople laughed. This Venetian must think that the inhabitants of Genoa were mad. Who could believe these

---

[6]Rosenthal, *Herb*, p. 136.
[7]See W. D. Drake, *The Connoisseur's Handbook of Marihuana* (New York: Straight Arrow Press, 1970), pp. 69–70.

incredible stories of cannibals, shark charmers, and houses built of gold and silver? But the laughter soon gave way to a hushed awe as the storyteller repeatedly checked his notes to make sure that his facts were accurate. His sincerity, if not his sanity, could not be doubted.

The storyteller was a merchant named Marco Polo. The year was A.D. 1297. Venice and Genoa were at war. Polo had been taken prisoner during a sea battle on his return from the Far East. Now, as he awaited his fate, he was recording memories of the eventful expedition he had just completed. Whatever his fate, he would leave behind a record of all the marvelous things he had seen and heard.

Even after his release from prison and the publication of his travel record, few people were willing to believe Polo sane. Nevertheless, the book was one of the most fascinating adventure stories of the day and it was widely copied and circulated. Two centuries later, it was to excite the imagination of an Italian visionary named Christopher Columbus and made him dream of a similar journey to these far-off lands. Only instead of going overland, he would go by sea, sailing westward around the world.

Columbus was not the only person to be influenced by Marco Polo's travelogue. Seven centuries after Polo's death, the Congress of the United States and the American public were once again treated to an excerpt from Marco Polo's writings. It was an excerpt that was widely cited in the 1920s and 1930s as proof that hashish was a drug that incited fanaticism, lust, and uncontrollable violence. The irony of this presentation was that Marco Polo himself had never even heard of hashish.

Marco Polo's Version of Paradise

As Marco Polo was passing through northern Persia on his way to China, the people of the area told him an amazing story about a legendary ruler known as the "Old Man of the Mountains" and his ruthless band of cutthroats known as the Assassins. For two centuries, beginning around A.D. 1050, these daggermen had struck fear into the hearts of even the most powerful Arab leaders. It was only in A.D. 1256 that their stranglehold over the Middle East was finally ended at the hands of the Mongols.

According to Marco Polo's diary,[8] the terrorist leader kept his minions blindly loyal to his will by brainwashing them; should they die in his service, they would be certain to enter Paradise. To convince skeptics

[8]H. Yule, ed., *The Book of Ser Marco Polo* (New York: Book League of America, 1929).

of his ability to make good such a promise, he gave each potential candidate a foreshadowing of what lay in store for him.

According to the legend, he accomplished this ploy through a beautiful garden landscaped in his mountain stronghold of Alamut, the "Eagle's Nest." The garden was filled with exotic flowers and fountains brimming with milk and honey. Sensuous girls strolled this oasis ready to grant even the slightest wish. Everything was designed for the immediate gratification of any whim. But before he could enter this magnificent garden spot, the potential convert was required to partake of a powerful drug which rendered him unconscious. In this comotose state he was carried into the garden. When he awoke, he could gratify himself to his heart's content.

After being allowed to savor "Paradise," the recruit was drugged once again and brought before the "Old Man." When he awoke, the novice begged to be readmitted. The "Old Man" promised to do so, provided his orders were followed meticulously and without question.

Such was the story told by Marco Polo. Although a mere fantasy, with little truth to it at all, there was an "Old Man of the Mountains," and there was a group of fanatics called the Assassins who were completely devoted to him. What, then, was the truth? Before answering this question, there are a number of points worth noting about Marco Polo's account, the most important of which is the mysterious potion referred to by the explorer.

The first point is that the potion is never identified. Marco Polo makes no mention of hashish at all, and yet most retellings of this story always identify it as hashish.

Second, whatever the drug, it was not given to anyone who was sent out on a mission. The potion was given only before entry into the garden and before being taken out.

Third, the mysterious potion was soporific. It put its users to sleep. There is no mention of delirium or excitement connected with the drug.

THE ORIGINS OF THE ASSASSINS

The roots of the fraternity of Assassins go back to A.D. 632, the year in which the prophet Mohammed died without leaving any designated heir. The religion of Islam, which Mohammed founded, began in the year A.D. 622, following the entry of the prophet into the city of Medina. It was the culmination of a meteoric career that saw a penniless unknown emerge to forge a religion that would unite a disorganized nation of nomads into one of the greatest empires of the world.

Born some time between A.D. 570 and 580, Mohammad became an orphan at a very early age and was raised in the city of Mecca by his grandfather. Although born into poverty, he became wealthy and respectable by marrying the widow of a rich merchant and taking over his business.

It was not until he was about forty years old that Mohammed began to feel the proverbial "call to religion." Dissatisfied with the tribal religions and idolatry of his fellow Arabs, and unable to accept either Judaism or Christianity, he began to preach against the evils of the old Arab religion and announced the coming of a new era. While he initially had no idea that he was beginning a new religion, he did succeed in converting a number of people to his way of thinking. Foremost among these new converts were his wife and his cousin Ali, who was later to become Mohammed's successor.

The more he criticized the existing religion, the more his activities came to the attention of the authorities, who looked with disfavor upon this challenge to their own position. Persecuted, Mohammed and his tiny band of converts fled to Abyssinia. From this relatively safe haven, Mohammed continued to preach his message, and the more he spoke, the more the people listened. When at last he felt that he had a strong enough following, Mohammed brought his religious message to Medina in present-day Saudi Arabia, an event celebrated today as the starting point in the Arab calendar. From that time on, the religion became so widely accepted that Mohammed was able to overcome all opposition.

THE BLOOD FEUD

The religion of Islam which Mohammed founded was based on the recognition of the one god, Allah, and his prophet, Mohammed. When Mohammed died in A.D. 632, the new religion faced the difficult problem of choosing a successor (caliph). Among those nominated was Ali, cousin to the prophet and one of his first converts. Also in Ali's favor was the fact that he was the husband of Fatima, Mohammed's only surviving daughter.

But Ali was not chosen. Instead, the office was given to an elderly man whom Mohammed had once asked to lead the daily prayers. This first caliph did not live very long, however, and a new successor had to be chosen. Again Ali was skipped over. Two more caliphs were elected before Ali was finally chosen in A.D. 656. Five years later he too was dead, the victim of a feud between Arab factions that supported him as caliph and those who refused to accept his appointment.

The bloodletting associated with the succession issue eventually split Islam into two main sects, the Sunnis and the Shiites. The Sunnis saw themselves as the upholders of orthodoxy in Islam. They contended that the people had a right to elect whomever they wished to be caliph. The Shiites, on the other hand, insisted that the only legitimate successors were those in whom the blood of the Prophet himself flowed. This meant Ali and his descendants.

Although the differences between the two parties appeared to rest on the problem of the rightful heir to the office of caliph, the animosities were much deeper and involved basic differences in racial background and ancient traditions. Racially, the Shiites were mainly Persians of Aryan ancestry. It was their custom, based on a tradition that reached back to the time of the great Persian empire, to be governed by a hereditary monarchy. The Sunnis, who represented the majority of Arabs, were Semitic in origin. Their custom was to elect leaders on the basis of personal merit, not blood line.

Since the Sunnis far outnumbered the Shiites, they exerted the dominant influence in Islam. The Shiites, however, refused to accept the caliphs chosen by the Sunnis, and instead pledged their allegiance to the family of the Prophet. These descendants were treated as divinely inspired and divinely appointed interpreters of the faith. Obedience to their commands, whatever these might be, was regarded as an integral part of the religion of Islam.

Ali's descendants were many in number, however, and while the Shiites agreed on the fundamental principle of hereditary succession, they were often unable to agree on who that legitimate successor ought to be. This internal disagreement resulted in a schism within the Shiite party which eventually led to the creation of the Ismaili sect, the party to which the Assassins belonged.

A HOUSE DIVIDED AGAINST ITSELF

The precipitating event in the Shiite schism occurred during the reign of Caliph Jafar-i-Sadiq. According to Shiite custom, the eldest son succeeded his father to the office of caliph. However, one day Jafar-i-Sadiq discovered his eldest son, Ismail, drinking some wine, an act expressly forbidden by the *Koran*, the holy book of Islam. Outraged at this abomination, the caliph announced that his eldest son was unfit to serve as his successor and he designated his younger son, Musa, for the job.

While most Shiites accepted the nomination, a small group remained loyal to Ismail, claiming that the succession belonged to the eldest son. In response to the accusation that Ismail had violated the proscription against drinking alcohol, these supporters pointed out that the successor-designate was divine and without sin. If he drank wine, it was to teach his followers that the statements in the *Koran* against drinking alcohol were to be taken figuratively, not literally. Wine, they argued, was a symbol for pride and vanity. It was these traits of character that the *Koran* forbade, not the juice of the grape.

But Ismail had few followers compared to the majority of Shiites who recognized Musa as leader. After his death, Ismail's supporters went underground and continued in relative obscurity while the faithful waited for a new leader to reveal himself and restore the House of Ali to its rightful heir. Their patience was finally rewarded in the tenth century when the Fatimids, a dynasty loyal to the Ismaili doctrine, seized the throne of Egypt. Soon after their accession to power, they began sending out missionaries throughout the Arab world to make converts to Ismaili orthodoxy. One of the converts eventually won over to their side was a young Persian named Hasan-ibn-Sabah, who was to become known to his enemies as the "Old Man of the Mountains."

THE OLD MAN OF THE MOUNTAINS

The two men strolled along the walls of the mountain fortress silhouetted against the clear Persian sky. The year was A.D. 1092. One of the men was a personal envoy of the sultan. His host was Hasan-ibn-Sabah, the "Old Man of the Mountains." The envoy had come to demand the surrender of the fortress. There was no use in resisting, he asserted, for the sultan had more than enough soldiers to capture the garrison. Surrender and he and his men would be treated with compassion; resist and they would meet Allah long before their time.

The ruler of the mountain stronghold listened to the offer in silence. When the envoy finished his message, Hasan pointed to a guard standing watch high atop a lookout post. The envoy watched as his host signaled the guard and blinked in disbelief as the man saluted and threw himself from his post down into the chasm a thousand feet below. There were 70,000 more like him, Hasan told the startled envoy, all prepared to lay down their lives at his slightest bidding. Were the sultan's minions any match for these devoted followers? Shaken, the envoy took leave of his host wondering if anyone would believe what he had just witnessed.

Apparently the sultan did not believe, for he sent his armies against Hasan. It was a mistake. Soon after the abortive attack he was murdered, poisoned by one of Hasan's devoted henchmen.

Who was this incredible leader for whom men were prepared to kill themselves and others at a mere wave of the hand? Although villainized by his enemies, there is no question that Hasan-ibn-Sabah was a man of exceptional abilities and self-discipline. He was intelligent, ambitious, and ruthless, a political opportunist who believed that the end justified the means. He was a man totally lacking in compassion. He demanded blind obedience and was prepared to sacrifice those who loyally served him without giving their deaths a second thought.

Born in A.D. 1050, Hasan was the son of a Shiite merchant who withdrew from society to a monastery and sent his son to an orthodox Moslem school. Two of Hasan's classmates were also destined for prominence in the Arab world. The first was Nizam-al-Mulk, prime minister to two sultans of the Arab empire, and the second was Omar Khayyam, tent maker, astronomer, and unparalleled poet of the Arab world.

One of the reasons his father had sent Hasan to this particular school was the widely held belief that all who studied there would eventually attain great importance. The students were also aware of this belief, and one day Nizam, Omar, and Hasan made a pact that whosoever of them would fulfill the prediction first would do his utmost to help the other two.

The earliest of the three to advance his career was Nizam-al-Mulk who rose to a high position in the court of the sultan. As he had promised, he tried to help his friends. When Omar Khayyam came to him for support, Nizam obtained a pension for the poet generous enough for him not to be burdened with earning a living, and the poet was able to compose his famous *Rubaiyat* poems without distraction.

Next, Hasan presented himself at court. Nizam cordially received his other friend and got him an interview with the sultan, who took an immediate liking to him and made Hasan his chamberlain. But Hasan was overly ambitious. And an ingrate. As soon as he had his foot in the palace door, he tried to undermine Nizam in the sultan's eyes and install himself in his erstwhile friend's place.

Hasan thought he saw his opportunity when the sultan asked Nizam to draw up a record of all the income and expenses of the empire. Asked how long such an undertaking would require, Nizam estimated a time no less than a year. At this point Hasan jumped in and challenged that he could do it in forty days. The sultan was greatly pleased at such a possibility and gave him the job instead.

True to his word, Hasan had the accounts ready within the designated period. But Nizam was not one to be brushed aside so easily. By some trick he managed to alter the records, and when Hasan presented the accounts to the sultan they were so distorted that he was banished from the court for his impertinence. Although he protested his innocence, Hasan could not explain how his records had been doctored since they were written in his own script.

Humiliated but not discouraged, Hasan next journeyed to Egypt where he allied himself with the Fatamids and was introduced into the secret doctrines of the Ismaili sect.

If Hasan had been searching for some way to gain power, Egypt was a well-chosen starting place. The Fatamids had founded a school in which they trained recruits in the Ismaili doctrine and in the art of assassination. The techniques he would learn at this school subsequently proved invaluable to Hasan.

The Egyptian rulers welcomed Hasan to their court when they learned of his arrival. A recent member of the sultan's personal retinue could bring only prestige to the Fatamid court. But Hasan once again involved himself in some chicanery at court and he was arrested and thrown into jail. But the moment he entered the prison, a minaret broke in two and crashed to the earth. The event was seen as a sign that Hasan was no ordinary man. Apprised of the coincidence, the Egyptian ruler immediately released Hasan and sent him away laden with gifts.

Hasan next made his way to Syria by boat. It was aboard this ship that he made his first two converts. These conversions renewed his confidence in himself, and immediately upon disembarking, he began to spread his message, which became known as the "New Propaganda."

Asserting that Islam and the Ismailis had grown decadent, Hasan promised to bring both back on a more righteous course, true to Allah's ways. There would have to be sacrifices, however. The Ismailis would have to renounce all worldly pleasures. They would have to rid themselves of all those things that other men found pleasurable. Since the Ismailis at that time were a poor, oppressed, discontented people seeking some meaning in a hapless existence, Hasan's injunctions entailed little self-denial on their part.

Hasan himself was no hypocrite. An ascetic for most of his life, years later he expelled one of his followers from the fold for flute playing, and executed his own son for a minor frivolity. He set the example, and he expected his disciples to follow it.

To those who asked how Allah's ways were to be made known to the Ismailis, Hasan answered that a true understanding of that divine plan was not possible for the ordinary mind to comprehend. It was only possible for a divinely appointed representative to understand and make known Allah's ways. Mohammed had been such an intermediary. He, Hasan, was another such representative.

Hasan repeatedly emphasized that Allah's ways were too profound to comprehend through reason. Utilizing techniques he had learned in Egypt, Hasan created doubt in the minds of his audiences concerning orthodox Islamic teaching. The more confusion he was able to sow, the more dependent on him would his followers become, since he was the only source of wisdom. Only through faith and blind obedience could they be assured of obtaining salvation.

Once he had convinced a small number of Ismailis that he alone comprehended Allah's ways, Hasan instructed them on how to win over new members. Each convert thus in turn became a proselytizer.

Captivated by Hasan's dynamic personality, his utter confidence in himself, his self-assurance, his conviction that Islam had grown decadent and that salvation could only come through him, converts began pledging their lives in increasing numbers, often leaving behind their wives and children to make their way without husband and father.

Hasan's next move was to order his men to infiltrate the mountain fortress of Alamut, the "Eagle's Nest," and make converts of the soldiers stationed there. Then, after carefully laying some preliminary plans, Hasan approached the commander of the garrison and offered him 3000 pieces of gold for all the land under his control that could be covered by the hide of an ox. The commander thought Hasan mad to make such an offer, but who was he to look Allah's gift horse in the mouth? A wide grin appeared on his face as the last gold piece was counted out and handed over to him. But the grin quickly disappeared as he watched Hasan cut the hide into thin strips. The bargain was off, he shouted, as he watched Hasan sew the strips together and then march around the fortress.

However, Hasan was prepared for such a contingency. After surrounding the fortress with the ox hide, he produced an order signed by a high-ranking government official, a secret convert to the "New Propaganda," which ordered the commander to honor the terms of the bargain. The commander dutifully obeyed and marched out, leaving Hasan in possession of an impressive stronghold. The year was A.D. 1090.

Immediately upon moving into Alamut, Hasan inaugurated a series of building measures to strengthen the fortification. Canals were dug to carry water to the fortress, the fields that surrounded it were irrigated, fruit trees were planted, and storerooms were erected.

The point of these improvements was lost on Hasan's enemies who, in later generations, mistakenly assumed that he was constructing a sort of Paradise to entice new followers to his ranks. These mistaken stories were eventually recorded by European travelers such as Marco Polo, and through them, Hasan's fortress became known to Western readers as a palacial mansion filled with lush and exotic plants and populated with beautiful and sensuous women.

There were other fantastic stories told about the ruses Hasan used to win over new converts. According to one legend, Hasan had a hole dug deep enough for a man to stand in with only his head above the ground. The hole was then filled in and a tray was fitted around his neck. To increase the effect, fresh blood was splashed around the "severed" neck.

Potential candidates were then brought into the room and, after fixing each man with his steely gaze, Hasan announced that the head would speak to them of the marvelous life that awaited them in the other world if they were to obey his commands without question. At this point, the confederate opened his eyes and began to tell them of the Paradise his soul had recently been admitted to as a result of serving Hasan.

The scene made a profound impression on all those who witnessed it, and they went away pledging their lives to Hasan. Shortly after they left the room, the confederate was actually decapitated and his head was prominently displayed so that no one would have second thoughts about having been duped. In this story, however, there is no mention of any drug being administered to either the initiates or the unfortunate victim.

THE "DEVOTED ONES"

With Alamut as his base of operations, Hasan began to organize his followers into various grades or degrees of office. At the top he naturally placed himself, giving his position the title of grand master. Next came the grand priors, the overseers, who directed the activities of the sect and apprised Hasan of all important developments. Below them came the dais, or missionaries, who disseminated the "propaganda" of the sect throughout the Middle East. The fourth and fifth orders made up the bulk of members of the sect. They admitted their allegiance to the grand master and supported the movement in various ways, usually through donations. The sixth group was called the fidais, the "devoted ones." These were the enforcers. It was their job to carry out the orders of their superiors.

Once a fidai received his orders, he was committed to only one purpose—carrying out those instructions, no matter what the obstacles or the consequences to his own life. He would perservere for months, waiting for the right moment to strike. No matter that he would be captured and killed on the spot. The only thing that mattered was the mission. To die in the performance of his duty was a privilege and a ticket to Paradise. This disregard for death made the Assassins the most feared gang of cutthroats in the Middle East.

Arab sultans, princes, and prime ministers as well as many eminent Crusaders all fell victim to these daggermen. With the assassination of Conrad, marquis of Monteferrat, however, the reputation of the "Old Man of the Mountains" spread far beyond the Middle East to the far reaches of Western Europe. The fidai responsible for the murder spent six months disguised as a monk in the camp of the Crusaders, waiting for just the right opportunity. Finally, the moment came and, in full view of the marquis's attendants, the assassin plunged his dagger into Conrad's body.

Once their reputation had spread throughout the Middle East, it was no longer necessary for the Assassins to liquidate their enemies. Often, all that was required was a threat. On one occasion, for example, Saladin, one of the most able Arab generals of that era, decided that the Assassins had to be put in their place and he mounted a campaign to take the Alamut fortress. Shortly before the seige, however, he awoke one night to find a dagger stuck in the ground beside him. Attached to the knife was a curt message advising him to reconsider. Saladin wisely changed his mind and directed his efforts elsewhere.

How was it that Hasan was able to enlist such a devoted band of selfless followers who were more than willing to lay down their lives at his bidding?

According to Marco Polo, Hasan kept his men blindly loyal to his will by convincing them that should they die in his service, they would be certain to enter Paradise.

This theme appears also in the story of the "severed" head and in an anecdote related by an emissary to the emperor Frederick Barbarossa in A.D. 1175. According to this report,

> [Hasan had] many of the sons of his peasants brought up from early childhood. . . . These young men are taught by their teachers from their earliest youth to their full manhood, that they must obey the lord of their land in all his words and commands; and that if they do so, he, who has power over all living gods, will give them the joys of Paradise. . . . When they are in the presence of the Prince, he asks them if they are willing to obey his commands, so that he may bestow Paradise upon them. . . . They throw themselves at his feet and reply with fervor that they will obey him. . . . Thereupon the Prince gives each one of them a golden dagger and sends him out to kill whichever prince he has marked down.[9]

In all the stories about Hasan's ability to instill blind loyalty in his followers, the one common element is the promise of entering Paradise in return for serving the grand master. Only in Marco Polo's account is there any mention of a drug.

What's in a Name?

One of the most puzzling questions about the Assassins is how they got their name. The members of the sect never referred to themselves as such. They called each other fidais, "devoted ones." Only their enemies called them Assassins.

[9]Quoted in W. Fleischhauer, "The Old Man of the Mountain," *Symposium* 9 (1955): 82–3.

In a report to Frederick Barbarossa, ruler of the Holy Roman Empire, they are called Heyssessini. William, Archbishop of Tyre, wrote that "both our people and the Saracens called them Assissini," but, he adds, "we do not know the origin of this name."[10]

By the thirteenth century, however, the word "assassin" and its variants were being used in Europe in the sense of a paid professional killer. The word was derived from the name of the sect, but no one suggested that they got that name because of their usage of hashish, although a twelfth-century friar, Abbot Arnold of Lubeck, did state that the Assassins used hashish: "hemp raises them to a state of ecstasy or falling, or intoxicates them. Their sorcerers draw near and exhibit to the sleepers, phantasms, pleasures and amusement. They then promise that these delights will become perpetual if the orders given them are executed with the daggers provided."[11]

Travel books such as the seventeenth-century *Purchas His Pilgrimis* repeated Marco Polo's story about a mysterious potion but made no mention of hashish. Another writer of that era, Denis Lebey de Batilly, wrote only that the name given to the sect by its enemies was Arabic for hired killer.

Various other explanations were subsequently proposed, among them that the name was derived from "asas," a word meaning foundation, which was applied to the religious leaders of Islam; that assassin was derived from the Arabic word *hassas*, which, among other things, meant "to kill;" or that the name was applied to the followers of Hasan.

THE TALE OF THE HASHISH EATER

Between A.D. 1000 and A.D. 1700, a collection of stories from the Arab world came into being which today are known as *The Thousand and One Nights*. Although loosely joined, the thread that holds the collection together is the delightful fantasy of how a wily young harem girl enchanted the sultan and saved her life. It was through these stories that most Europeans first learned of hashish.

According to the storyline, the sultan Shahriyar had ordained that each of his future wives was to be put to death the morning after consumating their marriage nuptials. This ritual went on through several wives until Scheherazade, the daughter of the grand vizier, tricked the sultan into revoking this postamatory rite.

The ruse she used consisted of telling the sultan an amusing story

[10]Quoted in C. E. Nowell, "The Old Man of the Mountain," *Speculum*, 22(1947):500, note 8.
[11]Quoted in L. Lewin, *Phantasica* (New York: E. P. Dutton, 1964), p. 110.

on the night of their marriage and then breaking it off in the middle, promising to finish it the next night. But each night she also started a new story, breaking that one off as well so that it would have to be ended the next night. In this way she succeeded in delaying her execution for a thousand and one nights, until at last the sultan became so enamored of this spinner of tales that he fell in love with her and decided to cancel his former edict.

One of the stories Scheherazade amused the sultan with was called "The Tale of the Hashish Eater," and in it she recounted the saga of a hashish user who had been reduced to poverty as a result of wasting his savings on his drug and on women. Yet by means of his cherished drug, he was able to escape into a dream world where he was no longer a beggar but a handsome and prosperous lover.

One day this pauper took some hashish in a public bath and dropped off into a dream in which he was transported into an enchanting room filled with beautiful flowers and the smell of exotic perfumes. All this time, however, he sensed that this was only a dream and that it would not be long before his presence in the public bath would be noticed and he would be beaten and thrown out. Even so, he continued to enjoy the dream.

As he fell deeper into his reverie, he saw himself being carried to another luxurious room filled with soft, plush cushions where he was sexually aroused by a sensuous slave girl. Just as he was about to embrace the girl, he was awakened from his dream by the laughter of the patrons in the bath who had become highly amused at the sight of this tumescent beggar. And just as he foresaw, he was beaten and ejected from the premises.

Readers of this story were not only amused by it, they were also able to appreciate the state of "double consciousness" the beggar found himself in as a result of taking hashish. In this state, the hashish user hallucinates, but is also aware that he is hallucinating—he does not lose complete touch with reality. Hashish causes him to dream, but it enables him to remain conscious of his dream so that he can appreciate the images and themes his mind is producing. It was this aspect of the hashish experience that was later to intrigue European writers, especially the French Romantic authors of the middle and latter part of the nineteenth century, for in this mysterious drug of the Arab world they saw untold possibilities of delving into the hitherto buried niches of the human mind.

The debasing influence of hashish was not the only theme in popular Arab literature. The ways in which the drug corrupted high officials also delighted audiences and readers. One such favorite anecdote tells of a hashish "pusher" who was apprehended and brought to court to appear before a judge presiding over a community that did not permit the use of hashish. This "pusher" had been fined on many occasions for his illegal activities, but to no avail. He simply paid his fine and went back to selling his illegal wares.

Fed up with this unrepentent drug peddler, the judge finally threatened him with a huge fine if he did not permanently cease his offensive activities. Faced with the threat of an exorbitant penalty, the "pusher" agreed to find another means of earning a living. To make sure that there would be no misunderstanding, the judge made the man swear an oath in which he enumerated all the different names and varieties of hashish. On hearing this list, the "pusher" observed that although he had heard of some of these names and preparations, many were completely new to him and he suggested that since the judge knew so much about the subject he ought to administer the oath to himself as well![12]

A similar story tells of the hypocrisy and quick thinking of a Moslem priest. During a wild and animated sermon in which he was haranguing his audience on the evils of hashish, his tunic opened and a bag of the vile drug fell to the ground right before the startled eyes of the onlookers. Without hesitating an instant, the priest pointed to the bag and shouted, "This is the demon of which I warned you; the force of my words have put it to flight, take care that in leaving me, it does not throw itself on one of you and enslave him." The crowd continued to listen to his sermon, but their eyes were glued on the hashish. Yet no one dared to pick it up. After the priest finished, the parishioners dispersed, leaving only the priest and the bag of hashish, which the holy man promptly picked up and stuffed back into his tunic.[13]

HASHISH AND THE ARAB WORLD: SUMMARY

Every culture has some kind of escape hatch, some ersatz respite from the overburdening realities of everyday existence. For over a thousand years, hashish has been this escape hatch for a large segment of Arab society.

The earliest groups to use hashish on a large scale were the Sufis, an economically and socially despised sector of Moslem society, who justified their use of the drug, to themselves at least, as a way of communing with their god.

The association of hashish with the Sufis had the effect of identify-

[12]Rosenthal, *Herb*, p. 39.
[13]Walton, *Marihuana*, p. 11.

ing it as a contemptible substance, a drug that sapped a man's energy and his willingness to work, a drug that made him a pariah rather than a contributor to his community. Hashish symbolized the ageless class antagonisms. The lowly social standing of the poor was attributed to their use of hashish, and the very term "hashish user" became an insulting epithet for what the upper classes regarded as the social misfits of their society. Thus, when the Arabs spoke of someone such as Hasan or his followers as "ashishin" (or Assassins, as the Crusaders pronounced the word), they were referring to them figuratively and abusively. Whether the Assassins did or did not use hashish was immaterial.

Nevertheless, it was because of the association of this term with the infamous gang of cutthroats, the resourceful terrorists of the Middle Ages, that many centuries later hashish gained for itself a reputation as a drug that inspired mayhem.

Curiously, the Arabs themselves have never regarded hashish as a drug which inspires violence. Perhaps the Arabs are simply too familiar with the actions of hashish to attribute violence to its seemingly endless list of effects. Yet in America, a country with a history of violence and little familiarity with cannabis as a mind-altering substance, hashish was to become known as the "killer drug."

II

THE HEMP ERA

3

Rope and Riches

In 1896, a German archaeologist, Hermann Busse, unearthed an ancient tomb at Wilmersdorf, near modern-day Brandenburg, which contained a funerary urn dating back to the Fifth century B.C. It was not the oldest grave to be discovered in Europe. People had been living in what is now Europe for thousands of years and remnants of their existence were not uncommon. The thing that made Busse's discovery unique was that the funerary urn that had lain buried in the earth for almost 2500 years contained various identifiable plant fragments, among them cannabis seeds.[1]

How did these seeds get there? Did the Scythians penetrate this far west in their restless search for new lands and people to conquer? Hiero II of Greece had sent men to the Rhone Valley in France in the third century B.C., but this discovery placed cannabis in northern Europe 200 years before that, and indicates that even at this early date, cannabis had acquired a special significance in the burial rites of the dead.

A thousand years later, the limestone tomb of the French queen Arnegunde, who was buried around A.D. 570 in Paris, likewise contained cannabis.

As was typical of the crypts in which the medieval French nobility were laid to rest, Arnegunde's tomb was lavishly furnished with precious objects. Gold coins, rich jewelry, and costly garments were all interred with the dead to guarantee that they would enjoy as comfortable a life in the next world as that from which their souls had just departed.

The buckles on her shoes and garters were made of silver. Around her neck was a gold broach. At the side of each of her temples were gold pins which held a veil of red satin over her face. On each ear was a gold filigree earring. Her body was dressed in violet silk and rested on a

---

[1]W. Reininger, "Remnants from Prehistoric Times," in *The Book of Grass*, ed. G. Andrews and J. Vinkenoog (New York: Grove Press, 1967), p. 14.

bright-red blanket over which was draped a cloth made from hemp,[2] a material apparently deserving of this place of honor among the rich and elegant burial wardrobe of the French nobility during the early Middle Ages.

Cannabis in one form or another has been found in other parts of Europe as well during this early period of history. Hempen ropes, for instance, have been found in a well from a Roman fort in Dunbarton-shire, England, which was occupied between A.D. 140 and 180. However, modern scientific studies of pollen in soil samples shows that cannabis was not cultivated in England until around A.D. 400[3] when the Anglo-Saxons migrated to the island from their homes in mainland Europe. Since they had no way of knowing if there would be enough cannabis in the lands they conquered to meet their needs, the Romans took hemp ropes with them. When these ropes wore out, orders were sent back home for replacements. The pieces of hemp rope from Dun-bartonshire were thus made elsewhere and sent to England as part of the supplies needed for the occupation.

Hempen ropes have also been found in Iceland among artifacts that date back to the early Middle Ages. These ropes were carried there by the intrepid Vikings, for whom strong rope often meant the difference between survival or disaster in the vast uncharted Atlantic. Pieces of cloth and fishing line made from hemp have also been discovered in Viking graves in Norway, and cannabis seeds have been found in the remains of Viking ships that date back to A.D. 850.[4]

Cannabis in its various forms was thus no stranger to Western Europe by the beginning of the Middle Ages. However, it was the Italians who began the first large-scale cultivation of the plant and eventually turned hemp into haute couture.

THE VIRGINS AND THE PIRATES

During the Middle Ages, the Italians ruled the seas and nothing surpassed the strength and durability of the hempen ropes with which their ships were outfitted. To maintain their supremacy on the seas, the Italians had to be assured that their supplies of hemp fiber would not be jeopardized by foreign control of hemp. Only by raising their own crop of the precious fiber could they be certain that Italian shipbuilders would

[2]J. Werner, "Frankish Royal Tombs in the Cathedrals of Cologne and Saint-Denis," *Antiquity* 38 (1964): 201–16.
[3]H. Godwin, "The Ancient Cultivation of Hemp," *Antiquity*, 41 (1967): 44.
[4]*Ibid.*, pp. 46–7.

never be blackmailed by foreign suppliers. Foremost among those who promoted domestic production of hemp were the merchants and shipbuilders from the city of canals and gondolas.

Although Venice emerged as one of Italy's most powerful city-states, initially it was but a swamp village at the head of the Adriatic Sea and it was only goaded into asserting its dominance by the abduction of its virgins by a gang of daring pirates.

The event that led to Venice's rise to a major sea power began inauspiciously enough on February 1, A.D. 945. For centuries, all Venetian marriages took place on the first day of February. It was an event celebrated with great pomp and ceremony by rich and poor alike. It was a day of expectation, excitement, anticipation—a day of love.

From all parts of the city they came, the young radiant girls of Venice and their proud mothers and fathers. Their destination—the Church of San Pietro di Castello in the eastern sector of the city. At the church door, the nervous bridegrooms rubbed their hands and shuffled their feet. Inside, the bishop was giving last-minute instructions to the choirboys. The doge (ruler) was seated in the front row, ready to give his blessing as well to the newlyweds.

The people of Venice were wealthy and respected, but they had their enemies. Among those who eyed their money with envy was a gang of resourceful pirates whose base of operations was the seaports of Dalmatia located opposite Venice on the other side of the Adriatic Sea. From these harbors the pirates ventured out in search of booty, plundering far and wide—the entire Mediterranean Sea their prey. No ship was safe once it left port. Even the Venetians paid extortion money when it was demanded, preferring to surrender some of their profits than to challenge the pirates and possibly lose everything.

Like most of the people who lived around the Adriatic Sea, the Dalmatian pirates knew of the annual nuptials about to be performed in Venice. Acting as much out of villainy as greed, the pirates decided to humiliate the Venetians by kidnapping their blushing brides on their wedding night. After all, what better time to attack? No one would be expecting them. The men would be too drunk to offer much resistance. And the women would both satisfy their lustful appetites and bring a bountiful ransom.

Silently, they meandered their ships into Venetian waters. A token force was left to guard the boats while the main group of pirates stealthily made their way toward the Church of San Pietro. In the distance, the pirates could hear the music and celebrations. They grinned at one another. The plan was going well.

They struck at midnight. Swooping down on the unsuspecting merrymakers, the pirates burst into the midst of the festivities, and before anyone realized what had happened, the pirates were back aboard their ships with the irate brides and a cargo full of expensive wedding presents.

The raid caught the Venetians by surprise, but somehow the tipsy bridegrooms managed to sober themselves. Soon the whole city was aroused. From every quarter the men rushed to the port, swearing revenge on the pirates. At the head of the rescue mission was the doge himself.

The Venetian ships skimmed over the waves. Not an inch of canvas was left unfurled. Not only was the virtue of their women at stake, the honor of Venice itself had been besmirched. The gap between the fleeing pirates and the pursuing bridegrooms finally closed at Carole. The Venetians were inflamed, but the pirates were wily fighters. The battle waged for hours. When the smoke finally cleared, however, the brides were back with their husbands and those pirates who had managed to remain alive were in full flight. From that day on, the scene of the battle was called the Porto della Damigelle, the Port of the Young Women.

The pirates had lost the battle, but the war was still unresolved. Finally, in A.D. 1000 the Venetians decided that they had had enough. They had beaten the pirates before, they could do it again. On Ascension Day, the doge assembled all the fighting men and all the ships in Venice and set sail toward Dalmatia. Up and down the coast they hunted their pirate quarry. Every city that gave the pirates refuge was attacked and punished. No longer would anyone dare to threaten Venetian shipping. Her enemies were no more. Venice was now undisputed sovereign of the Adriatic and the Mediterranean.

It was the Crusades, however, which saw the emergence of Venice from a Mediterranean to a world power. Owing to its strategic port location, Venice was able to demand huge fees to transport the Crusaders from Europe to the Holy Land. Venice supported the war against the Moslem infidels, but its Christian fervor had a price. With each Crusade, Venice's power increased. By A.D. 1200, Venice had control over all the trade in three-quarters of what remained of the ancient Roman Empire. Virtually anything that moved across the Adriatic, the Aegean, the Mediterranean, the Black Sea, and the Sea of Marmara sailed in Venetian ships. From outposts in the conquered Moslem cities of Sidon and Tyre, Venice also controlled the entire trade route from Constantinople to Western Europe. Venice had become the trade merchant of the world.

This preeminence among European powers continued until the middle of the fifteenth century. With the discovery of an Atlantic route around the Cape of Good Hope to the Far East in A.D. 1486, European ships no longer had to sail by way of the Mediterranean to gain access to the East. This discovery, more than any other single event, initiated

Venice's gradual decline to a second-rate power. Venice's demise did not happen overnight, however. The city still remained a wealthy and important influence in the world until almost the end of the eighteenth century when it was finally conquered in 1797 by Napoleon and was made into an Austrian possession.

The Venetian Hemp Guild

In Italy, hemp was once called *quello delle cento operazioni,* "the substance of a hundred operations," because of the many processes to which the plant was subjected before its fibers could be used.

Long before the days of automation, young girls would assemble in the houses where hemp was to be split and they would work well into the night preparing hemp for the craft industries. It was not easy work. Each girl took five or six stalks in one hand and what remained of the roots in the hollow of her other hand. Then, with a quick snap, she broke the stalk about twelve inches from the root. Next, she crooked the middle finger of her left hand and passed the fibers through the crook. While the thumb and forefinger of her right hand still held the unbroken part of the stalk, she grasped the woody part of the stem and pulled it away from the fibers.

The stripped fibers were held between the thumb and little finger of her left hand and they were twisted into a coil. The coils were then placed in piles to be beaten and swingled. Beating involved pounding the fibers to make them soft. First, the fibers were tied into tight round bundles. If the beating were to be done by hand, the bundles were placed on a stone and were either pounded manually with a heavy wooden mallet or flayed with a whip. In hemp mills, the pounding action was done by rolling a heavy millstone over the hemp manually or by a water wheel.

Next, the hemp was swingled. This was done by placing the hemp strands over a wooden board and removing any visible splinters. The last main step was combing—the separation of any fibers that still clung together by passing them through a rough and then a fine-toothed comb.

Very often these tasks were done in groups and they took on the atmosphere of a social get-together, much like the American sewing and quilting bees. In many villages, the townspeople worked on the hemp at night in someone's home and ended the evening on a festive note with games and dancing.

Whether hemp was processed in private homes or in large factories, the end product was fiber that was without equal for strength and durability. The Venetian Senate recognized the importance of hemp fiber for its shipbuilding and trade industries, and to ensure that Venetian hemp standards would remain high, it established a state-run factory called the Tana to oversee the quality of all the hemp that was processed into the rigging and anchor lines of the Venetian fleet. On "the manufacture of cordage in our home of the Tana," declared the Senate, rests "the security of our galleys and ships and similarly of our sailors and capital."[5]

According to Venetian statutes, all rigging for Venetian ships had to be manufactured from the highest grade of hemp. Unfortunately, the best hemp came from Bologna, and the Florentines who owned the Bolognese fields charged exorbitant prices for the commodity. Although it had no intention of using inferior hemp in its ships, the Tana tried to dupe the Florentines into believing that because of their high prices, Venice was going to import a lower and cheaper quality of hemp from Montagnana. The ruse worked and the Florentines lowered their prices, a compromise that fattened Venetian pockets considerably.

Even with the lowered price, however, Bolognese hemp was still more expensive than Montagnese, so the Venetians decided to try and cut their costs even more by improving the quality of hemp grown around Montagnana. As part of its plan, the Venetian Senate hired a Bolognese hemp expert, Michele di Burdrio, to teach the Montagneseans how to grow a better quality of hemp. Such corporate looting was not regarded very favorably by the people of Bologna, and for divulging the closely guarded secrets of his homeland, di Budrio was banished perpetually from his native city and all his property was confiscated. The Venetians, however, were prepared to compensate him for his losses, financial or otherwise. Di Budrio received a handsome salary, a monetary settlement equal to his losses, and his descendants were hired as salaried supervisors in the hemp fields for many generations thereafter.

Despite the improvements in Montagnese hemp that followed the hiring of di Budrio, the overall quality of the Montagnese product remained inferior to the Bolognese variety, and the Tana insisted the two varieties be clearly labeled. To ensure that the inferior product would not inadvertently find itself destined for one of the city's important shipping districts, procedures were implemented so that the two varieties of hemp would never be together in the same room. First-grade Bologna hemp also carried a white label attached to it, while first-grade Montagnana hemp was identified by means of a green label. In this way, the buyer was sure of the material he was purchasing.

Hemp spinners in Venice all belonged to a craft union and were

[5]Quoted in F. C. Lane, "The Rope Factory and Hemp Trade in the Fifteenth and Sixteenth Centuries," *Journal of Economic and Business History* 4 (1932): 834.

paid according to the quantity of work they produced rather than on the basis of an hourly or weekly wage. Those who were employed by the Tana were closely supervised by factory foremen. Each spinner was given a specially marked bobbin so that his work could be easily identified. Removal of these "trademarks" or the use of someone else's bobbin was considered a criminal offense punishable by whipping and/or dismissal from the craft for up to ten years. Foremen regularly inspected all ropes made by Tana spinners and inferior workmanship was also punishable by fines.

By insisting on only the highest grade of hemp and by enforcing rigid codes of excellence in her rope factories, Venice outfitted a fleet second to none in Europe. Any cargoes, whatever their value, had a better chance of reaching their destinations if carried by a Venetian ship than by any other vessel. Because of its superiority, the Venetian merchant marine dominated the Mediterranean for centuries, an accomplishment due in no small measure to the high quality of raw materials such as hemp which went into each and every one of her sea-going armada.

During the nineteenth century, Italy became one of the world's main hemp-producing centers, supplying hemp fiber to Switzerland, Germany, England, Portugal, and Spain. It was not for cord or heavy rope that Italian hemp was prized, however, but for the fine fabric and clothes that could be manufactured from its whitish fiber. In skilled Italian hands, hemp fiber was turned into a thread that almost equalled silk in its delicacy. It was much finer than cotton and certainly much stronger. Two and one-half pounds of hemp, for instance, could be spun into 600 miles of lace threads![6] For those who could afford them, tablecloths and specially designed dresses spun from fine Italian hemp were prized possessions.

Hemp Magic

In keeping with hemp's importance as a major agricultural crop, various customs and ceremonies based on the homeopathic magical principle that like begets like were performed during the Middle Ages expressly to influence the growth of the hemp plant in the forthcoming year.

In many parts of Europe, for instance, peasant farmers kindled huge bonfires and danced around or leaped over the flames. The idea was that just as the flames and dancers soared into the air, so too would

---

[6]S. S. Boyce, *Hemp* (New York: Orange and Judd, 1900), pp. 48–9.

68 CHAPTER 3

the hemp crop grow high into the sky. So seriously did the peasants regard these hemp dances, writes the noted anthropologist Sir James G. Frazer, that anyone not contributing to the fire could look forward to a bad crop next year and "his hemp in particular would not grow."[7]

In parts of France, to make doubly sure that the hemp harvest would be good, the women dancers performed their leaps while slightly drunk.[8] Unfortunately, we do not know if this drunkenness was another instance of the magical belief in like begetting like—the drunkenness of the women influencing the production of psychoactive plant material.

Another French custom designed to influence the hemp growth was for the farmer to hitch up his trousers as high as possible while he sowed his hemp seeds in the hope that the hemp plants would grow to the height he had raised his pants.[9]

In many parts of Europe, it was also customary for farmers to sow their hemp seeds on days dedicated to the celebration of saints remembered as being rather tall. By asking for the help of these tall saints, the peasants believed that their hemp would also be tall.[10]

Various other customs were followed to coax hemp into growing tall. In some countries, the hemp dances were performed on rooftops. In Germany, hemp seeds were flung high into the air in the hope that the stalks of these seeds would be able to find their way back into the air one day.[11]

Yet another quaint custom related to hemp growing involved the election of a King and Queen of the Bean on the Twelfth Day (the Epiphany, January 6). As part of this custom, which began in the sixteen century, a huge cake was baked on the eve of the Twelfth Day. Two beans were then inserted into the cake. Pieces of cake were then distributed and whoever got the beans became the King and Queen of the Bean.

As soon as the king and queen were chosen, they were saluted and hoisted onto the shoulders of their subjects so that they could make crosses on the beams of the houses. These crosses were supposed to protect the houses during the coming year against evil spirits. But the real point of the selection was augury: it was an attempt to peer into the future to determine what the next year's hemp crop would be like. If the king were taller than the queen, then the male plant would be taller than the female (and the fiber would therefore be better). If the queen were

[7]J. G. Frazer, *Balder the Beautiful* (London: MacMillan, 1920), p. 168.
[8]*Ibid.*, p. 109.
[9]J. G. Frazer, *The Magic Art* (London: MacMillan, 1920), pp. 137–8.
[10]S. Benet, "Early Diffusion and Folk Uses of Hemp," in *Cannabis and Culture*, ed. V. Rubin (The Hague: Mouton, 1975), p. 43.
[11]*Ibid.*

taller, then the female hemp plants would be taller and the fiber would not be as good.[12]

In the Balkans, an ancient folk ritual (still practiced in the early part of the twentieth century) involved not so much dancing as running through a circle of burning hemp. As the peasants scampered through the flames, they chanted in unison: "We have been in the fire and not been burnt, we have been in the midst of illness and not caught it."[13]

Behind this ceremony is the idea that fire has a cleansing action and can thus protect people from disease. The reason the fires were made of hemp is unknown, but no doubt it was because of hemp's connection with magic.

IN SEARCH OF GOLD

Between A.D. 1400 and 1700, Western Europe was gradually transformed from a backward provincial potpourri of motley nations into a nationalistically minded assembly of world-conquering and world-colonizing empires. The Cinderella-like metamorphosis came about largely as a result of a technological innovation. First introduced by the Mediterranean nations and subsequently copied and improved on by Western Europe, the innovation that changed the course of history was the triangular sail.

By suspending a triangular sail from an oblique yardarm, sailors could sail against the wind. Hitherto, the square sail was the only means of propelling a ship, and most vessels were outfitted with only a single mast. After the triangular sail, galleons with three or four masts became commonplace and European ships began embarking from the safety of their ports to challenge the winds and the oceans of the world.

The triangular sail opened up new possibilities. The Italians had a solid hold on the Mediterranean. North Africa and the Middle East were controlled by the Arabs. Below Egypt lay the vast wastelands of the Sahara. Caravans sometimes trickled across the hot sands with their precious chests of gold, spices, and silks, but the journey was too hazardous and too costly to rely on an overland route to India and the Far East. Until the heroic rounding of the Cape of Good Hope in 1488 by the Portuguese adventurer Bartholomew Diaz, Western Europe had to be satisfied with its subordinate position.

But the triangular sail altered the balance of power and allowed Europe to master the treacherous winds that hitherto had made long

[12]J. G. Frazer, *The Scapegoat* (London: MacMillan, 1920), pp. 314–5.
[13]P. Kemp, *The Healing Ritual* (London: Faber and Faber, 1935), p. 151.

voyages down the coast of Africa, and subsequently across the Atlantic, almost impossible feats of navigation. Beginning in the fifteenth century, the Portuguese king popularly known to history as Prince Henry the Navigator set out to break the monopoly of the Italians and the Arabs. Henry's ultimate goal was to make Portugal master of the trade routes to the East, and to accomplish his goal, he was prepared to meet any expense.

Portugal was not a large country, however. During the fifteenth century it had fewer than a million people, most of whom were peasant farmers. What land there was was not very fertile. Most of it was stony. Only the river valleys were productive. During the Middle Ages, much of Portugal's food had to be imported from other countries.

Portugal's main economic asset was its long coastline with its teeming schools of fish. But fishing did not give Portugal a positive trade balance and the country was deeply in debt. Portugal needed gold. The Italians had it; the Portuguese wanted it.

There were two ways to get gold: take it from the Italians, or find some new route to some country, hitherto inaccessible, where gold was produced or where goods were made that could be sold for gold. Portugal wisely chose the latter alternative.

To get the gold Portugal needed, Henry's plan called for Portugal to outflank the Arabs in Africa by joining with a legendary hero of the Christian world, Prester John, whose headquarters were believed to be located somewhere in Africa. Since Prester John was said to command an army of millions, an alliance with his forces would certainly lead to victory over the Arabs and would result in a transfer of the trade monopoly from the Arabs and their Italian business partners to the Portuguese.

The Portuguese never linked up with Prester John. They couldn't have. He didn't exist. But their search for the elusive champion of Christianity got Portugal the gold she needed—at least for a time.

Every time Portuguese captains touched port in Africa, a new Portuguese outpost was established. It was not long before Portuguese ships were returning to Portugal laden with gold, ivory, and spices, just as Henry had dreamed.

Ten years after Diaz successfully rounded the Cape of Good Hope, another Portuguese adventurer, Vasco da Gama, dropped anchor in the waters off Calcutta and laid claim to the whole subcontinent in the name of the Portuguese monarch.

The empire which Portugal established in Africa and India was not based on colonization, however. Instead, the Portuguese erected a string of forts and naval bases. In this way she hoped to beat off rival nations who might also be looking for some foothold in these lands.

But aspire to greatness though she might, the territories which Portugal claimed were simply too vast and far-flung for her to retain control over. Portugal was too small a nation with too small a population to govern and maintain her newly acquired colonies. In addition to establishing a bureaucracy in each territory, she needed ships and sailors to man a navy large enough to guarantee the safety of her merchant marine and defend her colonial possessions.

Even if Portugal had had the manpower, the resources necessary to govern such an empire would have cut deeply into the profits gained from exploitation of these colonies. When rival Western nations finally began to flex their muscles at the beginning of the seventeenth century, tiny Portugal was forced to consolidate its holdings, and claims to vast territories in Africa and India had to be abandoned. Into the power vacuum sailed the Dutch and the English.

The Confrontation

The Dutch were the first to challenge Portugal's domination of the East. Late in the sixteenth century, the Dutch East India Company established its overseas headquarters at Batavia on the island of Java. From this outpost, it quickly took control of the spice trade and deliberately destroyed plant life in the East Indies to dry up supply sources. The effect of an increasing demand for sugar, cinnamon, and other spices, and a market deliberately crippled through manipulation of raw materials, was a skyrocketing increase in prices. The wealthier the Dutch became, the harder they tried to keep other nations from securing a foothold of their own in the rich spice lands of the East.

While the Portuguese and the Dutch were staking claims to the East Indies and Spain was establishing colonies in the New World, England was slowly coming to the realization that she was being left out of one of the greatest moneymaking opportunities every to present itself to the European economy. One of the main reasons England was unable to compete was that she lacked the ships necessary for exploration and trade. To expand her economy and keep up with her European rivals, England had to build new ships and develop new trade routes. And if she hoped to be able to protect her merchant ships from attack, she had to have a navy capable of repulsing an enemy. To build such a fleet, she needed raw materials such as timber and hemp. Unfortunately, both were in short supply and England had to send abroad to purchase these raw materials. In 1562, both Holland and England sent ships to the Baltic countries for these supplies. The Dutch sent 1192 vessels. The English sent as many as they could muster—51.

The situation was acute and England rose to meet the challenge. Spurred on by hopes of sharing in the new riches of overseas trade, English mercantilists sponsored the building of more and more ships. A new mercantile industry, legalized piracy, or privateering as it became known, also stimulated the demand for ships, and huge profits from goods commandeered on the high seas whetted English business appetites even more.

With her growing successes on the seas, and her support for Protestant causes in Europe, the new upstart could no longer be ignored. Spain, whose ships dominated the Atlantic, began to make hostile overtures. A confrontation was brewing. In 1587, war was finally declared.

The great naval clash came in 1588. Under the swashbuckling privateer Sir Francis Drake, the English prepared to fight the Spanish for control of the Atlantic. The Spanish plan of attack had two objectives. The first was to gain control of the English Channel; the second was to land a large military force in England. The troops to be used in the invasion were to consist of soldiers brought from Spain and from Spanish garrisons in the Netherlands.

The Spanish sent out 130 ships carrying 29,305 sailors, oarsmen, and soldiers. Opposing them was an English fleet of 197 ships manned by some 16,000 men. The cannons carried by the Spanish were most effective at close range. The English relied more on small-caliber cannons that could demolish the rigging of enemy ships at a distance, thereby crippling them and making them vulnerable to attack.

Although outnumbered, the English crews were better trained than the Spanish and the English artillery was manned by more experienced gunners than those who manned the Spanish weaponry. The Spanish in their huge ocean-going galleons also found it difficult to maneuver in the stormy waters of the English Channel, and when the two navies finally met, the great Spanish Armada had its bows slung full of grapeshot by the smaller, more maneuverable English vessels.

The Spanish never recovered from the humiliation of that defeat and the victory established England as the leading naval power in Europe. Now there was nothing to prevent her from founding her own colonial empire across the seas.

England's Need for Hemp

Even before the fateful battle in the English Channel, the kings of England recognized the need for hemp if their realm were ever to compete with Europe. Initially, the monarchs tried to coerce their subjects to raise hemp. The first such fiat came in 1533 when King Henry VIII commanded that for every sixty acres of arable land a farmer owned, a quarter acre was to be sown with hemp. The penalty for not doing so was to be three shillings and four pence.

Thirty years later, and long before the clash with Spain, his daughter Queen Elizabeth I reissued the command, raising the penalty to five shillings.[14] Elizabeth may not have had the best interests of the realm in mind when she issue this proclamation, however. Most of the hemp seed in England was sold by a Lawrence Cockson, a man who enjoyed the queen's favor. If English farmers complied with the royal proclamation, he stood to make a lot of money.[15]

Despite the law, few Englishmen complied with the royal decrees. The simple fact was that any landowner or small farmer could make more money by raising almost any crop other than hemp. Not only were the prices they received too low for them to make a good profit, farmers also complained that hemp exhausted the soil and made it unsuitable for growing other crops. It also gave off a bad odor when retted:

> Now pluck up they hempe, and go beat out the seed,
> and afterward water it as ye see need.
> But not in the river where cattle should drinke,
> for poisoning them and the people with stinke.[16]

English farmers were also reluctant to substitute hemp seed for grain since they claimed the seed gave an "ill flavor to the flesh of the bird that feeds on it."[17]

Since ships needed hemp and English farmers refused to supply it, merchants had to go elsewhere for their supplies. Most of the hemp that found its way into English ships during this period came from the Baltic. The best quality of hemp came from Danzig, and on several occasions the British government ordered its agents in that city to buy all the hemp they could get their hands on so that England would have enough rope for her ships.[18] Toward the middle of the sixteenth century, growing competition from Russia lured English buyers away from Danzig to the Russian cities of Riga and St. Petersburg. By 1630, Russia was supplying over 90 percent of London's hemp. By 1633, almost 97 percent came from Russia.[19]

[14]E. Lipson, *The Economic History of England* (London: A. C. Black, 1931), 2: 183.

[15]Youngs, F. A. *The Proclamations of the Tudor Queens* (Cambridge: Cambridge University Press, 1976), p. 142.

[16]T. Tusser, *Five Hundred Points of Good Husbandrie* (London: 1580), p. 152.

[17]J. Thistle and J. P. Cook, eds., *Seventeenth Century Documents* (Oxford: Clarendon Press, 1972), p. 167.

[18]H. Zins, *England and the Baltic in the Elizabethan Era* (Manchester: Manchester University Press, 1972), p. 229.

[19]*Ibid.*, p. 232.

The Russian Brack

Russia was the world's major exporter of hemp since it alone, of all the major hemp-producing countries, was able to supply the most hemp and produce it at the cheapest prices. Since England had no other source of supply that could meet its needs, England was Russia's best customer, importing two-thirds of all of Russia's exports by the eighteenth century.[20]

The center of Russia's hemp industry was located in the Ukraine and in the countryside between Poland and Moscow. Farmers raised and cleaned their hemp for sale to wholesalers, who bought it from them and transported it retailers in the towns, who in turn shipped it to various ports such as Riga and St. Petersburg.

Since hemp was sold on the basis of weight, it was relatively easy to increase its cost either by adding stones, timber, rotten hemp, or rubbish to the bales, by wetting down the fibers, or simply by giving the buyer a false weight. Because of the widespread fraud among Russian retailers, the Russian government instituted a formal inspection office called the brack, consisting of local port officials whose job was to make sure that fraud was not being perpetrated on buyers. Brack inspectors were supposed to be financially liable to a buyer on proof of fraud, but it was almost impossible to prove fraud until the hemp was unloaded in England. In some ports such as Riga inspection was rigorous, whereas in ports such as St. Petersburg it was lax and fraud was rampant.

In 1717, English merchants became so fed up with Russian cheating, they complained loudly enough to Parliament to pressure the English secretary of state to threaten the Russian ambassador that unless the abuses stopped once and for all England would go elsewhere for its hemp, such as its American colonies. It was a bluff, but the czar fell for it. Believing that Russia was in danger of losing its lucrative export trade with the English, he ordered the abuses stopped, and offenders were threatened with loss of their property, hard labor in the mines, and even death.[21]

Conditions still remained unsatisfactory in most Russian ports, however, and despite efforts and negotiations to change the brack so that English buyers would also serve as brack inspectors, English buyers had to grin and bear the dishonesty. They simply needed the hemp and had nowhere else to get it. While Poland, Prussia, and France also were exporters, they were not able to sell enough to satisfy England's enormous needs for the product.

[20]D. K. Reading, *The Anglo-Russian Commercial Treaty of 1734* (New Haven: Yale University Press, 1938), p. 21.
[21]*Ibid.*, p. 205.

England's dependence on foreign hemp placed her in a precarious position should hostilities ever break out between her and Russia or with any third country that controlled the sea route to Russia. Without a reliable source of hemp, England could not build ships. Without ships, she would remain an island isolated from Europe and the rest of the world.

> The royal navy and the navigation of England under God, the wealth, safety and strength of this kingdom [Parliament lamented] depends on the due supply of stores necessary for the same, which [are] being now brought in mostly from foreign parts in foreign shipping at exorbitant and arbitrary rates. . . .[22]

A pamphlet written by a Sir Richard Haines spoke directly at England's need to become self-sufficient in hemp:

> a further advantage by this planting of hemp, etc., will accrue towards making of sails, cables, and other cordage necessary for shipping, of which may be made at home, without being beholden to our neighbors for a commodity so important to navigation, parting with our money to strangers for it, as we usually do to a very great yearly value.[23]

To induce hemp workers who were fleeing persecution in Europe to seek refuge in England, Parliament passed a law in 1663 that any foreigner who settled in England or Wales and established a hemp-related industry within three years would, upon taking the oath of allegiance to the king, be accorded the same rights and privileges as natural-born citizens.[24]

But despite all her efforts to induce her own farmers at home to comply with the laws to raise hemp, and the inducements she offered refugees abroad to come to England if they promised to practice their trades once they got there, there was never enough hemp. Faced with failure at home, the monarchy turned to her loyal subjects abroad for cooperation.

[22]Quoted in Lipson, *Economic History*, 2: 183.
[23]*Ibid.*, 109.
[24]Thistle and Cook, *Documents*, p. 91.

4

Cannabis Comes to the New World

Like her greedy European neighbors, England eyed the New World with Midas eyes. Spain's conquistadors were sending a stream of gold and silver booty from the Aztec and Inca Empires. The English believed that they too could become rich by looting the native empires to the north of the Spanish colonies. There was also the possibility that this northern part of the New World might contain a passageway to the South Seas that would take English ships on to the East Indies and their spice-laden treasures. With colonies solidly established in the New World, England could control such a passageway and would thereby be assured of a virtual monopoly in any trade with the East.

The dream never materialized. There was no gold, no silver, no passageway to the Indies. There was, however, a different kind of wealth to be extracted from the Americas. The natives, in their ignorance, were willing to exchange furs—beaver, otter, seal, deer—for a pittance. The country was thick with trees; the waters were teeming with fish. The possibilities for trade were boundless. And by promoting the production of raw materials in the New World badly needed at home, England might become self-sufficient.

Sir Walter Raleigh became especially excited at the prospect of harvesting hemp in the American colonies as early as 1585 after Thomas Heriot, his friend and tutor, told him that he had seen a hemp-like plant growing wild in what was to become Virginia. Heriot's hemp, however, was *Acnida cannabinum*, a plant which also yields a fiber suitable for weaving, but one that is far inferior in strength to cannabis.

Even when the American variety of hemp proved not to be the same as that grown in Europe, the possibility of raising cannabis in the American colonies sent imaginations soaring. If only the energies of the colonists could be directed toward raising hemp, England might yet free herself from her heavy commercial debts.

The first settlers who founded the colony at Jamestown, Virginia, in 1607, however, did not make the long journey across the Atlantic to become hemp farmers. Like most Englishmen, they came to America in the belief that the country abounded in gold and silver. These early colonists expected to make a quick and easy fortune and planned to return home as soon as possible. When they found no gold or anything else of material value, they became so discouraged they refused to work to support themselves. Had it not been for the friendliness of the Indians who gave them food and showed them how to raise some basic crops, they would have starved to death.

In 1611, formal orders to raise hemp were finally received in the colony.[1] Speaking to a motley gathering of His Majesty's loyal subjects, the new governor, Sir Thomas Dale, informed the colonists that the king expected them to grow hemp.

The colonists were indifferent to the royal proclamation. They cared as little about raising hemp as they did any other crop. Yet by 1616, colonist John Rolfe could boast that the inhabitants of Jamestown had raised hemp "none better in England or Holland."[2] However, Rolfe had also begun to experiment with growing tobacco, and it was not long before the demand for American tobacco was greater than anyone could have anticipated. Faced with a choice between raising tobacco and becoming rich or complying with the Crown's wishes that they grow hemp, the colonists planted tobacco in every nook and cranny of the Jamestown settlement.[3]

To combat this obstinance, in 1619 the Virginia Company directed every colonist in Jamestown to "set 100 [hemp] plants and the governor to set 5,000" and it alloted one hundred pounds to a Gabriel Wisher to hire skilled hemp dressers from Sweden and Poland at ten pounds, ten shillings per man, if they would emigrate to the new colony.[4]

Parliament was also prepared to offer sizable inducements. In 1662, Governor William Berkely was empowered to offer each colonist two pounds of tobacco for every pound of hemp delivered to market. Similar bounties for hemp production were also offered in Maryland in 1671, 1682, 1688, and 1698.

In 1682, Virginia tried to encourage hemp production by making

---

[1]L. C. Gray, *History of Agriculture in the Southern United States to 1860* (Gloucester, Mass.: Peter Smith, 1958), 1: 25.
[2]*Ibid.*
[3]J. L. Bishop, *A History of American Manufactures* (New York: Augustus M. Kelly, 1966), 1: 26.
[4]B. Moore, *The Hemp Industry in Kentucky* (Lexington, Ky.: James E. Hughes, 1905), p. 12.

hemp legal tender for as much as one-fourth of a farmer's debts. Similar laws were enacted by Maryland in 1683 and by Pennsylvania in 1706.[5]

While these laws and bounties had the effect of increasing hemp production throughout Virginia and Maryland, very little hemp ever found its way into English ports. If there was any extra hemp in the colonies, Yankee merchants wanted it. Hemp was so scarce in the north that supply could not keep up with demand and New England merchants were prepared to buy all the available hemp they could get their hands on.

HEMP IN NEW ENGLAND

The story of the Pilgrims is known to every schoolchild in America. Ostensibly, the Pilgrims left Europe to find a place in the New World where they could practice their religious beliefs in freedom. But not all the Pilgrims who landed at Plymouth in 1620 came to America because of religious convictions. In fact, most of the passengers on the *Mayflower* hoped to earn enough money through fishing or trading for them to return to their homeland without having to worry about the future. Few of the Pilgrims were prepared or were willing to spend even part of their lives providing raw materials for the enrichment of England's merchants.

Nevertheless, cannabis was among the first crops to be introduced into the Massachusetts Colony, and initially there was great hope that it might even become an economically viable staple in New England. The General Court of Massachusetts was particularly interested in urging hemp production on the colonists because of the possibility that, without fibers with which to make clothing, the colony might freeze to death during the winter. To forestall such a possibility,

> [it] desired and expected that all masters of families should see that their children and servants should bee industriously implied, so as the mornings and evenings and other seasons may not bee lost, as formerly they have beene, but that the honest and profitable custome of England may be practiced amongst us; so as all hands may be implied for the working of hemp and flaxe and other needful things for clothing, without abridging any such servants of their dewe times for foode and rest and other needful refreshings.[6]

In 1629, shipbuilding was started in the village of Salem, and if there was any hemp available, Salem's merchants were prepared to buy

[5]V. S. Clark, *History of Manufactures in the United States* (New York: McGraw-Hill, 1929), p. 34.
[6]Quoted in Bishop, *American Manufactures*, 1: 303.

all they could get their hands on. But hemp was so scarce that it had to be imported from abroad.[7]

Despite the exhortations of the Massachusetts court and the clamorings of Salem's business interests, production fell far short of administrative expectations, and in 1639 the court formalized its demands by passing a law requiring every householder to plant hemp seed.

In 1640, the General Assembly of Connecticut also tried to persuade its colonists to sow hemp "that we might in time have supply of linen cloth among ourselves."[8] Like her sister colony, the Connecticut Assembly feared that the colonists might die of exposure if they did not take steps to raise fiber-bearing crops such as hemp.

Clothes were not the only concern of the colonists. The growth of the New England shipbuilding industry was creating yet another demand for hemp in the form of rope. Without rope, shipbuilders could not make rigging to hoist sails, and without sails, ships were useless. Although rigging could be made from a number of other raw materials, the preferred material was hemp because of its strength and durability.

Although ropemaking had become an established and respected trade in England by the thirteenth century, few colonists were trained ropemakers. In 1635, the first ropewalk—a factory for making rope from hemp—was established in Salem. Rival businessmen in Boston soon recognized the advantage of having a local ropemaker and they invited John Harrison to come to Boston from England and set up shop. Harrison arrived in 1642 and went into business in the open lot next to his house on Purchase Street.

By the terms of the agreement he worked out with Boston's town fathers, he was to have a total monopoly on making rope until 1663. During that time, Harrison's business prospered and he raised eleven children. When the monopoly expired, a John Heyman "set up his posts" and began making fishing lines. Harrison immediately began to worry that the competition would cut into his own business and he successfully persuaded the town fathers to revoke Heyman's permit. Despite Boston's need for rope, the town fathers continued to honor Harrison's monopoly until his death.

In the meantime, however, ropewalks were being erected all up and down the seacoast to meet the incessant demand of the fledgling shipbuilding and fishing industries. By the time of the Revolution, almost every town on the eastern seaboard had at least one. Boston alone had fourteen ropewalks. It was the taunting of His Majesty's soldiers by

[7]Clark, *History of Manufactures*, p. 24.
[8]Connecticut, *Public Funds of the Colony of Connecticut*, comps. J. H. Trumball and C. J. Hoadly (Hartford, 1850), 1:61.

these Boston ropeworkers that eventually set off the "Boston Massacre" of 1770.

The early ropewalks were relatively primitive industries. All that was needed was a large open field, a number of posts to rap the rope around, and of course, a good supply of hemp fiber. The rope was made by turning two hemp strands in opposite directions around one another. When the strands untwisted they came apart somewhat, but the friction between them held them together and produced a strong durable cord. These cords were then twisted with another set, and on and on, until thick strong ropes were created.

Later on, when ropemaking became a major industry in America, the fields were enclosed in long covered alleyways, some of which stretched over 1,000 feet in length and 20 feet in width, with three or four ropemakers working side by side. The sight of one such enterprise later inspired Longfellow's poem, the "Ropewalk" (1854):

> In that building, long and low,
> With its windows all a-row,
> Like the port-holes of a hulk,
> Human spiders spin and spin,
> Backward down their threads so thin
> Dropping, each a hempen bulk.

The Life of the Hemp Farmer

One of the reasons that American farmers were unable to produce enough hemp to satisfy England and their own colonial needs was the scarcity and high cost of labor needed to harvest the crop. Both George Washington and Thomas Jefferson tried to raise hemp and both lost money doing so.[9] Exasperated at England's incessant demands that the colonies send her more hemp, Benjamin Franklin railed at Parliament's ignorance of the shortages of hemp in America: "Did ever any North American bring his hemp to England for this bounty. We have not yet enough for our own consumption. We began to make our own cordage. You want to suppress that manufacture, and would do it by getting the raw material from us. You want to be supplied with hemp for your manufactures, and Russia demands money."[10]

The shortage of labor in the colonies was only one of the reasons

[9]See G. Andrews and S. Vinkenoog, eds., *The Book of Grass* (New York: Grove Press, 1967), p. 34; and E. M. Betts, ed., *Thomas Jefferson's Farm Book* (Princeton: Princeton University Press, 1953), p. 252.

[10]Quoted in L. Carrier, *The Beginnings of Agriculture in America* (New York: Johnson Reprint Co., 1962), p. 96.

farmers were unable to raise enough hemp to meet domestic demand for the crop. Another important reason was that hemp farming was not the easiest of jobs.

To prepare his land for hemp seed, the farmer usually had to plow his acreage at least three times, once in the fall, a second time in early spring, and a third time just before sowing. Immediately before the seeds were actually planted, the ground had to be carefully raked to break up any clumps so that the seeds would be distributed evenly. Seeds would be scattered throughout the field beginning in late March until the end of June. Generally, a farmer sowed his land at least two or three times just in case his seeds failed to germinate. About forty to fifty pounds of seed were sown per acre, and unless his seed was less than a year old, the farmer could not expect a good crop. Hemp seed had to be fresh and had to have been stored properly. Because older seeds were so unreliable, most farmers refused to have anything to do with suppliers they did not know personally. Although England regularly shipped hemp seed to the colonies, it was usually stored improperly and was often too old to be any good. It was in no small measure due to the shortage of good hemp seed from England that the colonists were unable to meet the demand for hemp at home and in the mother country.

About four to six days after sowing, the cannabis seed began to germinate. Some young plants grew at an astounding rate of five to six inches per day. Once his plants began to grow, the farmer could forget about them since no weed was a match for hemp and insects rarely attacked the plants. Thirteen to fifteen weeks later, the plants turned from green to a yellowish brown, the leaves began to droop and fall to the ground, and the flowers began to release their pollen, filling the air with clouds of hemp dust. The plants were finally ready to be harvested. Now came the back-breaking toil dreaded by all hemp growers.

Initially, farmers pulled each plant out of the ground to get as much of the stem as possible. A farmer who uprooted his crop could clear about a quarter of an acre per day. If he used a knife and cut the stems above ground, he could clear about a half acre.

Once a number of stalks had been pulled or cut, the farmer tied them into sheaves about as thick as a man's leg. These bundles were then leaned against a fence or against each other and allowed to dry for two to three days. After drying came the rotting (or retting as it was usually called). Retting was done to weaken the glue-like resin that caused the outer fibers to stick to the stalk.

The colonists used one of three retting methods, and the law stated that a dealer had to specify the way his hemp had been retted. Water retting was considered to be the best method as far as the resulting quality of the hemp fiber was concerned. This involved immersing the hemp in a stream or pond for four to five days if done in summer, or thirty to forty days if done in winter. European hemp was usually water retted, but this was not generally done in America. Instead, Americans preferred winter retting.

Winter retting was easier than water retting and it did not require a nearby water source. To winter-ret his hemp, the farmer simply threw the stalks on the ground when it began to get cold, leaving the rain, frost, and snow gradually to loosen the gum binding the fibers. Winter retting generally took about two to three months, and the result was a fiber measurably inferior in strength to water-retted hemp.

The third method was dew retting. This was to become the most common practice in Kentucky, but in colonies such as Virginia it was not used very much. Dew retting involved spreading the hemp plants on the ground at night to catch the dew and then tying them together in the morning so that they would remain wet for as long as possible. It was both time-consuming and produced a very inferior grade of hemp. Shipbuilders refused to buy dew-retted hemp, but cotton growers preferred it because it was cheap. All they wanted it for was to bale their cotton shipments.

After the hemp was retted by one of these three methods, it was allowed to dry once more. Then came the most tedious job of all, the "breaking" or freeing of the outer fibers from the stalk. During the Middle Ages, breaking was done by hand. But this was too slow a process and eventually "hand brakes" were introduced into the hemp industry. The simplest of these devices usually consisted of several vertical boards attached end to end with a movable arm hinged at one corner to the top board. The hemp was placed over the stationary edge and the top arm, which was sharpened somewhat, was brought down onto the hemp stalks with enough force to cut the fiber but not enough to go through the entire stalk. It was a task that required a great deal of skill as well as strength and stamina. Thomas Jefferson, one of Virginia's major hemp producers, gave up on hemp because of the back pain his slaves experienced in connection with the herculean breaking process:

> The shirting for our laborers has been an object of some difficulty. Flax is so imperious to our lands, and of so scanty produce, that I have never attempted it. Hemp, on the other hand, is abundantly productive and will grow forever on the same spot. But the breaking and beating it, which has always been done by hand, is so slow, so laborious, and so much complained of by our laborers, that I have given it up.... [11]

Before slaves were put to work in the hemp fields, the English had toyed with the idea of shipping the "multitude of loyterers and idle

[11]Betts, *Farm Book*, p. 252.

vagabonds" to the New World "where they would be put to worke in beatinge and workinge of hempe for cordage" as they were in England. The Virginia Assembly had also considered the possibility of "seating all convicts that should be imported into Virginia, in a county by themselves, under the care of proper overseers, who should confine them from doing any hurt, and keep them to their labor by such methods as are used in Bridewell."[12]

In fact, jail was where a great deal of hemp was processed, as shown in William Hogarth's (1697–1764) *The Harlot's Progress*, a series of engravings depicting what to Hogarth was the insidious influence of city life on the morality of a country girl named Mary Hackbout.[13]

The fourth illustration in the series depicts Mary beating hemp in Bridewell Prison, a house of correction in Tothill Fields, Westminster, for harlots such as herself and other sundry immoral characters. Hogarth portrays her holding a large mallet in her hands while the hemp strands lie in front of her on two tree stumps. A prison officer is shown standing beside her drawing Mary's attention to the pillory, already occupied, which bears the warning: "Better to Work than Stand Thus." A little to the right of the pillory is a whipping post which also bears a message: "The Wages of Idleness." To the far right of the picture an effigy of a "Sr. J. G." is shown hanging from a gallows, a starkly realistic foreboding of one of the uses to which the hemp Mary is working on is to be put.

Mary herself is pictured dressed in finely designed clothing totally inappropriate to prison life, whereas close beside her another woman is shown destroying the vermin in her pest-ridden garments. Quite possibly, Hogarth may have got the idea for Mary's attire from the September 24, 1730, issue of the *Grub Street Journal* which contained an item concerning a Mary Muffet who had recently been sent to Bridewell. The lady was a "woman of great note in the hundreds of Drury," said the *Journal*, "who about a fortnight ago was committed to hard labor in Tothill-fields, Bridewell . . . where she is now beating hemp in a gown very richly laced with silver."[14]

In any case, it was commonplace for prisoners to be put to work breaking hemp by their jailers. The work was arduous and punishing. However, prisoners were not made to work on hemp to teach them remorse. The fact was that few English men or women would willingly do such work. Forcing prisoners to do so kept them busy and also

[12]Moore, *Hemp Industry*, p. 13.
[13]R. Paulson, ed., *Hogarth's Graphic Works* (New Haven: Yale University Press, 1970), 1: 146–7.
[14]Cited in R. Paulson, *Hogarth's Graphic Works* (New Haven: Yale University Press, 1970), p. 147.

provided their keepers with a product that could be sold in the marketplace. With the money they earned from exploiting their charges, jailers were expected to pay the prison food bill. More often than not, a little something extra wound up in the jailers' pockets at the expense of a little something extra in the prisoners' bellies.

Frequently, the very hemp prisoners broke in jail was used to snap a fellow inmate's neck. In fact, because rope was so often made of hemp, the word "hemp" gave rise to several slang terms and expressions that were once familiar in England and America, but which have now disappeared from our language. Among the more current terms of a bygone era were "hempen collar," meaning a hangman's noose, and "hempen widow," a woman widowed by the hangman's hempen noose. "To die of hempen fever" was another way of saying a man had been hanged. During the heyday of the American Wild West, vigilantes were sometimes referred to as "hemp committees," and "sowing hemp" was another way of saying that someone was on his way to a rendezvous with the hangman.

The Hemp Farmer's Wife

Once hemp had been splintered into shreds on the brake, it was ready for market. More often than not, however, the farmer kept his harvest for his own needs.

During pre-Revolutionary times, hemp fabric was one of the most common materials in the colonial homestead. Hempen cloth covered the backs of farmers and their entire families, hempen towels wiped their hands, hempen napkins and handkerchiefs moped their brows and faces, and hempen tablecloths graced their fine furniture. There was virtually no household that did not contain an item made from hemp.

The popularity of hemp and the consequent dearth of hemp fiber to leave the American colonies for England was in no small measure due to the enterprising and dedicated pioneer women of the colonies, who transformed the raw fibers from the fields into cloth and fine linen. It was not an easy task.

After her husband brought her the broken hemp fiber, the farmer's wife placed it across the top of a "swingling" block, a strong wooden board three to four feet high mounted on a sturdy wooden frame. She and her older daughters now began to pound the fibers as hard as they could with wooden paddles until it was beaten free of woody particles. The long fibers that survived this beating were then drawn through a hatchel, a wooden comb that removed remaining short fibers. Hatchel-ing was done several times, each time with a comb with teeth set more closely together than the previous one. After the final combing, the fine soft pliable threads were spun into cloth. Short fibers removed during the preliminary hatchelings were called tow, and were made into heavy thread for burlap and cord.

Spinning involved twisting loose fibers together to make a single strand. The pioneer woman who was lucky enough to own a spinning wheel sat facing her prized possession and pulled a few strands of hemp from a rod or spindle and twisted these onto a bobbin. The bobbin was then set revolving by pressing down on a foot treadle. As the bobbin turned, it caused the thread to be wound. After a number of bobbins had been filled, the thread was wound into skeins on a hand-turned reel. The number of strands per skein was determined by the number of times a projecting peg tripped another peg.

After "reeling," the yarn was bleached to give it color. This too was a time-consuming job. First, the yarn was submerged in running water. Then, it was covered with piles of ashes and hot water, rewashed, pounded again, and washed once more. Now it was ready for bleaching. To give the yarn a white color, it was soaked in flaked lime and buttermilk. Walnut bark gave a brown tinge; oak and maple gave purple; hickory bark produced a yellowish color; sumac berries produced pinks and reds; blueberries gave blue.

Once dyed, the yarn was ready for weaving. This step involved passing a horizontal or "weft" thread over and under alternating vertical or "warp" threads. There were various types of looms in the colonies and there were always improvements in loom technology. Basically, however, the loom was an elaborate tool that allowed the weaver to hook the weft thread over and behind warp threads faster than could possibly be done by hand.

MERCANTILISM AND THE "SPINNING BEE"

As long as spinning and weaving were primarily household activities, they were encouraged by Parliament. But when they developed to the point that colonial imports began declining due to homemade goods, England tried to restrict these activities.

The mercantile system which England adopted as an integral part of her policy toward her American colonies was basically one which required the colonists to be suppliers of raw materials to and consumers of finished goods from the mother country. By the eighteenth century, spinning and weaving had increased to such a degree that British merchants began complaining to Parliament that the colonists were not buying enough British-made goods given their alleged dependency on English manufacturing.

In response to this pressure from the business sector, Parliament passed the Wool Act in 1699 which essentially deprived the colonists of the right to import wool. To circumvent this restriction, the colonists made more and more use of hemp and flax fibers. In 1708, Calib Heathcote, a New York colonist seeking a contract from the British Board of Trade to supply naval stores to England, wrote that his neighbors "were already so far advanced that three fourths of the linen and woolen used, was made amongst them . . . and if some speedy and effectual ways are not found to put a stop to it, they will carry it on a great deal further. . . . "15

Parliament demanded an explanation from Governor Dudley of Massachusetts concerning the reluctance of the colonists to buy British goods. Dudley replied that Americans would be more than happy to buy and wear goods made in England if they could pay for them. But since they could not earn enough money from chopping wood and sawing lumber, they were forced to make and sell their own goods, leaving those that were made in Britain to more affluent New Englanders.

The event which ultimately transformed the colonies from part-time household producers of clothing to full-time manufacturers, and caused more than one ulcer in the British business community, was the arrival in Boston in 1718 of a number of professional spinners and weavers from Ireland. Although colonial women had been spinning their own thread for some time, their expertise was nowhere near that of professional European craftsmen. When these newcomers landed in Boston, the women of the town asked for advice on how to make better cloth. The immigrants were more than obliging, and soon Boston's women, young and old, rich and poor, were flocking to the Common where a makeshift spinning school had been set up to teach the colonists how to spin thread professionally. The whirr of spinning wheels soon filled the air from morning to night as each woman competed with her neighbor to produce more and better thread. Boston's womenfolk, it was said, had been bitten by the "spinning craze."

It was the passage of the Stamp Act in 1765, however, that really sent the women of New England to their spinning wheels in earnest. The new law promulgated by Parliament did more to crystalize opposition to the import and consumption of British goods in the colonies than did any other single measure. Businessmen refused to purchase any

15New York, *Documents Relative to the Colonial History of New York,* eds. E. B. O'Callaghan and B. Fernow (Albany, 1860) 5:63.

products made in England and colonists agreed not to wear any clothing except that manufactured domestically. In New England, the campaign not to buy British goods was led by a group of women who called themselves the Daughters of Liberty. To meet the expected demand that a boycott against English goods would create in the colonies, the Daughters turned to "spinning bees," as the "spinning crazes" were now called.

Between 1766 and 1771, women across New England met in churches, meeting halls, private homes, and anywhere else that was available, to spin in groups. Speaking of one such gathering held in Providence, Rhode Island, the *Boston Chronicle* on April 7, 1766, wrote that the women gathered there "exhibited a fine example of industry, by spinning from sunrise until dark, and displayed a spirit for saving their sinking country, rarely to be found among persons of more age and experience."

These spinning bees were not without results. Production of cloth materials increased in every town and village, and it was not long before there was more than enough homemade cloth to clothe anyone who wanted American-made garments.

The spinning bee soon spread to other colonies as well. In Philadelphia, a market was opened especially for the sale of domestic fabrics. In Virginia, George Washington erected a spinning house on his plantation. Even as far as South Carolina, domestic production of fabrics increased markedly as the spirit of resistance filtered down from New England to the southern colonies.

As a result of these spontaneous gatherings, the colonists became self-sufficient in clothes. When the Revolution came and textile materials from England were completely cut off, the colonists were not faced with the kind of predicament they might have been in had they not learned to manufacture their own household goods. Until trade relations could be started with other countries, the colonists were able to care for their own needs and were generally able to supply uniforms and basic clothing for their army.

More Valuable Than Cash

To maintain their newly declared independence, the American colonies not only had to field an army, they had to become self-reliant in all the resources necessary to support that army and the civilian population. Grain and beef suddenly became the chief priorities for the fledgling nation.

Once they were sure of food, the colonists could devote their efforts to raising raw materials for the war effort. Foremost among the raw materials being demanded was hemp. The Revolution's impact on the hemp industry was reflected in the prices for hemp fiber. Prior to the outbreak of hostilities, hemp sold for about twenty-seven to thirty-five shillings per hundredweight. Between 1780 and 1782, the price soared to three hundred shillings.[16]

Much of Virginia's hemp was produced by small farmers and was subsequently processed into rope and cordage. There were no fewer than eighteen "ropewalks" in Virginia transforming raw hemp fiber into badly needed rope during the Revolution, and there was still a shortage of rope. These ropewalks and various sailmaking factories sprang up all over the colony to supply the needs of the colonial navy. So important were rope and sail to the war effort that any man who worked at these jobs for at least six months was excused from military duty for the duration of the war.[17]

Virginia's ropewalks were also considered an important war industry by the British. In April 1781, when Benedict Arnold led a force of British infantry up the Jones River and penetrated as far as Richmond, one objective of his mission was the "Public Rope Walk" in Warwick, which he destroyed. This ropewalk was the biggest rope-manufacturing factory in Virginia and its loss dealt a considerable blow to Virginia's rope production for the war effort.

In addition to making clothes and rope from hemp, the Americans had another equally important need for the precious fiber during the Revolution—paper. Although hemp was a basic ingredient in the invention of paper, other materials such as flax and cotton had long since replaced it. However, in 1716, a pamphlet was published on the art of papermaking entitled *Essays for the month of December 1716, to be continued monthly by a Society of Gentlemen for the benefit of the people of England,* which urged papermakers to return once again to hemp. Detailed instructions were given as to how to prepare the hemp for the job and paper mill owners were invited to plant hemp in their yards so that they would have their own supplies of raw material.

In 1765, a dedicated English paper manufacturer named Jacob Christian Shaffer began writing a long and thorough text on the art of papermaking which was based on experiments he himself had made during his career in the paper industry. In going over the different materials that had been used to make paper in the past, Shaffer noted that while rags and wornout linen were the main raw materials for

[16]R. D. Mitchell, "Agricultural Change and the American Revolution: A Virginia Case Study," *Agricultural History* 47 (1973): 126.

[17]G. M. Herndon, "A War-Inspired Industry." *Virginia Magazine of History and Biography* 74 (1966): 304–5.

making paper in his day, "the dearth of this material is now complained of everywhere." To deal with this shortage Shaffer proposed hemp fiber as an alternative, and to prove its feasibility, he printed portions of the third volume of his textbook on pages made from hemp fiber.[18]

Several years after the publication of Shaffer's books on the art of papermaking, Robert Bell, an American printer who in 1777 identified his shop as "next door to St. Paul's Church, in Third Street, Philadelphia," likewise suggested that hemp be used as a raw material for making paper in the colonies, since now that they had declared their independence from England they could no longer count on cotton or flax imports.

The problem was, however, that once war broke out, hemp became just as scarce as any other fibrous materials. For a time American papermakers had to scrounge, beg, and plead for people to bring them their old rags so that the United States would have paper upon which money, business accounts, military commands, etc., could be written. The shortage did not last forever and after the War of Independence papermakers could choose what materials to use in producing paper. But for a time, the acute hemp and paper shortage threatened to undermine the American war effort.

One of the better known Virginia landholders who astutely anticipated both the war and the demand for hemp was Robert "King" Carter, an early ancestor of President Jimmy Carter. Although he owned more than 300,000 acres in Virginia, Carter was much more than just a wealthy land baron. During his career, he held many colonial offices among which were justice of the peace, member of the House of Burgesses, speaker of the House, colonial treasurer, and commander of the local militia. The Carters and the other Virginia aristocrat societies were leaders in every social, religious, and political event that took place in the colony. So held in awe was Carter that it was said that no Christian save the minister would think of entering Christ's Church on the Sabbath before "King" Carter arrived.

In 1774, on the eve of the Revolution, Carter took stock of the political situation in the colonies and decided that tobacco would no longer be a profitable concern. Accordingly, he wrote to one of his foremen, "I apprehend that tobacco which may be here, next summer will be in little demand. . . . [Therefore] in place of tobacco—hemp and flax will be grown."[19] At the same time, he erected a spinning factory on his plantation to process the future hemp crop.

---

[18]Quoted in D. Hunter, *Papermaking Through Eighteen Centuries* (New York: Wm. E. Rudge, 1930), p. 60.

[19]Quoted in L. Morton, *Robert Carter of Nomini Hall* (Williamsburg, Va.: Colonial Williamsburg Inc., 1941), p. 156.

Even with the hemp from his own vast farmlands, Carter did not have enough hemp to suit his needs. In 1775, he bought five hundred pounds from his stepbrother. In 1776, he bought two tons more. Much of this hemp was spun into osnaburg, a coarse fabric used to make shirts and trousers for workmen and the Revolution's soldiers.

Hemp was more than just fiber for clothes, however. It was also money. In 1781, Governor Thomas Jefferson received a note from David Ross, Virginia's purchasing agent, stating that his buyer in Philadelphia "writes me the 2,000 Stand of Arms will be ready this week." But to pay for them, he was "obliged to engage hemp" since there was "no encouragement from Congress that they can do anything for [us] in money matters. Tobacco will not do there and we have nothing to depend upon but our hemp."[20] In a later note, Ross acknowledged that Jefferson was reserving "the hemp in the back country . . . to be used in paying for articles bought in Philadelphia for the use of the Army. This is an article very much in demand in Philadelphia and a valuable Fund. . . ."[21] A year later, a Philadelphia businessman likewise noted that "hemp, tar, pitch, and turpentine command cash in preference to any other goods."[22]

The reason hemp was more valuable than cash was simple. Paper money had no value in the colonies. A thousand dollars in Virginia currency, for example, was only worth one dollar in silver. Because of the lack of faith in paper money, the American economy operated on the barter system. And because of hemp's "comparative uniformity, its comparative freedom from deterioration, the universal and steady demand for it, and its value, which exceeded all other raw produce," it "was recognized as the standard commodity for the first three or four decades" of the new American republic.[23] Anything and everything could be bartered for hemp, from the local newspaper to the services of stud racehorses.[24]

The American Revolution altered the lifestyles of the American people in many ways. Hitherto, the colonists had relied heavily on imports from England, especially for clothing. Had it not been for organizations like the Daughters of Liberty, whose enthusiasm and efforts encouraged colonial women to make their own clothes, the disastrous winter of 1778 at Valley Forge might have been typical of life throughout the northern colonies.

To make sure the army had uniforms and Americans did not freeze

[20]Herndon, "War-Inspired Industry," pp. 304–5.
[21]G. M. Herndon, "Hemp in Colonial Virginia," *Agricultural History* 37 (1963): 93.
[22]*Ibid.*
[23]Moore, *Hemp Industry*, p. 17.
[24]*Ibid.*, p. 22.

to death, Congress implored the colonists to raise as much hemp as possible so that clothing could be manufactured. Soldiers needed uniforms not only to keep warm, but also to keep up their morale. On at least one occasion, for instance, the Americans refused to fight alongside their French allies because they looked so pitiful next to the elegantly uniformed French.

KENTUCKY'S HEMP INDUSTRY

Although Kentucky was to become the nation's most productive hemp supplier, hemp production was not started there until 1775. By 1810, however, hemp had become "the grand staple of Kentucky." In 1850, there were 8327 hemp plantations in the United States, putting hemp second only to cotton and tobacco production.[25] Most of these plantations were located in Kentucky; the remainder were spread throughout Tennessee, Missouri, and Mississippi.

The major reason hemp production began to increase once again following the initial depression of the hemp markets after the Revolution was the import tariffs Congress levied against hemp brought into the United States from abroad. In 1792, the tariff was placed at twenty dollars per ton. During the war of 1812, it rose to forty dollars per ton, and by 1828, it was sixty dollars per ton.[26] These tariffs were first imposed at the urging of Alexander Hamilton, who as secretary of the treasury, saw these imposts against foreign hemp as a means of stimulating domestic hemp supplies and thereby making the United States independent of foreign nations for this essential military item. After Hamilton, the fight to retain the tariff was spearheaded by one of Kentucky's most distinguished spokesmen, the indefatigable Henry Clay.

Clay was not a native Kentuckian. He had been born in Virginia but had moved to Lexington in 1797 where he became a well-known trial lawyer and husband to Lucretia Hart, the daughter of a rich hemp manufacturer. Soon after his marriage, Clay began to espouse the cause of Kentucky's hemp farmers, a career that helped elect him to Congress where he was instrumental in promoting Kentucky's hemp industry through the tariff.

Not surprisingly, northern manufacturers and shipbuilders were opposed to these tariffs. Through Daniel Webster, their spokesman in Congress, they demanded an unrestricted supply of cheap raw hemp to

[25]C. Eaton, *A History of the Old South* (New York: Macmillan, 1966), p. 229.
[26]Clark, *History of Manufactures*, 1: 289.

make rope and cordage, and since they refused to use southern hemp because of its poor quality, they had to rely on imports. Placing a tariff on hemp from abroad hurt their business and they pressured their own congressmen to vote against these tariffs. But, more often than not, Clay and his supporters won out over Yankee business interests.

However, the tariffs did little to discourage imports from foreign countries. Their main effect was simply to increase prices to consumers. Before 1800, the United States imported about 3400 tons of hemp a year. At the time of the War of 1812, imports rose to 4200 tons, and by the 1830s they increased to 5000 tons per year.[27]

Northern manufacturers preferred foreign hemp, especially that from Russia, to domestic hemp because of the superior manner in which the fiber was processed abroad. In Russia, for example, the stalks were hung on rocks as soon as they were cut. If the weather remained dry, the stalks were not disturbed. If it rained, they were placed in a kiln. Regardless of how they were initially dried, on the third day after harvesting the plants were completely submerged in warm water for three weeks and then cold water for five weeks more. Then they were allowed to dry for two additional weeks, followed by a second kiln drying for twenty-four hours. Finally, the stalks were broken. The husks were torn off and the fiber was carefully hatcheled. The finished fiber was then placed in storerooms until it was sold.

In contrast to the Russian method of production, Kentucky growers left the chopped cannabis stalks on the ground to become dew retted. Water retting was discouraged because Kentucky farmers believed that fish and livestock that drank from a pond in which hemp had been placed would be poisoned. Then, too, the water smelled like rotten eggs after hemp had been soaking in it, "which was considered unhealthy for slaves and twice as bad for whites."[28]

Not only were the northern manufacturers reluctant to use dew-retted hemp, the United States Navy also refused to buy Kentucky hemp despite Congress's efforts to promote the industry. In 1824, Congress inquired as to the basis for this discrimination. The secretary of the navy's reply was that "cables and cordage manufactured from it [Kentucky hemp] . . . are inferior in colour, strength and durability to those manufactured from imported hemp, and consequently are not safe or proper for use in the navy."[29] An expert in rope making was quoted as

[27] Ibid., p. 326.
[28] A. W. Crosby, America, Russia, Hemp and Napoleon (Columbus: Ohio University Press, 1965), p. 21.
[29] American State Papers: Naval Affairs, 2: 27–9.

stating, "I would not use cordage made from Kentucky yarn or hemp, even if I could produce it at one half the price of cordage made from Russian."[30]

Actual experiments conducted in the 1820s aboard the U.S.S. *North Carolina* supported the navy's position. Although initially as strong as cordage made from Russian hemp and able to support a weight of 125 pounds when new, after eighteen months at sea cordage made from Kentucky-raised hemp could not even support a weight of 18 pounds![31]

HEMP AND SLAVERY

One of the industries to experience a sudden growth as a result of the shortage of labor and the demand for hemp was slavery.

Before the war there were only about 2500 slaves in Virginia's Shenandoah Valley. By 1790 there were 10,000.[32] Although the demand for hemp declined precipitously after the war, rope and cordage were still important commodities and large-scale hemp production required manpower. "Take away slaves," argued William C. Bullitt, a delegate to the Constitutional Convention of 1849 which debated the slavery issue, "and you destroy the production of that valuable article, which is bound to make the rich lands of Kentucky and Missouri still more valuable."[33]

After Virginia's farmers lost interest in raising hemp due to the drop in prices, Americans in other parts of the country decided to move into the hemp market. Foremost among these new hemp producers were the farmers of Kentucky. And like their neighbors in Virginia, Kentuckians found that the only profitable way to raise hemp was through slave labor.

"Without hemp," writes J. F. Hopkins in his *History of the Hemp Industry in Kentucky*, "slavery might not have flourished in Kentucky, since other agricultural products of the state were not conducive to the extensive use of bondsmen. On the hemp farm and in the hemp factories the need for laborers was filled to a large extent by the use of Negro slaves, and it is a significant fact that the heaviest concentration of slavery was in the hemp producing area."[34]

---

[30]*Ibid.*, p. 28.
[31]*Ibid.*
[32]Mitchell, "Agricultural Change," p. 126.
[33]Quoted in J. F. Hopkins, *A History of the Hemp Industry in Kentucky* (Lexington: University of Kentucky Press, 1951), p. 30.
[34]*Ibid.*, p. 4.

Kentucky hemp growers estimated that three slaves could cultivate about fifty acres. This resulted in a yield of about 35,700 pounds of fiber and a return of about thirty-five dollars per acre.[35]

Although working in the hemp fields was backbreaking toil, many slaves preferred it to other kinds of labor since it was task work. Under the task system, the slave was given a fixed amount of work for the day. If he finished his work, he could spend his remaining time as he wanted. A slave could even earn money on the task system, although his wages were minimal. For every pound of hemp over the 100 pounds he was required to break per day, the slave was paid one cent.[36] A good worker could break about 300 pounds,[37] so it was possible to earn about two dollars a day.[38] Some slaves earned enough money in this way to buy their freedom. Under the gang system, which was more common in the cotton fields, slaves worked in groups under the watchful eye of a driver whose job it was to get as much work out of each fieldhand as possible.

Labor in the hemp factory was also task work. A northern visitor to a Lexington ropewalk in 1830 wrote that there were "60 to 100 negro slaves, of all ages," working in the factory and they were "all stout, hearty, healthy and merry fellows, some of whom contrive to while away the time and drown the noise of the machinery by their own melody."

On another occasion, this same visitor remarked that

> every man and boy in this establishment, as I before mentioned, has his allotted portion or his stint to perform, and each one is paid for what he does beyond it. This keeps them contented, and makes them ambitious, and no one, who knows anything of mankind, will doubt but that more labor is obtained from the same number of hands than could possibly be forced from them by severity. . . . I have never seen a happier set of workmen than these boys; there was no overseer in their apartment; each boy placed his raw material beside his wheel, spun his thread the length of the room, returned to his place, and after winding the thread upon his reel, went on with his spinning with the utmost regularity and good order, singing the while with great earnestness, and not altogether without melody."[39]

Another surprised northerner told the readers of the *Boston Courier* on November 10, 1830: "I have no hesitation in saying that to the best of my knowledge, there is more real freedom of body, and quite as much

---

[35]C. P. Nettels, *The Emergence of a National Economy* (New York: Holt, Rinehart and Winston, 1962), 2: 198.

[36]J. W. Coleman, *Slavery Times in Kentucky* (Chapel Hill: University of North Carolina Press, 1940), p. 80.

[37]Nettels, *National Economy*, p. 198.

[38]Coleman, *Slavery Times*, p. 80.

[39]*Ibid.*, p. 83.

independence of mind, among the slaves of Kentucky, as there is to be found in any other portion of our country. . . ."[40]

These favorable reports were not welcomed by northern Abolitionists, who preferred to read and tell stories of beatings and torture. While such atrocities occurred, they were far less common than the Abolitionists contended. It would have been poor business to treat any slave brutally since this would have impaired his ability to work, and cheap labor was what slavery was all about.

Compared to his fellow workers in the cotton fields, however, the slave who worked in the hemp factory was far better off, and there are records showing that some of these laborers earned as much as nine hundred dollars under the task system.[41] This was more than many white workers were able to earn and save during their lifetimes.

One of the many slaves who worked in the Kentucky rope factories and who later wrote about his experiences was William Hayden. Born in Virginia in 1785, Hayden was separated from his mother and taken to Kentucky when he was only five years old. In 1803, he was hired out to the owner of a ropewalk in Lexington where he showed himself to be so proficient that he was taken into the foreman's home. It was during this time that he learned to read and write. In his memoirs, which he wrote as a free man in Cincinatti, Hayden boasted that not only was he very good at his work, he was actually "acknowledged to be the best spinner in the country," and when he asked for an increase in his wages to six dollars a year, his request was immediately granted.

Hayden's task quota was forty-eight pounds of spun hemp per day, which he proudly observes was "considered a good day's work for two men." Yet not only was he able to accomplish this work, he was so proficient that he was able to gain two days in every week, exclusive of the sabbath: "The proceeds of these two days amounted to three dollars, which it was optional with me to make, or devote my time to pleasure, if I saw fit so to do."

Hayden later went to work in Georgetown and "notwithstanding there was an experienced white man superintending the business, he could show me nothing that I did not already know, hence I soon became the foreman of the factory. From this time I was treated more as a white man than any thing else." By 1824, Hayden had saved enough money to purchase his freedom. Able to go where he pleased, he left the hemp factories of Kentucky and eventually moved to Cincinatti where he spent the remainder of his life working as a barber in his own shop.[42]

[40]*Ibid.*, p. 84.
[41]*Ibid.*, p. 83.
[42]W. Hayden, *Narrative* (Wilmington, Del.: Afro-American Historical Series, n.d.), pp. 27–38.

The Demise of the American Hemp Farms

The death blow to the American hemp industry came in the wake of the Civil War. Once trade broke off with the north, suppliers in the south lost a major market for bagging and cordage. Things were no better in the south. With no cotton to be shipped to the north or to Europe, the Confederate Congress prohibited the raising of cotton except for home use. Since no cotton was being baled, there was no need for bale rope and farmers lost their best customers.

While northern demand for hemp was unabated, businessmen had to rely exclusively on costly foreign fiber even for jobs that did not need high-quality fiber. With the loss of the cotton trade, an investigation was begun to consider the practicality of producing thread from hemp. Congress appropriated twenty thousand dollars to pay a Pennsylvanian congressman to look into the matter. His report was offered in 1865, too late to have any impact, and was ignored. Moreover, all the information he submitted was taken from contemporary encyclopaedias and from some letters written to the commissioner of agriculture.[43]

After the Civil War, hemp production never recovered. Faced with competition in the form of iron wire cables and bands, and cheaper jute bagging, many farmers simply gave up on hemp and turned instead to other agricultural staples such as wheat.

Yet hemp did not disappear from the American landscape. As late as 1890, thirty-three million dollars' worth of cordage was manufactured in the United States, and during World War I the hemp industry experienced a temporary revival. But the vast hemp plantations in Kentucky, Missouri, and Mississippi were gone forever. In later years it would even become illegal to grow hemp, as Americans learned that the once-commonplace plant was a "depraver of youth" and a "provoker of crime" called marihuana.

The Hemp Plant in Canada

Like their English rivals, when the French laid claim to North America in the sixteenth century, they too envisoned the New World as a vast repository of naval supplies, especially hemp and timber. These hopes were fueled by reports from her early explorers such as Jacques Cartier who, like many others, had mistaken *Acnida cannabina* for *Cannabis sativa*.

[43]P. W. Gates, *Agriculture and the Civil War* (New York: Knopf, 1965), p. 175.

Unlike the English, however, the French did not need to import hemp. They wanted more so that they could sell it to other countries. The earliest record of hemp in France goes back to around 200 B.C., when the Greeks brought hemp from the Rhone Valley to outfit their ships. The manufacture of French fabrics made from hemp is almost as ancient.

The export of hemp abroad began around the fifteenth century. By the sixteenth century, France was said to possess "two magnets" which attracted the wealth of Europe. One of these was wheat. The other was hemp. The yearly exports to England alone between 1686 and 1688 were over two million pounds. It was not without reason that the English complained so bitterly about the draining of their economy as a result of their imports of hemp from France.

"This most prosperous kingdom," declared the chancellor of France in 1484, "has a great number of provinces which, because of the beauty of the countryside, of the fertility of the soil, of the health-giving air, easily surpasses all the countries of earth."[44] To take advantage of these bountiful assets, French workers were continually urged to work harder to produce wool, flax, and especially hemp.

Ironically, despite the abundance of hemp, French merchants still imported large quantities of fiber from countries such as Italy and Sweden. The reason was that French merchants were able to make greater profits selling hemp abroad than they could possibly earn by manufacturing it and selling it domestically. Thus, while France sold enormous amounts of hemp to countries like England and Spain, she herself imported large quantities from other European countries. Consequently, when French merchants heard that hemp was growing wild in the New World, they sensed an opportunity for enormous profits. (Unfortunately, Cartier was a better explorer than a naturalist. The European variety of hemp did not grow wild in the New World.)

After the first disappointments subsided, the French thought they could still make a profit in hemp if they could simply persuade the colonists who were settling in New France to cultivate cannabis as a crop. To this end, Samuel Champlain, the great explorer and colonizer, brought hemp seeds with him on his early expeditions to New France. By 1606, hemp was growing in Port Royal in Nova Scotia under the watchful eye of the colony's botanist and apothecary, Louis Hébert.[45]

However, like their counterparts in the British colonies, the early French settlers were faced with an acute labor shortage and the pioneers

[44]Quoted in C. W. Cole, *Colbert and a Century of French Mercantilism* (New York: Columbia University Press, 1939), 1: 9.
[45]M. Lescarbot, *The History of New France* (Toronto: Champlain Society, 1914), 3: 247.

had trouble just trying to grow enough food to stay alive. For anyone to spend time clearing land to grow hemp would mean time lost growing food. To deal with such obstinance, Jean Talon, the wily finance minister of the Québec colony, confiscated all the thread in the colony and declared he would sell it only in return for hemp. At the same time, he gave hemp seed free to farmers with the understanding that they were to plant it immediately and replace the gift with seed from their next year's crop. Since their children had to be clothed, the women either persuaded their husbands to raise hemp or they bought it themselves and used it to barter with Talon. In this way, Talon created a demand for hemp and an industry to supply that demand.[46]

In the meantime, relations between France and England were rapidly deteriorating and eventually the two countries went to war. The French proved to be no match for the English, and in 1763 all of New France became an English domain. Almost immediately, England tried to promote hemp production in her new colony. When her initial entreaties failed, the new governor of Québec was told not to grant any land to any settler unless he promised to raise hemp on his new holdings. It was to no avail. Despite these efforts, England received only token amounts of hemp from the colonists in Canada.

After the American Revolution and the loss of her colonies to the south, England redoubled her efforts to promote hemp production in Canada. In 1790, 2000 bushels of Russian hemp seed were brought to Québec and were distributed free to all the agricultural districts of the province. Only fifteen farmers showed any interest.

By 1800, Russia was charging sixty-one pounds per ton of hemp. England reacted by urging her governors to offer more bounties. A public relations campaign of sorts was also initiated claiming hemp was a valuable economic commodity to colony and mother country alike. If hemp production increased, there would be more money and more employment. The standard of living would rise. Prosperity was within each colonist's grasp if only he would turn his efforts to growing hemp.

The appeal fell upon deaf ears. There were simply too few people to work in the hemp fields. Whatever manpower was available could be more profitably used clearing land to grow food crops essential for survival. An equally formidable problem was the Catholic church. Since hemp was exempt from tithes, the Catholic clergy refused to encourage their parishoners to grow hemp. Even had they had the time and will, French Canadians would not have listened to the English pleas. In Nova

[46]T. B. Costain, *The White and the Gold* (New York: Doubleday and Co., 1954), p. 273.

Scotia, the hemp shortage became so acute that the legislature complained that hangings had to be delayed![47]

Not easily discouraged, Parliament offered a deal to James Campbell and Charles Grece, two experts in hemp production. Should either of them sow twenty-five acres of land with hemp during their first year of settlement in Canada, and agree to continue cultivation on a scale thereafter deemed satisfactory to the local authorites, and should they also be willing to teach the settlers the fine points of hemp production and serve as inspectors for all finished hemp, they would be assured of a purchase price of forty-three pounds per ton for any hemp they raised, for five years. In addition, each man would be given an annual allowance of two hundred pounds, a loan of four hundred pounds which had to be forfeit if the contract were broken, free passage to Canada, money to pay hemp dressers, free seed, and 150 acres of land to use for experimentation. And as frosting on the cake, Parliament promised a lifetime annuity of two hundred pounds if the venture proved a success.

Alas, both men failed. Grece tried very hard to raise a crop the first year, but a combination of bad seed, late sowing, and poor weather was less than conducive to success. Campbell fared no better. What the spring floods left of his crop, the fall frost destroyed.[48]

Meanwhile, Napoleon's brilliant victories in Europe were beginning to pose a threat to England's Baltic hemp suppliers. If Napoleon defeated Russia, England would no longer have a reliable hemp source. In desperation, she once again turned to Canada. Promises of seventy pounds per ton and 300 acres of land were made to anyone who would raise five tons of hemp in a year. To make sure these offers were heard throughout the country, they were issued from church pulpits immediately after services were concluded. Yet, even with these substantial inducements, little hemp ever made its way from Canada to England.

Hemp in Latin America

Even before the English and the French were thinking about exploiting the New World, Spain was trying to promote hemp production in

---

[47]J. Howe, "Early Attempts to Introduce the Cultivation in Eastern British America," Paper read before the New Brunswick Historical Society, n.d.

[48]N. MacDonald, "Hemp and Imperial Defence," *Canadian Historical Review* 17 (1936): 385–98.

her colonies throughout Latin America. As early as 1545, hemp seed was sown in the Quillota Valley, near the city of Santiago in Chile. Most of the hemp fiber from these initial experiments was used to make rope for the army stationed in Chile. The rest was used to replace wornout rigging on ships that docked at Santiago. Eventual surpluses were shipped north to Lima, Peru.[49] Attempts were also made at cultivating hemp in Peru and Colombia, but only the Chilean experiments proved successful.

Hemp is believed to have been brought to Mexico by Pedro Cuadrado, a conquistador in Cortes's army, when the conqueror made his second expedition to Mexico. Cuadrado and a friend went into business raising hemp in Mexico and were very successful at it. In 1550, however, the Spanish governor forced the two entrepreneurs to limit production because the natives were beginning to use the plants for something other than rope.[50]

In the eighteenth century, Spain's economy began to plumet drastically and she began to turn to her colonies. In 1777, several hemp experts were sent to various colonial outposts in Spanish America to teach the inhabitants the fine points of growing and preparing hemp for market.[51] Three years later, special orders from the king instructed all viceroys to encourage hemp production throughout New Spain.

In Mexico, the authorities decided that the province of California would be an ideal place to begin hemp farming. But despite pleas to church prelates for cooperation, the missions and the individual farmers in the parishes preferred raising food crops and cattle to hemp.

When no hemp arrived for shipment to Spain, experts were sent to California to instruct the people how to grow and prepare hemp for market. The area around San José was chosen as an experimental farm area in 1801 and an earnest effort was made to raise hemp for market.

The first results were encouraging. By 1807, California was producing 12,500 pounds of hemp. About 40 percent came from Santa Barbara. Good harvests were also reported around San José, Los Angeles, and San Francisco. By 1810, California was producing over 220,000 pounds of dressed hemp.

Production would probably have continued to increase, but in 1810 a revolution in Mexico effectively isolated California from the main seat of government. As a result, the subsidies that had stimulated hemp

---

[49]A. Vasquez De Espinsoa, *Description of the Indies* (Washington, D.C.: Smithsonian Institute Press, 1960), pp. 453, 728.

[50]S. A. Mosk, "Subsidized Hemp Production in Spanish California," *Agricultural History* 13 (1939): 171–5.

[51]In the same year, Spain also sent experts to the Phillippines to encourage the natives to raise hemp (H. Hill, "The Ganja Problem in Singapore," *International Criminal Police Review* 23 [1968]: 211).

production were no longer available, and with the elimination of this incentive, commercial production of hemp ceased and was never started up again.[52]

No one knows for certain when cannabis was introduced into Brazil, Portugal's main colony in South America. The words for marihuana in Brazil include *maconha*, *liama*, and *diamba*, which closely resemble West and South African terms such as *riamba*, *diamba*, and *liamba*. On the basis of this linguistic similarity it is possible that Negro slaves abducted from their homes in Africa and brought to Brazil as plantation laborers may have brought some seeds with them to the New World. This is not very likely, however. The ships that crossed the Atlantic loaded with slaves did not afford any opportunity for comfort. Seeds that happened to be hidden in some clothing would have been eaten on ship, not saved for future farming. More probably the Portuguese themselves brought hemp seed to Brazil, since they too recognized its economic potential. Once sown, however, the slaves would have used the plant as they had in their native land. There was no need to invent new terms for plants already familiar to them.

The earliest actual reference to cannabis in Brazil dates back to the early decades of the 1800s. In 1808, the king and queen of Portugal fled to Brazil rather than risk capture by Napoleon who at that time was threatening to overrun the Iberian Peninsula. After Napoleon's defeat, the royal couple returned to Lisbon in 1814. Three years later the queen became ill and death was imminent. As she lay awaiting her death, she summoned a Negro slave who had accompanied her to Brazil and asked her to "bring me an infusion of the fibers of *diamba do amazonas*, with which we sent so many enemies to hell."[53] The slave concocted an infusion of marihuana and arsenic for her mistress which had such analgesic properties that the queen felt no further pain, and shortly before her death she sang and played her guitar.[54]

Although this anecdote casts a favorable light on marihuana, the sentiment was not shared by Brazilians. In 1830, for example, the Municipal Council of Rio de Janeiro prohibited importation of marihuana into the city. Anyone selling the drug was liable to a large fine and any slave found using it could be sentenced to three days' imprisonment.[55]

There is also no exact date for the importation of hemp to Jamaica. Around 1800, the British sent a Russian hemp expert to Jamaica to see if the plant could be profitably raised on the island, but the attempt failed

[52]Mosk, "Subsidized Hemp Production," p. 173.
[53]H. W. Hutchinson, "Patterns of Marihuana Use in Brazil," in *Cannabis and Culture*, ed. V. Rubin (The Hague: Mouton, 1975), pp. 173–83.
[54]*Ibid.*
[55]G. Greyre, *The Masters and the Slaves* (New York: Knopf, 1968), p. 317.

and production was abandoned.[56] Nevertheless, the plants began to grow wild. When indentured laborers from India came to work in Jamaica following the emancipation of the Negro slaves in the British Caribbean in the mid-nineteenth century, they found ganja already growing there.

In 1793, cannabis was brought to Cuba to see if it could be grown profitably on that island, but the planters were more interested in growing sugarcane and little effort was devoted to hemp production.[57] About the same time, hemp was introduced into Guatemala. Although serious efforts were made to cultivate the plant on a large scale in that colony, very little hemp was ever produced.

[56]V. Rubin and L. Comitas, *Ganja in Jamaica. A Medical Anthropological Study of Chronic Marihuana Use* (The Hague: Mouton, 1975), p. 15.
[57]R. J. Schafer, *The Economic Societies in the Spanish World* (Syracuse, N.Y.: Syracuse University Press, 1958), p. 322.

III

THE MARIHUANA AND HASHISH ERA

5

New Uses for the Old Hemp Plant

The discovery of the passage to the East Indies by way of the Cape of Good Hope was one of the great events of Western European history. Besides bringing great wealth, the explorations that followed the trade routes, the conquests, and the early settlements in the East helped to free Western Europeans from the shackles of medieval parochialism. Once their imaginations had been whetted, Europeans craved to know more and more about the people who lived in these far-off lands. What the people of India looked like, what they ate, how they dressed, acted, thought, etc., fascinated erstwhile provincially minded Europeans. Even the momentous landing on the moon pales before the excitement generated by the landings of the first explorers in the East Indies.

In the marketplace of ideas, the demand for news far outstripped supply and created an insatiable outlet for travelogues, or itineraries as they were often called. To supply this demand, anyone and everyone who visited these far-off places, and had the ability to put what he had seen into words, became the bestselling authors and the most sought after raconteurs of their day.

These books and storytellers were the eyes and ears of Europe. They were the entertainment media in an age of boredom. But the stories that were told did more than just entertain readers and listeners. They were grist for European brain mills to process into new thoughts and ideas. It was through these stories, for instance, that many Europeans learned that the hemp plants that grew wild in their fields were used as medicines by the people of India. Even more surprising, Europeans were told that the people in the lands to the east actually made a beverage from this plant which caused them to act as if they were drunk with wine!

Such revelations were startling. Had these same Europeans visited their own countryside and villages, or the urban hovels where the unskilled and uneducated lived, they would have known of such things long before they were written about in the travel books that poured off the printing presses. The people who craved vicarious adventure and escapism such as that offered by travelogues were mainly the well-to-do. Although European craftsmen and businessmen used enormous quantities of hemp, their familiarity with the cannabis plant was totally related to its fiber. Even the Italian hemp dealers and artisans who were so expert in evaluating the different grades of hemp fiber were totally unaware of the plant's other properties. The *Decameron*, Giovanni Bocaccio's ribald masterpiece of the Fourteenth century, refers at one point to the "Old Man of the Mountain," and to some mysterious potion, but Bocaccio never identifies the drug by name: "He sought out a powder of marvelous virtue which he had gotten in the parts of the Levant of a great prince who avouched it to be that which was wont to be used by the 'Old Man of the Mountain' when he would fain send anyone sleeping into Paradise."[1]

In the next century, the French writer and physician François Rabelais wrote at length about cannabis, calling it Pantagruelion. Pantagruelion, says Rabelais, "is sown at the first coming of the swallows, and is taken out of the ground when the grasshoppers begin to get hoarse." Its stalk is *"full of fibers, in which consists the whole value of the herb"* (italics mine). Following Pliny, he declares that the seeds produced by the male plant "destroy the procreative germs in whosoever should eat much of it often." Referring to Galen, he says, "still is it of difficult concoction, offends the stomach, engenders bad blood, and by its excessive heat acts upon the brain and fills the head with noxious and painful vapors."[2]

If Rabelais knew anything more about the effects of cannabis, he did not record them. Probably he did not. Beyond what he recorded from these classical sources, it is unlikely that Rabelais was in any way familiar with cannabis as a medicament or as a psychoactive agent.

The Witches' Brew

Away from the hustle and bustle of the major urban centers, in the relative peace and serenity of the countryside, or in the wretched shacks that housed the unskilled city dwellers, where superstition passed for truth, where magic and sorcery were a way of life, where witches revelled with the devil in hallucinatory stupor, hemp was appreciated for marvelous powers unknown to Bocaccio and Rabelais.

---

[1]G. Bocaccio, *Decameron* (New York: Blue Ribbon Books, (1931), bk. 3.8.
[2]F. Rabelais, *Pantagruel.*

"During the whole time that Catholicism had the spiritual direction of Europe," writes Émile Grillot de Givry, "a veritable Church of Evil opposed . . . the Church of God, a Church of the devil defying the Church of God. . . . like the latter [it possessed] it priests, its rites, its cult, its books, its congregations, and its supernatural visitants."[3]

The Church of Evil was the church of the discontented and the ungratified, men and women who looked upon the glories to God—his splendid churches, his powerful clergy, the pomp and ceremony dedicated to his worship—with awe and envy. Condemned to poverty and destitution through no fault of their own, they questioned the fairness of their plight and decided that if God were not on their side, then maybe they would be better off serving Satan. After all, Satan was the renowned master of mortal wealth. Serving him could lead to no worse adversity than that which they were already experiencing.

Many were content simply to worship the devil. Others aspired to higher satanic office and proclaimed themselves sorcerers (priests) and witches (priestesses). The main duties of these servants of the devil was to cast spells on those whose misfortune they desired. In so doing, they called upon the Prince of Darkness to do their bidding. Sorcerers and witches also officiated at the Black Mass—the Witches' Sabbath—an assemblage of worshippers of the devil presided over by Satan himself.

Invariably, whenever medieval artists turned to the subject of the Witches' Sabbath, they depicted a group of women, who were usually naked, compounding a mysterious drug in a large cauldron. As early as the fifteenth century, demonologists declared that one of the main constituents that the witches compounded for their heinous ceremony was hemp.

In 1484, Pope Innocent VIII issued a papal fiat condemning witchcraft and the use of hemp in the Satanic mass.[4] In 1615, an Italian physician and demonolgist, Giovanni De Ninault, listed hemp as the main ingredient in the ointments and unguents used by the devil's followers.[5] Hemp, along with opium, belladonna, henbane, and hemlock, the demonologists believed, were commonly resorted to during the Witches' Sabbath to produce the hunger, ecstasy, intoxication, and aphrodisia responsible for the glutinous banquets, the frenzied dancing, and the orgies that characterized the celebration of the Black Mass.

---

[3]E. G. De Givry, *Illustrated Anthology of Sorcery, Magic and Alchemy* (New York: Causeway Books, 1973), p. 25.

[4]A. De Pasquale, "Farmacognosia della 'Canape Indiana,'" *Estratto dai Lavori dell'Instituto di Farmacognosia dell'Universita di Messina* 5 (1967): 24.

[5]*Ibid.* Cf. also, Cornelius Agrippa, *De Oculta Philosphia* (n.d.), vol. 43; and Pierre d'Alban, *Heptameron seu Elementa Magica* (1567), p. 142.

Hemp seed oil was also an ingredient in the ointments witches allegedly used to enable them to fly.[6]

Jean Wier, the celebrated demonologist of the sixteenth century, was quite familiar with the exhilarating effects of hemp for sinister purposes. Hemp, he wrote, caused a loss of speech, uncontrollable laughter, and marvelous visions. Quoting Galen, he explained that it was capable of producing these effects by "virtue of affecting the brain since if one takes a large enough amount the vapors destroy the reason."[7]

Cannabis still retained its importance as a key ingredient in magical potions well into the nineteenth century. An occult French publication, *The Prophet's Almanac*, in its 1849 edition, for example, shows a crowd of people standing in front of a wizard who is gazing through a telescope into the future. Two of the men in the throng carry banners; one banner has "ether" printed on it, the other bears the word "hashish."[8]

Sorcerers and witches were not the only people to attribute magical properties to the marihuana plant. In the Ukraine, peasant farmers used to pluck marihuana flowers on St. John's Eve in the belief that this would keep the evil eye from hurting their farm animals.[9] Ukrainian girls of marriageable age used to carry hemp seeds in their pockets when they whispered magical spells designed to hasten their wedding day. After they pronounced these spells, they stripped naked and scampered around their homes to complete the magic.[10] In Ireland, young maidens sowed hemp seed during Halloween, believing that if they looked behind them while sowing, they would see the ghost of their future husbands.[11] In other parts of Great Britain, this rite was not confined to Halloween alone. For example, a love poem of bygone days states:

> A eve last Midsummer no sleep I sought,
> But to the field a bag of hemp-seed brought;
> I scatter'd round the seed on ev'ry side,
> And three times, in a trembling accent, cried
> This hemp-seed with my virgin hand I sow.
> Who shall my true love be, the crop shall mow.[12]

While occult in nature, the basis of these superstitious rites are lost in time.

Hemp was also mentioned in many medieval herbals as a medicinal

[6]P. Kemp, *The Healing Ritual*, (London: Faber and Faber, 1935), pp. 57, 198.
[7]Quoted in De Pasquale, "Farmacognosia," p. 24.
[8]*Almanach Prophetique pour 1849* (Paris: Aubert and Co., 1849).
[9]S. Benet, "Early Diffusion and Folk Uses of Hemp," in *Cannabis and Culture*, ed. V. Rubin (The Hague: Mouton, 1975), p. 43.
[10]*Ibid.*
[11]J. Brand, *Observations on the Popular Antiquities of Great Britain*. (London: Henry Bohn, 1848), 3: 395–6.
[12]*Ibid.*, p. 386.

agent. In 1530 and again in 1548, the English herbalist William Turner states that the plant was known as hemp in English, "hanffe" in Dutch, and "chanvre" in French, but he does not list any of its therapeutic properties.[13] About the same time, Mattioli, an Italian herbalist, described the characteristics of male and female hemp plants and listed the therapeutic properties of their seeds, roots, leaves, and sap.[14] In 1564, another Italian herbalist, Dioscobas Tabernaemontanus, wrote that hemp seeds and roots were used as medicinal agents and prescribed the application of an ointment of dry cannabis leaves and butter for burns and scalds.[15]

Hemp was also a particularly familiar ingredient in the folk medicine of Eastern Europe. In Poland, Russia, and Lithuania, peasant farmers relied on the vapor given off by smoldering hemp seeds to relieve their toothaches.[16] In some parts of Eastern Europe, doctors advised patients whose gums and teeth were thought to be infested with worms to inhale hemp seed fumes so that the worms would become intoxicated and fall out on their own![17] Other common folk uses for the plant were in easing childbirth; reducing inflamation, fever, and the swelling of joints; preventing convulsions; and curing jaundice and rheumatism.[18] Many of these uses later found their way into the pharmacopoeias of modern European medicine in the nineteenth century.

The use of cannabis in magic and folk medicine clearly shows that the European peasantry was well aware that the hemp plant had other important properties besides the marvelous virtue of its indomitable fiber. But this awareness of the plant's other uses seems not to have gone beyond the peasant farmers and the practitioners of the occult. Hence, it was a revelation for many Europeans to learn that in the Arab countries, and especially in India, the hemp plant was hardly valued at all for its fiber and instead was actually eaten and made into a beverage which was said to have the same intoxicating effects as alcohol.

The first reports came from Africa. In 1510, Leo Africanus, a Moroccan convert to Christianity, told his readers of a compound called "Lhasis" used by the people of Tunis which made them burst into laughter, caused them to act as if half drunk, and "provoked them into lust."[19]

[13]De Pasquale, "Farmacognosia," p. 24–5.
[14]Ibid.
[15]Benet, "Early Diffusion," p. 46.
[16]Ibid.
[17]Ibid.
[18]Ibid.
[19]Leo Africanus, The History and Description of Africa and of the Notable Things Therein (New York: Burt Franklin, n.d.), 3: 722.

Toward the end of the sixteenth century, a physician by the name of Prosper Alpini published a widely read book in its day entitled *The Medicines of the Egyptians* (1591), in which he stated that hashish caused men to revel in ecstasy. He compared the early stages of hashish intoxication to that of alcohol, but emphasized that the visions hashish users experienced were to an important extent dependent on their intelligence and their psychological state at the time they took the drug.

During the next two centuries, Europe entered a period of unprecedented colonialism. As more and more ships made their way down the coast of Africa and on to India, Europeans who remained at home were able to keep abreast of what was happening in these far-off lands through the various books that seemed to crop up everywhere. Many of these books were diaries and travelogues, written by adventurers, sea captains, wealthy travelers, priests, traders, administrators—in short, anyone who could write about the people of Africa and the East Indies did so. At home, the people eagerly awaited any and every bit of information that these returning voyagers might bring concerning the habits and customs of the people who lived in these "newly discovered" parts of the world.

Since Portugal was the first to establish outposts in India, it is not surprising that the earliest books to be written about life in the East Indies were authored by Portuguese writers. The first European book to deal with the effects and uses of marihuana was written by a Portuguese physician whose writings were posthumously burned in public because a secret he had carefully guarded all his life was finally revealed after his death.

A Closet Heretic in India

One of the many to be fascinated by the anecdotal tidbits about India that began filtering back to Portugal was a young doctor, Garcia Da Orta (1501–68). After hearing about India and its people, Da Orta decided to enlist in the Portuguese civil service as personal physician to the viceroy of the Indian provinces so that he could observe firsthand the truth of all these strange and exotic customs. Da Orta was also curious about the reports he had heard concerning strange new drugs that the people of India used and decided to record everything he could about India's *materia medica*. It was as a result of these writings that the people of Europe learned of a new and previously unimagined use for the familiar hemp plant. Although Da Orta's book subsequently became a classic in the literature of drugs, almost every copy was destroyed when the Portuguese church found out that he had been a closet Jew who had hidden his religion nearly all his life.

Da Orta was not a native-born Portuguese citizen but the son of Spanish Jews who had been forced into exile when Spain banished all Jews from that country in 1492. Like many other Spanish Jews, Da Orta's father sought refuge in neighboring Portugal. The king and the church allowed them to stay until 1497. In that year, Jews were once again faced with the threat of exile if they did not convert to Christianity.

Tired of flight, Da Orta's father let it be known that he had disavowed his Jewish heritage. This enabled him to remain in the country and allowed his son Garcia to enter the Spanish universities of Salamanca and Alcala de Henares where he studied arts and medicine. It was shortly after receiving his degree in medicine that Garcia left Europe to serve in Portugal's new territories in the east.

Da Orta got more than he bargained for, however, for in serving in India he was occasionally required to take part in military campaigns against the native populace. The life of a military surgeon seems not to have been to his liking, for as soon as his enlistment ran out he left the army and went into private practice in Goa, the Portuguese colony off the coast of India. It was during this period that he wrote his famous *Colloquies on the Simples and Drugs of India*, which was subsequently published in Goa in 1563.[20]

The book was to become the most important text on natural medicines since Dioscorides' herbal, hitherto the most influential text of its kind for the previous 1500 years.

The *Colloquies* is a landmark in the history of psychopharmacology. Written in the form of a dialogue between himself and a colleague from Salamanca named Ruano, Da Orta describes for his readers the effects of various hallucinogenic drugs commonly used in India. Among those which receive special attention are opium, datura, and of course bangue, the concoction made from cannabis.

Bangue, Da Orta said, makes a man laugh foolishly and lifts him above all cares and anxieties. It had aphrodisiac effects ("I hear that many women take it when they want to dally and flirt with men") as well as soporific actions ("I've heard it said, although it may not be true, that the great captains, in ancient times, used to drink it with wine or opium so that they could get some rest from their work, banish their cares, and get to sleep").

Da Orta also remarked on what was already a well-known phenom-

[20]G. Da Orta, *Colloquies on the Simples and Drugs of India* (London: Henry Southern, 1913).

enon regarding marihuana, namely that the drug's effects on mood depended on the user's feelings at the time he took it:

> I myself saw a Portuguese jester . . . eat a slice or two of the electuary and at night he was pleasantly intoxicated, his utterance not intelligible. Then he became sad, began to shed tears, and was plunged into grief. In his case the effect was sadness and nausea. . . . Those of my servants who took it, unbeknownst to me, said that it made them so as not to feel their work, to be very happy, and to have a craving for food. I believe that it is so generally used and by such a large number of people, that there is no mystery about it. But I myself have not tried it, nor do I wish to do so. Many Portuguese have told me that they have taken it and they experienced the same feelings, more especially female partakers.[21]

Da Orta's book created quite a stir when it first appeared in Europe. The book was widely read by his colleagues and by those interested in the customs of the people of India, and very often his observations were copied verbatim in subsequent medical treatises or travel narratives, often without giving any credit as to source. Owing largely to Da Orta's writings on the subject, physicians began to regard cannabis in a new light. Prepared properly, hemp could be made into a drug the actions of which included euphoria, sedation, stimulation of appetite, hallucinations, and aphrodisia.

However, Portuguese physicians were not able to keep Da Orta's book on their library shelves for very long. Soon after the author's death, his wife confessed to the Portuguese Inquisition that her husband had been secretly practicing his Jewish faith. He had only adopted the outward signs of Christianity to deceive the authorities.

When it heard this confession, the Inquisition had Da Orta's body exhumed and cremated in public as a lesson to all other Jewish apostates who thought that they might get away with deceiving the church as to their conversions. Furthermore, all copies of Da Orta's book that could be located were confiscated and burned as well. (Fortunately, a Flemish botanist discovered a copy in a Lisbon bookshop and kept it from being destroyed. The book was later republished in Latin, Italian, French, and English, and was widely quoted whenever any reference was made to the hallucinogenic plants of India.)

MORE ABOUT BANGUE

In 1578, a Portuguese colleage of Da Orta's, Cristobal Acosta (1524–94), published his own textbook, *On the Drugs and Medicines from the East Indies*, in which he dealt at some length with the properties of bangue.

[21] *Ibid.*, p. 53.

Acosta had also sailed to India in the service of the government. He too had had to take part in military campaigns against the native populace, and on one occasion was actually captured and imprisoned in Bengal. After his release, he traveled to Goa where he visited Da Orta, and the two doctors exchanged information on what they had learned about the exotic drugs of the Indies.

Like Da Orta, Acosta had found that bangue was used by different people for different reasons: "some take it to forget their worries and sleep without thoughts; others to enjoy in their sleep a variety of dreams and delusions; others become drunk and act like merry jesters; others because of love sickness."[22]

Also like Da Orta, Acosta noted that various other ingredients were added to bangue for various purposes. Gum areca (Indian betel nut), opium, and sugar were common additives. For those who wished to hallucinate ("enjoy a variety of dreams"), the recipe called for the addition of camphor, clove, nutmeg, and mace. Increased sexual potency could be had by adding amber, musk, and sugar.

The last major book of the sixteenth century to mention marihuana was written by a Dutchman, John Huyghen van Linschoten. Van Linschoten had been especially intrigued by Da Orta's descriptions of India and its exotic drugs. He realized the potential for success and wealth in catering to Europe's new appetitie for vicarious wanderlust by supplying more of the same.

Van Linschoten was a man of single-minded purpose. To visit India he had to be employed by the Portuguese since they still controlled the subcontinent. Consequently, he left his native Holland and took up residence in Portugal, learned the language, and eventually got a job in the Portuguese colonies. After his tour of duty, he returned to his native Holland and began to write about what he had seen overseas. His travel log, or *Itinerario* as he called it, was published in 1596 and was an instant bestseller.

But while he claimed to have written about things he himself had seen, much of the *Itinerario*'s description of the effects of bangue were taken almost verbatim from other books such as Da Orta's *Colloquies*. Van Linschotten was not content with simply copying Da Orta's text, however. In several instances he deliberately embellished or distorted the material he copied to make it more interesting. It was also through van Linschoten's *Itinerario* that many readers got the mistaken impression that bangue and opium were identical in their effects.

Fifty years later, in 1649, a Portuguese missionary, Fray Sebastien

---

[22]Quoted in F. Guerra, "Sex and Drugs in the 16th Century," *British Journal of Addictions* 69 (1974): 269–90.

Manrique, also mistakenly equated the two drugs in a book he wrote describing his own travels in India: "This country also produces a plant called Anfion resembling our own hemp [which is used by the people] to assist in the gratification of lust and lewdness, by increasing their sexual power. . . . Bangue and posto [cannabis spiked with opium] have a similar effect."[23]

Summing up his attitude toward these drugs and the people who used them, the friar said: "Being mere barbarians and people ignorant of our true and sacred religion, they think only of pleasure of the flesh, believing that the highest pitch of human beatitude lies in them [that is, in drugs such as opium and bangue]."[24]

Such errors were not peculiar to the Portuguese. In 1628, Peter Mundy, an employee of the British East India Company, wrote that bangue had the same effect as opium "soe that most commonly they [the natives] will call a druncken fellow either Amphomee [opium eater], Postee [opium drunkard] or Bangguee [hemp eater]. . . . "[25]

In 1698, John Freyer, a physician employed by the same British company, made a similar mistake. Freyer in fact believed that opium was made from bangue. "It [bangue] grows," he said, "as our hemp, the juice of whose seed ground in a bowl like mustard-seed, and mixed with any other liquor. . . [causes its users to develop] a craving for this poisonous drink . . . [and when mixed with belladona] bangue is the inebriating confection of the Post [opium]."[26] Apparently Freyer was under the impression that the cannabis in Post was more potent than the opium in it.

Freyer also describes a form of punishment Indian rulers meted out to subjects who were too important to execute outright:

> Upon an offence they are sent by the King's order, and committed to a place called the Post (from the punishment inflicted), where the Master of the Post is acquainted with the heinousness of the crime; which being understood, he heightens by a drink, which they first refuse, made of Bang (the juice of the intoxicating hemp), and being mingled with Dutry (the deadliest sort of Solanum or Nightshade) name Post, after a week's taking, they crave more than ever . . . [and die].[27]

The French journalist Bernier also remarked on this strange torture:

> [Miscreants] whose heads the Monarch is deterred by prudential reasons from taking off . . . [are brought] a large cup of this beverage . . . early in the

[23]S. Manorique, *Travels of Fray Sebastien Manorique (1629–1643)*. (Oxford: Hakluyt Society, 1927), p. 427.

[24]*Ibid.*

[25]P. Mundy, *The Travels of Peter Mundy, in Europe and Asia, 1608–1667* (Oxford: Hakluyt Society, 1914), 2: 247.

[26]J. Freyer, *A New Account of East India and Persia Being Nine Years' Travel 1672–1681* (Liechtenstein: Krauss Reprint Ltd., 1967), 1: 92.

[27]*Ibid.*

morning, and they are not given anything to eat until it be swallowed; they would sooner let the victim die of hunger. This drink emaciates the wretched victims, who lose their strength and intellect by slow degrees, become torpid and senseless, and at length die.[28]

The fact that opium was actually mixed with bangue may have been responsible for the notion that the two were one and the same or that bangue could be chemically transformed into opium. Whatever the basis for the error, the idea that bangue had the same addicting effects as opium began to take shape in the minds of Europeans.

THE WORLD OF BANGUE

As more and more travelers visited India, more and more began to be written about bangue and its effects. A well-known herbal of the eighteenth century in which bangue was given special attention was published in 1695 by a physician living in India named Rumphius. Rumphius remarked that bangue was widely used in India to treat all kinds of diseases from gonorrhea to diarrhea.

A particularly interesting account of bangue and its uses in Persia and India is contained in another seventeenth-century medical treatise by Englebert Kaempfer. Kaempfer was a German physician who was equally well known as a historian, political scientist, diplomat, and botanist. Very early in life, Kaempfer earned a reputation as a brilliant scientist, and so impressed the king of Sweden than he asked Kaempfer to be one of the ambassadors he was sending to Persia to coax the Persians to break ties with the Arab empire and begin trading with the West. After the unsuccessful delegation returned to Sweden, Kaempfer signed on with the Dutch East India Company as fleet surgeon. It was during this time that he observed a fascinating spectacle in India involving bangue:

> At the time of the sacrifices in honor of Vishnu, virgins pleasant to behold and richly adorned, were brought to the temple of the Brahmins. They came out in public to appease the god who rules over plenty and fine weather. To impress the spectators, these young women were previously given a preparation with a basis of hemp and datura, and when the priest saw certain symptoms, he began his invocations. The Devadassy (the term for these girls) then danced, leapt about yelling, contorted their limbs, and, foaming at the mouth, their eyes ecstatic, committed all sorts of eccentricities. Finally, the priests carried the exhausted virgins into a sanctuary, gave them a potion to destroy the effect of the previous one, and then showed them again to the people in their right mind, so that the crowd of spectators might believe that the demons had fled and the idol was appeased.[29]

---

[28]*Ibid.*, note 1.
[29]Quoted in F. J. Bouquet, "Cannabis," *Bulletin on Narcotics* 2 (1950), 14–30.

Although intrigued by such spectacles, Kaempfer was no stranger to cannabis. During his student days at the University of Cracow he says that he used to eat food made with cannabis, so he probably had some personal experience with its effects. He was also familiar with Pliny's description of the drug as well as its uses as a medicinal agent in ancient times, mentioning its properties as a soporific and an antispasmotic. From his writings, it appears that by the seventeenth century the medicinal properties of the plant were fairly well known to the medical profession.

Among the popular travel logs that entertained English readers was *A Geographical Account of Countries Round the Bay of Bengal,*[30] an interesting memoir published some time around 1680 by a wizened old sea dog named Capt. Thomas Bowrey.

Bowrey was a frequent visitor to India between 1669 and 1679, and had sailed up and down the subcontinent carrying supplies and goods to and from the various outposts that dotted the seacoast. Unlike many Europeans, who lived in India and observed the customs and foods of the native people without participating in what they saw, Bowrey often partook of the food and especially the intoxicating beverages of the country. His observations, as described in his book, were English readers' first detailed insight into the effects of bangue as experienced by a fellow Englishman.

Bowrey began his discussion by noting that bangue had different effects on different individuals depending on their temperament:

> It operates according to the thoughts or fancy of the Partie that drinketh thereof, in such manner that if he be merry at that instant, he shall continue soe with exceedinge great laughter for the before mentioned space of time [four to five hours], rather overymerry than otherways, laughinge heartilie at every thinge they discerne; and, on the contrary, if it is taken in a fearefull or melancholy posture, he shall keep great lamentation and seem to be in great anguish of spirit, takeinge away all manly gesture or thoughts from him.[31]

In the following excerpt from his travelogue, Bowrey describes his first reactions to bangue. Note the precautions he and his comrades took to keep from being observed, and the effect of the drug on the participants, especially the man who stuck his head in a jar:

> Eight or tenne of us to trye practice, wee wold needs drinke every man his pint of bangha, which we purchased in the bazar for the value of 6d English. I ordered my man to bringe alonge with him one of the Facheers (who frequently drinke of this liquor), promisinge him his dose of the same to come and compound the rest for us, which he cordially and freely accepted

---

[30]T. Bowrey, *A Geographical Account of Countries Round the Bay of Bengal, 1669 to 1679* (Nendeln, Liechtenstein: Kraus Reprint, 1967).
[31]*Ibid.,* p. 79.

of, and it was as welcome to him as a crowne in moneys. Wee dranke each man his proportion, and sent the Fackeer out of dores, and made fast all dores and windows, that none of us might run into the street, or any person come in to behold any of our humors thereby to laught at us.

The Fackeere sat without the street dore, callinge us all kings and brave fellows, fancyinge himselfe to be at the gates of the Pallace at Agra, singinge to that purpose in the Hardostan languadge.

It soon tooke its operation upon most of us, but merrily, save upon two of our number, who I suppose feared it might doe them harme not being accustomed thereto. One of them sat himselfe downe upon the floore, and wept bitterly all the afternoone, the other terrified with feare did runne his head into a great Mortavan Jarre, and continued in that posture 4 hours or more; 4 or 5 of the number lay upon the carpets (that were spread in the roome) highly complimentinge each other in high termes, each man fancyinge himselfe noe lesse than an emperor. One was quarrelsome and fought with one of the wooden pillars of the porch, untill he had left himselfe little skin upon the knuckles of his fingers. My selfe and one more sat sweatinge for the space of 3 hours in exceedinge measure.[32]

For his part, Bowrey regarded the effects of cannabis rather favorably, speaking of it as "theire so admirable herbe." But despite his praises for the drug, Bowrey seems to have suffered a mild withdrawal effect after he stopped using it regularly. "Taste it hath not any, in my judgement less faire water, yet it is of such a bewitchinge Scottish nature, that whoever use it but one month or two cannot forsake it without muche difficultie."[33] Judging from this mild dependency reaction, it is likely that Bowrey's bangue contained more than a little opium.

THE FRENCH ITINERARIA

The French also had their world travelers who brought back exotic tales of the East and their experiences with hashish.

Laurent D'Arvieux visited the Middle East in 1665–6 and described his adventures in *Voyage in Palestine, To the Grand Emir, Chief of the Arabian Princes of the Desert, Known as the Bedouins.* D'Arvieux relates that he took a drug called Berge which may have been hashish, but he identifies it at one point as opium and at another time as henbane.

In 1686, Jean Chardin, published an account of his adventures in the Middle East in *Voyages to Persia and Other Parts of the Orient,* a widely read book which was reissued several times. Like most of the European observers, Chardin did not experience the effects of cannabis firsthand, but merely related what he had seen and been told.

Regarding cannabis, Chardin distinguishes between the bueng

[32] *Ibid.*
[33] *Ibid.*

used by the Persians and that used in India. Persian bueng, he says, is actually a mixture of cannabis, opium, and nux vomica, which is also called "Poust." Like John Freyer, Chardin relates that "Poust" was given to "state criminals whose lives are to be ended, so as to take away their spirit," as well as to "children of royal blood whom they wish to render incapable of reigning. They say it is less inhumane than killing them, as is done in Turkey, or in blinding them as the Persians do." On the other hand, Indian bueng, he says, consists only of cannabis "but in all sects it is only the worthless people who drink it, particularly tramps and beggars."[34]

In 1681, another French traveler, Père Ange, who had journeyed to Persia to study the plants used by the people, also reported (*Pharmacopoea Persica*) that the Persians used a mixture of cannabis and opium which, he says, produced effects similar to those Herodotus described when he wrote about the Scythians.

THE DANISH EXPEDITION

With all the excitement and curiosity being generated by the fascinating accounts of life in other lands, the urge to send even more expeditions was infectious. Yet another monarch to be caught up in the ebullience of the times was the king of Denmark.

Less interested in staking claim to new territories than in learning more about the culture of the Arab world, the king agreed to finance an expedition to the unmapped regions of Yemen, a hitherto isolated region of Arabia once known as the Incense Trail.

In 1759, the expedition set out to make the long voyage to the south. The fact-finders were five prominent scholars—a botanist, a zoologist, a philologist, an artist, and a mathematician. Each was to exercise his skills as best he could in learning about Yemen and its people.

Yemen is an incredibly hot country. The temperature often soars to over 120°F. Parts of it are almost impassable. When the expedition arrived in the country, the villages were primitive outposts built either of stone in the highlands or of mud in the low regions.

The country took its toll. Of the five explorers, only one, the mathematician Carsten Niebuhr, survived, and even he contracted malaria. Seven years after he had first set out, Niebuhr finally returned to Denmark and filed his report to the king. In 1772, he formally published his observations in a book which he called *Travels in Arabia*.

Like many of his fellow explorers who had witnessed and been

---

[34]In A. C. Kimmens, ed., *Tales of Hashish* (New York: Wm. Morrow, 1977), p. 278.

intrigued by the widespread use of bangue or hashish, Niebuhr reflects in his book the European fascination with the popularity of these drugs among non-Europeans.

"The lower people [Sufis] are fond of raising their spirits to a state of intoxication," Niebuhr told his readers, explaining that they did so by smoking hashish, "which is the dried leaves of a sort of hemp." He explained:

> The smoke exalts their courage and throws them into a state in which delight-ful visions dance before their imagination. One of our Arabian servants, after smoking Haschisch, met with four soldiers in the street, and attacked the whole party. One of the soldiers gave him a sound beating, and brought him home to us. Notwithstanding his mishap, he would not make himself easy, but still imagined, such was the effect of his intoxication, that he was a match for any four men.[35]

Cannabis in Medicine

The seventeenth and eighteenth centuries marked the appearance not only of travel books dealing with cannabis, but also of "dispensatories" which began referring to cannabis as a medicinal agent. Typically, however, these texts were rather cautious in their advocacy of hemp as a therapeutic agent. In most instances, cannabis's antibiotic and analgesic properties were emphasized.

Although as early as 1621 Robert Burton had suggested that cannabis might be of value in the treatment of depression,[36] this proposal was never tried in England. The New London Dispensatory, published in 1682, contained only a brief reference to hemp seeds, claiming that they cured coughs and jaundice but filled the head with vapors," but the Complete English Dispensatory of 1720 took issue with the recommendation to use hemp seeds in treating jaundice, asserting that such recommendation is "not hitherto with authority enough to bring them into prescriptions of any kind."[37]

The New English Dispensatory of 1764 recommended boiling hemp roots and applying them to the skin to reduce inflammation, a folk medicinal treatment that had been popular in eastern Europe for centuries. Other uses for the concoction were in drying up tumors and dissolving deposits in the joints.

---

[35]C. Niebuhr, Travels in Arabia, in A General Collection of the Best and Most Interesting Voyages and Travels in All Parts of the World, ed. J. Pinkerton (London: Longman, Hurst, Ries, Orme, and Brown, 1811), 10: 153.

[36]R. Burton, The Anatomy of Melancholy (New York: Vintage, 1977), 2: 247.

[37]J. Quincy, ed., Complete English Dispensatory (London: A. Bell, 1720), p. 201.

The *Edinburgh New Dispensary* of 1794 carried a relatively long description of the effects of hemp in medicine, indicating that its popularity in this regard had begun to increase. "This plant," the text stated,
"when fresh, has a rank narcotic smell, the water in which the stalks are
soaked, in order to facilitate the separation of the tough rind for mechan-
ical uses [e.g., rope], is said to be violently poisonous, and to produce its
effects as soon as drunk." Regarding the seeds, the text claims that they
yield an "insipid" oil when pressed, and that when this oil is added to
milk, an emulsion is formed which is useful in treating coughs, "heat of
urine [venereal disease]," and "incontinence of urine." The authors also
state that cannabis was believed to be useful in "restraining venereal
appetites," but adds that "experience does not warrant their having any
virtue of this kind." The section on cannabis closes with a foreshadowing of the future: "Although the seeds only have hitherto been princi-
pally in use, yet other parts of the plant seem to be more active, and may
be considered as deserving further attention."[38]

A few years later, Nicholas Culpeper, the foremost herbalist of his
time, summarized all the conditions for which cannabis was reputed to
be an effective medicinal agent. Culpeper repeats many of the claims for
cannabis contained in the previously mentioned dispensatories and adds
a few from the classical writings of Galen and Pliny, including some of
his own recommendations. For example, he mentions that cannabis
"dries up the natural seed for procreation," and "being boiled in milke
and taken, helps such as have a dry hot cough." "It is held very good to
kill the worms in men and beasts; and the juice dropped into the ears
kills worms in them; and draws forth earwigs, or other living creatures
gotten into them." Furthermore, "the emulsion or decoction of the seed
stays lasks and continual fluxes, eases the cholic, and allays the trouble-
some humours in the bowels, and stays bleeding at the mouth, nose and
other places." Regarding its other effects, Culpeper mentions that "the
decoction of the root allays inflamation of the head, or any other parts;
the herb itself, or the distilled water thereof doth the like. The decoction
of the roots eases the pains of the gout, the hard humours of knots in the
joints, the pains and shrinking of the sinews, and the pains of the hips.
The fresh juice mixed with a little oil and butter, is good for any place
that hath been burnt with fire, being thereto applied."[39]

It was not until the middle of the nineteenth century that cannabis
was to be given serious consideration by the medical profession. Until
that time, it was sparingly used as a folk remedy for certain disorders,
but it never enjoyed any popularity and there is absolutely no indication

---

[38]*Edinburgh New Dispensatory* (Edinburgh: Wm Creech, 1794), p. 126.
[39]N. Culpeper, *Complete Herbal* (London: Richard Evans Co., 1814), p. 91.

that the English ever became intoxicated as a result of eating cannabis leaves or seeds. The variety of cannabis that grew in England did not produce enough resin for it inadvertently to intoxicate any proponent of the plant as a home remedy.

LINNAEUS VERSUS LAMARCK

In 1753, the hemp plant was christened *Cannabis sativa* by the Swedish botanist Carl Linnaeus, in his *Species Plantarum,* and it has borne this scientific name ever since.

However, almost as soon as Linnaeus dubbed hemp *Cannabis sativa,* other botanists began to argue that there were two distinct types of hemp plant and therefore it was a mistake to lump all hemp-like plants under one name. The most notable dissembler was the French biologist Jean Lamarck.

In 1783, Lamarck contended that the European hemp plant and the Indian hemp plant each warranted its own name. The latter, he noted, contained far more resin than the European plant and it also appeared noticeably different in other distinct ways. Because of these differences, Lamarck reserved the name *Cannabis sativa* for the European plant and gave the name *Cannabis indica* to the Indian plant—indica referring to its place of origin.

Lamarck was not the first or the only scientist to point out the differences between the two plants, but he was the first to contrast clearly the two types, and his arguments were very convincing.

This early argument as to whether there is one species of cannabis which includes many different varieties or several different species still remains to be settled.

6

The Indian Hemp Drug Debate

India was one of England's most lucrative colonial ventures. The English gentry made fortunes several times over from their investments in India. Exploitation of natural resources was assumed whenever European countries established territorial rights, and Parliament usually gave its blessing to any such enterprises in expectation of sharing in windfall profits.

Sometimes, however, despite the most stringent economic, social, and political regulations imposed on the native peoples of another country, business ventures failed. Such was the case with the British East India Company. The problem was not that the company did not make money—its profits were enormous. But many of the company's top executives were not adverse to pocketing a little extra money at the company's expense. Consequently, while the fortunes of the company's managers skyrocketed, the profits of the company and its stockholders plumeted. By 1770, the finances of the British East India Company were in such a dismal state that it was forced to ask Parliament for a loan so that it could avert bankruptcy.

Parliament debated the issue of extending money to such a poorly managed enterprise for some time, but finally agreed to underwrite such a loan. On condition—the company had to place its operation under direct Parliamentary control.

The company's directors had no other recourse. They had to agree. As soon as the arrangements were made, Parliament began to examine various options to get its money back and then some. Among the suggestions subsequently adopted was a tax directed at India's intoxicating hemp drugs, namely bhang, ganja, and charas.

According to the new law which came into effect in 1798, no one was permitted to manufacture or sell hemp drugs without first obtaining a license from the Zillah, the administrative office set up to collect such revenues. Such a regulation was adopted, the law stated, "with a view to check immoderate consumption, and at the same time to augment the public revenue."[1]

Although professing altruistic motives, the fact that the law also included substances such as tobacco and toddy in its list of taxable drugs indicates that the legislation was clearly motivated by economic consid- erations. Any thought for the welfare of the people of India was merely lip-service to pacify a small coterie of native Indian bureaucrats and the few English government workers who felt that widespread abuse of hemp drugs was endangering the population.

Among those who believed that hemp drugs were ruining the coun- try was the governor general. Drugs such as charas and ganja, along with opium and alcohol, "are of so noxious a quality, and produce a species of intoxication so extremely violent," he warned, "that they cannot be used without imminent danger to the individual as well as to the public."[2] The sale of all such drugs, he urged, ought to be totally prohibited in India. Poverty, ignorance, disease, crime, political corrup- tion, all of which were endemic to the country, were attributed to drug abuse, expecially bhang, ganja, and charas.

The Board of Revenue met to consider these allegations but decided that the dangers to the country and its people were not so dire as the governor general implied, and decided that if curtailment were in the best interests of the country, such curtailment ought to be achieved through taxation. These drugs, it declared, "are not for the most part represented as producing any very violent or dangerous effects of intox- ication except when taken to excess. . . . we do not recommend that the sale of any of them be altogether prohibited, but shall proceed to state what appears to us the best means of restricting the use of them, and improving the revenue by the imposition of such taxes as are best adapted to the nature of the cause."[3]

Such measures were routine answers to the country's problems. Back in England, thousands of miles away, Parliament's main interest in India was how to extract more money from the country. The people could intoxicate themselves as much as they liked. As long as England profited from their intoxication and the country remained peaceful, Par- liament could not have cared less.

England, in fact, was one of the world's main drug suppliers and cannabis was but a minor revenue-generating resource. The big money lay in opium, and India grew more opium than any other country. Thousands and thousands of pounds of opium were offered annually at

[1] *Indian Hemp Drugs Commission,* (Simla, India: 1893–4), 3: 16.
[2] H. C. Mookerjee, "India's Hemp Drug Policy Under British Rule," *Modern Review* 84 (1948): 447.
[3] *Ibid.*

public auctions to English merchants who bought the drug and resold it to the Chinese at an enormous profit. When the Chinese government tried to stop the flow of opium into the country, England sent gunboats into Chinese waters to protect British interests. Revenue, not altruism, was Parliament's concern.

In 1838, a survey of the agricultural products raised in East India was conducted under the auspices of the British government. In the course of his report, the official in charge of the survey noted that despite the taxes on ganja, it was still used daily by the natives. Furthermore, the drug was being sold illicitly in many places and the colonial office suggested that perhaps India's hemp drugs ought to be banned outright.

Parliament responded in its own inimitable fashion. It considered how to get more taxes out of the people. Since the revenues were not so great as had been anticipated, a new method of taxation was imposed, one based on the weight of drug sold instead of on potency. When this tactic failed to generate any noteworthy increases to the treasury, the overall tax was boosted once more.

In the meantime, Parliament began hearing reports that Sepoys, native Indian soldiers serving in the British army, were using ganja and, as a result, the efficiency of Her Majesty's armed forces was being undermined.

Criticism started mounting from other directions as well. Bhang, it was said, was causing indigestion, coughing, melancholy, impotency, insanity, idiocy, and most alarming of all, crime.

Behind the rising complaints against the drug was the nuisance, to England at least, of growing Indian nationalism.

In 1870, the financial secretary of the government of India added his voice to the growing condemnation of cannabis: "Every lunatic asylum report," he stated, "is full of instances of insanity and crime due to the use of ganja."[4]

Surprisingly, little was ever said against bhang or charas. For one thing, bhang was rather weak. It was a beverage consumed as nonchalantly as a cup of tea. A sizable quantity of bhang would have to be consumed before any serious effects would be experienced.

Charas was a different story altogether. It was the most potent of the three cannabis drugs, and one might expect that if any of these three would be accused of inducing abnormality, it would have been charas. But charas was also the most expensive of the three. It could only be afforded by the wealthy. Hence, the number of those using it to excess was comparatively few. Moreover, should a situation arise in which

[4]*Ibid.*, p. 448.

some well-to-do user did require special attention, relatives and friends could afford to keep him out of the public eye.

Ganja, on the other hand, was potent, not very expensive, and popular. Those who enjoyed it usually came from the lower classes. If they ran afoul of the law, there was no one to speak up for them. Generally, they were either thrown into jail or into an insane asylum.

When the outcry against cannabis could no longer be brushed aside, India's local administrators were instructed to look into the charges that cannabis was inciting the natives to criminal acts and insanity. On October 10, 1871, the secretary to the government of India issued a directive in which he stated the conditions that had prompted the inquiry and informed the administrators what they should concern themselves with:

> It has frequently been alleged that the abuse of ganja produces insanity and other dangerous effects. . . . you will be so good as to cause such investigations as are feasible to be carried out in regard to the efforts of the use or abuse of the several preparations of hemp. The inquiry should not be simply medical but should include the alleged influence of ganja and bhang in exciting to violent crime.[5]

The study was conducted without a great deal of fanfare and the report was submitted to the central office. After sifting through the correspondence, the government issued a statement to the effect that there was no proof that cannabis drugs specifically incited criminal activities to a greater degree than did any other drugs. On the insanity issue, the government admitted that while there was "no doubt that its habitual use does tend to produce insanity, the total number of cases of insanity is small in proportion of the population, and not large even in proportion to the number of ganja smokers. . . . "[6] No doubt a major consideration in weighing the evidence was that a substantial revenue from the taxes imposed on cannabis was finally beginning to be realized.

While local officials continued clamoring that cannabis was ruining the country, British lawmakers contended that total prohibition would only lead to contraband use. The only way to reduce consumption, the government asserted, was to increase the cost of these drugs to consumers. Such impositions, it admitted, would also raise more income for Her Majesty's coffers.

Local administrators refused to be silenced, however, and in 1877 enough pressure was brought to bear upon the cannabis issue that a special task force was commissioned to look into the problem. Once again the government admitted that excessive use of cannabis drugs was

[5] Ibid.
[6] Ibid.

harmful, and once again it insisted that the only way of reducing consumption was by increasing "the tax on this article as high as it can
possibly bear. . . . The policy of Government must be to limit its production and sale by a high rate of duty without placing the drug entirely
beyond the reach of those who will insist upon having it."[7]

The Indian Hemp Drugs Commission

Thus far, most of the demands for something to be done about the
alleged cannabis problem in India had come from local native administrators. These officials were drawn primarily from the middle and upper
classes, and although sincere in their beliefs about the dangers associated with cannabis drugs, they viewed the issue from the point of
view of class distinction. To these observers, it was not that the lower
classes were poor and destitute, not that their opportunities for better-
ment were minimal if not nonexistent, not that they lived in squalor and
often had to beg or steal to feed themselves and their families, not that
they were placed in insane asylums because of failing health due to
inadequate nutrition or disease. Instead, all these problems were blamed
on the use of ganja and other hemp drugs.

By 1890, however, more and more of the English bureaucracy
stationed in India were starting to agree with their local underlings and
they began to express their feelings in the newspapers. These statements could not be ignored or dismissed as the exaggerated claims of
ignorant native administrators. Nor could they be brushed aside as the
rantings of a rabble of dissidents whose criticism of British policy, whatever it might be, was their only interest. The authors of these statements
were respectable English gentlemen and as such they attracted attention
from other respectable English gentlemen.

Because these statements were issued by English administrators
and not Indians, they received a certain amount of attention in England.
The ganja menace, at it was being called, eventually caught the attention
of the Temperance League, and one of the leaders of that movement,
who also happened to be a member of Parliament, requested Lord Kimberly, secretary of state for India, to form a commission to inquire into
the cannabis issue in India with a view to determining whether cannabis
should be prohibited altogether in that country. Kimberly agreed, and
on March 16, 1893, he ordered such a commission to be appointed.

The committee that was finally chosen was composed of four English and three Indian members. Its mandate was extensive. It was to

[7] *Ibid.*

study the method used to cultivate cannabis, the kind of drugs made from the plant, and the effects of their consumption on the moral and social life of the people of India. In keeping with Parliament's primary concern, namely revenues, the committee was also instructed to inquire into "the various systems employed for taxing the drugs or cultivation of the plant . . . with special reference to the comparative incidence of this taxation in different parts of India and to the comparative efficacy of the taxation imposed in restricting consumption. . . . "[8]

Once they had dealt with the taxation issue, the committee members were to give special attention to two points:

> The first of these is the danger lest prohibition, or restrictive measures of a stringent character, may give rise to serious discontent, and be resented by the people as an unjustifiable interference with long-established social custom. . . . It is believed that in some parts of the country bhang is, in a special degree, the poor man's narcotic and the possible unpopularity of a measure which would deprive the very poorest of the population of the use of a narcotic to which they have always been accustomed should not be overlooked.
>
> Another point to which the attention of the Commissioners should be directed is the probability or possibility that, if the use of hemp drugs is prohibited, those who would otherwise continue to use them may be driven to have recourse to alcohol, or to stimulants or narcotics which may be more deleterious.[9]

Further directives required the commission to recommend "reforms and improvements . . . for controlling the cultivation of the hemp plant, and the manufacture, sale, and taxation of hemp drugs," should the evidence warrant the prohibition of any cannabis preparation. On this score, the commissioners were advised that "absolute prohibition, or repressive measures of a stringent nature, may involve inquisitorial proceedings of an unpopular character, and afford opportunities for the army of blackmail. . . . "[10]

The commission met on August 3, 1893, and remained in session until August 6 of the following year. During this time, it received written and oral testimony from 1193 witnesses from all provinces of India. These witnesses were either summoned directly or were sent by local authorities to give testimony. A number of witnesses also gave voluntary evidence.

Few of those who appeared before the commission had expertise in any matter about which they gave testimony. Most were individuals who were supposed to know something about the effects of cannabis

[8] *Indian Hemp Drugs Commission,* 3: 2–3.
[9] *Ibid.,* p. 3.
[10] *Ibid.,* pp. 3–4.

drugs because of contact with people who used them. Very few were, or admitted to being, actual users of cannabis drugs.

The majority of the witnesses were English and native physicians, civil and medical officials, magistrates and policemen, farmers, traders, and missionaries. The evidence which they gave consisted of their answers to carefully worded questions prepared by the commission.

So that the commissioners could better evaluate the answers received, all witnesses were requested to indicate the source of their information and how they had arrived at their opinions and statements.

Furthermore, the commissioners also made on-the-spot visits throughout the country to inspect firsthand, the role of hemp drugs in the lives of the people of India.

The commission's findings were recorded and published in a massive seven-volume report. While it is not possible to summarize the entire text, some of the more interesting conclusions are noteworthy:

Extent of Use. Although ganja was the main revenue-generating cannabis drug, bhang, which was not subject to taxation, was the most popular of the three cannabis drugs and was the most widely used drink among the Hindus.

Among the reasons cited for its popularity was that it was cheap, not very potent, and that it did not produce unpleasant effects even after consumption of large quantities. Charas, by contrast, was very expensive and could only be afforded by people of better means.

Usage of charas and ganja, the commission noted, was actually declining among the upper classes as a result of its rising cost. In its place, a newly acquired taste for alcohol, which sold at a substantially lower price, had begun to develop among the well-to-do.

Social and Religious Usage. Although none of the religious books of India required devotees to use cannabis drugs, there was a long-standing tradition of such usage in connection with religious ceremonies throughout the country. Ganja was especially associated with worship of the god Siva. Devotees of this cult believed that ganja was a special attribute of this god and their partaking of ganja in connection with his worship was akin to communion in the Catholic church. The same held true for the Sikh religion. During a holiday called Dasehra, every Sikh was required to drink bhang in commemoration of the founder of the Sikh religion, Gobind Singh.

Effects. To the commission's surprise, neither the native nor the European witnesses had any real knowledge or familiarity with cannabis's effects. Casual users of these drugs could not be readily identified. Moderate users were generally unknown except to those who also used these drugs. Since it was not customary to use cannabis drugs in the presence of someone considered to be inferior, few witnesses would admit using or knowing users of these drugs. The only users who were easily identifiable were the public inebriants who usually appeared intoxicated and dissipated.

Despite the fact that most witnesses readily admitted being unfamiliar with the effects of moderate usage of cannabis drugs, the commission was astounded to find them more than willing to express dogmatic opinions.

> Some witnesses know only the medical use of the drugs and are prepared to say nothing but good of them, being really ignorant of their use as intoxicants. There are also witnesses who do not know the use of the drugs as intoxicants, but know only moderate use. They have nothing to say of the drugs as would be said of alcohol by the man who only had seen a glass of wine taken at his own table or at the table of a friend. He knows nothing of the effects of excess. Others again have only experience of excessive consumption. The moderate consumer has not attracted their attention. The ruin wrought in certain classes by excess alone attracted their attention. They feel towards these drugs as that man feels towards alcohol whose experience had been mainly gained among the social wrecks of the lowest parts of a great city.[11]

Any understanding of cannabis's effects, the commission concluded, had to take into account frequency of usage and potency of preparation. Furthermore, the fact that cannabis drugs also contained other substances such as opium, datura, and hyoscyamis, made it extremely difficult to determine whether the adverse effects attributed to ganja and charas were valid. With respect to addiction, the commission noted that while most witnesses believed that moderate usage eventually developed into excessive usage, this belief was based primarily on a general opinion that such progression occurred for all intoxicants.

Adverse Physical Effects. Few witnesses were willing to state that moderate use of cannabis drugs was harmful to the body. On the other hand, most witnesses stated categorically that excessive consumption was dangerous. The evidence for this assertion, as was the case for most of the claims the commission heard, was based on casual observation of very few heavy users. In fact, the commission was singularly impressed with the dearth of such claims: "The most striking feature of the medical evidence is perhaps the large number of practitioners of long experience who have seen no evidence of any connection between hemp drugs and disease."[12]

Adverse Psychological Effects. The alleged connection between cannabis and insanity was a particularly controversial issue. Although most asylum superintendants stated categorically that excessive cannabis

---

[11] *Ibid.,* p. 168.
[12] *Ibid.,* p. 223.

usage led to insanity, the commission noted that these officials "know nothing of the effects of the drugs at all . . . and they have generalized from the few cases that were brought to them in which the patient's illness was attributed to cannabis usage. . . . the opinions they have expressed in stereotyping the popular opinion and giving it authority and permanence"[13] had only added to the confusion.

Since the testimony of medical experts was so contradictory and vague, asylum statistics were examined. However, this effort proved valueless because of a lack or a concealment of information, lack of agreement as to diagnosis, and simple bureaucratic bumbling. The available information, the commission noted, usually consisted of guesses by police officers regarding the background and habits of friendless and homeless wanderers.

An examination of 222 cases of insanity reported in 1892, allegedly precipitated by cannabis revealed that in only 61 cases could a reasonable claim for cannabis-related insanity be made. To this the commission cautiously added that "it must be borne in mind that it is impossible to say that the use of hemp drugs was in all the sole cause of insanity, or indeed any part of the cause." Despite this admission, the commission still endorsed such a link: "Taking these accepted cases as a whole, we have a number of instances where the hemp drug habit has been so established in relation to the insanity that, admitting (as we must admit) that hemp drugs as intoxicants cause more or less of cerebral stimulation, it may be accepted as reasonably proved, in the absence of evidence of other causes, that hemp drugs do cause insanity."[14]

Crime. In exploring the relation between cannabis and crime, the commission separated premeditated crimes such as robbery and unpremeditated crimes such as assault arising as a consequence of intoxication.

No connection between cannabis and premeditated criminal behavior could be substantiated. The view that such a relationship existed was based on the fact that those who used cannabis drugs to excess were usually people from low social and economic status groups.

In the case of unpremeditated crimes, especially in crimes of violence, most witnesses were of the opinion that, rather than increasing the likelihood of violence, habitual users became timid and quiet. A number of witnesses did insist, however, that they knew of many cases in which cannabis usage led to "temporary homicidal frenzy." When questioned further on this point, however, these witnesses invariably stated that they could not give any examples of such behavior. The

[13] *Ibid.,* p. 226.
[14] *Ibid.,* p. 250.

witnesses have "a more or less vague impression that hemp drugs and violent crime have been occasionally associated, but they cannot recall cases," the commission noted.[15]

When an inspector general of police was questioned concerning his statement that "running amok is always the result of excessive indulgence [in cannabis]," he admitted that "I have never had experience of such a case. I only state what I have heard." Such "witnesses also are typical of a considerable class," the commission added, "who refer to hearsay, to rumor, and to newspapers as the basis of their opinion."[16]

A third class of witness was also identified "who do not profess at all to require any basis of fact for their opinion. They speculate on probabilities." Since alcohol incited some people of a naturally violent temperament, they imagined that cannabis drugs were equally capable of a similar effect. "All this," the commission concluded, "tends greatly to lessen the weight of evidence in support of the affirmative answer to this question and to strengthen the impression that it is but rarely that excessive indulgence in hemp drugs can be credited with inciting to crime or leading to homicidal frenzy."[17]

Conclusions. Having examined the evidence, the commission concluded: (1) Moderate use of cannabis drugs had no appreciable physical effects on the body. As with all drugs, excessive use could weaken the body and render it more susceptible to diseases. Such circumstances were not peculiar to cannabis, however. (2) Moderate use of cannabis drugs had no adverse effects on the brain, except possibly for individuals predisposed to act abnormally. Excessive use, on the other hand, could lead to mental instability and ultimately to insanity in individuals predisposed by heredity to mental disorders. (3) Moderate use of cannabis drugs had no adverse influence on morality. Excessive usage, however, could result in moral degradation. Although in certain rare cases cannabis intoxication could result in violence, such cases were few and far between.

In summarizing the evidence overall, the commission remarked that the facts showed "most clearly how little injury society has hitherto sustained from hemp drugs."[18]

Recommendations. Taking all the evidence into consideration, the commission felt that suppression of bhang would be "totally unjustifiable" because its usage was so much a part of the social and religious life of India, and in moderation it was harmless. Moreover, usage of bhang

---

[15]*Ibid,* p. 258.
[16]*Ibid.,* p. 258–9.
[17]*Ibid.,* p. 259.
[18]*Ibid.,* p. 264.

would be difficult to suppress, suppression would be very unpopular, and finally, should suppression occur, it would have the effect of causing the people to turn to more harmful drugs. Although charas and ganja were potentially harmful if taken in excess, the commission felt that suppression of these drugs was also unadvisable.

As to the tax issue, the commission felt that the government's policy of trying to restrict the use of cannabis through taxation was the best plan possible: "In the opinion of the Commission, the general principle may be fearlessly asserted that it is right to tax intoxicants; and the higher they are taxed the better. . . . If it is necessary to put briefly in words a description of what the policy of the Government should be in regard to the hemp drugs, it would be somewhat as follows: To control their use, and especially their harmful use, in such a manner as to avoid a worse evil, and subject to this proviso, to tax them as fully as possible."[19]

The report of the Indian Hemp Drugs Commission has been widely praised for its thoroughness and impartiality. "The most complete and systematic study of marihuana undertaken to date," one critic has said.[20] Another has described the report as "by far the most complete collection of information on marihuana in existence."[21]

Without detracting from the report's merits, the fact is that all of the evidence submitted to the commission was in the form of opinions, and these came from persons who had had very little direct contact with cannabis users. As such, it has many shortcomings. Its major contribution lies not in the information which it collected, but rests instead on its cognizance and insight into the many problems that must be addressed in gathering and evaluating such information.

Since the data the commission had to evaluate was so biased, the only conclusion that ought to have followed was that the opinions it had heard were of dubious value. Without comparisons of cannabis users and nonusers from the same social and economic background, there was simply no way to evaluate issues such as cannabis's relationship to physical health, adverse psychological impact, criminal behavior, etc.

At the time it was issued, it was indeed the most comprehensive study of cannabis ever conducted. But it was merely a first step in collecting relevant information, no more than that.

[19] *Ibid.*, p. 288.
[20] T. H. Mikuriya, "Physical, Mental, and Moral Effects of Marijuana: The Indian Hemp Drugs Commission Report," *International Journal of the Addictions* 3(1963): 253.
[21] J. Kaplan, *Report of the Indian Hemp Drugs Commission, 1893–1894* (Silver Springs, Maryland: T. Jefferson Pub. Co, 1969), p. vi.

The Hashish Problem in Egypt

In addition to its territorial possessions in India, England was also entrenched in Egypt, although its hold on that country was not so tight-fisted as in the eastern subcontinent. Furthermore, in contrast to its Indian hemp policy, the English Parliament supported local attempts in Egypt to eradicate cannabis. In this regard, it is worth noting that England received no revenues from the use of cannabis drugs in Egypt.

As in India, local officials in Egypt were alarmed at the large numbers of inhabitants who used hashish directly or in confections, many of which were exported to Europe. Among the variety of confectionary treats containing hashish that were sent abroad were "Turkish Delight," square pieces of hashish containing sugar and gelatin which were a particular favorite of the students at Cambridge University in England.[22] Other well-known treats were "Sesame Sweetmeat," flat pieces of hashish, sesame seeds, and honey; "Bird's Tongue," black gelatinous pieces of hashish coated with sugar; "Saffron," an orange-colored slab of hashish, saffron, and spices; "Banana," small banana-shaped pieces of hashish and sugar; and "Crocodile's Penis," a black paste made of hashish. (The last derived its name from the belief that the penis of the crocodile was a potent aphrodisiac and that hashish was capable of infusing the amorous spirit in its users.)

An initial attempt to suppress the sale of hashish was made in 1868 when the Egyptians passed a law making possession a capital offense. However, in 1874, importation of hashish into Egypt was permitted provided a duty was paid, but possession was still prohibited!

In 1877, the sultan of Turkey, who still ruled over Egypt, ordered a nationwide campaign to confiscate and destroy the drug. This fiat was followed in 1879 by another law making importation illegal. In 1884, cultivation of cannabis became a criminal offense, but instead of destroying confiscated hashish, customs officers were allowed to sell the drug abroad. The money from such sales was to be divided among informers and customs officers responsible for the seizures.

These laws had very little effect on the use of hashish in Egypt. Nevertheless, they were reissued in 1891 and 1894. In 1898, over 10,000 kilos of hashish were seized and over 500 businesses were closed because their proprietors had allowed hashish to be used on the premises. In 1908, there were almost 2000 such closings. Yet all the attempts to outlaw hashish in Egypt during the nineteenth century were as unsuc-

[22]T. C. Allbutt, *A System of Medicine* (New York: Macmillan, 1900), 2: 903.

cessful as the earlier attempts of the thirteenth and fourteenth centuries had been. They were failures all.

Whatever measures officials adopted to keep hashish from being grown or imported, they were no match for the ingenuity of the hashish dealers. For example, one method used by smugglers to bring hashish into the country was to wrap the drug in waterproof bags attached to sacks of salt. If a government cruiser happened to come across some smugglers, the cargo was quickly dropped overboard. Weighed down by the bags of salt, the contraband sank to the bottom. In a few days, after the salt had dissolved, the bags rose to the surface and were picked up by the smugglers.

HASHISH IN GREECE

Despite the subjugation of Greece by the Ottoman Turks during the Middle Ages, the Greeks were almost totally unaware of hashish and its effects prior to the nineteenth century. The first mention of the drug in a Greek pharmocopoeia occurred in 1837 and this was based on a Bavarian text.[23] In an 1855 pharmacology text, cannabis is described as "a plant, indigenous in the East and especially in Persia, but cultivated in many areas of Europe and Greece. . . . "[24] Apparently, the author was familiar with hemp fiber but not hashish. It was not until 1875 that the plant's medicinal and narcotic properties were alluded to in Greek medical texts.[25]

The entry of hashish into mainland Greece occurred some time between 1870 and 1880 following the development of Piraeus as a major trade depot in the Aegean. Immigrants from Egypt, Cyprus, and various Mediterranean countries streamed to the port city in search of work, and not surprisingly they brought with them their hashish habit.

Hashish usage, however, was confined primarily to the poor. The drug, in fact, was nicknamed the "weed of the poor,"[26] and was a favorite among dock workers, shippers, cargo carriers, wagoners, deckhands, and barmen.[27] Local demand among the working classes became so great for the drug that cultivation of cannabis became a major enterprise, with enough grown for export to other countries.

[23]C. Stefanis, C. Ballas, and D. Madianou, "Sociocultural and Epidemiological Aspects of Hashish Use in Greece," in *Cannabis and Culture*, ed. V. Rubin (The Hague: Mouton, 1975), p. 310.

[24]*Ibid.*

[25]*Ibid.*, p. 311.

[26]*Ibid.*, p. 313.

[27]M. G. Stringaris, *Die Haschischsiet* (Berlin: Springer-Verlag, 1972), p. 46.

Middle-class Greeks, however, quickly became concerned about the spreading use of hashish. They saw the drug as a social danger and they regarded hashish users as degenerates and criminals. "Criminal," in fact, soon became a popular term for users of hashish.[28]

By 1890, the authorities became so alarmed at the widespread use of hashish that they officially outlawed the cultivation, importation, and usage of the drug.[29] But the law was not strictly enforced and hashish usage was only minimally affected.

After World War I, a dramatic rise in hashish usage occurred in Greece prompted by the return of Greek soldiers and the repatriation of about a half million Greek citizens from Asia Minor. These soldiers and citizens had been living in areas where hashish was accepted and cultivation was a normal part of life. When these people returned to the Greek mainland, they brought their acquired habits and familiarity with hashish with them.[30]

During the 1920s, Greece became a major producer of hashish. According to one chronicler of the times, it was not uncommon for women returning from the hashish harvest to enter their villages covered with flowers and singing and dancing as if they were drunk. Their unconventional behavior at such times was generally attributed to their being overcome by the fumes from ripe cannabis blossoms.[31]

Although hashish use is still prevalent in Greece, its popularity fell after the German occupation of World War II, primarily because most of the users died of starvation.[32]

[28]Ibid.
[29]Stefanis et al., "Sociocultural and Epidemiological Aspects," p. 314.
[30]Stringaris, Die Haschischsiet, p. 47.
[31]Ibid.
[32]Ibid., p. 48.

7

The African Dagga Cultures

Long before greed and ambition prompted the countries of Western Europe to send their armies to conquer the New World, Europeans were exploring and exploiting Africa. The incentives that beckoned the white race to the "dark continent" were many, but chief among them were precious goods such as gold, ivory, and spices. Once they began to colonize the New World, however, European interest focused on yet another African treasure—the slave. The growth of the plantation systems in both North and South America had created a sudden demand for cheap and obedient labor, and to meet this demand Europeans looked to Africa.

Africa was no stranger to the slave trade. Human bondage is one of man's earliest atrocities. It was commonplace throughout the ancient and early medieval worlds. But until the coming of the Europeans, slavery had existed on only a relatively small scale. Once the people of Western Europe "discovered" the continent, however, slavery became big business. Approximately ten million natives were taken from their homes between the middle of the fifteenth to the end of the nineteenth century to destinations sometimes halfway around the world, to be dispassionately sold like chattel.

By virtue of their early conquest of the treacherous seas off the African coast, the Portuguese were the first to establish outposts in Africa, but it was not long before the Dutch, the English, and the French began to challenge Portugal's claim to Africa and her domination of the slave trade. Unable to retain its grip over the entire continent, Portugal had to content herself with a few territories while her European rivals each staked claim to different parts of Africa. Ironically, Portugal was the last of the great European powers to maintain a colonial empire in Africa.

The trading posts and settlements that were subsequently established throughout the continent soon brought the Europeans into intimate contact with the different native tribes of Africa. And just as Europe craved to know all about the lives of the savages of India and the New World, so too did they eagerly await any news of the quaint and curious customs of the African aborigines.

What intrigued Europeans most about these native peoples was their primitiveness. They had no police and no jails. Their law was uncomplicated: a man who committed a crime was either fined if his offense were not serious by tribal standards, or he was executed. Their religion was pagan. They had never heard of Jesus. They were neither Moslems nor Jews. Instead, they worshipped many gods and paid homage to the spirits of the dead. They ate human flesh and they offered human sacrifices. Their lives were painfully simple. They had no books. They lived in mud huts without windows and shared their cramped living quarters with their animals. They sat on wooden stools. They ate with their fingers. They wore few garments, and those that they did wear were made of animal skins. Their women did all the work; their men hunted, looked after the cattle, farmed a little, and occasionally went to war. Surely, Europe rationalized, God had ordained such people to be slaves to the superior white race.

One of the native customs that seemed especially unusual to the European mind was their peculiar penchant for eating and smoking hemp leaves. To a part of the world that thought of hemp only as a source of fiber, this strange practice seemed particularly puzzling and fascinating.

The Cannabis Habit in Africa

When the natives first began using cannabis as a drug is not known. The plant is not indigenous to Africa. The only way the African natives could have learned about it would have been through their contact with outsiders, and the most likely point of contact was the Arabs.

The earliest evidence for cannabis in Africa outside of Egypt comes from fourteenth-century Ethiopia, where two ceramic smoking-pipe bowls containing traces of cannabis were recently discovered during an archaeological excavation.[1] From Ethiopia, cannabis seeds were carried to the south by Bantu-speaking natives who originally lived in North Africa, and from them the use of cannabis as an intoxicant spread to other native Africans such as the Bushmen and the Hottentots.[2]

---

[1]N. J. Van der Merwe, "Cannabis Smoking in 13–14th Century Ethiopia," in Cannabis and Culture, ed. V. Rubin (The Hague: Mouton, 1975), pp. 77–80.
[2]J. Walton, "The Dagga Pipes of Southern Africa," Research of National Museum 1 (1963): 85–113.

One of the first books about the people of Africa to mention the cannabis habit was written by a Dominican priest, João dos Santos, in 1609. The plant, he said, was cultivated throughout Kafaria (near the Cape of Good Hope) and was called bangue. The Kafirs were in the habit of eating its leaves, and those that used it to excess, he said, became intoxicated as if they had drunk a large quantity of wine.

Far from cowering before the white man, these Kafirs were a proud and confident people whose king received his white visitors as vassals rather than conquerors. Speaking of their chief, Quiteve, dos Santos writes: "if the Kafirs have a suit, and seek to speak with the king, they crawl to the place where he is, having prostrated themselves at the entrance, and look not upon him all the while they speak, but lying on one side clasp their hands all the time and having finished they creep out of doors as they came in." Visiting Europeans such as dos Santos were required to act in like manner. Those the chief desired to entertain were offered food and intoxicating spirits which "they must drink, although against their stomach, not to condemn the king's bounty."[3] One of these intoxicating spirits was bangue.

In 1658, Jan van Riebeeck, the first governor of the Dutch colony at the Cape of Good Hope, described the use of cannabis by yet another tribe, the Hottentots. These were a yellowish-skinned people who spoke a "click" language. They were not a "pure" native tribe, but rather the offspring of Egyptian soldiers who had deserted their posts in Ethiopia around 650 B.C. and Bushmen women.

Although they had once been a warrior race, by the time the Dutch came to Africa the Hottentots were a tribe of cattle and sheep herders. The Dutch called them "beachcomers" because the Hottentots frequented the shoreline searching for any edible meat still on the carcasses of seals and whales stranded on the beaches. This curious scavenging for meat in the midst of herds of cattle intrigued the Dutch, as did the Hottentot's reluctance to trade his cattle.

The explanation was simple enough, as the Dutch soon learned. To the Hottentots, cattle were status symbols. The more a man owned, the more respectable his position in the tribe. Frustrated at not being able to buy cattle from these natives at a reasonable price, the Dutch brought their own cattle to the Cape Colony, along with farmers (Boers) to look after them. The coming of the Boers, it turned out, signaled the enslavement of the Hottentots.

At first, the Dutch and the Hottentots got on fairly well together. But as more and more Boers came to the Cape Colony, more and more of

[3]Quoted in B. Laufer, W. D. Hambly, and R. Linten, "Tobacco and Its Uses in Africa," *Field Museum of Natural History* 1 (1930): 13.

the Hottentots' land was expropriated, including their valuable grazing fields. The Boers were not merely content with robbing the Hottentots of their land, they also began raiding their herds.

The Hottentots offered only a token resistance. They were herders, not warriors; and their spears were no match for gunpowder. To preserve their precious cattle, many of the Hottentots moved further north into the interior. Those who tried to make a fight of it were either killed or taken prisoner and made to serve as domestic servants for the rest of their lives.

The Hottentot custom that most intrigued the Dutch, judging by the frequency with which they refer to it, was their unique use of hemp, which they called dagga.[4] Dagga, van Riebeeck incredulously noted, was valued more than gold by the Hottentots, adding that it "drugs their brains just as opium.[5] Since the Hottentots had no pockets, they carried their dagga in small leather pouches which they pushed under the ivory rings they wore around their arms.[6]

In 1661, a Dutch surgeon named van Meerhof, who had married a Hottentot girl who spoke both Dutch and Portuguese, stated that the Hotttentots had tried to smoke dagga but they could not master the technique. By 1705, however, both the Hottentots and their neighbors, the Bushmen, were smoking, having been taught the art by the white man.

Lighting Up

Once the natives learned the technique of smoking, the inhalation of burning dagga leaves quickly spread from tribe to tribe. The popularity of smoking even created a new demand for pipes, and a new skill, pipe making, came into being.

Intoxication by means of smoking instead of chewing also altered African culture. No longer was dagga consumed alone. Smoking transformed the taking of dagga into a communal event, especially among those tribes that had few pipes.

Pipe bowls were made of various materials such as wood, stone, bone, or pottery, and were often fitted to a horn filled with water.

---

[4]The Dutch referred to both *Cannabis sativa* and *Leontis leonurus* as daccha (dagga), so it is possible that much of what was written about cannabis may not have pertained to it at all. However, the descriptions seem to fit cannabis, and, therefore, they have been treated as such.

[5]Quoted in J. E. Morley and A. D. Bensusan, "Dagga: Tribal Uses and Customs," *Medical Proceedings* 17 (1971): 409–12.

[6]J. Schreyer, "Diary," in *Cape of Good Hope*, ed. R. Raven-Hart (Capetown: 1971), A. A. Balkewa, p. 126.

At the start of a typical native "smoke-in," a quantity of water was put into the horn, the mouth was applied to the large orifice of the horn, and the smoke, after being drawn through the water, was inhaled quickly three or four times and then exhaled in a violent fit of coughing, causing tears to stream down the cheeks: "This was considered the height of ecstasy to the smoker. The process continued until the fumes of the dagga produced a kind of intoxication or delirium and the devotee commenced to recite or sing, with great rapidity and vehemence, the praises of himself or his chief during the intervals of coughing or smoking."[7]

Quite often, however, a tribe could not afford the luxury of a bowl and instead the natives improvised as best they could. Sometimes this took the form of a hole in the ground into which the dagga was placed. The drug was then mixed with burning manure and tunnels were dug into the sides of the mound. To inhale the fumes, the smokers lay down with their mouths over the holes. These earthen pipes were very common among the Hottentots, the Bushmen, and the Bantus.[8]

By the end of the eighteenth century, the natives had also begun to use tobacco, but they found it too weak for their tastes and usually mixed it with dagga. Wrote the Dutch explorer C. P. Thunberg,

> Hemp [is] a plant universally used in this country, though for a purpose very different from that to which it is applied by the industrious Europeans. The Hottentot loves nothing so well as tobacco, and, with no other can they become so easily enticed into a man's service; but for smoking and for producing a pleasing intoxication, he finds this poisonous plant not sufficient strong; and therefore in order to procure the pleasure more speadily and deliciously he mixes his tobacco with hemp chopped very fine.[9]

In 1818, the English explorer, G. Thompson wrote that

> the leaves of this plant [hemp] are eagerly sought after by the slaves and Hottentots to smoke, either mixed with tobacco or alone. It possesses much more powerfully stimulating qualities than tobacco, and speedily intoxicates those who smoke it profusely, sometimes rendering them for a time quite mad. This inebriating effect is, in fact, the quality for which these poor creatures prize it. But the free use of it, just like opium, and all such powerful stimulants, is exceedingly pernicious, and gives the appearance of old age in a few years to its victims.[10]

---

[7]E. W. Stowe, *The Native Races of South Africa* (Capetown: Juta and Co., 1910), pp. 52–3.
[8]Morley and Bensusan, "Dagga," p. 410.
[9]C. P. Thunberg, *An Account of the Cape of Good Hope and Some Parts of the Interior of Southern Africa* (1795), in *A General Collection of the Best and Most Interesting Voyages and Travels in All Parts of the World*, ed. J. Pinkerton (London: Longman, Hurst, Ries, Orme, and Brown, 1811), 16: 31.
[10]G. Thompson, *Travels and Adventures in Southern Africa* (Cape Town: Van Riebeeck Society, 1967).

Despite his disapproval of the drug, Thompson says that the white landowners cultivated cannabis for their servants, even though its intoxicating and deleterious effects were not in the best interests of the whites. The reason for this anomaly, explains Thompson, was that the white man used dagga "as an inducement to retain the wild Bushmen in their service. whom they have made captives at an early age . . . most of these people being extremely addicted to the smoking of dacha (dagga)."[11]

There were some whites such as evangelist Hugo Hahn who shared Thompson's belief that continued use of dagga was not in the best interests of the natives. Hahn had come to Africa to save the souls of the savages. Their use of dagga, Hahn felt, was a vile habit that would keep their souls from ever entering heaven. Not one to sit idly by while souls were at stake, Hahn raided Boer hemp farms, burning the wicked plants wherever he found them. His actions did little to endear him to either the natives or the white settlers of the area.[12]

Although he could not have cared less about the souls of the natives, another crusader who condemned the natives' indulgence in dagga was the famous American journalist Henry M. Stanley, whose rendezvous with the English missionary, David Livingston in 1871 is immortalized in his terse greeting: "Mr. Livingston, I presume."

Unlike the compassionate Livingston, Stanley had little regard for the African native whom he described as "wild as a colt, chafing, restless, ferociously impulsive, superstitiously timid, liable to furious demonstrations, suspicious and unreasonable. . . ."[13]

Stanley was in fact totally prejudiced against the native African. Regarding the natives' use of cannabis, which he believed weakened their bodies and made them unfit to carry his cumbrous cargo, he wrote:

> Certainly most deleterious to the physical powers is the almost universal habit of vehemently inhaling the smoke of the *Cannabis sativa* or wild hemp. In a light atmosphere, such as we have in hot days in the Tropics, with the thermometer rising to 140 Fahr. in the sun, these people, with lungs and vitals injured by excessive indulgence in these destructive habits, discover they have no physical stamina to sustain them. The rigor of a march in a loaded caravan soon tells upon their weakened powers, and one by one they drop from the ranks, betraying their impotence and infirmaties.[14]

Had Stanley had the misfortune to encounter the Zulus during his adventurous treks through the African jungle he might have thought otherwise of cannabis's devitalizing effects. According to at least one

---

[11] *Ibid.*
[12] H. Vedder, *South West Africa in Early Times* (New York: Barnes & Noble, 1966).
[13] H. M. Stanley, *Through the Dark Continent* (New York: Harper & Bros, 1879), 1:71.
[14] *Ibid.*, p. 86.

142   CHAPTER 7

white explorer, A. T. Bryant, whose intimate contact with the Zulus is
described in his book *The Zulu People*, "young [Zulu] warriors were
especially addicted [to dagga] and under the exciting stimulation of the
drug were capable of accomplishing hazardous feats."[15] Some historians
have even suggested that the Zulus were intoxicated with dagga when
they attacked the Dutch at the Battle of Blood River in 1838.[16]

The Zulus were not the only tribe to smoke cannabis before going
into battle. Speaking of the Sothos, David Livingston wrote that the
warriors "sat down and smoked it [hemp] in order that they might make
an effective onslaught."[17]

Apparently, the unwillingness of the natives to risk their lives and
to break their backs so that Stanley could become famous was not due to
dagga's weakening of their spirits. Yet, for the most part, both white
man and black man agreed that indulgence in cannabis was not in the
best interest of the individual or his tribe. Contrary to the Zulus, for
instance, the Ja-Luo tribe of eastern Uganda prohibited their warriors
from smoking dagga.[18] In some tribes, the men forbade their wives to
smoke dagga "on account of some evil effect it is said to have upon her
or her child, should she be about to become a mother."[19]

In his *Life of a South African Tribe*, Henri Junod mentions that the
Thonga likewise did not condone the use of dagga. To coax their sons off
the dagga habit, they "break the pipe and take a little of the soot which is
found inside and mix it with their food without their being aware of it.
When this has been done three times it is said to fill them with disgust
for hemp."[20]

Despite attempts to eradicate the cultivation of dagga by both the
white settlers and the natives, the dagga habit was too much a part of
the African natives' way of life. Some tribes such as the Bergdama of
South West Africa, for example, carried on a regular trade with
neighboring tribes in which they bartered dagga for valuable commodities such as cattle, goats, iron, and copper. And when the Berg-

---

[15]A. T. Bryant, *The Zulu People*, cited in T. James, "Dagga: A Review of Fact and Fancy,"
Medical Journal 44(1970): 575–80.
[16]*Ibid.*
[17]D. Livingstone, *Missionary Travels and Research in South Africa* (London: John Murray,
1857), p. 540.
[18]E. W. Hobby, *Eastern Uganda* (London: Anthropological Institute of Great Britain, 1902),
p. 30.
[19]J. P. Purvis, *Through Uganda to Mt. Elgon* (London: Fisher Unwin, 1909), pp. 336–7. This
is the only reference to possible birth defects resulting from maternal smoking of cannabis that I have come across in the anthropological and sociological literature.
[20]H. A. Junod, *The Life of a South African Tribe* (Neuchatel, Switzerland: Attinger Bros.,
1912), pp. 342–5.

dama paid annual tribute to their overlords, the Saan, they did so in the form of dagga cakes.[21]

Smoking dagga was a recreational activity for many tribes, which in turn spawned its own recreational games. One such game played by the Zulus and the Thonga was a spitting contest. Two contestants deeply inhaled the smoke from a dagga pipe and held it in their lungs as long as possible. Each player then spit what saliva he could muster onto the ground, sometimes with the aid of a reed, the object being to form a circle of bubbles around his opponent. The bubbles symbolized the warriors of an army and the idea was that, once surrounded by this army of bubble soldiers, the opponent was trapped and thus defeated.[22] The real achievement of the game came from the ability to spit, since cannabis has the effect of drying up the secretions of the mouth, much like atropine, thereby making it extremely difficult to produce any saliva at all.

In the French Congo, the Fang had a different use for dagga. Before Fang warriors went out to battle, the witch doctor erected an altar in the forest. A human sacrifice, usually a captive from a neighboring tribe, was then dragged out into the forest and tied to the altar. The binding of the victim was the signal for the chief to pronounce a ritual chant while the warriors began painting themselves and dancing around the altar. After the dance was over, the victim was forced to his knees, a white line was drawn across his neck, his arms were grasped firmly behind him, his head was jerked backward, and a single slash severed his head from his body. To prevent any struggling, the hapless victim was given a concoction containing dagga shortly before his sacrificial offering to the Fang war gods.[23]

THE AFRICAN HEMP CULTS

Perhaps the most interesting anecdote concerning cannabis in Africa relates the way in which the drug transformed the Bashilange from a tribe of feuding miscreants to one dedicated to peace and goodwill. The storyteller is a German explorer, Herman von Wissman.

The Bashilange were originally a very warlike people, Wissman tells us:

> One tribe with another, one village with another, always lived at daggers drawn.... The number of scars which some ancient men display among their tatooings gives evidence of this. Then, about twenty-five years ago [ca.

[21]Vedder, *South West Africa*, p. 175.
[22]Junod, *Life*, pp. 311–4.
[23]R. P. H. Tulles, "Totemism Among the Fang," *Anthropos* 1 (1912): 1–26.

1850]. . . a hemp-smoking worship began to be established, and the narcotic
effect of smoking masses of hemp made itself felt. The Ben-Riamba, "Sons of
Hemp," found more and more followers; they began to have intercourse
with each other as they became less barbarous and made laws.[24]

The transition from feud to friendship was only one of the changes initiated by the hemp cult. An entire religion came into being based on *riamba*, the Bashilange word for cannabis, which became the symbol of peace, comaraderie, magic, and protection. Tribesmen were no longer permitted to carry weapons in their villages, they called each other friend, and they greeted one another with the word *moyo*, meaning "life" and "health." Although formerly cannibals, they abjured their previous custom of eating the bodies of their captured enemies.

For their religious ceremonies, which occurred nightly, the men stripped naked and shaved their heads. Then they sat in a large circle and smoked cannabis from large pipes. Those who did not take part in the communal smoke-in were charged with beating drums, blowing ivory trumpets, and chanting. In addition to these nightly get-togethers, cannabis was smoked on all important holidays and at the conclusion of all alliances.

Although widely used by the men, Bashilange women were rarely allowed to smoke cannabis. The prohibition was a matter of tribal policy and reflected the position of the female in Bashilange society. It was she who was required to perform all the routine jobs in the village and her busy schedule allowed her no time for idleness, especially of the kind engendered by dagga.

Following the adoption of the cannabis cult, the Bashilange also began to believe in reincarnation. The appearance of von Wissman in their village was in fact greeted as proof that the dead could return. This white man, they believed, was the reincarnation of their dead chief Kassongo. The German, the people said, had lost his black skin in the big water. When the joyful reconciliation ended, the natives brought von Wissman his old "wife," informing him that his other wives and his former property would be returned to him as well. Unfortunately, von Wissman did not record his reaction to his new matrimonial status.

Cannabis also assumed a special importance in Bashilange jurisprudence. Any native accused of a crime was required to smoke dagga until he either admitted his crime or lost consciousness. In cases of theft, the robber had to pay a fine, consisting of salt, to each person who witnessed his smoking. The crime of adultery required that the guilty male

[24]H. von Wissman, *My Second Journey Through Equatorial Africa* (London: Chatto & Windus, 1891), p. 312; cf: K. Zetterstrom, "Bena Riamba, Brothers of the Hemp," *Studia Ethnographica Upsaliensia*, 26 (1966): 151–65.

smoke dagga as well. However, there was no fine. The amount of dagga to be smoked depended on the status of the man who had been cuckolded. If the latter were important, the guilty man had to smoke until he lost consciousness. He would then be stripped, pepper would be dropped into his eyes and/or a thin ribbon would be drawn through his nasal bone. More serious crimes were accompanied by additional punishments.

Not all the Bashilange were favorably disposed toward the new cult. For one thing, many Bashilange began to take advantage of the leniency of the new laws. Before the cult, the seduction of a woman carried a heavy fine, and inability to pay the fine usually resulted in bloodshed. The new law of the *bena riamba* forbade the payment of any such fines, much to the annoyance of many disgruntled fathers.

The Bashilange nobility was also upset by the new changes. Hitherto, high-status tribesmen were permitted to wear cotton garments. The new laws of brotherhood did away with such class distinctions. Now anyone who could afford them could wear such clothes.

The Bashilange also suffered a great loss of wealth after the adoption of the cult. Previously, neighboring tribes that were vassals of the Bashilange had paid them tribute. Now that their former masters had renounced the spear for the dagga pipe, these vassals refused to continue paying tribute, and without going to war the Bashilange had no way to enforce their demands.

All these problems came to a head around 1876 when a serious rebellion against the chief broke out. The chief, his brother, and his sister were accused of having killed a man by sorcery. It was a trumped-up charge, but the accused had to smoke dagga until they became unconscious. When finally they fell to the ground, they were attacked and stabbed by their enemies. Had it not been for the intervention of some of the other villagers, they would have been killed. Having failed in their attempt to assassinate the royal family, the leaders of the rebellion deserted the village, but they soon returned to their homes and were never punished for their crime.

The end was near at hand, however, and it was not long before the anticannabis forces mustered enough support to overthrow the riamba cult. The tribe returned to many of its old customs, but many of the changes initiated as a consequence of the adoption of the cult remained. The Bashilange ceased their warlike activities against their neighbors, much of the legal system was preserved so that harsh penalties were rarely applied, and cannabis still remained an integral part of their daily lives.

Another African hemp cult about which very little is known was located in the Sudan. The founding of the cult was attributed to a mysterious woman named Sirdar. Its purpose is not well known, but it appears that that the participants shared feelings of opposition to the local chiefs in the area.

Directly under Sirdar were two lieutenants known as her mudirs. These officers had their own subordinates who supervised yet another group further down the hierarchy. The lowest level of the echelon was charged with establishing cliques to promote the smoking of dagga throughout the district. Sirdar's organization and her message, whatever it was, was apparently a huge success for gifts regularly poured into her camp from locales as far as two or three days' journey from her headquarters. Yet, like the riamba cult, Sirdar's influence in the Sudan eventually declined and the hemp cult she introduced also disappeared.[25]

THE "COOLIE" PROBLEM

By the time the white man came to Africa, dagga had become a part of the native's way of life. In the quest for altered consciousness and escape from the humdrum characteristic of nearly all societies, primitive or highly industrialized, Africa had become a country of dagga cultures whereas Europe besot itself in alcohol. Like alcohol, dagga was a relaxant, a social lubricant, an integral part of religious ceremony, and a drug of abuse. Since Europe sat in judgment of Africa alcohol was rarely given a second thought, whereas the natives' use of dagga was considered by many to be morally reprehensible. As long as dagga was taken primarily by the black man, white Africa took little interest, other than amusement, in these peculiar drug cults. When cannabis subsequently took root in their own cities, however, the fear of contamination by such foreign practices began to alarm segments of white society. The change in attitude occurred shortly after 1843, when the Republic of Natalia (Natal), on the northeast coast of South Africa, was annexed by England and made a part of the Cape Colony. Following the development of the sugar industry in the new province, more and more laborers were needed to work the fields. When native manpower proved unequal to the task, workers were sought from other countries, especially from the British colony of India, and about 6000 mainly low-caste Indians entered the country.[26]

Although brought over expressly to work in the sugar fields, these "coolies," as they were called, left the fields as soon as they were able to

[25]P. M. Larken, *An Account of the Zande* (Khartoum: McCorquodale & Co., 1926), 1: 93.

[26]B. M. Du Toit, "Historical and Cultural Factors Influencing Cannabis Use Among Indians in South Africa," *Journal of Psychedelic Drugs* 9 (1977): 235–46.

satisfy their indenture obligations and they sought jobs in other industries. Many became semiskilled laborers, domestic servants, farmers, storekeepers, fishermen, etc. But while they fitted into the European way of life, they never became a part of it. Their dark skins, culture, social and religious background, and language set them apart from both the Europeans and the native Africans.

Europeans were also suspicious of them because of their use of cannabis, a habit which they brought with them from India. Cannabis, the Europeans believed, made the "coolies" sick and lazy and therefore unable to work, and also led them to commit criminal acts.

The Indian emigrées had not had to import cannabis seeds with them; cannabis was already a popular drug among the natives and it was probably from them that the Indians obtained their cannabis. It was not long, however, before legal steps were adopted to curtail such usage. By 1870, European settlers became so alarmed at the alleged dangers of cannabis to South Africa that they passed a law "prohibiting the smoking, use, or possession by the sale, barter, or gift to, any coolies whatsoever, of any portion of the hemp plant (Cannabis sativa). . . ."[27]

But just as identical laws in other countries had no effect on the use of cannabis, so too was it ignored in Africa. In 1887, the Wragg Commission (named after its chairman, Supreme Court Judge Walter Wragg) concluded that the "coolies" were still using cannabis and that the drug posed a danger to white South Africans. Again, measures were taken to outlaw the sale, cultivation, possession, and use of cannabis. Such laws were no more successful than previous ones.

In 1923, South Africa tried to enlist the aid of the League of Nations in outlawing cannabis on an international scale, but to no avail. Five years later, the country passed yet another anticannabis law. This was followed by still more anticannabis laws. The result was always the same—try though they might to legislate cannabis out of existence, South African lawmakers were never a match for the plant's tenacious hold over its devotees.

[27]Quoted in *ibid.*, p. 241.

8

The Hashish Club

For twenty years Napoleon had led his loyal minions against the armies of Europe. His spectacular victories, often against overwhelming odds, filled France with a feeling of pride and ebullience. No matter that the cost of victory had been two million French casualties. These dead were heroes.[1]

Despite his ultimate defeat and the terrible price of the transient glory he gave France, Napoleon would always be remembered for what he did on the battlefield and for what he accomplished on the domestic front, especially in the area of civil liberties.

Although it had not been his intention to do so, Napoleon's military exploits were also responsible for introducing thousands of French soldiers to hashish. The initiation came about as a consequence of the French invasion of Egypt in 1798 and caused Napoleon some concern that his troops might become dissipated and unruly because of their indulgence in the drug.

Then, as now, army life was basically a series of endless routines and insurmountable boredom. To pass the time, some men will drink themselves into oblivion. But in Moslem Egypt, alcohol was not the intoxicant of choice. The Egyptians preferred another drug, and that drug, of course, was hashish. So widespread did the hashish habit become among his men that in October 1800 Napoleon issued the following ordinance to the French army of occupation:

> It is forbidden in all of Egypt to use certain Moslem beverages made with hashish or likewise to inhale the smoke from seeds of hashish. Habitual

---

[1]These citizen soldiers, Alexandre Dumas later wrote, "typified the devotion, the courage, the honor of the noblest, the warmest, the purest blood of France! They embodied twenty years of struggle against all of Europe; they were of the Revolution, our mother; they were of the Empire, our nurse; they were not the French nobility, but the nobility of the French people."

drinkers and smokers of this plant lose their reason and are victims of violent
delirium which is the lot of those who give themselves full to excesses of all
sorts.[2]

The soldiers heard the order, probably nodded in agreement, and
went right on using hashish. Along with the soldiers, three French
scientists—Silvestre de Sacy, Rouyer, and Desgenettes—whom Napoleon had brought with him to study the country and its people, also
began using hashish, ostensibly to see for themselves what this drug did
to the human body. Intrigued by their experiences with hashish, they
sent some back to France for their colleagues to conduct further experiments in their laboratories.

The first of these studies to be published appeared in 1803 by a Dr.
Virey, who made various extracts of hashish, hoping to track down the
drug's elusive active principle. After studying the drug at length, it was
Virey's opinion that hashish was nothing less than the mysterious
nepenthe used by Helen of Troy to drug her guests into a stupor of
forgetfulness.

Soon after the army's return, the French began hearing about the
incredible effects of hashish from both the soldiers who had used it
themselves and from the country's scientists who had had an opportunity
to study the drug and its mystique while serving with the army in Egypt.
It was shortly after the army's return to France, for instance, that Silvestre
de Sacy, the foremost Arabic scholar in the world at that time, announced that he had at last solved the long-baffling mystery of the
origin of name of the Assassins—the Arabic gang of cutthroats who had
terrorized the Middle East during the time of the Crusades. In an address to the Institute of France in 1809, Silvestre de Sacy claimed that the
word "assassin" was derived from hashish, a common term for herbage
or grass in the Arab world. He then argued that cannabis was considered to be like grass and that the mysterious potion mentioned by Marco
Polo was in fact hashish:

> The intoxication produced by the hashish [can lead to a] state of tempor-
> ary insanity [such that] losing all knowledge of their debility [users] commit
> the most brutal actions, so as to disturb the public peace . . . it is not impossi-
> ble that hemp, or some parts of that vegetable, mixed with other substances
> unknown to us, may have been sometimes employed to produce a state of
> frenzy and violence.[3]

In 1818, a Viennese writer, Joseph von Hammer-Purgstall, capitalized on European interest in the Assassins and the stories of hashish,

[2]Quoted in P. Allain, *Hallucinogens et société* (Paris: Payot, 1973), p. 184.
[3]M. Silvestre de Sacy, "Memoir on the Dynasty of the Assassins, and on the Origin of their
Name," *The History of the Assassins,* edited by J. von Hammer-Purgstall (New York: Burt
Franklin, 1968), p. 235.

the exotic drug of the Arab world, by publishing the first full-length book to be written about the sect. Originally published in German, the book became so popular it was soon translated into French (1833) and English (1835). The link between hashish and the Assassins became firmly soldered in cannabis folklore from that time on.

Drugs and Dreams

Prior to 1800 there were only about ten references to cannabis in all of French literature, travel books, or botanical books. Between 1800 and 1850, no fewer than thirty articles and books were published on the subject in France. *The Thousand and One Nights,* with its tales of hashish intoxication, drug-induced hallucinations, and "double consciousness," topped the bestseller lists for many years. Famed Orientalist Silvestre de Sacy's warning that hashish produced ecstasy, delirium, insanity, and even death, only whetted the public's appetite for more.

Among those to become enthralled by the furor over this strange drug were a number of young writers, poets, and artists, who thought that hashish's peculiar effects on the mind might be a way to enhance their creativity.

The post-Napoleonic era in France and throughout the rest of Europe was a time of soul searching. People seemed disenchanted with the achievements of the "rational age" which had only made war more terrifying, and searched instead for the hidden, irrational, emotional self that was buried deep within the human mind. Writers and artists of this period were especially haunted by this hidden psychic entity, this doppleganger of the mind, whose activity could be glimpsed only in dreams. If only they could discover the entrance to this hidden world, they could communicate with the unconscious.

At first they relied on opium. Opium's potential for psychic enlightenment came to the attention of the literary world as a result of a series of articles appearing in *London Magazine* in 1821. Thomas de Quincey, the author of these *Confessions of an Opium Eater,* had held his readers spellbound with descriptions of his weekly excursions into the world of this mind-altering drug and the excruciating torment he later suffered as a consequence of his addiction. For many writers, opium promised to be the key that would unlock the invisible bonds shackling them to the mundane world of the conscious self. Once freed, perhaps it might be possible to conjure up the hidden muse of creativity. Out of drug-inspired dreams and altered consciousness might come plots for stories, images for poems, ideas for art.

It was especially the potential for producing dreams that first at-

tracted novelists, poets, and artists to opium, Many of the major literary
giants kept notes of their dreams and used these notes in their work.
Browning, Coleridge, Poe, Wordsworth, etc., all kept pad and pen beside their beds to record their nightly visitations from their dream
muses. Not to be able to remember a dream was a regretable loss to a
writer's creativity. The drug-induced dream promised enhanced creativity with each swallow.

But many who chose this route to the hitherto inaccessible regions
of the human mind later regretted their decision; De Quincey was not
the only one to experience the agony of addiction. Their experiences in
opiate hell led to the search for some other drug, some other type of
chemical concoction with opium's desirable effects, yet free of its nightmarish properties.

There were stories of such a drug. Veterans of the Egyptian campaign used to tell about a drug right out of the pages of the *Arabian
Nights,* a drug known as hashish. There were also rumors that a well-
known doctor in Paris was asking for volunteers to test this drug.

HASHISH AND MADNESS

Dr. Jacques-Joseph Moreau (1804–84) had studied psychiatry under
one of its most important innovators, Jean Esquirol. It was due to Esquirol's influence, for instance, that psychiatrists began to recognize that
the events preceding mental breakdown sometimes held the key to the
mystery of mental illness. It was also due to Esquirol's influence that
psychiatrists such as Moreau became intrigued with hallucinations, believing that if psychiatry could only determine what caused them, it
might be able to get at the cause of insanity itself.

Duly impressed with his teacher's emphasis on causality and hallucinations as the keys to understanding and treating mental illness,
Moreau pondered how to experience insanity without first suffering a
mental breakdown:

> To understand an ordinary depression it is necessary to have experi-
> enced one; to comprehend the ravings of a madman, it is necessary to have
> raved oneself, but without having lost the awareness of one's madness,
> without having lost the power to evaluate the psychic changes occurring in
> the mind.[4]

By knowing what a patient was experiencing, Moreau felt that he
might eventually understand the psychotic state and devise a method to
treat it. His tool for producing this "model psychosis" was to be hashish.

[4]J. J. Moreau, *Hashish and Mental Illness* (New York: Raven Press, 1973), p. 17.

Moreau had first tried hashish during a trip through the Arab countries in the 1830's. He was no doubt already familiar with some of the properties of hashish through the writings of other doctors, but it was not until 1840 that he became intrigued at hashish's potential for exploring the mind after reading a scientific article by Dr. Aubert Roche entitled "Du typhus et de la peste en Orient" (Concerning Typhus and the Pestilence in the Orient). Although Roche had only claimed that the Egyptians were less susceptible to diseases that plagued Europeans because of their indulgence in hashish, Moreau began to think seriously of other uses for the drug.

"There are two modes of existence—two modes of life—given to man," Moreau mused. "The first one results from our communication with the external world, with the universe. The second one is but the reflection of the self and is fed from its own distinct internal sources. The dream is an in-between land where the external life ends and the internal life begins."[5] With the aid of hashish, he felt that anyone could enter this in-between land at will.

During the course of his studies with hashish, Moreau began to notice a peculiar relationship between the amount of drug he administered and its effects. A small dose produced a sense of euphoria, calmness, lassitude, and apathy. A little higher dose and attention began to wander. Ideas appeared at random. Time sense was distorted; minutes became hours. Thoughts rushed together. Sensory acuity seemed greater. More drug yet, and dreams began to flood the brain. These dreams, Moreau felt, were like the hallucinations of insanity.

Moreau's experiments with hashish led him to the conclusion that insanity was not due to brain damage, as many of the leading psychiatrists of his day maintained, but was instead due to a change in the way the brain functioned, a change that was caused by a chemical alteration in the nervous system. A hundred years later, psychiatrists working with LSD would come to a similar conclusion.

Because his supply of hashish was limited, Moreau decided not to explore possible therapeutic applications to which hashish might be put. Instead, he decided to follow through on his initial idea to use the hashish experience as a model psychosis. To conduct such studies, however, he had to be able to observe the effects of hashish objectively. By experimenting on himself, he had gained some insight into what the drug did to the mind. But perhaps these subjective impressions were inaccurate? Hashish distorted time sense; might it not also distort other impressions? Only by enlisting the aid of volunteers could he observe the drug's effects on others while he himself was free of hashish's rev-

[5]*Ibid.*, p. 21.

erie. It was in this role as the dispassionate scientist that Moreau became drug dispenser to the Hashish Club, a coterie of France's leading
writers, poets, and artists.

Although Moreau's work in psychopharmacology is now recognized for its pioneering approach to the study of the way drugs affect the
brain, his own colleagues failed to recognize the value and importance of
his studies.

In 1846, a year after the publication of his 439-page book, *Diu
Hachish et de l'alienation mentale—études psychologiques* (Hashish and
Mental Illness—Psychological Studies), Moreau decided to enter it in a
competition sponsored by the French Academy of Sciences. The other
entries consisted of other medical, surgical, and neurological books. Six
of these entries received prizes; two received honorable mentions,
among them Moreau's book. Even this distinction might have eluded
him had not one of the judges been impressed with the intriguing relationship between drug dosage and subjective effects. Were it not for
Théophile Gautier and the Hashish Club, Moreau would probably be
even less known than he already is, although he was one of the earliest
scientists to study hashish and to propose drugs as tools in the study of
mental aberrations.

Far from being disinterested in hashish, however, French scientists
seemed very curious and intrigued about its therapeutic potentials. In
1847, the Pharmaceutical Society of Paris posted a prize for the isolation
of the active principle in cannabis, which was eventually won in 1857. In
1848, the first doctoral thesis on hashish was written by DeCourtive,
whose pharmacopoeia Charles Baudelaire later relied on for much of his
information about hashish.

Hashish's Advance Man

Among the luminaries of the French world who sought in hashish
the key to expanded consciousness was Pierre Jules Théophile Gautier.
A failure as a painter and poet, Gautier became an overnight sensation
in 1835 at the age of twenty-four with *Mademoiselle de Maupin,* the story
of a transvestite, hailed by one critic as "the most daring novel... that
ever a full-fledged Romanticist could write."[6]

Gautier's view of life is best stated in the preface to this novel. A
special award ought to be given to people who invent new pleasures, he

[6]Quoted in L. Grinspoon, *Marihuana Reconsidered* (Cambridge, Mass.: Harvard University
Press, 1971), p. 64.

tells his readers, "for enjoyment seems to me to be the end of life, and the only useful thing in the world."[7]

No doubt, one of the first recipients of such an award, had Gautier had his way, would have been Moreau, who introduced him to the wonders of hashish. As a result of this encounter with Moreau, Gautier subsequently founded the famous Hashish Club (Club des Hachichins) which met on a monthly basis in the elegant Hôtel Lauzun in Paris's Latin Quarter. It was during these sessions that Moreau dispensed dawamesk (a mixture of hashish, cinnamon, cloves, nutmeg, pistachio, sugar, orange juice, butter and cantharides) to such notables as Alexandre Dumas, Gérard de Nerval, Victor Hugo, Ferdinand Boissard, Eugène Delacroix, and Gautier himself.

Gautier's own interest in hashish stemmed in large part from curiosity. He had heard the gossip of the French soldiers who had first tried the drug in Egypt and was intrigued by their stories. Gautier was also astute enough to realize that the French public would be just as interested as he himself was in hashish. They too had heard stories of this mysterious drug, and the popularity of books about the Arab countries such as *The Thousand and One Nights* was proof enough that articles of this kind would sell.

In 1843, François Lallemand anonymously published *Le hachych*, the first book to incorporate hashish as a plot device. The book became popular enough to warrant reissue in 1848 and this time it carried Lallemand's name as the author. But it was Gautier's "Le hashish," also published in 1843, which captured and held imaginations. It was a relatively short article describing the various hallucinations Gautier experienced while under the influence of the drug—the changes in colors and designs; the disfigurement of bodies; and the sensation of being able to hear colors and see sounds (a phenomenon known as synesthesia)—and its popularity encouraged Gautier to write another.

His second article appeared in the *Revue des Deux Mondes* in 1846 and was titled "Le Club des Hachichins." Although it contained relatively little concerning his experiences under the influence of hashish that he had not already described, it was to become the better known of his writings on the subject because of his description of the Hôtel Lauzun and the members of the club that gathered there.

The hotel immortalized by Gautier was built in 1657 by the duc de Lauzun as his personal palace, and he lived there until his death at the age of ninety in 1723. In its time it was a magnificient architectural feat, but by the 1840s it was more rundown than remarkable. When first erected, the building's three stories made it one of Paris's skyscrapers.

[7] *Ibid.*

Its large windows, tiny panes of glass, and stone balcony were city landmarks. To the left of the front door were red, bright-yellow, and gold-colored iron posts. At about the level of the first floor was a gargoyle dragon that looked down on all who called upon the duke. The popularity of Gautier's writings on hashish, it has been said, was not so much due to his descriptions of the hashish experience as to the moody atmosphere of the gathering place of the Hashish Club and the eminent people who assembled there to partake of the drug.

The fascination evoked by Gautier's article is immediate. Gautier sets the mood with deliberation. It is night. A fog drifts in off the Seine. Nothing is discernible. Shapes are indistinct, fuzzy, there and gone. When at last Gautier finds the hotel and knocks at the door, he is met by an old porter who points the way with a "skinny finger stretched outwards."

Among those who greet him at the top of the stairs is a mysterious doctor (Moreau) who hands him a "morsel of paste of greenish jam about as large as a thumb from a crystal vase," as he cautions that "this will be deducted from your share in Paradise."[8]

Gautier then goes on to tell his readers about the Old Man of the Mountain and the Assassins, declaring that the "green paste that the doctor had just passed out among us was precisely that which the Old Man of the Mountain used to administer to his fanatics . . . that is, hashish, whence comes hashisheen or hashish-eater, the root of the word 'assassin,' whose ferocious meaning is readily explicable of the bloodthirsty habits of the votaries of the Old Man of the Mountain."[9]

The sinister relationship between hashish and death is further developed in Gautier's description of his table fellows—"long-haired, bearded, moustached or singularly shorn guests, brandishing sixteenth century daggers, Malayan drisses or navajas. . . . "[10]

As the meal draws to a close, Gautier begins to hallucinate. The faces of the people at the table change shape and color, and "madness, like a wave foaming against a rock, which withdraws to hurl itself once more, entered and departed my brain, at length altogether invading it."[11]

The guests retire to the drawing room. Gautier sinks into a chair by the fireplace and surrenders himself to the drug. Totally absorbed in his thoughts, he knows that others are with him in the room, but he sees no

[8]T. Gautier, "The Hashish Club," *The Marihuana Papers*, ed. D. Solomon (New York: Signet, 1966), p. 166.
[9]*Ibid*
[10]*Ibid.*, p. 167.
[11]*Ibid.*, p. 168.

one. He is completely wrapped up in himself, his mind filled with grotesque characters whose faces and bodies are monstrously contorted. The rest of his narrative contains much the same material. The images which Gautier calls to mind are thoroughly at home in the Gothic interior of the Hôtel Lauzun. The grotesque shadows which lace through his thoughts as he hallucinates owe much to his surroundings. From Gautier's description, the reader senses that hashish is indeed the boatman ferrying passengers across the Styx of imagination to the netherworld of insanity.

Hashish's Troubadour

Without doubt the best known member of the Club des Hachichins was the brooding melancholic Charles Baudelaire. Baudelaire was no stranger to drugs. During his youth he lived in the Latin Quarter, a section of Paris like San Francisco's Haight-Asbury district of the 1960s, inhabited mainly by students, writers, artists, and thieves. The streets were narrow, dimly lit, and foul smelling. Students "hung out" at cafes and restaurants carousing and boasting about real and imagined sexual conquests. They drank to excess and indulged themselves in all the latest vices, among which were opium and hashish.

Baudelaire first met Gautier toward the middle of 1849 thanks to a mutual friend, the artist Fernand Boissard. Boissard and Gautier were both tenants at the Hôtel Lauzun, and in the course of things Baudelaire was invited to attend the meetings of the Hashish Club. Yet, always the loner, Baudelaire rarely accepted the invitation.

In the preface to his *Flowers of Evil* (Fleurs du Mal), published in 1868, Baudelaire confesses that he usually avoided these clandestine soirées and that when he did attend, it was only as an observer. Gautier corroborates this confession:

> It is possible and even probable that Baudelaire did try hascheesh once or twice by way of physiological experiment, but he never made continuous use of it. Besides, he felt much repugnance for that sort of happiness, bought at the chemist's and taken away in the vest-pocket, and he compared the ecstasy it induces to that of a maniac for whom painted canvas and rough drop-scenes take the place of real furniture and gardens balmy with the scent of genuine flowers. He came but seldom, and merely as an observer, to the meetings in Pimodan House [Hôtel Lauzun], where our club met....[12]

Gautier himself gave up hashish "after trying it some ten times or so, . . . not that it hurt me physically, but because a real writer needs no

---

[12]T. Gautier, "Charles Baudelaire," in *The Works of Théophile Gautier*, ed. F. C. De Sumichrast (New York: George D. Sproul, 1890), 23: 100–1.

other than his own natural dreams, and does not care to have his throught controlled by the influence of any agency whatever."[13]

In the introduction to *The Artificial Paradises*, his best known work on hashish, Baudelaire candidly admits that for much of his information concerning the actions of the drug, he relied on the detailed notes he had accumulated in talking to his friends who had been using hashish for a long time. Two other major sources were Silvestre de Sacy's writings, and a popular pharmaceutical text of the day, *L'Officine ou répertoire général de pharmacies practiques* (The Laboratory or General Encyclopedia of Practical Pharmacy), parts of which he copied verbatim. The latter was first published in 1844 by the pharmacist Dorvault, and became a standard reference manual on drugs (it was reprinted and expanded in 1847, 1850, and 1855). Baudelaire incorporated approximately three-quarters of the material on hashish from Dorvault's 1850 edition in the *Artificial Paradises* which he published in 1858, although no mention of Dorvault appears anywhere in Baudelaire's writings.

The *Artificial Paradises* is divided into two parts. The first contains Baudelaire's "Poem of Hashish"; the second is a translation of de Quincey's *Confessions of an Opium Eater*. Baudelaire's inclusion of these two works into a single volume was due to his feeling that both drugs produced very similar effects. Indeed, it is sometimes impossible to tell whether Baudelaire is writing about opium or hashish in various parts of his "Poem of Hashish."

Although widely hailed as one of hashish's most articulate and analytical devotees, as well as one of its most tragic victims, Baudelaire was neither devotee nor victim of hashish. He was merely an observer of hashish's effects, and he died not from overindulgence in hashish but from syphilis. Nevertheless, aside from the bitter recriminations expressed at the end of his essay, Baudelaire's *Artificial Paradises* is unsurpassed as literature's most poetic description of the hashish experience. Gautier later wrote of the book:

> Medically speaking *The Artificial Paradises* constitute a very well written monograph of hascheesh, and science might find in it reliable information; for Baudelaire piqued himself on being scrupulously accurate, and not for the world would he have allowed the smallest poetic imagery to slip into a subject that was naturally adapted to it.[14]

Baudelaire begins his discussion by refuting the notion that hashish will transform anyone into an entirely different person. One "will find in hashish nothing miraculous, absolutely nothing but an exaggeration of the natural," he says. "The brain and organism on which hashish

[13] *Ibid.*, p. 101.
[14] *Ibid.*, p. 103.

operates will produce only the normal phenomena peculiar to that individual—increased, admittedly, in number and force, but always faithful to the original."[15]

Next he cautions that the user must be in the right frame of mind to take hashish, for just as it exaggerates the natural behavior of the individual, so too does hashish intensify the user's immediate feelings. Obligations that require attention will keep the user from enjoying the otherwise pleasurable effects of the drug and instead he will be tortured with worry and subjected to unbearable agony.

Once he has been properly prepared, the hashish user will pass through three successive phases. The first comes on rather slowly, almost imperceptibly. Because the novice has in all likelihood been previously told something of the effects of hashish, Baudelaire advises his readers that they are likely to feel impatient. This impatience, he warns, must be overcome for it could throw the novice into a state of anxiety. An indication that the drug is beginning to work, regardless of what the user says, is uncontrollable laughter. The most trivial remark assumes new meaning. A sense of incongruity, of puns on words, of ridiculous situations, are all characteristic of the mirth of hashish. A second indication that hashish is beginning to act is an inability to maintain a train of thought. Ideas race through the mind, becoming disjointed, fragmented, isolated; conversation is no longer possible.

The second stage of intoxication is characterized by a feeling of coldness in the extremities and general lassitude. There is a sense of stupor and stupefaction. The mouth feels parched with incredible thirst. A heightened feeling of sensory acuity begins to be imagined. The senses are scrambled. Sounds have colors; colors contain music. It is now that one begins to see and hear things that are not there.

The final stage is marked by a feeling of calmness. Time and space have no meaning. There is a sense that one has transcended matter. In this state, one final supreme thought breaks into consciousness—"I have become God."

Having traced the stages of hashish intoxication, Baudelaire concludes his essay with a chapter entitled "moral." Here Baudelaire deals with the after effects of hashish. Although he states that there are no dangerous physical consequences from hashish, he contends that the same cannot be said for the user's psychological health. Although hashish increases creativity and elevates imagination, the individual who has come to rely on the drug for inspiration may become its prisoner, unable to think creatively at all unless drugged with hashish. Moreover, hashish's weakening of the will makes the user unable to

[15]C. Baudelaire, "The Artificial Paradise," *The Marihuana Papers*, ed D. Solomon, p. 181.

profit from any creative insights he may derive from the drug. If one can instantly realize all the pleasures of heaven and earth through hashish, he asks, why should anyone actively pursue such goals?

Baudelaire moved out of the Hôtel Lauzun shortly after a botched suicide attempt. He was suffering from syphilis, he drank heavily, and he was constantly resorting to opium to help himself deal with a deep-seated feeling of despondency and self-hatred. Although respected by fellow writers and critics, Baudelaire considered himself a failure. He died in 1866, his brain decayed by the syphilitic bacterium he had contracted as a youth.

Balzac and Flaubert

Baudelaire was not the only well-known nonparticipant to attend the meetings of the Hashish Club. As Baudelaire noted, Honoré de Balzac also preferred to watch the proceedings without personally partaking of the "green paste" handed out by Moreau:

> Balzac no doubt held the belief that there is no deeper shame nor worse suffering for a man than to renounce control over his own will. I saw him once at a meeting where the prodigious effects of hascheesch were being discussed. He listened and asked questions with amusing attention and vivacity. Those who knew him will readily guess that he was interested. But the idea of thinking in spite of himself shocked him deeply; he was offered some dawamesk; he examined it, smelt it, and returned it without touching it. The struggle between his almost childish curiosity and his dislike for abdication exhibited itself on his expressive face in a striking manner. The love of self-dignity won the day.[16]

Gautier recalls that occasion:

> I was at Pimodan House that night, and I am in a position to certify to the absolute accuracy of the story. I will merely add this characteristic trait: as he handed back the spoonful of dawamesk that had been offered him, Balzac remarked that it would be of no use to make the test, for he was sure that hascheesch would have no effect upon his brain.[17]

Balzac's curiosity finally got the better of him, however, and in a letter dated December 23, 1845, addressed to a Madame Hanska, he confesses that he finally took some hashish at one of the gatherings of the Hashish Club, adding that as he was leaving the group, he began to hear celestial voices and see divine paintings.[18]

One of France's well-known writers who was profoundly influ-

---

[16]Gautier, "Charles Baudelaire," pp. 101–2.
[17]*Ibid.*, p. 102.
[18]H. Balzac, *Letters to Madame Hanska* (Boston: Little, Brown, 1900), p. 689.

enced by Baudelaire's description of the hashish experience, and who like Balzac had certain misgivings about trying the drug himself, was Gustav Flaubert. Baudelaire had sent Flaubert a personal copy of *Artificial Paradises*, and in a return letter, Flaubert confessed that "these drugs have always aroused great longing in me. I've got some excellent hashish made up for me by Gastinel, the chemist. But it terrifies me! I blame myself bitterly for this!"[19]

Although frightened at the prospect of taking hashish, Flaubert nevertheless took issue with Baudelaire's characterization of the drug as something evil. To Flaubert, Baudelaire's condemnation of hashish had ruined what was otherwise an excellent essay. "It seems to me," Flaubert wrote, "that in a subject treated so eminently, in a work that is the beginning of science, in a piece of natural observation and induction, you have emphasized too greatly the spirit of evil. I would have preferred that you would not have accused hashish and opium of excesses. It was not the drugs that were evil, but rather the misuse of these substances."[20]

Shortly before his death, Flaubert had begun outlining a novel of his own entitled *La Spirale*, based on Baudelaire's description of hashish's effects. Flaubert's notes depict a tormented hero who is eventually confined to an institution for the insane. The cause of his mental breakdown is hashish, a drug habit he had acquired during a visit to the Arab countries, and an exceptional imagination and disposition for reverie upon which the drug acted. Saturated with hashish, his brain manufactured ecstatic visions and plunged him into a state of "permanent somnabulism" which rendered him insensible to pain.

Hashish's Tragic Apostle

Gérard de Nerval was another prominent French writer who belonged to the Hashish Club and who wrote about the drug in his books. Like Baudelaire, Nerval was plagued with fits of melancholy. Most of his life he lived in poverty and dissipation. Also, like Baudelaire, Nerval tried to kill himself. Unlike Baudelaire, he succeeded.

Nerval had met Théophile Gautier while they were both students in Paris and the two remained friends for the rest of their lives. It was through Gautier that he became a member of the Club des Hachichins.

Nerval's first major literary triumph was a translation of *Faust*, pub-

[19]P. Dimoff, "Autour d'un projet de roman de Flaubert: La Spirale," *Revue d'Histoire et de Littérature* 48 (1948): 314.
[20]*Ibid.*

lished when he was only twenty. The story of the man who sold his soul to the devil appealed to his mystical interests and was only one of many such stories to set his mind on a cryptic transcendental course. During a trip to the Near East which he described in his *Voyages to the Orient* (1847), Nerval got the idea for his "Story of the Calif Haken," a singularly exotic tale of hashish and double consciousness.

The main character of the story lives a dual existence. By day, he is the caliph, the ruler of Egypt; by night, he dresses in slave's clothes and wanders among the common people. As the story opens, the caliph enters an *okel*, "one of those houses where taking no heed of the prohibition (against intoxication), infidels came to make themselves drunk with wine, Bouza [beer] or hashish." He orders some hashish which is brought to him in the form of a "greenish paste," and has some with a companion whom he has just met. As the drug is brought to them, the other man says that "this box contains the paradise your prophet Mohammed promised to his believers. . . . "

Nerval describes the various feelings the caliph experiences, the uncontrollable laughter, the languor, the rapid whirl of ideas, the visions, and the feeling of total relaxation. During this unique experience, the caliph announces that he is God, a remark that turns the other patrons against him for this act of blasphemy, and they beat him severely. Although he is forgiven because he has not mastered the hashish experience as yet, this idea remains fixed in his mind and he is thrown into an insane asylum. While he is a patient there, he is visited by the famous Arab physician Avicenna, who dismisses his protestations and his insistence that he is the caliph as the ravings of a hashish-crazed lunatic.

The high point of the story comes when the caliph escapes from the asylum and sees someone else upon the throne who resembles himself so closely that it can only be his doppleganger. This is another part of his existence previously unknown to him. In the end, by a set of peculiar circumstances, the caliph is physically killed while his spiritual being, the being that sits upon the throne, continues to rule over Egypt.

The point of Nerval's allegory is that under the insidious influence of hashish, reality and illusion cannot be separated. The hashish user is cast under a spell in which an idea is fixed in his mind to the exclusion of everything else and this idea determines how one sees oneself on a number of different levels. The hashish user assumes both a physical and a spiritual entity. Mind and body dissociate; yet all the while the soul consciously and dispassionately observes what happens to each.

Nerval also wrote several stories in which opium played a prominent part. Like Baudelaire, he was no stranger to drug abuse. His last years were spent in poverty and misery. Unable to cope any longer after a number of tragic love affairs exacerbated his already thread-bare sanity, he hanged himself.

ALEXANDRE DUMAS

The fourth prominent member of the Club des Hachichins whose writings deal with hashish was Alexandre Dumas, one of the most prolific and entertaining of the French writers of the mid-nineteenth century. Although well acquainted with the effects of hashish through attending the gatherings at the Hôtel Lauzun, there is no indication that Dumas ever used hashish or any other drug to excess. Like Gautier, Dumas was astute enough to realize that hashish had a mystique about it that fascinated the French reading public, and he heightened the interest of one of his best known stories. *The Count of Monte Cristo,* by making hashish a part of the plot. In a chapter from *Monte Cristo* entitled "Sinbad the Sailor," Dumas tells of the meeting of Franz with a mysterious stranger who lives on a deserted island and refers to himself only as Sinbad.

Franz has come to the island, which is sometimes used as a base for smuggling, to do some hunting. He encounters some smugglers and is invited to dine with their leader Sinbad, whose quarters are located somewhere beneath the island. To prevent any outsiders from finding the entrance to these quarters, Sinbad blindfolds Franz and then leads him into an underground palace, magnificently furnished with articles from around the world.

After a sumptuous meal, a servant places a cup on the table. Franz lifts the lid of the cup and sees a "greenish paste." "Taste this," his host says, offering the paste, "and the boundaries of possibility disappear, the fields of infinite space open to you, you advance free in heart, free in mind, into the boundless realms of unfettered reverie."

Sinbad takes some of the paste himself, and while they are resting he tells Franz the story of the Assassins. The mystery of the green paste now becomes clear to Franz. "It is hasheesh!" he cries.

His curiosity soaring, Franz also takes some of the drug and the two men retire to another lavishly furnished chamber where they relax and talk about visiting the great cities of the Arab world.

Franz experiences the various effects of hashish and then finally falls asleep. When he awakens, he finds himself above ground and alone. He tries to find the entrance to the palace so that he can return, but it is too well hidden. He then begins to doubt the whole adventure, but his servant, who has been waiting for him, points to a boat sailing off in the distance. Peering at the vessel through a telescope, Franz is able to make out the figure of Sinbad standing alone on the deck of the ship. It was not a dream. The experience had been real.

Franz's enounter with his mysterious host, the underground palace, the blindfold, his initiation to hashish, the visions he experiences, and his dream-like impressions are all calculated to hold the reader's interest. They are examples of Dumas's expertise as a storyteller. And they are also examples of Dumas's subtle and masterful craftsmanship, for what the reader has actually been treated to is a rerendering of Marco Polo's story of the Old Man of the Mountain and his band of Assassins.

The mysterious Sinbad is none other than Hasan. The cave is the Alamut stronghold. The smugglers are the Assassins. The magnificent palace is the Paradise of the legend. Franz is blindfolded; the candidates (fidais) are given a potion to render them unconscious before they can enter the grounds, and like Franz they are taken from the grounds in an unconscious state. The analogy is so well executed that even the reader who is acquainted with Marco Polo's narrative is unaware that he is encountering the very same legend in the story of *Monte Cristo*.

Hashish in England

The lurid accounts of the hashish experience by the popular French literati did not go unnoticed across the Channel, and it was not long before English writers and students were also experimenting with the drug.

In 1845, Thomas de Quincey obtained some "bang" and said that he would shortly be describing his reactions to it for the English reading public, much the same as he had done in the case of opium. For some unknown reason, his plan never materialized. However, he does state that

> one farmer in Midlothian was mentioned to me eight months ago as having taken it, and ever since annoyed his neighbors by immoderate fits of laughter; so that in January it was agreed to present him to the sheriff as a nuisance. But for some reason the plan was laid aside and now, eight months later, I hear that the farmer is laughing more raptuorously than ever, continues in the happiest frame of mind, the kindest creature and the general torment of his neighborhood.[21]

In 1848, an anonymous article appeared in *Chamber's Edinburgh Journal*, a widely read literary periodical of the era, in which the author warned his readers that a menace was ravaging France. Indulgence in

---

[21]Quoted in R. P. Walton, *Marihuana* (Philadelphia: J. B. Lippincott, 1938), p. 62.

hashish, he said, had spread from physicians and medical students to that nation's "poets, idealists, and all the lovers of novelty." After describing the effects of the drug, the "alterations" produced "upon the perceptive powers, the imagination, and the reason," he concludes with a grave warning to those Englishmen who may have been contemplating their own hashish romp of the senses: "It may be emphatically said that none of nature's law can be violated with impunity, nor can that reason which renders man pre-eminent be misapplied without a punishment."[22]

This dour admonition seems to have been ignored since the popular press and the medical journals began to carry more and more articles on the effects of hashish. In 1850, David Urquhart, a member of Parliament, published a two-volume book entitled *The Pillars of Hercules* in which he added his own experiences regarding hashish to the literature on the subject.[23] The use of such a drug by a member of the government convinced many readers that the dangers attributed to hashish had probably been exaggerated, although the number of people who decided to try some for themselves as the result of such books was never great. It was personal contact with other users, not books, that increased the growing coterie of hashish patrons.

The anonymous author of an 1858 article in *Little's Living Age Magazine* comforted his readers that

> the English are in no danger whatever of becoming a nation of opium or hashish debauchies; and we feel no compunction in placing before them an account of some of those exceptional cases in which the results have been sufficiently delightful to constitute a temptation to one of the most ruinous species of debauchery.[24]

Following this pronouncement, the author cites some interesting statistics regarding the use of hashish and other drugs throughout the world at that time: "Tobacco is the one universal narcotic; the others are consumed by the human race in the following proportions; opium by four hundred millions, hemp by between two and three hundred millions, betel by one hundred millions, and coca by ten millions."[25] Interestingly, he makes no mention of alcohol in spite of the fact that alcohol abuse was a major problem in England in the mid-nineteenth century.

Despite all the evidence to the contrary, English writers repeatedly

---

[22]"The Hashish," *Chamber's Edinburgh Journal*, 10 (1848): 344.
[23]D. Urquhart, *The Pillars of Hercules, A Narrative of Travels in Spain and Morocco* (London: R. Bentley, 1850), pp. 81–90.
[24]"Hashish," *Little's Living Age*, 56 (1858): 450.
[25]*Ibid.*

denied that any of their fellow Englishmen were turning to hashish. In 1877, for example, a W. Laird-Clowes wrote in the magazine *Belgravia* that "as far as I am aware—and my researches have been tolerably extensive—no professional Englishmen (non-physician) has hitherto noted down the latter drug [hashish]."[26] Apparently, Laird-Clowes was unfamiliar with Urquhart's *Pillars of Hercules* or what was being written in other popular English magazines about hashish. But he had read enough to know that hashish was being blamed for the frenzied killings committed by the Assassins. To the charge that hashish inspires violence, Laird-Clowes says that as far as his own personal experience with the drug was concerned, he had never had the urge to go out and kill anyone.

> Perhaps I am not of a violent nature [he says in his concluding remarks], certainly I have no inducement to commit a murder; and probably a man's inborn tastes in great measure direct the effect that hashish will exert on his mental faculties . . . anything more foreign to the effects of the drug than the "creation of unpleasantness," either in thought, word, or deed, I cannot conceive.[27]

Other Englishmen concurred with Laird-Clowes's contention that the English were in no danger of becoming hashish addicts or even experimenting with the drug on a large scale. "The temperament which is unsuceptible of exultation by narcotics into a rapturous or vision-beholding condition, seems happily to be rare in northern climates," was how one writer put it.[28] Another wrote that "the Theater of Seraphim, with its gay marionette-version of human experience is open to all at the price of almost inevitable physical and moral degradation," a condition foreign to the English temperament.[29]

It was not that the English were above using drugs that altered consciousness, but rather that they were more content with alcohol, and saw little need to experiment with other mind-altering drugs. Those who did were either members of minority groups, artists, writers, criminals, or students. It was the isolated cases that came to the attention of the press and gave the impression that hashish was rampant in parts of England.

One such case took place in 1886 in the dormitories of staid old Cambridge University. According to a newspaper report, some students had obtained "Turkish Delight," and not being experienced users of the

---

[26]W. Laird-Clowes, "An Amateur Assassin," *Belgravia* 31 (1877): 353.
[27]*Ibid.*
[28]"Hashish," *Living Age*, p. 352.
[29]"Confessions of a French Hashesch Eater," *Once A Week* 18 (1868): 351.

hashish-laden confection, had taken an overdose and become ill as a result.[30] Oxford also had its share of cannabis users.[31]

In a footnote to "The Tale of the Hashish Eater," Richard Burton likewise commented that "I heard of a 'Hashish-orgie' in London which ended in half the experimentalists being on their sofas for a week. The drug is useful for stokers, having the curious property of making men insensible to heat. Easterns also use it for 'Imsak' prolonging coition, of which I speak presently."[32] This observation was published in 1885 so it must have occurred some time earlier.

While the medical journals began to teem with articles concerning possible therapeutic uses of the drug and adverse reactions occurring in those who took overdoses, the only nineteenth-century book to deal with hashish in England was an anonymous work entitled *Confessions of an English Hashish-Eater*, published in 1884, which was patterned after De Quincey's bestseller of years gone by.

The "Decadents"

Around the turn of the twentieth century, the spirit of ennui that had gripped the French Romantic writers of the mid-nineteenth century crossed the English Channel and settled on a coterie of English writers such as Arthur Symons, William Butler Yeats, Ernest Dowson, Oscar Wilde, and Havelock Ellis. Yeats called them the "Tragic Generation."

Like their French forebears, this new generation of creators sought new sensations, visions, and ideas to write about, and agreed with Gautier that "art [should be] for art's sake" rather than moral reform. Because they eschewed morality in their works, they were called the "decadents." And just as their French forebears had sought inspiration and escape from boredom in drugs, so too did the "decadents." Absinthe was a favorite with many of these writers such as Oscar Wilde, mescaline was preferred by Havelock Ellis and W. B. Yeats, although Yeats was not adverse to hashish;[33] Dowson preferred hashish in his youth,[34] but gave it up for alcohol. Their French counterparts, Arthur Rimbaud and Paul Verlane, "intoxicated themselves with both absinthe

[30]R. C. Albutt, *A System of Medicine* (New York: Macmillan, 1900), 2: 903.

[31]M. Longaker, *Ernest Dowson* (Philadelphia: University of Pennsylvania Press, 1945), pp. 42–3.

[32]R. F. Burton, *The Thousand Nights and a Night* (Benares: Burton Ethnological Society, 1885), 3: 91.

[33]W. B. Yeats, *Autobiography* (New York: MacMillan, 1953), p. 209.

[34]K. Beckson, ed. *The Memoirs of Arthur Symons* (University Park: Pennsylvania State University Press, 1977), p. 84.

and hashish and wrote poems of hellish and heavenly music,"[35] the best known of which is Rimbaud's *Illuminations,* and its memorable lines— "This is the time of the Assassins . . . it began with the laughter of children, it will end with it."

For Rimbaud and many of his contemporaries, hashish was, however, a means to an end, not an end in itself. "The Poet," he wrote, "makes himself a voyant through a long, immense reasoned deranging of all his senses. All the forms of love, of suffering, of madness; he tries to find himself, he exhausts in himself all the poisons, to keep only their quintessences."[36]

While the "decadents" used hashish and other drugs as much as Gautier, Baudelaire, Nerval, and the other members of the Hashish Club, they did not make drugs a formal part of their socializing, and there was no Gautier or Baudelaire to chronicle or exploit their drug-oriented activities. Moreover, their use of drugs seemed nothing out of the ordinary.

CANNABIS IN WESTERN MEDICINE

While the French were the first to begin experimenting with hashish on a relatively large scale, the introduction of cannabis into Western medicine is credited to a now obscure Irish physician, Dr. William Brooke O'Shaughnessy. Although known today for his pioneering experiments with cannabis, during his own lifetime he was best known for introducing intravenous fluid and electrolyte-replacement therapy in the treatment of cholera. His major achievement, however, had nothing at all to do with medicine. Instead, after leaving the medical profession for engineering, O'Shaughnessy was instrumental in introducing the telegraph system into India—an accomplishment for which he was knighted in 1856 by Queen Victoria. O'Shaughnessy retired from military service in 1861 at age fifty-two and returned to England, where for some unknown reason he changed his name to William O'Shaughnessy Brooke. Although he lived for another twenty-eight years, he never returned to medical research and spent his retirement engaged in other activities.

O'Shaughnessy first came to India in 1833 as a thirty-year-old surgeon in the employ of the British East India Company. He also held the position of professor of chemistry at the Medical College of Calcutta.

---

[35]T. B. Swann, *Ernest Dowson* (New York: Twayne Publishers, 1964), pp. 21–2.
[36]Quoted in E. R. Peschel, *Arthur Rimbaud. A Season in Hell, The Illuminations.* (New York: Oxford University Press, 1973), p. 7.

Apparently, he became intrigued at cannabis's therapeutic potential almost as soon as he arrived in India, and in 1843 he reported a summary of his studies of the drug[37] which so captured the interest of his medical colleagues in England that it was not long before they were clamoring for him to supply them with cannabis for their own medical practices.

O'Shaughnessy began his article by observing that while the intoxicating and medicinal effects of cannabis were known throughout the countries of the East, the drug was practically unknown in the West. Following a brief history of the use of the drug in India and in the Arab countries, O'Shaughnessy described the experiments he had conducted on animals, noting an observation that has not since been commented upon nor subjected to further study. In O'Shaughnessy's words, the experiments he had conducted "led to one remarkable result—That while carnivorous animals, and fish, dogs, cats, swine, vultures and crows, and adjutants, invariably and speedily exhibited the intoxicating influence of the drug, the graminivorous, such as the horse, deer, monkey, goat, sheep, and cow, experienced but trivial effects from any dose we administered." O'Shaughnessy had been nothing if not thorough in his preliminary studies on animals, judging by this statement.

Confident that cannabis posed no danger to the well-being of his animal subjects, O'Shaughnessy went on to test its curative potential in some patients who were plagued with rheumatism. After treatment with the drug, O'Shaughnessy found that many reported an easing of their pain and a "remarkable increase of appetite," "great mental cheerfulness," and a feeling of aphrodisia.

The capacity to make these patients euphoric led him next to try to alleviate the terrible symptoms associated with rabies in one of his patients. Although the man soon died of the disease, O'Shaughnessy was intrigued to find that the drug did relieve some of the patient's agony and did enable him to swallow some juice and moistened rice. O'Shaughnessy also experimented with cannabis in the treatment of cholera, tetanus, and epilepsy, reporting that in all cases his patients experienced relief from the symptoms of these disorders.

When O'Shaughnessy returned to England in 1842, he brought back a quantity of cannabis and turned it over to pharmacist Peter Squire to convert to a form suitable for medical usage. This preparation came to be known as Squire's extract, and launched Squire and his sons into

---

[37]W. B. O'Shaughnessy, "On the Preparation of the Indian Hemp or Gunjah (Cannabis Indica): The Effects on the Animal System in Health, and Their Utility in the Treatment of Tetanus and Other Convulsive Diseases," *Transactions of the Medical and Physical Society of Bombay* 8 (1842): 421–61.

prominence as the main and most reliable suppliers of cannabis extract in England.[38]

Soon after Squire's extract became commercially available, physicians began to prescribe it for almost any physical difficulty. One of the earliest conditions for which it was administered was childbirth. Dr. John Grigor, a pioneer in the obstetrical use of cannabis, wrote that while the drug was not effective in increasing labor contractions or reducing the pain of childbirth for all women, "it is capable of bringing the labor to a happy conclusion considerably within a half of the time that would otherwise have been required, thus saving protracted suffering to the patient, and the time of the practitioner."[39]

Other conditions for which the drug was often prescribed were loss of appetite, inability to sleep, migraine headache, pain, involuntary twitching, excessive coughing, and treatment of withdrawal symptoms associated with morphine and alcohol addiction.

Menorrhagia (excessive menstrual bleeding) was yet another condition for which cannabis was liberally administered, often with positive results. Dr. John Brown, an English obstetrician, stated that "there is no medicine which has given such good results . . . the failures are so few, that I venture to call it a specific in menorrhagia."[40] His colleague, Dr. Robert Batho, concurred. In his experience, cannabis had proven itself "par excellence the remedy for that condition . . . it is so certain in its power of controlling menorrhagia, that is a valuable aid to diagnosis in cases which it is uncertain whether an early abortion may or may not have occurred. . . . "[41]

Among the most prominent of English doctors to administer cannabis to his patients was Dr. J. R. Reynolds, court physician to dour old Queen Victoria.[42] Unfortunately, no one knows whether the drug's euphoric properties were ever experienced by the queen while she was being treated for any of cannabis's other therapeutic effects.

While a great many doctors could not say enough about cannabis's medicinal virtues, many others were reluctant to use the drug because of the variability of its actions. To overcome this problem, chemists

---

[38]In addition to Squire, the major commercial suppliers of cannabis to Europe were the pharmacies of Smith in Edinburgh, De Courtive and Personne in Paris, and Gastinel in Cairo.

[39]J. Grigor, "Indian Hemp as an Oxytocic," *Monthly Journal of Medical Science* 15 (1852): 124–5.

[40]J. Brown, "Cannabis Indica. A Valuable Remedy in Menorrhagia," *British Medical Journal*, May 26, 1883, p. 1002.

[41]R. Batho, "Cannabis Indica," *British Medical Journal*, May 26, 1883, p. 1002.

[43]J. R. Reynolds, "On the Therapeutic Uses and Toxic Effects of Cannabis Indica," *Lancet* 1 (1890): 637–8.

throughout the country attempted to identify and extract the active principle in cannabis so that it could be standardized as to purity and potency.

In the 1890s, a group of chemists at Cambridge University, Wood, Spivey, and Easterfield, succeeded in obtaining a relatively pure extraction of cannabis which they called "cannabinol." The discovery was not without mishap, however. While working on the project, Easterfield and Spivey were each blown to bits in chemical explosions. Wood, the third member of the group, almost perished under similar circumstances. While working in his laboratory, he took some cannabinol and lost consciousness. A chemical he was working with ignited some time later and the laboratory burst into flames. Luckily, someone smelled the smoke and ran to his assistance, rescuing him from the engulfing inferno.[43]

[43]R. P. Walton, *Marihuana* (Philadelphia: J. P. Lippincott, 1938).

Hashish in America

Although hemp had been a valuable and commonplace agricultural staple in the United States from the time of the first settlement in Virginia, the early Americans were totally unaware of the kaleidoscope of sensations lurking within the sticky resin that covered the plant. In fact, it was not until they read the exploits of their own Marco Polo, Bayard Taylor, that Americans learned of the existence of drugs such as hashish. But even then, they failed to make the connection between this exotic drug and the hemp weeds that grew in the vacant lots of their neighborhoods. Yet, because of Taylor's popularity, many of his impressionable thrill-seeking readers were prompted to try some of this strange electuary for themselves to see if they too could experience the bizarre sensations described by one of the country's favorite writers. So fashionable did the hashish habit become that even foreigners began to remark on the growing popularity of the drug in America.

HASHISH IN AMERICAN POETRY

Among the first Americans to write about hashish was not a novelist or a physician, but a poet—John Greenleaf Whittier. In "The Haschish," a short poem in his *Anti-Slavery Poems* (1854), Whittier writes of hashish-induced hallucinations and muddled thinking, but it is improbable that he himself had experienced the effects of the drug at the time he wrote the poem. The point of the poem, in fact, was not to describe the effects of hashish at all.

Although hashish is more potent in its ability to induce hallucinations than opium, and makes "fools or knaves of all who use it," says Whittier, when it came to enslavement hashish had to take a back seat to cotton. Whereas hashish enslaved the individual, cotton had enslaved a whole race of man.

The American Marco Polo

Whereas Whittier had written about hashish to emphasize his feelings about slavery, American writers and poets who followed him were
more interested in hashish as a plot device and therefore something to
be sensationalized. Among the first to write about hashish in this way
was one of the best known literary figures of the mid-nineteenth
century—Bayard Taylor. Poet, novelist, translator, music lyricist, war
correspondent, world traveler, secretary to the American legation to
Russia, ambassador to Germany—Taylor was ever in search of recognition. Yet, except for his translations of German classics such as *Faust*, for
which he was awarded the position of nonresident professor of German
literature at Cornell University, his writings were never regarded as
anything beyond mediocre by the nation's critics. Parke Godwin, editor
of the *New York Evening Post*, for instance, said that Taylor had "travelled
more and seen less than any man living."[1] The reading public, as is
often the case, ignored the critics and Taylor became rich and famous as
a writer.

In 1851, heartbroken over the death of his wife of three months and
exhausted from overwork, Taylor left the United States to travel in the
Middle and Far East. It was during this time that he first became acquainted with hashish, an experience he described for his readers in two
of his books, *A Journey to Central Africa* (1854) and *The Land of the Saracens; or, Pictures of Palestine, Asia Minor, Sicily, and Spain* (1855).[2]

Taylor's initiation to hashish took place in Egypt. The "exquisite
lightness and airiness," the "wonderfully keep perception of the ludicrous," and "the fine sensations which spread throughout the whole tissue of my nervous fiber, each thrill helping to divest my frame of its
earthly and natural nature," are briefly mentioned in *Journey to Central
Africa*. In *Land of the Saracens*, he delves more deeply into the hashish
experience, cloaking it in a sensationalistic wrap calculated to entertain
his readers.

Taylor begins by introducing the legend of the Assassins, a ploy
used by most writers to arouse in their readers' mind an anticipation of
uncontrollable passions and violence unleashed by this mysterious un-
guent of the Arab world. The theatrics are then carried one step further
as he tells of "a dark Egyptian," sent to obtain some of the drug with the
admonition: "And see that it be strong and fresh."

[1]Quoted in D. Ebin (ed.), The Drug Experience (New York: Grove Press, 1961), p. 41.
[2]B. Taylor, *A Journey To Central Africa* (New York: G. P. Putnam 1854); *id., The Land of the
Saracens; or, Pictures of Palestine, Asia Minor, Sicily and Spain* (New York: G. P. Putnam &
Sons, 1855).

Amid friends, Taylor retires to a quiet room. He swallows one tea-spoon of the mixture, the amount being roughly equal to that he had previously taken in Egypt. The lozenge is more bitter than he previously remembered—an intimation that it may also be more potent than that which he took in Egypt. But after an hour, none of the group felt any different.

When some of those present "loudly expressed their conviction of the humbug of hasheesh," Taylor advised a second teaspoon, "though not without some misgivings, as we were all ignorant of the precise quantity which constituted a dose, and the limits within which the drug could be taken with safety."

Not long after this second helping, Taylor senses "the same fine nervous thrill" that he had previously experienced in Egypt. But this time the sensation comes on suddenly and far more intensely. Now, he feels a kind of astral projection taking place: "The walls of my frame were burst outward and tumbled into ruin; and, without thinking what form I wore—losing sight even of all idea of form—I felt that I existed through a vast extent of space."

The sensation is too much for Taylor. His curiosity is satisfied. He wants to stop. But, instead, the "thrills which ran through my nervous system became more rapid and fierce. . . ." He loses control of his sensibility and bursts out in "an agony of laughter."

His senses are hurled into a rampage of conquest. "The spirits of height, color, odor, sound, and motion were my slaves; and, having these, I was master of the universe." Time has no meaning. "Though the whole vision was probably not more than five minutes in passing through my mind, years seemed to have elapsed. . . . One set of nerves was thrilled with the bliss of the gods, while another was convulsed with unquenchable laughter at that very bliss."

Next comes the second wave of intoxication. He begins to feel "a painful tension throughout my nervous system—the effect of over-stimulus." Illusions become "grotesque." A burning sensation smolders in the pit of his stomach and his mouth and throat feel "as dry and hard as if made of brass." Although he frantically pours water into himself, he can find no relief. The nightmarish illusions continue for several hours more. Taylor convulses uncontrollably and finally falls into a stupor.

The next day he is so incapacitated he cannot even dress himself and he crawls back into bed. On the morning of the second day, having slept about thirty hours, he is able to remain awake but "with a system utterly prostrate and unstrung, and a brain clouded with the lingering images of my visions. I knew where I was, and what had happened to me, but all that I saw still remained unreal and shadowy."

A servant prepares him a hot bath, and while he is relaxing he is brought a glass of "very acid sherbet," which he claims, brings him "instant relief," although for the next two or three days he continues to experience "frequent involuntary fits of absence, which make me insensible, for the time, to all that was passing around me. . . ."

"Fearful as my rash experiment proved to me, I did not regret having made it," he confesses to his readers. "It revealed to me depths of rapture and of suffering which my natural faculties never could have sounded. It has taught me the majesty of human reason and of human will, even in the weakest, and the awful peril of tampering with that which assails their integrity."[3]

Bayard Taylor's description of his experience with hashish was, for most Americans, their first introduction to the drug. Written intentionally for an audience that sought vicarious adventure and enjoyed reading about the customs of far-off peoples, Taylor's books were entertaining and extremely popular. Taylor gave America its first impression of the hashish experience. It was an impression that would last for quite some time.

FITZ HUGH LUDLOW

Among the many readers to be captivated by *The Land of the Saracens* and Taylor's experience with hashish was a young resident of Poughkeepsie, New York, Fitz Hugh Ludlow. Born in 1836 the son of an Abolitionist minister, Ludlow read extensively as a boy and was profoundly influenced by De Quincey's *Confessions of an Opium Eater*, and Taylor's *Land of the Saracens*. Ludlow was particularly impressed by De Quincey's book and he deliberately patterned his own book, *The Hasheesh Eater: Being Passages from the Life of a Pythagorean*, which he anonymously published in 1857, on De Quincey. "I am deeply aware that, if the succeeding pages are read at all," he tells his readers, "it will be by those who have already learned to love De Quincey."[4]

Ludlow was only sixteen years old when he first came under the spell of cannabis. Intrigued by the smells of medicines, he used to loiter about the apothecary shop of a pharmacist friend, a man named Anderson. The smells in the shop, he says, were "an aromatic invitation to scientific musing." Ludlow did more than muse, however. Not content merely to inhale the odors of the various concoctions that stood on the shelves, "with a disregard to my own safety, I made upon myself the

<hr>

[3]Taylor, *Land of Saracens*, p. 161.
[4]F. H. Ludlow, *The Hasheesh Eater: Being Passages from the Life of a Pythagorean*. (New York: Harper & Bros., 1957).

trial of the effects of every strange drug and chemical which the laboratory could produce." Among those he sampled were chloroform, ether, and opium.

"In all these experiences," he tells his readers, "research and not indulgence was my object, so that I never became the victim of any habit in the prosecution of my headlong investigations. When the circuit of all the accessible tests was completed, I ceased experimenting. . . ."[5]

One day, some time after his sampling of these medicinal wares, his pharmacist friend directed him to a new drug, *Cannabis indica* by name, which the pharmacist described as "a preparation of the East Indian hemp, a powerful agent in cases of lockjaw," manufactured by the Tilden Company.

Without giving it a second thought, Ludlow prepared to sample some of this new drug when the pharmacist suddenly shouted, "Hold on, do you want to kill yourself? That stuff is deadly poison." Shaken by this warning, Ludlow returned the bottle to its place on the shelf.

But Ludlow was not one to be deterred for long. An examination of the pharmacist's dispensatory informs him that large doses of the drug are indeed lethal, but moderate doses are rarely so. This extract, he concludes, is the hashish mentioned by Bayard Taylor whose experience with it "had moved me powerfully to curiosity and admiration."

So as not to alarm his friend, Ludlow surreptitiously removed some of the drug when the pharmacist was out of sight. The dose produced no effect, however, and several days later he took some more, but again experienced no effects. Finally, several days later still, he took a much larger dose and when nothing happened immediately thereafter, he concluded that he was "unsusceptible of the hasheesh influence."

Disappointed, he went to visit a friend. About three hours later, he suddenly began to experience unusual sensations. His first reaction was "one of uncontrollable terror—a sense of getting something I had not bargained for."

Following this unpleasant response, Ludlow resolved never to take cannabis again: "The glimpse which I had gained in that single night of revelation of hitherto unconcerned modes of uncharted fields of spiritual being," he says, "seemed enough to store the treasure-house of grand memories for a lifetime."

But his resolve was fainthearted. A little more than a week later, he was back at Anderson's. "Censure me not harshly, ye who have never known what fascination there is in the ecstasy of beauty," he entreats his readers. "There are baser attractions than those which invited me."[6]

[5] *Ibid.*, p. 17.
[6] *Ibid.*, p. 46.

Among the effects he now experiences are depersonalization, hallucinations, altered time perception, anxiety, and panic. Particularly interesting to him is the sensation of synesthesia, "the interchanging of the senses... the hashish eater knows what it is... to smell colors, to see sounds, and, much more frequently, to see feelings." The uncontrollable laughter, the rapid flow of ideas, the feeling of unquenchable thirst, the "awakening of perception which magnifies the smallest sensation till it occupies immense boundaries"—all are duly noted and recorded.[7]

Ludlow continued to take cannabis on a regular basis until he became psychologically dependent on it. Much of his youth, he says, was spent in a state of perpetual cannabis intoxication. Although he attempted to give up his habit, he found that abstinence caused him considerable suffering. Unable to give it up "cold turkey," he tried reducing the amount he took gradually, but this did not help. He finally did kick the habit with the help of a physician, but not without difficulty.

Ludlow states that his motivation for writing his book was De Quincey's description of the sufferings that writer had experienced with opium and the fact that no such warning was available for cannabis. To alert others of the dangers of habitually using cannabis, it was necessary to do for cannabis what De Quincey had done for opium.

Ludlow was not solely an altruist, however. In September 1856, *Putnam's Magazine* carried an article entitled "The Apocalypse of Hasheesh," which bore more than a superficial resemblance to parts of Ludlow's book. Ludlow acknowledged his familiarity with this anonymous article and says he came across it in a bookstore in Niagara Falls. The article contained "such startling analogies to... [my] own past experience that cold drops started upon... [my] forehead." Unbeknownst to one another, both "had walked the valley of awful shadows side by side." The fact is, Ludlow wrote the anonymous magazine article "to give credence to his own exaggerated report and to bolster sales of his soon-to-be published work..."[8] and actually plagiarized portions of Taylor's book in doing so!

Ludlow graduated from Union College in 1856, one year before he published *The Hasheesh Eater*, and he settled for a short time in Watertown, New York, to teach high school. He stayed at this job for only a short time and then resigned to study law. But the legal profession also held little interest for him and he abandoned that as well, seeking instead to earn his living as a drama critic, artist, and music

[7] *Ibid.*, p. 72–3.

[8] L. Grinspoon, *Marihuana Reconsidered* (Cambridge, Mass.: Harvard University Press, 1971), p. 96.

writer. He did rather well as a writer and became friends with some of the well-known writers of his time, among them the man whose books had so influenced his early years, Bayard Taylor.

In 1863, he moved to California for health reasons, but by this time he was a sick man. In 1870, he left the United States for Switzerland, hoping that he might yet regain his health in a sanatorium in that country. It was too late. He died that same year, one day after his thirty-fourth birthday. Although his death was attributed by many to his indulgence in hashish, the actual cause was tuberculosis.

Ludlow's *The Hasheesh Eater* still remains the best known book on hashish by an American, and contains many valuable insights into the peculiar effects of the drug. Besides pointing out the pharmacological relationship between dose and response, Ludlow also called attention to the importance of the conditions under which the drug might be taken, and the particular feelings of the user as bearing significantly on his reaction to the drug: "At two different times, when body and mind are apparently in precisely analogous states, when all circumstances, exterior and interior, do not differ tangibly in the smallest respect, the same dose of the same preparations of hasheesh will frequently produce diametrically opposite effects," he told his readers.[9] Even more so in individuals of differing personalities. "Upon persons of the highest nervous and sanguine temperaments hasheesh has the strongest effect; on those of the bilious occasionally almost as powerful a one; while lymphatic constitutions are scarcely influenced at all except in some physical manner, such as vertigo, nausea, coma, or muscular rigidity."[10]

Ludlow also called attention to a phenomenon known as "reverse tolerance." The characteristics of this condition is that the more one uses a drug such as hashish, the more sensitive one becomes, so that each time it is taken, less and less is needed to obtain the sought-after effect. "Unlike all other stimuli with which I am acquainted," Ludlow notes, "hasheesh, instead of recuiring to be increased in quantity as existence on it proceeds, demands rather a diminution, seeming to leave at the return of the natural state . . . an unconsumed capital of exaltation for the next indulgence to set up business upon."[11] (This phenomenon has been reported by many cannabis users and has intrigued scientists due to its pharmacological uniqueness. However, when subjected to rigid test conditions, the phenomenon disappears.)

Although *The Hasheesh Eater* is now recognized as a minor classic, and has earned the author the honor of having the Fitz Hugh Ludlow

[9]*Ibid.*, p. 66.
[10]*Ibid.*, p. 122–3.
[11]*Ibid.*, p. 104.

Library in San Francisco named after him, during his own era his book was generally unknown to the American reading public. A critic who reviewed it in 1857 for *Harper's Magazine* was less than enthusiastic. Although he did express his dismay at the effects of cannabis as described by Ludlow, nevertheless, he took considerable comfort in declaring that Americans were fortunately "in no danger of becoming a nation of hasheesh eaters."[12]

HASHISH COMES TO AMERICA

In 1857, the same year that Ludlow's book appeared on the bookseller's shelves, a physician named John Bell noted in the *Boston Medical and Surgical Journal* that "the various periodicals of this country have abounded, during the last few years, with accounts of hashisch; every experimenter giving the history of the effect it has had upon himself."[13]

Unfortunately, Bell did not mention any of the periodicals he had come across so there is no way of knowing what he meant by "abounded." It seems, however, that, at least in Bell's mind, a growing number of Americans were beginning to experiment with hashish.

Another comment from Bell's article is also worth noting. According to the learned doctor, specimens of hashish that he had obtained from Damascus contained about 25 percent opium! It is likely, therefore, that many of the effects attributed to hashish by American writers like Taylor and Ludlow, or French writers like Baudelaire, were in large part due to opium and not hashish.

One of the Americans Bell may have had in mind when he alluded to the growing use of hashish in the United States was a medical quack from Philadelphia, Frederick Hollick. Hollick claimed that his research had taught him that the central ingredient in all known aphrodisiacs and exhilarants was none other than hashish. Accordingly, readers of his *Marriage Guide* (1850) were advised to use hashish as a sexual stimulant if their marriages were in trouble.

Hollick was not only an author and lecturer, he also manufactured aphrodisiacs as a sideline. In one of his advertisements, he told potential customers:

> The true aphrodisiac, as I compound it, acts upon the brain and nervous system, not as a stimulant, but as a tonic and nutritive agent, thus sustaining its power and the power of the sexual organs also, which is entirely dependent upon the nervous power.

[12]Cited by L. J. Bragman, "Weed of Insanity," *Medical Journal and Record* 122 (1925): 418.
[13]J. Bell, "On the Haschish or Cannabis Indica," *Boston Medical and Surgical Journal* 56 (1857): 209–16.

> For convenience, I have it [the aphrodisiac] so put up, in a dry form, air and water tight, that it can be kept uninjured, for any length of time, in any climate, and under any circumstances. It can also be taken without the inconvenience of measuring, using liquids, or any other troublesome requirement, thus ensuring secrecy and facility of use, let a man be situated however he may. A gentleman can keep it in his vest pocket without any fear of detection from smell, or appearance. It will go anywhere by post, with perfect safety, and in such a form that no one through whose hands it passes would ever suspect its nature, or that it is anything peculiar![14]

Would-be purchasers were assured that they could not obtain this secret preparation from any retail dealer. Only by writing to Hollick personally could they hope to receive this potent elixir of sexual nirvana. "I do this," Hollick explained, "to avoid trouble, and also to prevent counterfeiting which would be sure to be practiced if it were generally sold through agents."

By the 1860s, so much hashish was being used in America that an English writer, Mordecai Cubitt Cooke, told his readers:

> Young America is beginning to use the "bang" so popular among the Hindoos, though in a rather different manner, for young Johnathan must in some sort be an original. It is not a "drink," but a mixture of bruised hemp tops and the powder of the betel, rolled up like a quid of tobacco. It turns the lips and gums of a deep red, and if indulged in largely, produces violent intoxication. Lager beer and schnaps will give way for "bang" and red lips, instead of red noses [Cooke predicted, will] become the style.[15]

In 1869, the periodical *Scientific American* carried a report to the effect that hashish, "the Cannabis indica of the U.S. Pharmacopoeia, the resinous product of hemp, grown in the East Indies and other parts of Asia, is used in those countries to a large extent for its intoxicating properties, and is doubtless used in this country for the same purpose to a limited extent."[16]

In that same year, Louisa May Alcott, author of *Little Women*, published a short story entitled "Perilous Play," in which she describes the effects of marihuana. The story begins ominously with Bell Daventry's plea: "If someone does not propose a new and interesting amusement, I shall die of ennui!" Rising to the challenge is a Dr. Meredith, who produces a box of "bonbons." "Eat six of these despised bonbons, and you will be amused in a new, delicious and wonderful manner," he promises. As the story progresses, the main characters lose their self-control

---

[14]Quoted in A. Hechtlinger, *The Great Patent Medicine Era* (New York: Grosset & Dunlop, 1970), pp. 164–5.

[15]M. C. Cooke, *The Seven Sisters of Sleep* (London, 1860), cited in T. Kupferberg, ed., *Birth Book* 1, no. 3 (1960): 50.

[16]*Scientific American* 21 (1869): 183.

as a result of taking the "bonbons." Rose, for example, exclaims after kissing Mark, "Oh what am I doing? I am mad, for I, too, have taken hashish."[17]

In 1874, hashish was once again the subject of a poem. This time the poet was Thomas Bailey Aldrich. In "Hascheesh," a short poem which appeared in *Cloth of Gold and Other Poems*, Bailey first describes the beautiful visions he dreamt while under the influence of the drug. In the midst of all this beauty, he suddenly is seized with a sense of terror. Ugly creatures begin appearing from a black hole and start crawling toward him. "Away, vile drug! I will avoid thy spell," he cries, "Honey of Paradise, black dew of Hell!"[18]

Aldrich's attitude toward hashish in this poem probably epitomized the attitude of many Americans to pleasure in general—it had to be paid for, and often the price was not worth the few moments of delight.

Critical though they might be about those who flaunted the mores of the times, the American reading public still loved to read about the sinners in its midst and the national tabloids satisfied their appetities. "Secret Dissipation of New York Belles: Interior of a Hasheesh Hell on Fifth Avenue" ran the caption to an *Illustrated Police News* (December 2, 1876) drawing showing five young women, elegantly dressed, and languishing on divans in a stuporous condition.[19]

In 1883, *Harper's New Monthly Magazine* ran a short article on the new hashish pastime entitled "A Hashish House in New York, The Curious Adventures of an Individual Who Indulged in a Few Pipefuls of the Narcotic Hemp."[20] Although anonymous, the author is generally believed to be H. H. Kane, a prominent American physician of the era who published several books on what he regarded as the growing drug menace in the United States.

The article begins with a conversation in which a friend tells the writer that "there is a large community of hashish smokers in this city [New York] who are daily forced to indulge their morbid appetites, and I can take you to a house up-town where hemp is used in every conceivable form, and where the lights, sounds, odors, and surroundings are all arranged so as to intensify and enhance the effects of this wonderful narcotic."

[17]L. M. Alcott, "Perilous Play," 1869, reprinted in A. C. Kimmens (ed.) *Tales of Hashish* (New York: Wm. Morrow, 1977), p. 228.

[18]T. B. Aldrich, *The Poems of Thomas Bailey Aldrich* (New York: Houghton, Mifflin & Co., 1882), p. 36.

[19]This drawing was reprinted in the *New York Times Magazine*, Dec. 13, 1970, p. 26.

[20]"A Hashish House in New York, The Curious Adventures of an Individual Who Indulged in a Few Pipefuls of the Narcotic Hemp," *Harper's New Monthly Magazine* 67 (1883): 944–9.

The following evening the two men visit this hashish house, whose address is given as near Forty-second Street and Broadway. The clients "are about evenly divided between Americans and foreigners . . . all the visitors, both male and female, are of the better classes and absolute secrecy is the rule. The house has been opened about two years, I believe, and the number of regular habitués is daily on the increase."

According to the author, there were about six hundred of these "habitués" in New York City alone. Other cities boasting comparable hashish dens were Boston, Philadelphia, Chicago, and especially New Orleans. In Baltimore, there was no need for secrecy since hashish devotees could purchase the drug in the form of candy in the city's business district.[21]

In Philadelphia, during the American Centennial Exposition of 1876, some pharmacists carried ten pounds or more of hashish on stock in case Americans or foreigners had a yen for the drug during the festivities.[22]

Why there should have been any secrecy about hashish at all is puzzling, since there certainly were no laws against the drug at this time.

As these magazine and newspaper articles and books on the drug circulated around the country, more and more Americans began experimenting with commercial cannabis preparations which were easily obtained from local pharmacies. The extent of these personal experiences is more than evident from the many reports of "cannabis poisonings" that began to fill the nation's medical journals and the "provings" that filled the homeopathic medical journals such as *American Provers' Union*, *American Journal of Homeopathy*, and the *American Homeopathic Review*. In fact, the sheer bulk of these reports was enough to persuade many doctors that cannabis was a dangerous drug.

CANNABIS IN AMERICAN MEDICINE

Even before O'Shaughnessy published his pioneering studies of cannabis, the drug was familiar to European and American practitioners of homeopathy, a branch of medicine based on the principle that like cures like. In 1839, the homeopathy journal *American Provers' Union*

---

[21]G. W. Grover, *Shadows Lifted or Sunshine Restored in the Horizon of Human Lives: A Treatise on the Morphine, Opium, Cocaine, Chloral and Hashish Habit* (cited in T. Kupferberg, *Birth Book 1*, no. 3 (1960): 48.

[22]R. H. True and G. F. Klugh, "American Grown Cannabis Indica," *Proceedings of the American Pharmaceutical Association* 67 (1883): 944–9.

published the first of many reports on the effects of cannabis.[23] In 1842, the *New Homeopathic Pharmacopoeia and Posology or the Preparation of Homeopathic Medicines* was published from an earlier German text. "To make the homeopathic preparation of hemp," the author explained, "we take the flowering tops of male and female plants and express the juice, and make the tincture with equal parts of alcohol; others advise only to use the flowering tops of the female plants, because these best exhale, during their flowering, a strong and intoxicating odour, whilst the male plants are completely inodorous."[24]

Cannabis was first mentioned as a medicinal agent in a "formal" American medical text in 1843.[25] In 1846, Dr. Amariah Brigham, the editor of the *American Journal of Insanity*, brought the drug to the notice of American psychiatrists with a review of Moreau's book and experiments. Brigham was very excited about the prospect of using cannabis to treat insanity (homeopathy?), and he sent to Calcutta for some of the drug which he subsequently administered to several patients at the Lunatic Asylum in Utica, New York. "From our limited experience," he concluded, "we regard it as a very energetic remedy, and well worthy of further trial with the insane, and thank M. Moreau for having called attention to its use."[26]

By 1854, the U.S. Dispensatory began to list cannabis among the nation's medicinals:

> *Medical Properties.* Extract of hemp is a powerful narcotic, causing exhilaration, intoxication, delirious hallucinations, and, in its subsequent action, drowsiness and stupor, with little effect upon the circulation. It is asserted also to act as a decided aphrodisiac, to increase the appetite, and occasionally to induce the cataleptic state. In morbid states of the system, it has been found to produce sleep, to allay spasm, to compose nervous inquietude, and to relieve pain. In these respects it resembles opium in its operation; but it differs from that narcotic in not diminishing the appetite, checking the secretions, or constipating the bowels. It is much less certain in its effects; but may sometimes be preferably employed, when opium is contraindicated by its nauseating or constipating effects, or its disposition to produce headache, and to check the bronchial secretion. The complaints to which it has been specially recommended are neuralgia, gout, tetanus, hydrophobia, epidemic cholera, convulsions, chorea, hysteria, mental depression, insanity, and uterine hemorrhage. Dr. Alexander Christison, of Edinburgh, has found it to

---

[23]T. F. Allen, ed., *The Encyclopedia of Pure Materia Medica* (New York: Boericke and Tafel, 1875), p. 448.

[24]G. H. G. Jahr, *New Homeopathic Pharmacopoeia and Posology or the Preparation of Homeopathic Medicines* (Philadelphia: J. Dobson, 1842), p. 137.

[25]J. Pereira, *The Elements of Materia Medica and Therapeutics* (Philadelphia: Lea and Blanchard, 1843).

[26]A. Brigham, "Review of Moreau de Tours, J: 'Du Hachisch et de l'Alienation Mentale,'" *American Journal of Insanity* 2 (1846): 275–81.

have the property of hastening and increasing the contractions of the uterus in delivery, and has employed it with advantage for this purpose. It acts very quickly, and without anesthetic effect. It appears, however, to exert this influence only in a certain proportion of cases. . . .[27]

However, in recommending cannabis, the Dispensatory cautioned physicians that "alarming effects" were possible if large doses were prescribed, owing to the variability in potency of commercially available preparations.

In 1859, Dr. John P. Gray, a future president of the American Psychiatric Association, described his clinical experiences with the drug and noted that there had been a widening interest in cannabis during the previous three to four years.[28]

In 1860, the Ohio Medical Society catalogued conditions in which cannabis had been successfully used. Among those mentioned were neuralgia, nervous rheumatism, mania, whooping cough, asthma, chronic bronchitis, muscular spasms, tetanus, epilepsy, infantile convulsions, palsy, uterine hemorrhage, dysmenorrhea, hysteria, withdrawal from alcohol, and loss of appetite—an imposing list of disorders drawn mainly from O'Shaughnessy's and other reports published in England. Little notice of the drug, however, seems to have filtered down to American doctors since cannabis was used only to a very limited extent during the Civil War, the most frequent applications being for the treatment of diarrhea and dysentery among soldiers.

After the war, when the number of "cannabis poisonings" began to attract notice, physicians found themselves in a quandry as to how to treat these drug overdosings. Many recommended forced vomitings followed by hot coffee, lemon juice, ammonia, strychnine, atropine, or nitrous oxide. Some physicians also recommended electric shock and artificial respiration.

But despite the frequency of such "poisonings," physicians frequently noted, "an overdose has never produced death in man or the lower animals. Not one authentic case is on record in which Cannabis or any of its preparations destroyed life. . . . Cannabis does not seem capable of causing death by chemical or physiological action."[29]

Nevertheless, American doctors were never very excited by cannabis for drug therapy. It had too many shortcomings. The potency of commercially available preparations differed considerably from pharmacist to pharmacist. Quite often a given dose of drug obtained from

[27]G. B. Wood and F. Bache, *The Dispensatory of the United States* (Philadelphia: Lippincott, Brambo & Co., 1854), p. 339.

[28]J. P. Gray, "On the Use of Cannabis Indica in the Treatment of Insanity." *American Journal of Insanity* 16 (1860): 80–9.

[29]V. Robinson, "An Essay on Hasheesh," *Medical Review of Reviews* 18 (1912): 159–69.

one supplier would have no noticeable effects whereas the same amount obtained from another supplier would be far above the amount which produced unpleasant effects.

Doctors were also at a loss to deal with the perplexing variability in the response of different patients to the same amount of drug. Some patients reported that they felt much better after taking the drug; others complained of delirium and hallucinations.

There were other drawbacks to contend with. Cannabis was not soluble in water and consequently it could not be given by injection. Compared with a fast-acting pain killer such as morphine, which was water soluble and could therefore be given by syringe, the action of cannabis was extremely slow and a doctor might have to remain with his patient for more than an hour after he swallowed the drug to make sure that not only was it having a desired effect, but also that the dosage had not been too high.

Faced with such uncertainty of drug action, a lack of pure compounds, difficulties in administering the drug except by mouth, and a long delay before the drug took effect, doctors understandably retained little interest in the possible therapeutic benefits of cannabis preparations.

Nevertheless, the pharmaceutical industry continued trying to turn cannabis into a viable medicinal agent. By 1896, several new cannabis derivatives were developed, among them cannabin, cannabindon, cannabine, and cannabinon. Cannabis was also included along with other drugs in various preparations such as "Chlorodyne" (a stomach remedy manufactured by Squibb Co. which mainly contained morphine), Brown Sequard's Antineuralgic Pills, and Corn Cololdion.[30] Most corn remedies, in fact, contained cannabis as a main ingredient, but it was only included as a coloring agent.

At the turn of the century the U.S. government was particularly interested in the therapeutic potential of marihuana and planted cannabis as well as opium and henbane along the banks of the Potomac near Washington. "The plants selected for culture in this government garden," the Boston Sunday Globe (Jan. 10, 1904) told its readers, "are those that yield the deadliest of known poisons.... The most striking feature of the poison garden... is a patch of Indian hemp, from which the

---

[30]M. Sassman, "Cannabis Indica in Pharmaceuticals," Journal of the Medical Society of New Jersey 35 (1938): 51–2. At least thirty different pharmaceutical preparations contained cannabis. Among the companies manufacturing these over-the-counter remedies were Parke Davis (Casadein, Colic Mixture, Veterinary, Utroval), Eli Lilly (Dr. Brown Sedative Tablets, Syrup Tolu Compound, Syrup Lobelia), and Squibb (Corn Collodium). Cannabis was finally removed from the U.S. Pharmacopoeia and National Formulary in 1941.

famous drug called 'hasheesh' is obtained." The *Globe* then went on to explain: "Most people have read of that remarkable secret society in the Orient, organized for wholesale and systematic murder whose members called themselves Hashhashin—hence our word 'assassin'—and stimulated themselves for their deeds of atrocity by doses of this drug."

The experiment was short-lived, however. In the wake of controversy over the "doping" of Americans that prompted the Food and Drug Act of 1906, the federally sponsored project was terminated and the "dope" fields were eradicated, to be occupied years later by the Pentagon.[31]

Some eminent American psychologists were also very interested in marihuana's effects and tried it on several occasions. James McKeen Cattel (1860–1944) during his student days at The Johns Hopkins University in Baltimore (1882–1883) took hashish on several occasions. However, years later, Cattel, who eventually became president of the American Psychological Association, regretted having done so. "On reaching years of somewhat greater discretion I was not altogether proud of my enterprise," he confessed in his person journal.[32]

Another prominent psychologist who experimented with cannabis around the turn of the century was Edmund Burke Delabarre (1863–1945), Director of the psychology laboratory at Brown University in Rhode Island. Delabarre began experimenting with cannabis in 1893 and continued studying the effects on himself until 1931. In 1898, Delabarre described some of his early work at the annual meeting of the American Psychological Association in New York, and, later that year, he spoke before the Art Club in Providence on his hashish experiments. Apparently, these reports were listened to with a great deal of interest, but for some unknown reason, most psychologists were not motivated enough to conduct their own studies with the drug.

---

[31]M. A. Aldrich, "Marijuana," *The Dope Chronicles,* ed. G. Silver (New York: Harper and Row, 1979), p. 255.
[32]Quoted in J. A. Popplestone and M. W. McPherson, "A Historical Note on Cannabis," *Catalogue of Selected Documents on Psychology* 4 (1974): 7.

IV

A NATION OF DRUG TAKERS

America's Drug Users

We here offer a perfectly safe and reliable cure to those addicted to the habit of using opium or morphine in any manner whatever.

This advertisement appeared in the 1905 Sears, Roebuck & Company catalogue. The price per bottle for this cure: sixty-nine cents.

At the turn of the century when this notice first appeared, about one million Americans were addicted to drugs such as opium and morphine. Most Americans have an image of the drug addict as a decadent denizen of a dirty inner-city metropolis. Not so during America's adolescent years. In the early 1900s, when most Americans still lived in the country, the typical addict lived in a small town or on an isolated farm, he attended church regularly on Sunday, and would have been astounded if anyone intimated that because of his addiction he was a degenerate, a deviate, or a criminal.

Opium, in fact, had been part of the American home-remedy drug cabinet almost from the time of the first settlements in America. Morphine, the active ingredient in opium, had been isolated in 1803. Inexpensive, potent, and reliable, morphine became a staple of the family drug arsenal as early as the 1830s. The invention of the hypodermic syringe in 1845 eventually led to such indiscriminate administration of this powerful pain killer during the Civil War that withdrawal came to be known across the nation as the "army disease."

After the war, the ranks of the addicted were swelled as well-meaning but ill-informed physicians, many of them little more than quacks, dispensed morphine at the sound of the faintest moan. To the doctor, morphine was a panacea that relieved pain and earned him a patient's gratitude and respect. Other sufferers, too isolated or poor to see a doctor, could treat themselves, as many did, with a variety of nostrums, usually laced with morphine, opium, or alcohol, which were available through the mails or from traveling medicine men.

The fact is that America is now, and has always been, a nation of pill poppers. At the same time, it is a nation that prides itself on the virtues of temperance and hard work. In advertising another of its elixirs, "White Star Secret Liquor Cure," for instance, Sears claimed that this potion "has saved many from that awful monster, Drink, and has protected thousands against a life of disease, poverty and degradation . . . a higher moral tone is upheld; in a word, it makes him a man among men."

Unlike opium, morphine, or alcohol, cannabis was a relatively obscure drug. The so-called hashish vice was still confined to the large cities and to a minority of writers, students, thrill seekers, and the bored upper classes. Had it not been for certain social and economic changes and an ambitious bureaucrat who saw the marihuana issue as a way to save his dying department and his job as czar of narcotics enforcement, most Americans probably would not have heard about marihuana or hashish until the 1960s.

Drugs and Minority Oppression

The story of how marihuana and hashish, drugs about which most Americans were totally ignorant and could not have cared less about at the time they were outlawed, begins in the latter half of the nineteenth century with the events that led to the unprecedented criminalization of the drug user in America.

In the latter part of the 1860s, thousands of Chinese immigrants poured into the American west to work on the railways that were beginning to tentacle across the country. By the end of the 1870s, the construction boom petered out and there were more men than jobs. The railway and mining companies, the large farm owners, and manufacturers took advantage of the situation and offered the lowest possible wages for whatever work they had available. Although white laborers were unwilling to accept the pittances being offered, the Chinese had no such scruples. They needed to survive and they took what they could find. White laborers reacted by blaming the Chinese for ruining the economy and taking jobs away from native Americans.

Most of the Chinese held menial jobs, but some saved enough to become shop owners and eventually became wealthy businessmen. Some became rich by opening brothels. With men outnumbering women by a ratio of almost twenty to one, these flesh stops did a thriving business. Still others became well-to-do by opening up opium houses where drug-induced stupor assuaged the loneliness and despair of these impoverished immigrants, strangers in a land thousands of miles away from homes and families.

Whether the Chinese immigrant had a taste for opium before he crossed the Pacific, or whether he developed the habit once he settled in America, the fact is that the opium den became the visible symbol of the Chinese presence on the West Coast and as such became the target of anti-Chinese sentiment. "Opium and the Chinese, to the mind of your average newspaper reader, are inseparable," wrote one newsman.[1]

The growing spectre of the opium den in the Chinatowns of many of the nation's cities kindled the resentment of many Americans toward what they regarded as a backward race of degenerates. An editorial in the February 13, 1882, edition of the *Tombstone Epitaph* did not mince its bigotry:

> The Chinese are the least desired immigrants who have ever sought the United States.... the almond-eyed Mongolian with his pigtail, his heathenism, his filthy habits, his thrift, and careful accumulation of savings to be sent back to the flowery kingdom. The most we can do is to insist that he is a heathen, a devourer of soup made from the flagrant juice of the rat, filthy, disagreeable, and undesirable generally, an incumbance that we have determined shall not increase in this part of the world.[2]

In 1875, San Francisco passed the first city ordinance against the smoking or possession of opium in America. A year later, Virginia City, Nevada, enacted a similar law. Ostensibly, the reason for these laws was the adoption of opium smoking by young white boys and girls. Oregon's legislators gave their own reason for enacting its state law against opium: "Smoking opium is not our vice, and therefore, it may be that this legislation proceeds more from a desire to vex and annoy the 'Heathen Chinese' in this respect than to protect the people from the evil habit."[3]

When they passed these laws against opium, city and state lawmakers were merely adding one more restriction to those already aimed at ignobling the Chinese such as the queue ordinance of 1870, which required all prisoners in San Francisco's county jails to have their heads shaved.

It was not so much the seduction of children by opium, although this was a concern if not a reality, which was on the mind of many Americans when the country became opium conscious. Rather, it was the growing realization that middle-class America was in danger of decadence through overindulgence in drugs. Besides opium and morphine,

[1]H. W. Morgan, *Yesterday's Addicts* (Norman: University of Oklahoma Press, 1974), p. 32.
[2]Quoted in S. M. Lyman, "Strangers in the Cities: The Chinese on the Urban Frontiers," in *Ethnic Conflict in California History*, ed. C. Wollenberg, (Berkeley: University of California Press, 1970), p. 36.
[3]Quoted in R. J. Bonnie and C. H. Whitebread, *The Marihuana Conviction* (Charlottesville: University of Virginia Press, 1974), p. 14.

chloral hydrate was reputedly enslaving Americans. College students were allegedly being corrupted by ether and chloroform fumes. Cocaine was reported to be inciting southern blacks to mayhem. Not for want of reason had America been christened "a nation of drug takers."[4]

With the increasing publicity being given to the looming menace of drug abuse, state governments were pressured to do something, especially where the opium problem was concerned. Unless steps were taken to restrict opiates, critics warned that "soon, the residents of our American cities will all be opium slaves."[5]

THE PURE FOOD AND DRUG ACT

To some extent, the antiopium laws adopted by various states were not meant solely to harass the Chinese, but were instead a reaction to what many saw as a real drug menace in America. The Chinese were merely the scapegoats.

Most of the laws promulgated by individual states attempted to curtail availability of drugs by requiring prescriptions for any opiates purchased. Pharmacists were obliged to retain these records for at least a year in some states. However, the Proprietory Association of America, which manufactured the opiate-laden over-the-counter drugs, was able to obtain a number of exemptions to various state laws whereby limited amounts of narcotics could still be sold in patent medicines without need for a prescription. These patent medicines were readily available and were liberally used for any and all illnesses, imagined or real, from headaches to alcoholism.

The more the public relied on these nostrums, the more dependent on their contents they became. While various states attempted to control the dispensing of narcotics by physicians through the presciption process, the restraints on the patent-drug industry were minimal. Restrictions on the medical profession were similarly lax and doctors could evade them in different ways.

"Dope doctors" who had no desire to comply with the law or who resented the paperwork involved in recording their drug dispensations, merely ordered drugs from companies in other states that had no such restrictions. These drugs could then be sold directly to patients without disobeying the law. Other doctors, who resented the competition of the patent-medicine manufacturers and the exclusion of proprietory

---

[4]Morgan. *Yesterday's Addicts*, p. 8.
[5]V. G. Eaton, "How the Opium Habit Is Acquired," *Popular Science Monthly* 33 (1888): 663–7.

medicines from state control, began to consider legal means to regulate the distribution of drugs at the national level.

The Constitution, however, made no provision for the regulation of drugs by the federal government. The only powers Congress might use involved the authority to regulate interstate commerce and impose taxes. After a long and involved examination of the problem, it was decided that the mandate over interstate traffic was authority enough to oversee the patent-medicine business.

On the premise that Americans were addicting themselves simply because they were unaware of the contents of the nostrums they were taking, the Pure Food and Drug Act of 1906 required that all patent medicines shipped across state lines had to list their ingredients if they contained more than a specified amount of opium, morphine, heroin, cocaine, alcohol, chloral hydrate, or cannabis. Three years later, Congress would adopt a second major drug law. This time, however, the impetus for such a law would come from international considerations.

FEDERAL ANTIOPIUM LAWS

In 1882, anti-Chinese feeling had risen to such a point that Congress passed the Chinese Exclusion Act which prohibited Chinese laborers from entering the United States for the next ten years. China reacted to this insult to its citizens by adopting an embargo against American manufactures. Faced with the loss of the lucrative Chinese market, and aware of China's efforts to eradicate its own domestic opium problem, President Theodore Roosevelt convened an international conference in 1909 in Shanghai to help China eradicate the problem of opium addiction among its inhabitants. By trying to impress China with its goodwill and concern about her drug crisis, the United States hoped to change China's attitude toward American goods.

It was with some degree of embarrassment, however, that the United States delegates to the Shanghai convention realized that their own country had no federal laws prohibiting the smoking of opium. To avoid being accused of hypocrisy, Congress quickly enacted such a law. Henceforth, importation of opium into the United States except at specific entry points, and then only with the provision that it was to be used exclusively for medical purposes, was prohibited. It was now a crime for anyone to buy or sell opium in the United States. By making the opium user a criminal, Congress attempted to suppress opium traffic in America.

Coming as it did while the Shanghai conference was in session, the delegates were greatly impressed with America's earnestness to deal with the problem. However, the various representatives attending the conference had not been empowered by their governments to write or adopt any international treaty for the control of world traffic in opium, so all they could do was congratulate the Americans and promise to make recommendations to their respective governments concerning such a global measure.

But the United States had not achieved its primary objective of gaining access to the Chinese markets, and so in 1911 the United States urged a second international meeting, this one to be held at The Hague. The British were cool to the proposal since India, its territorial province, was still supplying enormous quantities of opium to the Chinese market. Any restrictions on the opium trade would cut off this lucrative trade. Persia and Turkey were less than enthusiastic for the same reason.

Undeterred, the Americans pressed on. Said Hamilton Wright, the American delegate: "Our move [the Shanghai conference] to help China in her opium reform gave us more prestige in China than any of our recent friendly acts toward her. If we continue and press steadily for the [Hague] Conference, China will recognize that we are sincere on her behalf, and the whole business may be used as oil to smooth the troubled water of our aggressive commercial policy there."[6]

To gain this foothold in China, Wright pressured Congress to adopt wide-sweeping antinarcotics laws. His appeal was aimed at American prejudices. Opium smoking in America, Wright declared, had been introduced by the Chinese and "one of the most unfortunate phases of the habit... was the large number of women who have become involved and were living as common-law wives and cohabiting with Chinese in the Chinatowns of our various cities."[7]

Wright also incited latent racial fears. "It has been authoritatively stated," he said, "that cocaine is often the direct incentive to the crime of rape by the Negros of the South and other sections of the country."[8]

As initially proposed, the law required retail pharmacists to purchase tax stamps for narcotics, including cannabis, and demanded that they keep meticulous records of purchases of such drugs, regardless of amount.

The National Wholesale Druggist Association (NDWA) vehemently objected to such measures since the use of stamps and detailed record keeping would greatly increase the cost of doing business. The NDWA also objected to the inclusion of cannabis on the proscribed list. Dr.

[6]Quoted in D. F. Musto, The American Disease (New Haven: Yale University Press, 1973), p. 39.
[7]Quoted in ibid., p. 43.
[8]Ibid., pp. 43–4.

Charles West, their spokesman, said that there was no reason to consider cannabis in the same class as opium, morphine, and cocaine, since it was not habit forming. Dr. William Muir, spokesman for the New York Pharmaceutical Association, pointed out that cannabis was a major ingredient in corn cures. Having to keep detailed records of every sale of corn cures was ridiculous.

Eventually, the retail interests won out and the proposed legislation was defeated. Wright accurately foresaw the course of events at The Hague conference now that the United States was in the position of advocating international control of narcotics without having its own domestic laws against such drugs. Other nations that had such laws accused the United States of hypocrisy, since without such domestic restrictions the United States would not have to abide by any international agreements to ban narcotics. Wright assured his fellow delegates that adoption of such legislation was only a matter of time, but he was not persuasive enough and the conference disbanded without agreement.

THE HARRISON ACT

Disappointed but not yet beaten, Wright persuaded Congressman Francis Burton Harrison to introduce an amended antinarcotics bill in the House. The newly drafted legislation considerably simplified the record-keeping process, which pleased the pharmacists. However, the law did require pharmacists dispensing narcotics to register with the Bureau of Internal Revenue and pay for a tax stamp. By framing the law as a revenue measure, Congress felt that it could constitutionally oversee a law whose real intention was to regulate possession of opiates. When Congress adopted its antimarihuana law, this tax stamp pretext was again resorted to so that the federal government could constitutionally regulate possession and use of that drug as well.

The tax stamp measure also enabled federal officers to keep track of all legal dispensations of narcotics and placed enforcement of the law under the Internal Revenue Branch of the Treasury Department. Private individuals were not allowed to purchase these tax stamps, and therefore they were unable to obtain narcotics lawfully on their own. Possession of such drugs by a nonmedical individual was henceforth permitted only if prescribed by a physician or dentist. Physicians, however, were permitted to dispense narcotics directly to their patients while attending them, without having to record such actions.

Known as the Harrison Act, the statute was eventually adopted and became law in December 1914. Although it evolved into America's foremost drug-abuse law, the intention of the Harrison Act at the time of its conception and passage was really never directed toward the eradication of narcotic drugs but was merely a save-face piece of legislation, a law passed to honor American pledges given at The Hague convention that the United States would take steps to curtail criminal control of drug traffic. It was never meant to stand in the way of any addict who wanted to continue using drugs. It was merely to be a record-keeping bill, a piece of legislation that would cause a minimum of bother to all concerned.

The legislators did not intend to make addiction illegal. Addicts could obtain all the drugs they wanted, provided they got them through registered suppliers. The Narcotics Division of the Internal Revenue Bureau was created not as a law enforcement body, but as a bookkeeping department to supervise collection of tax stamp monies.

But Congress got more than it bargained for. The bureaucrats who moved into the department began to feel the need to justify their existence beyond that of mere bookeepers and they began to look for ways to expand and prove their worth. One way of becoming important was to take a more active part in overseeing the Harrison Act. But to do so, the terms of the act had to be broadened. To expand, there had to be an issue, one that Congress could understand and appreciate and at the same time see the need to bolster the Narcotics Division.

The plan began with a media campaign aimed at the alleged evils of narcotics. The idea was to stir up the public, make it appear that the country was on the verge of a drug-induced moral collapse. The themes were calculated to arouse fear and apprehension: children were being victimized; narcotics were lethal and enslaving; drug users were criminals. The campaign was such an overwhelming success in spreading panic that the bureau resorted to the same ploy years later when it sought to outlaw marihuana.

At the same time as it began waging its media campaign, the Bureau of Narcotics also prepared a second front aimed at increasing the scope of the Harrison Act through judicial reinterpretation of its terms. While the courts held that federal authorities had no right to arrest physicians for prescribing narcotics to known addicts in *U.S. vs. Jim Fuey Moy* (1916), it also ruled that physicians were not immune to paying the tax on narcotics in *U.S. vs. Doremus* (1919). This meant that doctors had to keep records of their dispensations. In a second ruling rendered the same day, the court also held in *U.S. vs. Webb et al.* that it was unlawful for a doctor to give opiates to narcotic addicts merely to keep them from experiencing withdrawal. Only in cases of senility or intractable pain could an addict legally receive narcotics.

These two decisions were to haunt the medical profession. Henceforth, many reputable physicians were closely watched by overly zeal-ous Treasury agents. Harassment was inevitable; humiliation was com-monplace. On the slightest suspicion, doctors were hauled into court to answer charges concerning their medical practices.

The medical profession also began to feel that the courts were inter-fering with the prerogatives of the doctor to treat his patient in a manner best suited to that patient's welfare. A new fear also began to emerge: the country appeared to be moving toward state-controlled medicine and possibly compulsory health insurance.

Once bitten, the American Medical Association was twice shy. Years later, when Congress debated outlawing marihuana, Dr. William Woodward, representing the AMA, was one of its most vigorous oppo-nents.

By making narcotics illegal, the price skyrocketed and addicts were forced to commit petty crimes to pay for their habit. Whereas they had previously been able to obtain narcotics from pharmacists and doctors, these outlets were no longer available. To meet their needs, addicts turned to the underworld and banded together, forming a drug subcul-ture in various sections of the nation's large cities.

Branded a criminal, faced with soaring costs for drugs, the addict began to live up to the bureau's labeling of him as a degenerate and a parasite. The more the public read of crimes allegedly committed by addicts, the more they were willing to believe that mind-altering drugs of any sort transformed normally law-abiding citizens into criminals.

For its part, the Bureau of Narcotics's campaign to expand its pre-rogatives and jurisdiction was a huge success. Each year the bureau grew in prestige and manpower. The mark of its achievement is most clearly seen in its budgetary allotment, which skyrocketed from a mere $292,000 in 1915 to $1,708,528 in 1932, an increase of over 400 percent.

PROHIBITION

Shortly after the adoption of the Harrison Act, the United States also passed the Eighteenth Amendment, outlawing the sale, manufac-ture, and transportation of alcohol across state lines. (Consumption, on the other hand, was still legal.)

Although following in the footsteps of the antinarcotics legislation, the crusade against demon rum had been going on long before there was any interest or concern over narcotics addiction. But coming in the af-termath of the Harrison Act, Prohibition became part and parcel of the new attitude toward drugs that would eventually draw marihuana into its nets of legalized morality.

In contrast to the antinarcotics laws, however, Prohibition came about with little debate. But like the Harrison Act, Prohibition continued the pattern of using federal authority to dictate morality to Americans and of placing enforcement of the law under the watchful eye of the Bureau of Internal Revenue.

The successes of the antinarcotics and temperance movements had the effect of encouraging other reformist groups to "clean up" America. The next targets were tobacco, dancing, and jazz. The cigarette was branded as evil. There was no "energy more destructive of soul, mind and body, or more subversive of good morals, than the cigarette. The fight against the cigarette is a fight for civilization." While some states in the south and west eventually did adopt laws outlawing cigarettes, these statutes were soon rescinded, too unpopular to enforce.

The new dance crazes were another bugaboo of the reformists. Accused of encouraging sex on the dance floor, the tango, hesitation waltz, turkey trot, black bottom, and the Charleston were all denounced as licentious.

Jazz was similarly censured as causing "mental drunkenness." Many agreed with the superintendant of schools in Kansas City, Missouri, who said, "This nation has been fighting booze for a long time. I am just wondering whether jazz isn't going to be legislated against as well."

The reformist sentiment represented village America's resentment of urban America. Village America was WASP land, home of white, middle-class, Protestantism, home of morality, fundamentalist religion, and rural-minded respectability. Men beat their wives and children, but did it in the privacy of their own homes and toolsheds, not in any crowded tenement where their neighbors could see and hear. When they drank to excess, their wives or a neighbor would fetch them home, not the police. Rural Americans, who far outnumbered urban Americans in their rate of drug addiction at the turn of the century, cast not the mote from its own eye. Instead, they denounced minority groups, such as the Chinese and the Negros for their addiction to opium and cocaine, and the Italians and the Irish for their boozing. These immigrants had been pouring into America by the millions. They had different cultures, different religions, and they spoke different languages. They crowded into cities and lived in squalid tenements, scratching for survival and looking for a way to escape their poverty.

What if they should take it into their heads to start a revolution? What if they rose en masse and tried to take by force what native-born Americans had struggled so hard to achieve? Ordinarily, the likelihood of anything like that was not very great, but what if they lost their senses as a result of taking drugs?

The spectre of class warfare loomed behind the actions of the anti-drug sentiment in America. Years later, when the focus of attention would be centered around the dangers of marihuana, the antidrug reformist would rant and rave about the infamy of the heinous Assassins who were provoked into a frenzy of uncontrollable violence by their indulgence in hashish. In an effort to anticipate, suppress, or eliminate the imagined danger of an uncontrollable mass of foreigners caught up in a paroxysm of drug-inspired violence, the watchdogs of American morality took it upon themselves to obliterate these evils from the nation. Caught up in the furor and fears of the drug menace scare that was sweeping the country, marihuana, a drug that most Americans had never heard of, let alone seen, smelled, tasted, or smoked, was about to become the victim of America's next drug witch hunt.

The attitude toward marihuana during the 1920s and 1930s was a logical extension of the class conflict and the fears surrounding opium abuse that arose during the latter half of the nineteenth century.

Behind the efforts to outlaw marihuana was the belief that this drug could potentially release the inner decadence of minority groups and America's own destitute poor. When the majority of addicts had been upright middle-class citizens, the country envisioned little danger to American society as a whole. However, when the bulk of the addict population began to be lower class, the danger seemed imminent. A society that harbored within it a body of indigent lazy men and women whose ways were contrary to the American work ethic seemed on the brink of economic chaos.

The attitude toward the drug addict changed overnight once he became a criminal. Drug addiction, which hitherto had been merely a personal vice, was now seen as a moral pestilence, a plague that destroyed the spirit and left the body to rot. Such was the campaign against addiction that all that was necessary to see marihuana as a threat was to brand it a narcotic. Automatically, it too became a diabolical substance, a drug that could enslave a man in its addiction, destroy his moral fiber, turn him into a degenerate and a parasite, and unleash the mad dog that hitherto had been securely restrained in his erstwhile healthy body.

11

Reefer Racism

Even when it was not against the law, marihuana was used by very few Americans. Those who used it were typically from minority groups like the Mexicans and the Negros, and this made them and their drug preferences highly visible. The fact that these people smoked marihuana for pleasure made marihuana a vice that was doubly suspect, since the American work ethic never recognized anything like an "artificial paradise."

At the root of America's preoccupation with the potential dangers of drugs such as marihuana was a xenophobia that seems to characterize the history of the country almost from its very beginnings. Although settled by foreigners, native-born Americans blamed newcomers to the United States for many of the country's ills. In the late nineteenth and early twentieth century, newly arrived foreigners were blamed for the sprawling urban slums, depressed paychecks, and labor unrest—conditions beyond the ken of frontier America's whelps. Although America was built by the sweat of toiling immigrants, the newcomers were seldom welcomed. This was especially true when the blue-eyed, blond-haired, fair-skinned, Protestant migrations gave way to the brown- and green-eyed, black-haired, swarthy, non-Protestants from Southern and Eastern Europe who settled in the coastal cities of America.

Penniless when they arrived, they were grateful for whatever jobs they could get. Their readiness to toil for the lowest of wages was seen by native Americans as a stab in the back. These foreigners, they felt, were nothing less than strikebreakers.

In the southwest, the sudden increase in Mexican immigration to the United States around 1910 set off yet another round of ethnic confrontation. The Mexicans were lower-class immigrants. They were crude, loud, uneducated. They lived in dirty shanties, ate strange food, and spoke a foreign language. The more resentful of these foreigners

Americans became, the readier they were to attribute other negative characteristics to the Mexican. The fact that the Mexicans were Catholics made their situation even more touchy since Protestant America considered Catholicism a religion of dark superstition and ignorance.

The Mexican was the Negro of the southwestern United States. While not a slave or a sharecropper, he was a peasant. The stereotype of the Mexican was that of a thief, an untamed savage, hot-blooded, quick to anger yet inherently lazy and irresponsible.

When revolution broke out in Mexico in 1910, it was inevitable that the fighting would spill across the Rio Grande. When Pancho Villa attacked the tiny outpost at Columbus, New Mexico, in 1916, the attitude toward the Mexicans worsened considerably. As General Pershing's army crossed the Rio Grande into Mexico in pursuit of the bandit, his soldiers marched to the tune of a song that reflected America's attitude toward all Mexicans:

> It's a long way to capture Villa
> It's a long way to go;
> It's along way across the border
> Where the dirty greasers grow.[1]

(Villa's followers rode to a different song "La Cucaracha"—the cockroach who can't walk any longer because he doesn't have any marihuana to smoke:

> La cucaracha, la cucaracha
> Ya no puede caminar
> Porque no tiene, porque no tiene
> Marihuana que fumar.

The song was adopted as Villa's battle hymn after his capture of Torreon and subsequent overthrow of the Mexican government because many of his men had smoked marihuana before going into battle, much like other soldiers drinking alcohol before battle.

When the 1930s devastated the American economy, the Mexicans bore the brunt of the scapegoat mentality in the southwest. Everything about them was abhorrent to many Americans, and there was a general hew and cry to kick them out of the country. Harassment was commonplace. The Mexicans were censured for almost everything they did or failed to do, including smoking marihuana. Marihuana, in fact, became the pretext for vexing the Mexicans just as opium had been the pretext for vexing the Chinese years before.

---

[1]Quoted in P. Jacobs and S. Landau, eds., *To Serve the Devil* (New York: Vintage, 1971), 1: 241.

Outlawing Marihuana

The campaign to outlaw marihuana in America began unexpectedly. Hamilton Wright, chief U.S. delegate to the international conference at The Hague in 1911, had wanted an expert on international law as part of his team, but was forced to accept a California pharmacist, Henry J. Finger, instead, by Secretary of State P. C. Knox (Finger's appointment was an act of patronage to Knox's brother). During the conference, Finger unexpectedly rose from his seat to plead that cannabis be put on the list with opium and other narcotic drugs to be censured on a worldwide basis. The reason for such an unprecedented move, he said, was San Francisco's concern over the "large influx of Hindoos," who were introducing "whites into their habit."

Italy was also in favor of restrictions on cannabis, and in fact stipulated that only if the cannabis issue were placed on the agenda would it attend the conference. Italy's interest in cannabis was anything but altruistic. Although it had no cannabis problem of its own (and in fact was one of the world's major producers of fine hemp fabric), the Italians had just gone to war with Turkey and had won jurisdiction over the African colonies of Tripolitania and Cyrenaica, where such a problem did exist.

The other delegates, however, did not view San Francisco's plight or Italy's consternation seriously, and no recommendations regarding cannabis were adopted.

At the same time, the U.S. House Ways and Means Committee, which also met in 1911 to hear proposals for federal antinarcotics legislation, were presented with arguments regarding whether cannabis should be outlawed domestically. Heading the anticannabis forces was Charles B. Fauns, a well-known director of a drug and alcohol hospital in New York City. Fauns berated those who minimized the dangers of cannabis. "To my mind it is inexcusable," he told the congressional hearing, "for a man to say that there is no habit from the use of that drug. There is no drug in the pharmacopoeia today that would produce the pleasurable sensations you would get from cannabis, no not one—absolutely not a drug in the pharmacopoeia today, and of all the drugs on earth I would certainly put that on the list. . . ."[2] Dr. William J. Schieffelin concurred with Fauns, although he felt that Fauns had overstated the case. Although very little cannabis was being used in the United States, he had heard that New York City's Syrian colony were smoking it and therefore perhaps it should be outlawed.[3]

Charles A. West, chairman of the National Wholesale Druggists'

[2]Quoted in R. J. Bonnie and C. H. Whitebread, *The Marihuana Conviction* (Charlottesville: University of Virginia Press, 1974), p. 41.
[3]Cf. D. F. Musto, *The American Disease* (New Haven: Yale University Press, 1973), pp. 217–8.

Association, and Albert Plaut, representing Lehn and Fink, a New York pharmaceutical firm, spoke against the proposal, claiming that the notion that cannabis was in any way a harmful drug was based more on literary fantasy such as that found in *The Count of Monte Cristo* than on fact. West and Plaut were the more convincing speakers and cannabis was not even included in the subsequent debate over national restrictions on narcotic drugs.

Unable to secure national support to outlaw cannabis, various state legislatures moved on their own to prohibit its possession unless prescribed by a physician. In 1915, California passed the first such law. Shortly thereafter, nearly every state west of the Mississippi followed California's lead, e.g., Utah (1915), Wyoming (1915), Texas (1919), Iowa (1923), Nevada (1923), Oregon (1923), Washington (1923), Arkansas (1923), and Nebraska (1927).

Yet, references in the newspapers to the adoption of these laws clearly show that the marihuana was relatively unknown, even in states with considerable Mexican populations. In Texas, for instance, the *Austin Statesman* explained to its readers that "marihuana is a Mexican herb and is said to be sold on the Texas Mexican border."[4]

Many northern states, however, also had anticannabis laws as early as 1915. To the legislators of Maine, Vermont, Massachusetts, and New York, a narcotic was a narcotic, whatever its name. Cannabis was considered a narcotic and therefore was accorded the same status as opium, morphine, heroin, and codeine, all of which were proscribed. Thus, when New York City's Board of Health prohibited cannabis from the city's streets in 1914, the *New York Times* (July 30, 1914) reported that the drug was a "narcotic [with] practically the same effect as morphine and cocaine . . . [and] the inclusion of cannabis indica among the drugs to be sold only on prescription is only common sense. Devotees of hashish are now hardly numerous here to count, but they are likely to increase as other narcotics become harder to obtain."

The motive behind these antimarihuana laws was obvious. Finger had alluded to San Francisco's "Hindoos" and Schieffelin had had New York City's "Syrians" in mind when they spoke out against the drug. But the Mexican connection was to outshadow these groups by far in future laws enacted against marihuana.

The Mexican Connection

In 1910, the revolution south of the Rio Grande drove thousands of Mexicans north into the United States. The main border crossings were

---

[4]Quoted in R. J. Bonnie and C. H. Whitebread, "Forbidden Fruit," *Virginia Law Review* 56 (1970): 1014.

El Paso, Texas; Nogales and Douglas, Arizona; and Calexico, California. The immigrants who passed through these points of entry usually
took up temporary residence on the outskirts of these towns, and the
Mexican ghetto or barrio became a common sight in parts of the southwest.

At first the newcomers were welcomed, especially by the wealthy
landowners and the railway companies. These people were willing to
work for cheap wages. As bad as the pay was, it was still worse in
Mexico. While many Mexicans were ferried as far north as Chicago to
work in the rail yards, most were recruited as fruit and vegetable pickers
in California's Imperial and San Joaquin Valleys, in Texas's Rio Grande
Valley, in Arizona's Salt River Valley, and in the sugar beet fields of
Colorado. So valuable a labor commodity were the Mexicans that big
business pressured Congress to exclude them from the literacy test and
head-tax payments that had been written into the Immigration Act of
1917.

Small businessmen also reaped dollars from the newcomers, and as
late as 1930 they fought all attempts to restrict Mexican immigration.
Said one Los Angeles shopkeeper:

> Mexican business is for cash. They don't criticize prices. You can sell
> them higher priced articles than they intended to purchase when they came
> in. They spend every cent they make. Nothing is too good for a Mexican if he
> has the money. They spend their entire paycheck. If they come into your
> store first, you get it. If they go to the other fellow's store first, he gets it.[5]

The reaction of the townspeople, however, was less favorable:

> The evils to the community at large which their presence in large num-
> bers almost invariably brings may more than over-balance their desirable
> qualities. Their low standards of living and morals, their illiteracy, their utter
> lack of proper political interest, the retarding effect of their employment
> upon the wage scale of the more progressive races, and finally their tendency
> to colonize in urban centers, with evil results, combine to stamp them as a
> rather undesirable class of residents.[6]

Small farmers, unable to compete with large growers because of the
cheap wages paid to the Mexicans, were being driven out of business.
Labor unions likewise complained of the competition from cheap labor.
Local governments were unhappy about the numbers of Mexcians on
relief. Business interests countered that the Mexicans were the most
preferable of all the cheap labor available and were more suited than
American whites at working at menial tasks. Caught in the middle, the

[5]W. Moquin, ed., *A Documentary History of the Mexican Americans* (New York: Praeger,
1971), p. 295.
[6]Quoted in A. Hoffman, *Unwanted Mexican Americans* (Tucson: University of Arizona Press,
1974), p. 15.

Mexicans became the scapegoats for the economic conflict between business and labor. It was largely in this role of monkey-in-the-middle that the habits and customs of the Mexicans began to be attacked as un-American, and at the top of the list of un-American-like activities was their use of marihuana.

THE AMERICAN HEMP DRUG COMMISSIONS

As the numbers of Mexican immigrants began to increase, especially in the border towns of the southwest, they were the object of close scrutiny by the townsfolk. Suspicious and often resentful of these newcomers, the townspeople humiliated, harassed, and abused them to make them feel as unwelcome as possible. When the Mexicans lashed back at their tormentors, their actions were often attributed to the influence of marihuana, which to many Americans symbolized the Mexican presence in America.

As early as 1914, the town of El Paso passed a local ordinance outlawing the sale or possession of marihuana. Like the outlawing of opium, the ordinance was meant to annoy and harass a class of people. The pretext for the law was said to have been a fight started by a Mexican who was allegedly under the influence of the drug, but the real reason was dislike, if not hatred, of the foreigners from across the Rio Grande.

Relations between Americans and Mexicans were not helped very much by the antics of the Mexican revolutionary Pancho Villa. Villa frequently led his bandits on raids against towns on the American side of the Rio Grande and then fled back into Mexico. When finally the Americans had had enough, they sent General "Black Jack" Pershing in pursuit of the elusive bandit.

When Pershing returned from Mexico, there was some concern that marihuana had infiltrated the American ranks, although an official inquiry failed to turn up any proof to that effect. However, in 1921, the commandant of Fort Sam Houston expressly forbade marihuana anywhere on the grounds of the military post, ostensibly because American soldiers were smoking the drug while on duty.

In 1916, military authorities in the Panama Canal Zone began to suspect that army personnel were also smoking marihuana, but little attention was given to the issue at that time.

Six years later, in 1922, the provost marshall became concerned about reports that American soldiers were smoking marihuana and were becoming disobedient as a result. The following year, the army prohibited possession of marihuana by American personnel in the Canal Zone.

On April 1, 1925, a formal committee was convened to investigate the traffic in marihuana in the Canal Zone and to consider steps to prevent its usage. The committee invited army officers to express their opinions on the use of the drug by American soldiers, and at a hospital for the insane the committee watched while some soldiers, four physicians, and two policemen smoked marihuana in their presence. The committee also examined the military records of delinquent soldiers for any evidence that marihuana had produced unruliness.

A Colonel Chamberlain spoke for most of the committee's members when he concluded: "I think we can safely say, based upon the samples we have had smoked here and upon the reports of the individuals concerned, that there is nothing to indicate any habit forming tendency or any striking ill effects. All of the statements to the effect that two or three puffs produce remarkable effects are nonsense, judging from our experience."

A Mr. Johannes concurred and added that Dr. Cornell, a physician participating in the experiment, "was about the only man who was actually affected."

A third member of the committee, a Dr. Hesner, explained, however, that Dr. Cornell "had previously seen a marihuana smoker at my place and I think he must have had similar symptoms to what he would have had if he had smoked any other kind of cigarette."

"In other words," Colonel Chamberlain noted, "the same effects might have been produced by any other kind of vapor."

To which Mr. Johannes replied: "I have seen firemen on ships' fires overcome by smoke, overcome by peculiar symptoms, run around without knowing what they were doing, acting peculiarly, and lacking coordination."

Up to this point, the committee seemed admirably objective in their assessment of the evidence. They had witnessed an experiment which allowed them to observe the effects of marihuana firsthand and had found nothing to be alarmed about. But a Colonel Rigby now interjected the possibility that marihuana "seems to affect some individuals pretty seriously and doesn't seem to affect others."

In response to a suggestion by Dr. Hesner that if the committee could get some other men to use it, they might be able to observe some "susceptible cases," a Mr. Calhoun proposed what would eventually become a clandestine military practice. "It might be well," opined Calhoun, "to have some who would not know whether they were smoking it or tobacco for the purpose of ascertaining exact effects." To his credit, a Dr. Bates recognized the ethical implications and denounced such a scheme. "I feel that if the matter can be demonstrated scientifically," he replied to Calhoun, "it should be so demonstrated rather than by sneaking up on them."

On the basis of the testimony given, their own personal observation, and examination of military files, the committee finally concluded that marihuana was not habit forming nor did it have "any appreciable deleterious influence on the individual using it." Previous orders forbidding possession of marihuana were subsequently rescinded in 1926.

Despite the thoroughness of the probe, some high-ranking army officers refused to accept the committee's findings and ordered that a new investigation be conducted. In 1929, the department surgeon in charge of the new inquiry reported that "use of the drug is not widespread and . . . its effects upon military efficiency and upon discipline are not great. There appears to be no reason for renewing the penalties formerly exacted for the possession and the use of the drug."

Nevertheless, in December 1930 the department commander ordered that since "the smoking of marihuana impairs the efficiency of the soldiers [it] is forbidden. Soldiers smoking marihuana or using it in any way will be brought to trial for each and every offence."

In June 1931, a third Canal Zone investigation was begun. Once again the committee found no evidence to link marihuana with problems of morale or delinquency. "The evidence obtained," the committee said, "suggests that organization Commanders in estimating the efficiency and soldierly quality of delinquents in their commands have unduly emphasized the effects of marijuana, disregarding the fact that a large proportion of the delinquents are morons or psychopaths, which conditions themselves would serve to account for delinquency."

But the army brass would not be deterred. Morale was down and a scapegoat had to be found. Orders forbidding possession of marihuana on military installations were to be continued in force.

MARIHUANA AND VIOLENCE

As the most conspicuous users of marihuana, Mexicans were oftentimes accused of being incited to violence by the drug. A letter written in 1911 by the American consul at Nogales, Mexico, stated that marihuana "causes the smoker to become exceedingly pugnacious and to run amuck without discrimination."[7] A Texas police captain claimed that under marihuana's baneful influence, Mexicans become "very violent, especially when they become angry and will attack an officer even if a

[7]*Canal Zone Papers*, p. 106.

gun is drawn on him. They seem to have no fear, I have also noted that when under the influence of this weed they have enormous strength and that it will take several men to handle one man while under ordinary circumstances one man could handle him with ease."[8]

Prison officials throughout the southwest had no doubt about marihuana's capacity to provoke violence. In the words of the warden of the state prison in Yuma, Arizona: "Under its baseful influence reckless men become bloodthirsty, terribly daring, and dangerous to an uncontrollable degree."[9]

The *Butte Montana Standard* reflected the thinking of the state's legislators when they outlawed marihuana in 1927:

> When some beet field peon takes a few traces of this stuff... he thinks he has just been elected president of Mexico, so he starts out to execute all his political enemies."[10]

When challenged, these statements were never supported. Dr. M. V. Ball, one of America's few authorities on marihuana, visited the border towns in 1922 as a representative of the American Medical Association to get a firsthand look at the alleged dangers of marihuana to the citizenry. Ball had previously noted that whenever cannabis drugs were mentioned in the old scientific literature, they were invariably mixed with opium,[11] and he was skeptical of the reports he had heard about the drug as far as its criminogenic properties were concerned.

During a site visit to a Texas jail, the warden gave an inmate a marihuana cigarette to smoke so that Ball could see for himself what it did to a man. "To the surprise of the American Prison Physician and the jailer who assured me three wiffs would drive fellows so wild that they become exceptionally difficult to subdue," the smoker remained calm and unperturbed. "There is no evidence whatever that I can discover," Ball subsequently reported, "to warrant the belief that marihuana smoking is on the increase among Americans or that it is prevalent or common, there is no evidence worthy of belief that marihuana is a habit forming weed or drug, or that its use is increasing among Mexicans in Mexico or in America."[12]

Four years later, Dr. W. W. Stockberger, a scientist at the U.S. Bureau of Plant Industry, issued a similar statement. "We have had

[8]Bonnie and Whitebread, *Marihuana Conviction*, p. 34.
[9]*Ibid.*, p. 12.
[10]Quoted in *ibid.*, p. 40.
[11]M. V. Ball, "Marihuana: Mexican Name for Cannabis, Also Called Loco Weed in Certain Parts of Texas," *Canal Zone Papers*, p. 62.
[12]M. V. Ball, "The Effects of Haschisch Not Due to Cannabis sativa," *Therapeutic Gazette* 34 (1910): 777–80.

correspondence with El Paso and other border cities in Texas for a good many years about this situation," he said. However, "the reported effects of the drug on Mexicans, making them want to clean up the town, do not jibe very well with the effects of cannabis, which so far as we have reports, simply causes temporary elation, followed by depression and heavy sleep. . . ."[13]

Several years later still, Dr. Walter Bromberg clearly demonstrated the carelessness of police officers in attributing criminal activity to marihuana. Among ten patients whose cases he pulled from the files of the Federal Bureau of Narcotics, Bromberg became especially interested in a J. O., a prisoner "described as having confessed how he murdered a friend and put his body in a trunk while under the influence of marihuana." Bromberg had J. O. brought to his clinic for a detailed interview. The interview convinced Bromberg that J. O. was no more a user of marihuana than was the commissioner of the Bureau of Narcotics. "Although he [J. O.] was a psychopathic liar and possibly homosexual," Bromberg concluded, "there was no indication in the examination or history of the use of any drug. The investigation by the probation department failed to indicate use of the drug marihuana."[14]

Yet another example of the way facts were deliberately falsified or distorted is a case cited by Dr. Lawrence Kolb.[15] As reported by the press, a fight which ended in the death of one of the combatants was described as a vicious, marihuana-induced murder. The facts, as best Kolb could uncover them, were that two men who were drinking heavily smoked one marihuana cigarette during the night. Sometime later a quarrel ensued. A fight erupted and one of the men was killed. Since marihuana had been used, the newspapers attributed the death to marihuana although there is little doubt that if any drug were responsible for what happened, it was alcohol.

During the 1930s the most sensationalistic of all the crimes to be attributed to marihuana's baneful influence was that of the death of a Florida family. On October 16, 1933, Victor Licata axed his mother, father, two brothers, and a sister to death in their Tampa home. The following day the Tampa chief of police declared "war on the marihuana traffic here," after reading the investigating officer's report that "the weed used as a cigarette had been indirectly to blame for the wholesale murder of the Michael Licata family. . . ."[16] The link between the crime

---

[13]Quoted in "Our Home Hasheesh Crop," *Literary Digest* 89 (1926): 64.

[14]W. Bromberg, "Marihuana: A Psychiatric Study," *Journal of the American Medical Association* 113 (1939): 4–12.

[15]L. Kolb, *Addiction* (Springfield, Ill.: Charles C Thomas, 1962).

[16]Quoted in J. Kaplan, *Marihuana* (New York: Pocket Books, 1972), p. 98.

and marihuana was that Victor Licata had been a known user of marihuana.

On October 20, a *Tampa Times* editorial blared: "Stop This Murderous Smoke": ". . . It may or may not be wholly true that the pernicious marihuana cigarette is responsible for the murderous mania of a Tampa young man in exterminating all the members of his family within his reach—but whether or not the poisonous mind-wrecking weed is mainly accountable for the tragedy its sale should not be and should never have been permitted here or elsewhere."[17]

Victor Licata was subsequently turned over to a psychiatrist for evaluation. The examining psychiatrist found that not only was Licata criminally insane, but that he had a history of insanity in his family and many of his relatives had been committed to mental institutions. In fact, the Tampa police had made an attempt to have Licata committed to an institution a year earlier (and a half year prior to his using marihuana), but his parents argued that they could take better care of him in their own home and he was remanded to their custody.

Licata was ultimately sentenced to the Florida state mental hospital, where he was again examined and diagnosed as suffering from a long-lasting psychosis which was probably responsible for his crime. In 1950, Licata hanged himself.

Although there was no evidence to show that Licata had killed his family while under the influence of marihuana, Harry Anslinger, the commissioner of the Bureau of Narcotics, cited the case during the hearings on the Marihuana Tax Act of 1937 as just one example of the dangers of marihuana:

> In Florida a 21-year old boy, under the influence of this drug killed his parents and his brothers and sister. The evidence showed that he had smoked marihuana.[18]

In his book *The Murderers*, Anslinger once again turned to the Licata case:

> Much of the most irrational juvenile violence and killing that has written a new chapter of shame and tragedy is traceable directly to this hemp intoxication. . . . A sixteen-year-old [sic] kills his entire family of five in Florida. . . . Every one of these crimes has been preceded by the smoking of one or more marihuana "reefers."[19]

Anslinger's attitude was typical of other police officers in regard to the marihuana issue. Without any evidence to back them up, more than a few law enforcement officers adamantly denounced marihuana as a "killer drug."

The campaign against the drug picked up especially during the Depression as marihuana became yet another issue on which to harass Mexican immigrants. The Mexicans were accused of spreading the marihuana vice throughout the nation:

> While the plant is a native of the Torrid Zone, its cultivation has been taken up through the United States and it is, at the present time, to be found in practically every state in the Union—in fact wherever Mexicans are located. So far north and east of its natural habitat has the weed spread under cultivation, that the New York Narcotics Forces have discovered patches of it which were grown within the city limits. Again the Mexican influence is shown, the supply being found near the Pennsylvania Railroad Yards, in the Borough of Queens, where the Mexicans are employed.[20]

Labor groups and antiforeigner groups like the American Coalition badgered California's legislators to kick the Mexicans out of the state on grounds that marihuana was undermining American morality. Said C. M. Goethe, a spokesman for the coalition:

> Marihuana, perhaps now the most insidious of our narcotics, is a direct by-product of unrestricted Mexican immigration. Easily grown, it has been asserted that it has recently been planted between rows in a California penitentiary garden. Mexican peddlers have been caught distributing sample marihuana cigarets to school children. Bills for our quota against Mexico have been blocked mysteriously in every Congress since the 1924 Quota Act. Our nation has more than enough laborers.[21]

A report from the Missionary Educator Movement in California also called attention to the widespread usage of marihuana among the Mexicans and its alleged connection with lack of morality:

> The use of marihuana is not uncommon in the colonies of the lower class of Mexican immigrants. This is a native drug made from what is sometimes called the "crazy weed." The effects are high exhilaration and intoxication, followed by extreme depression and broken nerves. [Police] officers and Mexicans both ascribe many of the moral irregularities of Mexicans to the effects of marihuana.[22]

Los Angeles's chief of detectives, Joseph F. Taylor, likewise hammered away at the crime-inducing effects of marihuana on the Mexican:

> In the past we have had officers of this department shot and killed by marihuana addicts and have traced the act of murder directly to the influence of marihuana, with no other motive.[23]

---

[20]Moquin, *Mexican Americans*, p. 295.
[21]Quoted in Musto, *American Disease*, p. 220.
[22]Quoted in J. Helmer, *Drugs and Minority Oppression* (New York: Seabury Press, 1975), p. 63.
[23]Quoted in M. H. Hayes and L. E. Bowery, "Marihuana," *Journal of Criminology* 23 (1933): 1086–98.

Elsewhere throughout the southwest, where there were heavy con-
centrations of Mexicans, newspapers carried on a vigorous campaign
against marihuana, aimed ostensibly at the evils of the drug but the real
object of their indictment was crystal clear: "Four men, including a deputy sheriff, were seriously injured last night by a marihuana-raged Mexican before the bullets of another officer killed him, as he charged this
officer with a knife."[24]

In 1933, the arrest of a "dope ring" specializing in marihuana, in
Longmont, Colorado, prompted the remark from one journalist that
marihuana was "highly intoxicating and constitutes an ever recurring
problem where there are Mexicans or Spanish-Americans of the lower
classes."[25]

Readers were likewise informed that while "appalling in its effects
on the human mind and body as narcotics, the consumption of
marihuana appears to be proceeding, virtually unchecked in Colorado
and other Western states with a large Spanish-American population."[26]
And if this were not dire warning enough, readers were also told that
marihuana was "kin to loco weed . . . [and] when mixed with hay causes
death to horses!"[27]

In 1931, the California State Narcotic Committee reported that
marihuana usage was "widespread throughout Southern California
among the Mexican population there,"[28] and cited statistics from the city
of Los Angeles that marihuana was frequently listed as being involved in
criminal arrests. On the other hand, although "widespread" among the
Mexicans, no other city in the state could produce comparable statistics.
In fact, surveys of crime and delinquency among the Mexicans clearly
demonstrated that they exhibited "delinquent tendencies less than their
proportion of the population would entitle them to show."[29] When the
records of one officer who had been adamant in his denunciation of the
Mexican crime wave were examined, it was discovered that he had
overestimated the proportion of Mexican arrests by 60 percent![30]

It was not their antisocial behavior nor their use of marihuana that
made the Mexicans *persona non grata*. As long as the economy had been
viable, differences between the Mexicans and the Anglos were rarely
belligerent. When the Depression hit, however, jobs in the city disap-

[24]*Tulsa Tribune*, June 11, 1930.
[25]*New York Times*, December 3, 1933.
[26]*New York Times*, September 16, 1934.
[27]Helmer, *Drugs*, p. 63.
[28]*Ibid.*, p. 58.
[29]*Ibid.*, p. 59.
[30]*Ibid.*

peared. Anglo workers now began looking to farm labor as a means of livelihood. It was then that real competition for jobs became an issue.

Relief programs for the unemployed were a related issue. During the 1920s, the Mexican population in Los Angeles alone increased by 226 percent.[31] By 1930, there were over 97,000 Mexicans in the city. When these immigrants lost their jobs and went on relief, the business sector, which had once regarded them as an exploitable asset, now began to view them as an intolerable burden.

To reduce the relief burden, labor groups led by the AFL began urging that the Mexicans be shipped back across the border. Repatriation became law in the 1930s, and beginning in 1931 thousands of Mexicans were shipped back across the Rio Grande. The cost to repatriate one Mexican to Mexico City was $14.70. An average family ran about $71.14, including food and transportation. Los Angeles County paid out $77,249.29 to repatriate one covey of 6024 Mexicans and figured it had got itself a bargain compared to the $424,933.70 it estimated charitable relief would have cost had these people remained.[32]

Mexicans who did not wish to return voluntarily were subjected to varying forms and degrees of harassment. Many were charged with vagrancy. Others were arrested for violation of state marihuana laws. When they began to resist efforts to jail and deport them, their resistance was attributed to the influence of marihuana and these charges lent further weight to the accusation that marihuana incited violence.

[31]According to the 1930 U.S. Census, there were over 360,000 Mexicans in California, over 680,000 in Texas, over 114,000 in Arizona, and over 50,000 in Colorado and New Mexico.
[32]Moquin, *Mexican Americans*, p. 295.

12

The Jazz Era

Around the turn of the century, New Orleans became the Marseilles of America, a cosmopolitan port filled with sailors, traders, gamblers, prostitutes, thieves, con men, and gangsters of every nationality. Although every major city in America had its red-light district, New Orleans's Storyville was the best known of all the nation's bawdy houses for not only were customers entertained by exotic ladies of the night, they were also treated to the strains of a new kind of music called jazz, played exclusively in these whorehouses by black musicians.

It was in these bordellos, where music provided the background and not the primary focus of attention, that marihuana became an integral part of the jazz era. Unlike booze, which dulled and incapacitated, marihuana enabled musicians whose job required them to play long into the night to forget their exhaustion. Moreover, the drug seemed to make their music sound more imaginative and unique, at least to those who played and listened while under its sensorial influence.

Jazz musicians in New Orleans's whorehouses were not the only ones smoking marihuana. "Moota," as the drug was known in the city, was popular throughout the red-light district, and eventually its association with this part of town came to the attention of the city's moral crusaders who began to warn of its dangers to the community as a whole.

The alarm was first sounded in 1920 by Dr. Oscar Dowling, president of Louisiana's State Board of Health, after learning of the conviction of a musician who had been caught forging a doctor's signature on a prescription to obtain some marihuana.[1] Marihuana, he warned Louisiana's governor John M. Parker, is "a powerful narcotic, causing exhilaration, intoxication, delirious hallucinations, and its subsequent

---

[1] R. J. Bonnie and C. H. Whitebread, *The Marihuana Conviction* (Charlottesville: University of Virginia Press, 1974), p. 43.

action, drowsiness and stupor..."[2] and urged that something be done about its threat to the city.

At the same time, he dashed off a plea to the surgeon general of the United States asking that action be taken to control traffic in marihuana on a national level. The surgeon general, Dr. Hugh Cummings, replied that he fully agreed with Dowling's assessment of the dangers associated with marihuana, but no further action was taken.[3] Prohibition Commissioner John F. Kramer likewise took no action after receiving a letter from Governor Parker late in November 1920 informing him that "two people... [had been] killed a few days ago by the smoking of this drug, which seems to make them go crazy and wild."[4] While sympathetic, federal authorities were far too busy enforcing the ban on morphine to think about widening the sphere of proscribed drugs they would have to deal with.

It was not long before the newspapers began to realize that the marihuana issue could boost circulation, and in 1926 the *New Orleans Morning Tribune* ran a series of articles ballyhooing the growing menace of the drug.

Mostly sensationalistic in tone, the headlines blared revelations to the effect that "SCHOOL CHILDREN FOUND IN GRIP OF MARIJUANA HABIT BY INVESTIGATORS," "WORKMEN OF CITY LURED BY MUGGLES, " "WELFARE WORKERS ARE POWERLESS TO COPE WITH SINISTER TRAFFIC."

One article claimed that schoolchildren were buying marihuana from "unscrupulous peddlers [who] openly sell the drug to boys of tender age who appear on streets under its influence." An interview with sixty children, all under age fifteen, revealed that all of them knew what marihuana was, where it could be purchased, and that all had used it. The reporter failed to mention that the children were Mexican or black, and that marihuana was something not very new or out of the ordinary to them.

When the marihuana peddlers were reported to be working out of saloons and pool halls, large-scale raids were carried out. Most of the 150 people caught in the roundup were from the poorer, lower classes, and the underworld. Satisfied that at last something was being done, Dowling repeated his "warning to parents, guardians and teachers of children against this menace."[5]

Always on the lookout for moral decay in America, the Women's

---

[2] D. F. Musto, "The Marihuana Tax Act of 1937," *Archives of General Psychiatry* 26 (1972): 101–8.

[3] *Ibid.*

[4] Quoted in D. F. Musto, *The American Disease* (New Haven: Yale University Press, 1973), pp. 218–9.

[5] Quoted in Bonnie and Whitebread, *Marihuana Conviction*, p. 44.

Christian Temperance Union began attacking "soft drink" stands and "corner drug stores which have taken the place of the saloon as a social meeting place. Here is where marihuana and liquors can sometimes be bought."[6]

The alleged marihuana menace in New Orleans was subsequently forgotten for about five years. Then, as happened in the southwest, an antimarihuana campaign followed in the footsteps of the Depression.

To carry on where his colleague Dr. Dowling had left off was a hellfire-and-brimstone physician, Dr. A. E. Fossier, who resurrected all the old myths including that of the Assassins, to ensure that his message would not be lost on his listeners:

> During the time of the Crusades, [the Assassins] resorted to every kind of violence. Their utter disregard for death and the ruthlessness of their atrocities presented a formidable obstacle to the arms of the Christians, because under the influence of hashish those fanatics would madly rush at their enemies, and ruthlessly massacre everyone within their grasp.[7]

Having set the proper mood, Fossier then lashed out at the contemporary problem as he saw it:

> The underworld was quick to realize that marihuana was an ideal drug to quickly cut off the inhibition, especially in the light of inadequate personality. Under the influence of cannabis indica, these human derelicts are quickly subjugated by the will of the master mind. The moral principles or training initiated in the mind from infancy deter from committing willful theft, murder or rape, but his inhibition from crime may be destroyed by the addiction to marihuana.[8]

Dr. F. F. Young, who was in the audience when Fossier delivered his views on marihuana, urged a note of caution regarding marihuana's link with crime. All the marihuana users he had seen, he said, "were defective in the brain and nervous structure before they began smoking this weed. . . . these smokers are criminals before they become addicted to the weed."[9]

Most law officers dismissed opinions such as Young's without a second thought. Eugene Stanley, district attorney for New Orleans, for example, relied heavily on Fossier's description of the dangers of marihuana in an article he wrote for the *American Journal of Police Science* in 1931:

---

[6]Bonnie and Whitebread, *Marihuana Conviction*, p. 44–5.
[7]A. E. Fossier, "The Marihuana Menace," *New Orleans Medical and Surgical Journal* 44 (1931): 247.
[8]*Ibid.*, p. 249.
[9]F. F. Young, Discussion of Fossier's "The Marihuana Menace," *New Orleans Medical and Surgical Journal* 44 (1931): 251.

> It has been the experience of Police and Prosecuting Officials in the South, that immediately before the commission of many crimes the use of marihuana cigarettes has been indulged in by criminals, so as to relieve themselves from the natural restraint which might deter them from the commission of criminal acts, and to give them the fake courage necessary to commit the contemplated crimes.[10]

Stanley then called upon the federal government to help eradicate the menace:

> Inasmuch as the harmful effects of the use of marihuana are daily becoming more widely known, and since it has been classified as a narcotic by the statutory laws of seventeen American States... the United States Government, will unquestionably be compelled to adopt a consistent attitude towards it, and include it in the Harrison Anti-Narcotic Law, so as to give Federal aid to the States in their effort to suppress a traffic as deadly and as destructive to society as that in the other forms of narcotics now prohibited by this act.[11]

Dr. Frank Gomila, New Orlean's public safety commissioner, felt that the main difficulty in eliminating the marihuana vice in the city was that the drug's effects were too well known, "especially among the negro population. Practically every negro in the city can give a recognizable description of the drug's effects."[12] According to Gomila, tons of marihuana were processed and sold in warehouses and storerooms throughout the city.

To what extent the New Orleans campaign against marihuana was racially motivated is difficult to judge. From Gomila's remarks, it is clear that he, at least, was motivated by racial prejudice. Fossier, perhaps the most influential of the marihuana demagogues, also revealed his biases:

> The debasing and baneful influence of hashish and opium is not restricted to individuals but has manifested itself in nations and races as well. The dominant race and most enlightened countries are alcoholic, whilst the races and nations addicted to hemp and opium, some of which once attained to heights of culture and civilization have deteriorated both mentally and physically.[13]

Which "races" Fossier had in mind he never stated. He could not have meant the Mexicans since by 1930 there were only 991 Mexicans in all of New Orleans, a mere two-tenths of 1 percent of all the people in

[10]E. Stanley, "Marihuana as a Developer of Criminals," *American Journal of Police Science* 2 (1931): 255.
[11]*Ibid.*
[12]F. R. Gomila and M. C. G. Lambow, "Present Status of the Marihuana Vice in the United States," in *Marihuana: America's New Drug Problem*, ed. R. Waton (Philadelphia: J. P. Lippincott, 1938), p. 29.
[13]Fossier, "Marihuana Menace," p. 257.

the city.[14] Although Gomila indicted the blacks, 25 percent of the Negro propulation across the state had moved north by this time.[15] Moreover, arrest figures for the city argued against his racial theory of drug-inspired deterioration. In 1928, for instance, 75 percent of all those arrested for violation of Louisiana's 1924 law against sale or possession of marihuana were American-born whites.[16] Nevertheless, blacks had the worst criminal records in the city,[17] and Fossier was probably of the same mind as Gomila in his indictment of "races... addicted to hemp."

Interestingly, Fossier, Stanley, and Gomila each enjoyed greater credibility in other parts of the country than in his own state or city. In 1933, Stanley's article was cited in *Utah vs. Navaro* as proof that marihuana provoked crime and insanity, and in 1937 it was again cited during the congressional hearings on federal prohibition of marihuana, along with Fossier's article.

In New Orleans itself, and throughout Louisiana, the populace could not have cared less. Blacks were no economic threat, most whites had no idea what all the fuss was about, and no one paid any attention to the WCTU.

New York

The next major American city in which marihuana was allegedly epidemic was New York. While Mexican immigrants had been pouring into the south and midwest, New York's Harlem was the scene of a vast influx of Negroes from the West Indies and the southern United States. By 1930, New York's black population numbered over 300,000. More blacks lived in New York than in Birmingham, Memphis, and St. Louis combined.[18]

Some of these newcomers eventually became prominent business and civic leaders in the community; most found opportunities as limited as they had been back home. Unable to better their condition, they sought ways of making the intolerable tolerable. Some resorted to music with its "charms to soothe the savage beast." Others resorted to drugs such as heroin and especially marihuana, a drug that was no stranger to the West Indian. On July 30, 1914, the *New York Times* had commented that "devotees of hashish are now hardly numerous enough here to

[14]J. Helmer, *Drugs and Minority Oppression* (New York: Seabury Press, 1975), p. 78.
[15]*Ibid.*
[16]*Ibid.*, p. 77.
[17]*Ibid.*
[18]G. Osofsky, "Harlem Tragedy: An Emerging Slum," in *The Ordeal of Twentieth Century America* ed. J. A. Schwarz (Boston: Houghton Miffin, 1974), pp. 89–111.

count." By January 11, 1923, it proclaimed that marihuana had become the city's "latest habit forming drug." Even *Scientific American* noted an increase in the use of marihuana in the city.[19] By 1932, the Bureau of Narcotics also felt that it was widespread enough in the city to warrant at least passing mention in its annual report on "Traffic in Opium and Other Dangerous Drugs for the Year Ended December 1931":

> The abuse of the drug is noted among the Latin-American or Spanish-speaking population. The sale of cannabis cigarettes occurs to a considerable degree in States along the Mexican border and in cities of the Southwest and West, as well as in New York City, and, in fact, wherever there are settlements of Latin Americans.[20]

Most of the marihuana users in the city lived around 110th Street and Fifth Avenue, with some spillover into the Broadway area above 42nd Street. Hundreds of marihuana dens were said to be flourishing in Harlem. Some estimated that there were more "tea pads" than there had been speakeasies at the height of Prohibition.

Most of the drug in Harlem was distributed either through independent peddlers or in the "tea pad." By the 1940s, three different grades were available. The cheapest, known as "sass-fras" was made from American-grown plants and was rather weak. Connoisseurs would resort to it only if nothing else were available since a lot of it had to be smoked before a good "high" could be reached. The second, and more potent variety, was called "mezzrole" or "messrole." Moderately priced, it was the favorite variety of Harlem's marihuana users. Its country of origin was usually somewhere in Central or South America, and it was sold by the "Baron Munchausen of jazz," Milton "Mezz" Mezzrow.

Mezzrow was a white musician who called himself a "voluntary Negro." He moved to New York from Chicago in 1929 and soon began selling marihuana on the streets of Harlem. "Overnight I was the most popular man in Harlem," he says in his autobiography, *Really the Blues.*[21]

Mezzrow, in fact, became a fixture in Harlem known as the "White Mayor of Harlem," the "Link Between the Races," and the "Man that Hipped the World." A new word for marihuana was coined after his name—"mezz"; a "mezzrole" was a fat, well-packed marihuana cigarette. Eventually, "mezz" transcended its literal meaning and came to mean anything genuine or superior in Harlemese.

The third and most potent grade of marihuana came from Africa.

---

[19] *Scientific American* 139 (1921): 14–5.
[20] Federal Bureau of Narcotics *Report by the Government of the United States of America for the Calendar Year Ended December 31, 1931; on The Traffic in Opium and Other Dangerous Drugs.* Washington, D.C. 1932, p. 51.
[21] M. Mezzrow, *Really the Blues* (New York: Random House, 1946), p. 89.

Called "gungeon," it was the most expensive variety of the three and only those whose incomes were above average could afford the luxury of smoking such a high grade of drug.

The "tea pads" were rooms or apartments located throughout Harlem. These were the speakeasies or social clubs of the marihuana aficionado, places where one could relax and talk with strangers or friends over a "reefer," sanctuaries wherein one could escape the realities of the outside world for a moment. The ambience was always one of peace and tranquility. Any sign of belligerence was squelched immediately; the patron either relaxed or he was forceably ejected.

Each "tea pad" was furnished in line with the clientele it served. Usually there was a radio, a record player, or a jukebox to entertain the customers. The furniture was comfortable and soft, the lighting dim. Burning incense mingled and flirted with marihuana smoke. The walls were typically covered with lewd pictures, but rarely was sex offered on the premises.

For those who preferred to buy their marihuana from independent peddlers on the street, the favorite places to smoke the drug were dance halls where both musicians and those who listened to their music lit up. Theaters were another popular spot to relax in.

In the 1930s, "reefer" songs were the rage of the jazz world. Distinctive and characteristic, it was music written and played by black musicians for black audiences. The music had a special feeling. It was a tangible medium through which minority experiences could be shared by large numbers of people dispersed throughout the country. It gave musicians and their audiences a sense of solidarity.

Among the tunes that topped the black hit list of the era were Louis Armstrong's "Muggles," Cab Calloway's "That Funny Reefer Man," Fats Waller's "Viper's Drag," and many more, by lesser known artists, like "Viper's Moan," "Texas Tea Party," "Smokin' Reefers," "Mary Jane," and the "Mary Jane Polka," recorded by studios like Columbia, Victor, and Brunswick. Even Benny Goodman got into the act with "Sweet Marihuana Brown."

In 1932, a musical number "Smokin' Reefers" opened in a review on Broadway starring Mr. Belvedere, Clifton Webb. Lyrics from the song called marihuana "the stuff that dreams are made of," a line later used by Humphrey Bogart in reference to the Maltese Falcon. Another line from the show acknowledged marihuana as "the thing that white folks are afraid of."

It was not an idle statement. White folks were becoming concerned over what marihuana might do to blacks. To emphasize the menace to white society, *American Mercury* carried an article by A. Parry entitled "The Menace of Marihuana," in which the author cited an incident calculated to arouse white readers. As described by Parry, a Negro man was arrested and brought to a New York hospital after threatening two white women in the street. His actions were attributed to a marihuana-induced dream in which he saw "a bunch of naken wimmin, some of 'em in bed, black an' white together, like dey was expectin' men."[22]

The relationship between marihuana and jazz reached across the Atlantic to England, where it began to alarm the white music establishment. On February 22, 1936, the English music periodical *Melody Maker* carried a full-page exposé on the use of marihuana by British musicians. In an ominous tone, the article reported that

> The time has come for light to be thrown on an astonishing situation which is likely to become a serious menace to the jazz world on two continents. This concerns the "reefer" or dope habit which is spreading rapidly amongst musicians, and has been going on comparatively secretly for a number of years.[23]

The magazine traced the spread of the marihuana habit from Mexico to New Orleans and from there on to Chicago, quoting as its source a clarinettist who, it said, "is now in an insane asylum in Louisiana."

According to the *Melody Maker*, the marihuana traffic in New York was run by "a celebrated hot clarinettist" who "has sent supplies to coloured musicians touring Europe."[24]

Later that year, when the senior surgeon of the U.S. Public Health Department visited the Bureau of Narcotics to obtain information about the dangers of marihuana, Commissioner Harry Anslinger produced this issue of the *Melody Maker* from the bureau's files to prove that the dangers of this drug had not been exaggerated.[25]

Although marihuana had found a home in Harlem, the rest of New York's boroughs were relatively free of the drug. The police, in fact, had had such little contact with it that they had to be given special classes to enable them to recognize it if they came across it growing in vacant lots.[26]

After these classes New York's finest discovered an estimated three million dollars worth of the drug in Brooklyn and set it ablaze. Commissioner Valentine, who supervised the conflagration, stated that "this is an extremely dangerous weed. . . . it causes temporary insanity. It is a great menace to our young people and we'll do everything in our power to stamp it out."[27] Later that year, "squads of WPA workers specially

[22]A. Parry, "The Menace of Marihuana," *American Mercury* 36 (1935): 489.
[23]"Dope Cigarette Peddling Among British Musicians," *Melody Maker*, February 22, 1936.
[24]*Ibid.*
[25]R. R. Spencer, "Marihuana," *Health Officer* 1 (1936): 299–305.
[26]"Marihuana," *Journal of the American Medical Association* 107 (1936): 107.
[27]*New York Times*, August 14, 1933.

trained to recognize marijuana" were likewise educated to spot the drug and were "placed on duty in the boroughs of the Bronx, Brooklyn, Queens, and Richmond to eradicate the weed from vacant lots."[28]

Elsewhere throughout the country, various newspapers and magazines also began heralding the spread of marihuana to other cities. Gary, Indiana, Kansas City, Kansas, and Chicago were all allegedly infested by the weed. Sensationalistic news items became the order of the day. Typical was the following from the October 24, 1926, issue of the *Chicago Herald-Examiner:*

> A Kansas hasheesh eater thinks he is a white elephant. Six months ago they found him strolling along the road, a few miles out of Topeka. He was naked, his clothes strewn along the highway for a mile. He was not violently insane, but crazy—said he was an elephant and acted as much like one as his limited physique would let him. Marihuana did it.

In 1925, shortly after Mexico, the country from which most of the marihuana that entered the United States originiated, officially outlawed cultivation of marihuana, the correspondent for the Associated Press who covered the story reported that "scientists say its effects are perhaps more terrible than those of another drug."[29]

The Assassins in America

For more than a century after its publication, Joseph von Hammer-Purgstall's book on the Assassins remained the standard reference on the murderous gang of cutthroats who allegedly used hashish before going out on their errands of mayhem. During the early twentieth century, anyone calling for the prohibition of marihuana merely had to cite the connection between hashish and the Assassins to get across the point that marihuana—the American counterpart of hashish—was capable of inciting uncontrollable violence.

One of the earliest American writers to arouse the public concerning the perils of marihuana was a physician, Dr. Victor Robinson. Robinson's sensationalistic account of the Assassins, published in the 1912 *Medical Review of Reviews*, set the tone for all subsequent treatments of the subject in the American press:

> When a Devoted One was selected to commit murder, he was first stupefied with hasheesh, and while in this state was brought into the magnificent gardens of the sheikh. All the sensual and stimulating pleasures of the erotic Orient surrounded the excited youth, and exalted by the delicious

[28]"Marihuana," *Journal of the American Medical Association*, p. 107.
[29]*New York Times*, December 28, 1925.

opiate he had taken, the hot-blooded fanatic felt that the gates of heaven were already ajar, and heard them swing open on their golden hinges. When the effect of the drug disappeared and the Devoted One was reduced to his normal condition, he was informed that through the generosity of his superior he had been permitted to foretaste the delights of paradise. The Devoted One believed this readily enough—disciples are always credulous—and therefore was eager to die or to kill at a word from his master. From these hasheesh-eaters, the Arabian name of which is hashashin, was derived the term "assassin."[30]

In this lurid account, Robinson is generally true to Marco Polo's original story. The Assassins do not kill while the under the influence of hashish but only after they have savored the delights of paradise revealed to them by the drug. The murders they commit are not the acts of frenzied psychotic butchers, but the cool, calculating, premeditated deeds of a loyal and devoted gang of trained killers.

Fifteen years later, Robert Kingman further developed the theme of the hashish-crazed killer for readers of the *Medical Journal and Record*. Although not suggesting that the Assassins killed while under the influence of hashish, Kingman wrote that the drug was given to assuage any doubts the killer might have concerning the morality of his mission.[31]

By the 1930s, however, hashish itself had become the instigator of the Assassins' murders:

Dr. A. E. Fossier, *New Orleans Medical and Surgical Journal* (1931): "Under the influence of hashish those fanatics would madly rush at their enemies, and ruthlessly massacre every one within their grasp."[32]

William Wolf, *Popular Science magazine* (1936):

> . . . "assassin" has two explanations, but either demonstrates the menace of Indian hemp. According to one version, members of a band of Persian terrorists committed their worst atrocities while under the influence of hashish. In the other version, Saracens who opposed the Crusaders were said to employ the services of hashish addicts to secure secret murders of the leaders of the Crusades. In both versions, the murderers were known as "haschischin."[33]

In 1937, readers of *American Magazine* were aroused by yet another hysteria-rousing version, this time written by the commissioner of the Federal Bureau of Narcotics, Harry Anslinger:

> In the year 1090, there was founded in Persia the religious and military order of the Assassins, whose history is one of cruelty, barbarity, and

---

[30]V. Robinson, "An Essay on Hasheesh," *Medical Review of Reviews* 18 (1912): 159–69.

[31]R. Kingman, "The Green Goddess: A Study in Dreams, Drugs, and Dementia," *Medical Journal and Record* 126 (1927): 126.

[32]Fossier, "Marihuana Menace," p. 84.

[33]W. Wolf, "Uncle Sam Fights a New Drug Menace: Marihuana," *Popular Science Monthly* 128 (1936): 15.

murder, and for good reason. The members were confirmed users of hashish, or marihuana, and it is from the Arabs "hashashin" that we have the English word "assassin."[34]

The more often the story of the Assassins was told, the more ludicrous it became. The image of the demented, knife-wielding, half-crazed hashish user running senseless through the streets, slashing at anyone unfortunate enough to cross his path, became part of the American nightmare of lawlessness. As a nation raised on violence, Americans soaked up these tales of mayhem like a sponge. Mutilation, dismemberment, uncontrollable passion, fanaticism—in short, anything that evoked terror, came to be associated with hashish through the embellishment of the Assassin story.

Although frequently denounced in the Western world as an inciter of violence, there is, however, virtually no mention of disorderly conduct on the part of hashish users in any Arab writings for the past thousand years. Modern scholars have concluded that the identification of hashish as the mysterious potion referred to by Marco Polo cannot be proven.[35] Nor is there any historical basis for the connection between hashish and the murderous activities of the Assassins. The Assassins may have used hashish, but not before they took anyone's life. To do so would have jeopardized their mission.

Nevertheless, hashish, murder, and treachery became inextricably interwoven in cannabis folklore. For example, even as late as 1962, although he clearly acknowledged that "we do not know of any objective study showing a direct or causative relationship between marihuana and violent crime in a significant number of cases," Victor Vogel, chief medical officer of the Narcotics Treatment Center in Lexington, Kentucky, still offered the etymological premise that the words "assassin" and "hashish" are connected to argue in favor of such a relationship:

> Any remarks concerning the relationship of marihuana to crime should be prefaced with the note that marihuana is a form of hashish, a most dangerous drug in its unadulterated form. We get the word assassin from the Italian *assassina* which in turn is derived from the Arabic *Hashshashin*, meaning one who uses hashish; this etymology reflects rather accurately the cultural pedigree of the drug, which has been known for centuries to release impulses toward violence.[36]

---

[34]H. Anslinger and C. R. Cooper, "Marihuana, Assassin of Youth" *American Magazine* 124 (1937): 150.

[35]*Eq.*, M. G. S. Hodgson, *The Order of Assassins* (S'Gravenhage, Holland: Mouton, 1955); B. Lewis, "The Sources for the History of the Syrian Assassins," *Speculum* 27 (1952): 475–89.

[36]D. Maurer and V. Vogel, *Narcotics and Narcotics Addiction* (Springfield, Ill.: Charles C Thomas, 1962), p. 327.

Marihauna and the Law

Between 1926 and 1936, eight major cases came before state courts in which marihuana was an issue.[37] The decisions rendered in these cases are noteworthy for the fact that typically the judgments relied on mythology and opinion rather than on any scientific evidence of the dangers of marihuana.

In 1931, for example, a Louisiana court quoted the story of the Assassins to support its finding that marihuana posed a threat to the community (*State vs. Bonoa*).[38] In a 1933 decision in the Utah courts (*State vs. Navarro*), an ariticle by a Wichita detective was cited as evidence for the criminogenic properties of the drug.

"The courts, like the legislatures," two University of Virginia law professors have recently concluded in reference to these decisions, "assumed marihuana caused crime and insanity, and assumed that had popular opinion crystallized on the question it would have favored suppression of a drug with such evil effects."[39]

What these decisions also show was that the lurid sensationalistic copy of the day was read by the nation's lawmakers and the courts, and that these carried a certain amount of weight insofar as general policy toward marihuana was concerned.

Seducing the Young

By far the most emotional issue surrounding marihuana was the contention that schoolchildren were being seduced into using it by drug pushers who, more often than not, were identified as foreigners, Mexicans, or blacks.

Nowhere was the seduction issue ballyhooed more loudly than in New Orleans where the *Item* and the *Morning Tribune* ran a series of sensationalistic articles describing marihuana's infiltration into the city's schools. According to Dr. Frank Gomila, commissioner of public safety for the city, the marihuana wholesalers in New Orleans were "made up mostly of Mexicans, Italians, Spanish-Americans and drifters from ships."[40] The inference was obviously that American children were being seduced by foreigners.

---

[37]R. J. Bonnie and C. H. Whitehead, "Forbidden Fruit," *Virginia Law Review* 56 (1970): 1022.
[38]Bonnie and Whitebread, "Forbidden Fruit," pp. 1022-3.
[39]Bonnie and Whitebread, "Forbidden Fruit," p. 1026.
[40]Gomila and Lambow, "Present Status," p. 30.

Other newspapers were soon running similar stories. The September 10, 1929, issue of the *Tulsa Tribune* described the arrest of a Mexican "hot-tamale salesman" who, the paper claimed, had been selling marihuana to girls and boys in school. Two years later, a Tulsa attorney got so caught up in the marihuana scare that, in his opinion, "the general use of this drug among young people is making it imperative that the state or the government of the United States take immediate steps to cope with this deadly drug, the dope which is used by murderers."[41]

As early as 1928, the *Kansas City Star* had begun publishing reports of boys and girls using marihuana. By 1933, Detective L. E. Bowery of the Wichita Police Department claimed that

> no denial can be made of the fact that marihuana smoking is at present a common practice among the young people of the city, and that it is constantly becoming more prevalent. Due to its relatively recent introduction into this territory, habitual smoking is at present almost exclusively confined to young persons among the white people. It is interesting to note that the habit has recently spread among the negroes and that they are known to be trafficking in it.[42]

In Gary, Indiana, 25 percent of the Mexican population were said to be smoking marihuana, and of these, many were said to be earning their livings by peddling the drug.[43]

On June 22, 1929, the *Chicago Examiner* reported on the antimarihuana crusade of the local United States attorney, who had moved against storehouses in the city from which marihuana was being "sold to school pupils and other youthful thrillseekers." Of the nine men arrested, "most of them [were] Mexicans."

The *Chicago-Tribune* also took up the issue. The marihuana habit, it said, on June 3, 1927, had been introduced into the city by Mexicans and "has become widespread among American youths... even among school children."

In September 1934, a *New York Times* correspondent described the widespread use of marihuana in Colorado and quoted "some authorities" to the effect that "it is being peddled to school children."

In 1935, the *New York Times* quoted a Sacramento crusader who claimed that "Mexican peddlers have been caught distributing sample marihuana cigarettes to school children."

In 1936, in an article on marihuana ominously prefaced: "Public Health Enemy No. 7," author C. M. Weber reviewed the alleged dan-

[41]Quoted in Bonnie and Whitebread, *Marihuana Conviction*, p. 71.
[42]M. H. Hayes and L. W. Bowery, "Marihuana," *Journal of Criminology* 23, (1933): 1093.
[43]Bonnie and Whitebread, *Marihuana Conviction*, p. 46.

gers of the drug to Americans and repeated previous news reports that about two hundred New Orleans school children were "demand[ing] their reefers."[44]

In Detroit, an "American woman" was said to be peddling marihuana for local Mexicans. "She gives the reefers to her own children to sell to their schoolmates."[45]

"A few years ago," declared an anonymous writer, "the startling discovery was made in St. Louis that scores of youngsters of high school age had been victims of the weed." Quoting an unnamed marihuana peddler, the writer added, "the worst thing about that loco weed is the way these kids go for them. Most of them, boys and girls, are just punks and when they get high on the stuff you can write your own ticket." The writer added that one of the effects of marihuana is that it unleashes uncontrollable passions in the young, backing this up with what to him was a horrible turn of events. "A boy and a girl who had lost their senses so completely after smoking marihuana," he said, actually "eloped and were married"![46]

Feeling that the elopement may not have been shocking enough, the writer dropped his final bombshell: "While it cannot be proved, the increasing number of suicides by jumping from tall buildings may have in fact resulted from the use of this drug. Once started, an addict may be led to commit all of the previously mentioned crimes and the end may be in the gallows, as has been so often the case in recent years."[47]

In Richmond, Virginia, readers of the *Times-Dispatch* were told that "school children were being induced to become addicts of marihuana cigarettes and that the weed was being cultivated in and near the city on a wide scale.... A youth who said he was a former addict of the drug testified before the Council that inhalation of one of the cigarettes would produce a 'cheap drunk' of several days duration."[48]

In *Here's to Crime*, author Courtney R. Cooper, who collaborated with Anslinger on at least one antimarihuana article, charged that

> there is only one end for the confirmed marihuana smoker, and that is insanity. Therefore, it might be of interest to know that one of the main selling places of marihuana in the United States is in the vicinity of high schools....
>
> The use of marihuana has spread within the last few years so rapidly as to constitute a menace which should receive the attention of every thinking parent in America.

---

[44]C. M. Weber, "Mary Warner," *Health Digest* 3 (1936): 77–80.

[45]*New York Times*, May 14, 1936.

[46]"The Menace of Marihuana," *International Medical Digest* 77 (1937): 183–7.

[47]*Ibid.*, p. 184.

[48]Quoted in Bonnie and Whitebread, "Forbidden Fruit," p. 1040.

Having caught the unsuspecting student's attention, the pusher then makes his pitch: "Forthwith the peddler extends a hand filled with marihuanas, and says persuasively; 'Try one of my cigarettes. They are a new special kind; got a real kick in 'em. You'll like 'em; take two or three."[51]

In all fairness to the Rowells, they were not racially motivated when they spoke out against marihuana. Rowell senior was an active campaigner against all vices. He had started out as northwestern organizer and lecturer for the White Cross National Anti-Narcotics Society and later took up the post of state organizer and lecturer for the California branch of the White Cross. While vehemently an antinarcotics group, the White Cross differed from most other institutions, however, in that it supported local treatment of addicts in narcotic clinics rather than sending them to prison. The group was rather influential during the 1920s and 1930s, but it disappeared after World War II.

It was while he worked for the White Cross that Rowell paraded up and down the southwest lecturing against marihuana. But although he claimed that he had been "on the trail of marihuana" since 1925, and had given more than 4000 lectures in forty states, and had personally uprooted and burned many thriving marihuana fields, in an earlier book titled *Battling the Wolves of Society*, which was published in 1929, Rowell included only one paragraph on marihuana and most of that was a quote from De Quincey's *Confessions of an Opium Eater*.[52]

While Rowell may have gotten carried away on the extent of his evangelistic stumping throughout the southwest, he and those like him who crusaded against marihuana were no doubt responsible for the mounting pressure to place legal restrictions on the drug.

MARIHUANA AS A PLOT DEVICE

Newspapers and news magazines were not the only media to exploit and sensationalize the marihuana issue. Having exhausted the drug diaries and confessions of the hashish user genre that had been so popular among the French, inventive novelists and pulp magazine writers saw that they could still use marihuana to sell their works.

In 1900, James Lane Allen's *The Reign of Law* dealt with the history of the Kentucky hemp fields, but the book had nothing to say about

---

[51]E. A. Rowell and R. Rowell, *On the Trail of Marihuana, the Weed of Madness* (Mountainview, Calif.: Pacific Press, 1939), p. 16.
[52]E. A. Rowell, *Battling the Wolves of Society* (Mountainview, Calif.: Pacific Publishers Association, 1929), pp. 35–6.

marihuana. The first of the modern marihuana horror stories appeared in 1915, in what in retrospect is an amusing story entitled "The Poison Ship," published in *Harper's* Magazine. The author, Morgan Robertson, had heard that the hemp plant had narcotic-like effects when smoked, but he knew little else. To him, all hemp was *Cannabis sativa* and in his story he has "burning jute (New Zealand hemp)" giving "off the soporific fumes of hashish" which "produces drowsiness, then wild dreams and waking ecstasy."

In Robertson's imaginative story, a passenger ship carrying jute in its hold catches fire and the fumes overwhelm and intoxicate the passengers. First, they become excited and talkative, but soon they are thrown into a stupefying frenzy. The crew is likewise rendered senseless and unable to function. Most of those on board perish, but a few are rescued.

A 1917 thriller by Carl Moore appeared in *Spicy-Adventure Stories* and is just as ridiculous. Set in London, it has Scotland Yard detectives surreptiously getting a murder suspect to take some hashish. Overcome by the drug, the suspect loses consciousness, convulses, and subsequently reenacts the crime he has been arrested for (rape and murder). Convicted by the evidence, he is later hanged.

Sax Rohmer, the well-known author of the *Fu Manchu* mysteries, also used hashish to heighten the excitement of *Dope* (1919), one of his books in which the Chinese (but not Fu Manchu) are the villains. Although about opium and its effects, Rohmer intimates that hashish is far more evil. In a scene in which Mrs. Sin is entertaining Mollie, Mollie says she just read Hector France's *Musk Hashish, and Blood* (published in 1900):

> "Hashish!" said Mrs. Sin, and laughed harshly. "One night you shall eat the hashish, and then—"
> "Oh really? Is that a promise?" asked Mollie eagerly.
> "No, no," answered Mrs. Sin. "It is a threat!"[53]

Other writers also tried to add mystery to their characters by having them use hashish. Carl Van Vechten's *Peter Whiffle* (1925) was an avid experimenter with mind-expanding drugs, among which was hashish. Whiffle had been told that hashish causes uncontrollable laughter but his reaction is only one of melancholy and despair. The experience so upsets him that his "nerves revolved under the strain" and he is forced to remain in bed for four days to recover.

Thomas Burke's *Tai Fu and Pansy Greers* presents another picture of hashish.[54] Capitalizing on the anti-Chinese sentiment in Britain so well

---

[53]S. Rohmer, *Dope* (New York: McKinlay, Stone and MacKenzie, 1914), p. 154.
[54]T. Burke, "Tai Fu and Pansy Greers," *Limehouse Nights* (New York: R. M. McBride & Co., 1926).

After describing the dangers of marihuana, Cooper next indicted
every apartment building owner in the United States: "Apartments are
run by ghoul-minded women; in such apartments high school students
gather on the promise that reefer-smoking will put music in their souls
and a release from all moral restrain; nothing is said about eventual
insanity."

Cooper then introduced the sexual promiscuity theme:

> Then suddenly a girl wanted to dance. Immediately everyone wanted to
> dance. . . . The movements were of sensuosity. After a time, girls began to
> pull off their clothes. Men weaved naked over them; soon the entire room
> was one of the wildest sexuality. Ordinary intercourse and several forms of
> perversion were going on at once, girl to girl, man to man, woman to wo-
> man.
>
> This is one of the great reasons why girls who are little more than
> children are now being placed in whorehouses by members of prostitution
> syndicates, why young boys of otherwise straight habits suddenly join up
> with dangerous gangs, why there are constantly more murders committed by
> youth. . . .[49]

It was gutsy stuff. Although he meant to scare readers away from
marihuana, Cooper's prose probably pricked the curious to try the drug
for themselves more than it frightened anyone.

An article by Dr. Arthur La Roe, president of the American Narcotic
Defense Association, in the *American Weekly* (1940), is deserving of recognition as the most ludicrous of the marihuana seduction literature.
The article, entitled "Growth of the Marihuana Habit Among Our
Youth," shows a posed photograph of a "slick," as La Roe calls him,
loitering outside a school waiting for the students to leave. This "slick"
is described as "dapper" and "suave" and is shown wearing a sport
jacket and tie. He is, however, only a decoy for the seedy pusher. It is
his job to lure students to the pusher who is waiting at a table somewhere for his naïve prey. Once seated at the table, the "slick" and the
pusher "then smoke the reefers; inhalation of the smoke in the room
'pre-conditions' the 'guests' so that moral resistance is lowered."[50]

Another popular example of the unsuspecting youth and diabolical
pusher motifs appeared in *On the Trail of Marihuana, the Weed of Madness,*
a short, hysterical antimarihuana polemic written by Earle Albert Rowell
and his son Robert. According to this father and son duo, "one of the
methods used in making marihuana users is for the peddler, with an
unlighted marihuana cigarette in his hand, to step up to a high-school
boy or girl who is smoking a tobacco cigarette and say, 'Give me a light, I
haven't a match.' "

[49]C. R. Cooper, *Here's to Crime* (Boston: Little Brown, 1937), pp. 333–8.
[50]A. La Roe, "Growth of the Marihuana Habit Among Our Youth" (1940), reprinted in
Stone Mountain, *Pot Art* (Tucson, Ariz.: Apocrypha Press, 1970), pp. 4–5.

exploited by Sax Rohmer, Burke's Tai Fu is depicted as a repulsive Chinese denizen of London's underworld who has many vices, among which is hashish.

Algernon Blackwood's *A Psychic Invasion* gives hashish black magic veneer. In this story, hashish is a drug which "has partially opened another world to you by increasing your rate of psychical vibration, and thus rendering you abnormally sensitive" to the spirit world,[55] the main character informs his client who has come to him because he has become disturbed by strange things that go bump in the night. He has been sensitized to these poltergeists as a result of taking hashish.

The *Dope Adventures of David Dare* marks the high or low point in this genre.[56] Written by Earle Albert Rowell, the novel is set in middle America amid a quintessential all-American-boy-next-door, apple-pie mom-and-motherhood setting. David Dare exposes the marihuana menace in his hometown and is rewarded by being made an honorary police officer.

While the impact of these naïve stories was less than minimal, they show that during the early decades of the nineteenth century familiarity with marihuana, even on the part of those who wrote about the drug, was negligible and the attitudes toward the drug were all negative.

The movies also capitalized on the marihuana-evil sentiment. In 1927 *Notch Number One* appeared on the silver screen starring Ben Wilson as a ranch foreman intent on keeping his cowhands from falling victim to marihuana's heinous spell. As the audience watched the drama unfold, Wilson holds a marihuana cigarette out for a headstrong cowpuncher to inspect, cautioning him that he is holding "a devilish narcotic" in his hand, which if smoked, will send him to "the bughouse, loco... [and will make him] want to raise H - - - in general." The ranchhand does not take the fatherly advice, however, and tries it out—and sure enough, he goes berserk.[57]

JANEY CANUCK

Across the Forty-ninth Parallel in the Dominion of Canada, marihuana was virtually unknown, although hemp was a fiber crop across the country until the days of the Depression. Up until 1908, in fact, there were no national restrictions against any drugs. But an economic crisis and anti-Chinese sentiment in the province of British Co-

[55]A. Blackwood, "A Psychic Invasion," *The Tales of Algernon Blackwood* (New York: E. P. Dutton, 1939).
[56]E. A. Rowell, *The Dope Adventures of David Dare* (Nashville: Richwook & Co., 1937).
[57]J. Kane, "Dope in the Cinema," *High Times*, no. 79, (1977), p. 74.

lumbia on the west coast stirred racist fires. Stories of white women and children being lured into opium dens, rumors of huge profits in opium, and moral indignation over drug abuse in general, eventually caused Deputy Minister of Labor (who would latter become Prime Minister) William Lyon Mackenzie King to recommend to the House of Commons suppression of opium traffic in Canada. There was little opposition to such a proposal, and in 1908 it became illegal in Canada to import, manufacture, sell, or possess for sale opiates for nonmedical use. As in the United States, however, possession for personal use was not outlawed since Canadians were not as yet ready to make criminals out of drug users.

In 1908, Canada also passed the Patent and Proprietary Medicine Act. Like the American Pure Food and Drug Law of 1906, the Canadian law required the labeling of certain ingredients in medicines. Although the presence of opiates had to be indicated, the amount of alcohol limited, and cocaine banned outright, no restrictions were placed on cannabis.

In 1909, Canada participated in the international conference on opium in Shanghai. As a result of his previous activities in the outlawing of opiate traffic in Canada, Mackenzie King was included in the Canadian delegation. The fact that Canada did not support the American and Italian initiatives to include cannabis in the list of proscribed drugs being considered by the delegates likewise indicates how little importance Canada attached to marihuana during these early years. In 1911, Canada passed the Opium and Drug Act. The new law broadened the ban against opium by adding morphine, cocaine, and their derivatives to the list of proscribed drugs. Again, cannabis was not mentioned.

Marihuana continued to be ignored in the 1910s and would have remained so in the 1920s had it not been for a Canadian crusading feminist who wrote under the pen name of "Janey Canuck."

Janey's real name was Mrs. Emily F. Murphy. She was a tough-minded woman who had the persistence and aggressiveness to overcome the barriers placed against women in her time. As a feminist, she fought for the right for women to be tried in court by other women and before female judges, and for her efforts, in 1916 she was appointed the first woman judge in the British Empire.

In 1920, the Canadian government indicated that it was once again about to amend its drug laws, and *Maclean's magazine* asked Judge Murphy if she would be willing to write some pieces on the drug problem in Canada. Murphy was more than willing.

Although sincerely interested in helping many of those who appeared before her, Murphy had no sympathy for drug sellers or users. Writing under the name of "Janey Canuck," her indictment of these "dregs of humanity," as she called them, was pure racism. These people, she told her readers, were mostly nonwhite (Chinese and Negroes) and non-Christians, who, next to drugs, craved nothing better than the seduction of Canadian women. Behind these outcasts, she maintained, was an international conspiracy of yellow and black drug pushers whose ultimate goal was the domination of the "bright-browed races of the world." Among her recommendations for dealing with these drug fiends were long prison sentences, whippings, and deportations if the offenders were aliens.

In anything, Janey was consistent. She was against all drugs associated with minorities, even marihuana, a drug that was totally unknown in Canada. Quoting American authorities, she said that marihuana drove its users completely insane: "The addict loses all sense of moral responsibility. Addicts to this drug, while under its influence, are immune to pain.... While in this condition they become raving maniacs and are liable to kill or indulge in any form of violence to other persons, using the most savage methods of cruelty without, as said before, any sense of moral responsibility."[58]

So sensational and popular were Janey's writings on the drug evil in Canada that they were eventually collected into a book, *The Black Candle* (1922). More significantly, Janey single-handedly succeeded in altering Canadian views of drugs and drug users. Hitherto, drug users had been merely been regarded as moral degenerates. After Janey's exposé, they became public enemies, bent on the destruction of the White race. And whereas Canadians had never heard of marihuana before Murphy, after reading about marihuana in *Maclean's* and *The Black Candle*, Canadian lawmakers were quick to add it to the list of regulated substances in the Opium and Narcotics Drug Act of 1929.

According to a 1934 editorial in the *Canadian Medical Association Journal*, the first indication that marihuana had entered the country occurred in 1931. By 1932, the drug had worked its way to Ottawa, Ontario, the nation's capital. In Windsor, across the border from Detroit, "it was learned that some thirty young people in that city were addicted to marihuana. These cigarettes," the editorial noted, "were peddled in dance halls" and were being brought in from across the border in Detroit. By 1933, the drug had spread to Montréal, and by 1934 it had even worked its way to Toronto "the Good [city]."

In assessing marihuana's inroads into Canada, the editorial warned that

the menace is a serious one, for the experience of all countries is that the hashish habit has a special appeal to the young, not, necessarily, that they

[58]E. F. Murphy, *The Black Candle* (Toronto: Coles Publishing, 1973), pp. 332–3.

crave for the drug, at least at first, but they use it with the desire to appear "smart." Then comes the urge for more, and a dangerous habit is created.[59]

There were also reports on the international scene of marihuana's inroads into Canada. In 1933, the Advisory Committee on Traffic in Opium and Other Dangerous Drugs of the League of Nations noted in its annual report that "a smuggling trade in cigarettes containing Indian hemp ('marijuana' cigarettes) appears to have sprung up between the USA, where it grows as a wild plant freely, and Canada."[60]

Despite Janey Canuck's dire warnings and the marihuana "menace" uncovered by the Canadian Medical Association, and League of Nations, there were only twenty-five convictions in Canada for marihuana possession between 1930 and 1946.[61] The Royal Canadian Mounted Police (Canada's counterpart to the FBI), note that "prior to 1962, isolated cases of cannabis use were encountered, but generally in connection with entertainers and visitors from the United States. Although marihuana arrests were effected sporadically in the middle 40s, its use on a more frequent basis appeared in Montreal only in 1962, in Toronto in 1963 and in Vancouver in 1965."[62]

Although cannabis could no longer be legally grown in Canada without a permit after 1938, it was still dispensed in pharmacies as an over-the-counter medicinal until 1939 and was used in prescriptions until 1954.[63]

In 1961, cannabis was included in the Narcotic Control Act and stringent penalties were applied for possession. In 1970, the law was amended and sentences were considerably softened. In 1972, revisions in the Canadian Criminal Code fixed the penalty for simple possession at a minimal fine.

THE INTERNATIONAL DEBATE

The United States was not the only country to become overly concerned with marihuana during the early decades of the twentieth century. The government of South Africa was also concerned lest drugs turn its black population into an unruly mob. Dagga was a popular

[59]Editorial, "Marihuana," *Canadian Medical Association Journal* 31 (1934): 545.
[60]Quoted in K. Bruun, L. Pan, and I. Rexed, *The Gentlemen's Club* (Chicago: University of Chicago Press, 1975), p. 184.
[61]M. Green and R. D. Miller, "Cannabis Use in Canada," in *Cannabis and Culture*, ed. V. Rubin (The Hague: Mouton 1975), p. 498.
[62]Quoted in *ibid*.
[63]Green and Miller, "Canada," p. 498.

intoxicant with natives throughout Africa and the government of South Africa felt that it posed a tangible danger to the white minority. Accordingly, when the Advisory Committee of the League of Nations met in 1923, the South African delegation urged that the League classify cannabis as a habit-forming narcotic and recommended that international traffic in the drug be brought under the control of The Hague convention.

Anxious that such a measure might affect England's cannabis revenues in India, the British delegate managed to block adoption of such a measure by urging that more information be obtained on such a motion and that the issue be taken up again at the next meeting of the Second Geneva Opium Conference scheduled for 1925.

Owing to some maneuvering by England, the matter was not even included in the agenda in 1925, but nevertheless the issue was introduced by M. E. Guindry, who headed the Egyptian delegation. Like the South African government, Egypt was also concerned about the social impact of cannabis on its people.

Steven Porter, the head of the American delegation, likewise spoke on behalf of a resolution to ban international traffic in cannabis, but his support was given mainly in the spirit of "reciprocity," as he put it, for the support the other nations had given the United States in its crusade against opium. If the United States had a cannabis problem, Porter was not aware of it.

Next came the turn of countries opposed to such a policy. The delegation from India pointed out that cannabis held a unique place in Indian life and emphasized that "there are social and religious customs which naturally have to be considered, and there is doubt whether the total prohibition of drugs easily prepared from a wild-growing plant could in practice be made effective."[64]

Sir Malcolm Delevigne took a different tack. He protested that the delegates had not been prepared for any discussion regarding cannabis and consequently they had not been given any instructions on how to vote on such an issue by their governments.

Bourgeois, the French delegate, concurred with Delevigne on the inappropriateness of adopting such a measure without first having time to consider it in detail. Furthermore, he contended that while it might be possible to outlaw the use of cannabis in France, it would be impossible to do so in the French Congo where there were "several tribes of savages and even cannibals among whom the habit is very prevalent. It would

---

[64]Quoted in W. W. Willoughby, *Opium as an International Problem* (Baltimore: Johns Hopkins University Press, 1925), p. 382.

therefore be hypocritical on my part," he told the gathering, "to sign a Convention laying down strict measures in this respect."[65]

The issue was ultimately referred to a subcommittee which later reported certain major problems associated with placing sanctions on cannabis: "It should ... be remembered that all derivatives of hemp are capable of providing, in addition to products injurious to public health, fibers which can be used in industry (cloth, cordage, matting, etc.) and that the oil seeds may also be employed for domestic purposes. That being the case, it would not appear to be any easy matter to limit the amount grown."[66]

After due consideration was given to these various problems, a recommendation was offered whereby export of cannabis resin would be prohibited to any country unless the recipient signed a special import certificate stating that such importation was to be used exclusively for medical or scientific purposes.

The recommendation was voted on and approved but the proposal was not signed by all the delegate nations, thereby making international control unworkable. Among the nations not signing the proposal were the United States and Egypt, which had brought the problem up in the first place.

[65] Ibid.
[66] Ibid, p. 383.

13

Outlawing Marihuana

On August 12, 1930, the Federal Bureau of Narcotics was created as an independent unit in the Treasury Department and Harry J. Anslinger was appointed the bureau's first commissioner of narcotics by President Hoover.

During its earliest years, the bureau's primary concern was violation of the Harrison Act. Although mounting attention was being directed at the marihuana issue in the southwest, Anslinger felt that the problem was relatively negligible. The only people using marihuana to any great extent were the Mexicans and it was only from local law enforcement officers that the bureau heard any complaints. Policing the traffic in narcotics left little time to worry about the use of marihuana by some Mexicans. Yet by 1937 Anslinger was able to persuade Congress to adopt draconian federal antimarihuana legislation. There have been many explanations for this dramatic turn of events, none of them satisfactory. But one thing is certain. Without Harry Anslinger, the marihuana maelstrom might have been just a passing breeze.

HARRY J. ANSLINGER

Although Anslinger has been accused of single-handedly manufacturing the marihuana problem in the United States, much of what he did was the result of a sincere conviction that drugs such as marihuana did pose a danger to the country. Few people ever doubted his sincerity or his devotion to the office of commissioner of narcotics when he spoke out against drugs. He was, however, not above exploiting controversial issues to achieve what he felt was in the best interest of the American people and the bureau which he headed.

When Anslinger assumed the position of Bureau of Narcotics chief, he was already a hard-liner on drug abuse. For example, in dealing with violation of the Prohibition Act which outlawed only the sale, manufacture, and transportation of liquor for sale, but not its purchase, Anslinger contended that if it were up to him, the law would be changed so that buyers would also be subject to punishment. And no small punishment at that. For a first-time conviction he thought that a jail term of not less than six months and a fine of not less than $1000 was appropriate. A second violation, he felt, deserved imprisonment for two to five years and a fine of $5000 to $50,000.

Had Anslinger had his way there might have been many more Americans in jail. It was Anslinger's opinion, an opinion that he later carried over to his new post as commissioner of the Bureau of Narcotics, that the only way to force the public to obey the liquor and drug laws was to impose stiff penalties on those who broke these laws. While his suggestions for heavy fines and imprisonment were never endorsed in the case of buyers of alcoholic beverages, they were accepted in dealing with violation of the narcotics and later the marihuana laws which did make consumers liable for their actions.

Anslinger developed this hard-line attitude toward drug users during his youth and early career in the Treasury Department. Born in Altoona, Pennsylvania, in 1892, he spent his early years attending school and working summers for the Pennsylvania Railroad as an assistant to the railway police. He says that he first became alerted to the evils of narcotics when a friend of his, a choirboy, "died from smoking opium."[1]

In 1917, after the United States entered World War I, Anslinger became an ordinance officer in the War Department supervising government contracts. Unhappy with this domestic duty, he applied to the State Department for overseas assignment and was sent to Holland as attaché in the American legation.

After the war, he remained in the foreign service until 1926, serving as consul in Hamburg, Germany; La Guaira, Venezuela; and Nassau, Bahamas. It was as consul in this latter post that the Treasury Department first took notice of him for it was through his efforts that England agreed to keep a fleet of rumrunners from heading out to the high seas and eventually carrying their cargoes to the United States. For helping to plug this hole in the smuggling side of Prohibition, he was appointed to the Treasury Deparment's Prohibition Unit. Three years later, in 1929, he became assistant commissioner of Prohibition.

In 1930, Anslinger's career was given a major boost as a result of a scandal that toppled many of the bureau's key figures. A number of

[1]H. J. Anslinger and W. Oursler, *The Murderers. The Story of the Narcotics Gangs* (New York: Farrar, Straus, 1961), p. 9.

agents attached to the New York office of the Narcotics Division of the Prohibition Bureau had been caught padding their arrest records to make themselves look better, and all hell broke loose. A grand jury investigation found that these agents had been falsifying arrest records on orders from Assistant Deputy Commissioner William Blanchard. Blanchard in turn incriminated Deputy Commissioner L. G. Nutt. It was the grand jury's finding that these actions had been carried out to hide a dismal arrest record which it attributed to probable collusion between federal narcotics agents and drug distributors.

Not long thereafter, Congress stripped control over narcotics from the scandal-torn Prohibition Unit and created an entirely new department, the Bureau of Narcotics, under the auspices of the Treasury Department with Harry Anslinger as its first commissioner.

When Anslinger took command of the Bureau of Narcotics, he inherited a philosophy of law enforcement regarding narcotics that he could willingly endorse, namely that "strong laws, good enforcement [and] stiff sentences" were the bureau's best weapons in the fight to eradicate addiction. It was a philosophy that would characterize the bureau's attitude toward drug issues for years to come.

While Anslinger was undoubtedly a dedicated and conscientious public servant who worked hard and long at combatting what he felt was a national and international menace, he was above all an astute and calculating bureaucrat. It was because of his astuteness that he was initially cool to those who pressured him to join the fight against marihuana.

For one thing, past experience enforcing Prohibition and the Harrison Act had taught him that the federal courts had limited jurisdiction in prosecuting alcohol- and drug-related offenses. They could not, for instance, prosecute buyers of alcohol. Such prosecution could only be handled at the state level. Similarly, although the intention of the Harrison Act had been to curtail the unsanctioned use of narcotic drugs, the law was basically a taxing measure. The law did not prohibit possession.

A second reason for Anslinger's initial reluctance to join in an antimarihuana campaign on a federal level was that there was no federal law under which marihuana offenses could be prosecuted. The Harrison Act did not apply since it encompased only drugs not grown in the United States such as opium.

A third reason may have been Anslinger's realization, even in the early 1930s, that it would take far more men than the bureau could spare to enforce any laws against marihuana. Until some way could be found to get around those administrative problems, Anslinger had second thoughts about putting the bureau's weight behind any antimarihuana measures:

> A great deal of public interest has been aroused by newspaper articles appearing from time to time on the evils of the abuse of marihuana, or Indian hemp, and more attention has been focussed upon specific cases reported of the abuse of the drug than would otherwise have been the case. This publicity tends to magnify the extent of the evil and lends color to an influence that there is an alarming spread of the improper use of the drug, whereas the actual increase in such use may not have been inordinately large.[2]

This communiqué was issued in 1932. Later that same year, Anslinger began to reassess his stand on the marihuana issue, not because of any change of mind regarding the drug's alleged menace, but because the Bureau of Narcotics was in danger of floundering.

THE BUREAU JOINS THE FIGHT

Deep in the throes of the Depression, Congress began to examine budgetary requirements from all federal agencies, and the Bureau of Narcotics was no exception. Requests for even small amounts of money had to be supported with documentation of the need for such spending. The bureau's budget was cut by $200,000, the number of agents on the payroll was reduced, and Anslinger began to fear that the bureau itself was in danger of emasculation.[3] To maintain its virility, Anslinger had to prove that there was a new drug menace threatening the country, one that required immediate federal attention, one that the Bureau of Narcotics could deal with if only its hands were not tied. To prove the reality of the menace, Anslinger was prepared to spare no effort or guile.

A great believer in the force of public opinion, Anslinger reverted to the type of media campaign that had proven so successful when the Narcotics Division sought to expand in 1915—he began to supply information to organizations like the WCTU, community service clubs, and the popular press concerning alleged atrocities committed by people under the influence of marihuana. The bureau made no secret of this publicity campaign:

> Articles were prepared in the Federal Bureau of Narcotics, at the request of a number of organizations dealing with this general subject [uniform state drug laws] for publication by such organizations in magazines and newspapers. An intelligent and sympathetic public interest, helpful to the administration of the narcotic laws has been aroused and maintained.[4]

[2]Quoted in S. Meisler, "Federal Narcotics Czar," *The Nation* 190 (1960): 160.

[3]D. T. Dickson, "Bureaucracy and Morality: An Organizational Perspective on a Moral Crusade," *Social Problems* 16 (1968): 143–56.

[4]U.S. Bureau of Narcotics, *Traffic in Opium and Other Drugs* (Washington, D.C.: U.S. Government Printing Office, 1934), p. 61.

Whereas only two such articles appeared in the American popular press between 1920 and 1929, after 1930 they began to appear on the market in a steady stream. Among the titles appearing on the newstands were: "Youth Gone Loco" (*Christian Century*), "Marihuana: Assassin of Youth" (*American Magazine*), "Uncle Sam Fights a New Drug Menace—Marihuana" (*Popular Science Monthly*), "One More Peril for Youth" (*Forum*), "Sex Crazing Drug Menace" (*Physical Culture*), "The Menace of Marihuana" (*American Mercury*), "Tea for a Viper" (*New Yorker*), and "Exposing the Marihuana Drug Evil in Swing Bands" (*Radio Stars*). Although most of these articles appeared after enactment of federal antimarihuana legislation, most of them drew their information from the files of the Bureau of Narcotics just before Anslinger prepared his assault on Capitol Hill.[5]

Typical of the lurid sensationalistic prose in which Anslinger wrapped his message is the following excerpt from an article written for *American Magazine* in 1937 by Anslinger himself:

> The sprawled body of a young girl lay crushed on the sidewalk the other day after a plunge from the fifth story of a Chicago apartment house. Everyone called it suicide but actually it was murder. The killer was a narcotic known to America as marihuana, and history as hashish. It is a narcotic used in the form of cigarettes, comparatively new to the United States and as dangerous as a coiled rattlesnake.[6]

This was typical of the bureau's "educational campaign describing the drug, its identification, and its evil effects. . . ."[7]

Meanwhile, Anslinger began to urge that marihuana be included in the Uniform State Narcotic Act that was making the rounds of various state legislatures. This law gave each state the power to arrest addicts for possession of oulawed drugs, and in so doing effectively closed the loophole that undermined the Harrison Act. Had it not been for Anslinger's campaign against marihuana, few of the states adopting the act would have included marihuana in its provisions. For example, by 1935 only three states out of the twelve that had adopted it included marihuana in its list of proscribed drugs. This was well before Anslinger's machine was operating at maximum efficiency. By 1936, all eighteen of the states that adopted the act that year included marihuana.

---

[5]Of the seventeen articles dealing with marihuana indexed in the *Reader's Guide to Periodical Literature* from July 1937 to July 1939, ten acknowledged the help of the Bureau of Narcotics in supplying information (H. Becker, *Outsiders* [New York: The Free Press: 1963], p. 141).

[6]H. J. Anslinger and C. R. Cooper, "Marihuana: Assassin of Youth," *American Magazine* 124 (1937): 19.

[7]Anslinger and Oursler, *Murderers*, p. 10.

Yet, far from being whipped into a panic over the "killer drug," most Americans seemed totally unconcerned or aware that there was a drug menace threatening the country. Many congressmen likewise were ignorant of the bureau's efforts to arouse the nation over marihuana, and Anslinger felt that he had to do something else to capture their attention.

Looking back over the way in which the Opium and Harrison Acts had come into being, Anslinger realized that one way to pressure Congress into moving against marihuana was to embarrass the nation's lawmakers. By making the United States a party to international restrictions on the drug, it would be placed in the position of agreeing to international sanctions without having domestic sanctions. Once the United States became a signatory to an international treaty, Anslinger felt that Congress would have to adopt federal antimarihuana legislation despite opposition on constitutional grounds to any law restricting cannabis on the basis of current federal tax or interstate laws. Once the U.S. was party to an international drug agreement, Anslinger suggested that the Treasury could overcome constitutional opposition by citing the precedent of the Migratory Bird Act, a law that had been declared constitutional even though it called for overstepping state police powers because it was part of an international treaty with Canada and Mexico, as a way of overriding any opposition.[8]

To that end, Anslinger traveled to Geneva in 1936 to attend the Conference for the Suppression of Illicit Traffic in Dangerous Drugs. As one of the American delegates to the conference, he urged the other members to include control of cannabis in any drug treaty that they, as representatives of their respective governments, might adopt. The other delegates refused to agree to such a request since a subcommittee charged with looking into the cannabis question indicated that not enough was known about the physiological, psychological, or psychopathic effects, addictive properties, or cannabis's relation to crime, to warrant any such proposal.

Anslinger left Geneva despondent, refusing to sign any of the resolutions adopted by the convention because no provisions had been adopted for punishment of "illegal cultivation and gathering of cannabis" and because the provisions that had been adopted were "inadequate as far as cannabis was concerned."[9]

[8]D. Musto, "The Marihuana Tax Act of 1937," *Archives of General Psychiatry* 26 (1972): 105.
[9]A. Lander, "The International Drug Control System," in *Drug Use in America: Problem in Perspective* (Washington, D.C.: National Commission on Marihuana and Drug Abuse, 1973), 3: 25.

"I Believe It Is a Narcotic of Some Kind"

After consultation with Anslinger, the Treasury Department began to prepare its case to Congress for outlawing marihuana. The hearings were set for the spring of 1937. In January of that year, Anslinger met with the department's legal and medical experts to review how the case would be presented.

Typical of the kind of evidence the department was going to depend on is a question put to Anslinger by one of the department's lawyers: "Have you lots of cases on this?—Horror stories, that's what we want."[10]

Horror stories were Anslinger's strong suit. He had files and files of them. There would be no problem along those lines, he assured the legal staff. Then, as if to belie all that he himself had written on the marihuana issue, Anslinger turned to the department's drug authority, Dr. Carl Voegtlin, and asked in all sincerity whether the doctor thought that marihuana really did produce insanity![11]

The actual hearings took place in late April and early May of that year. As presented to Congress, the antimarihuana bill stipulated that all handlers of cannabis had to be registered and pay a special occupational tax. Written forms had to be submitted and filed for every transaction involving cannabis, and payment of a transfer tax of one dollar per ounce had to be paid each time the drug was delivered to an authorized recipient.

The bill was introduced by Clinton M. Hester, the Treasury Department's assistant general counsel. Hester told the House Committee on Ways and Means that the Treasury Department had taken it upon itself to call for federal laws against marihuana after a two-year study by the Bureau of Narcotics revealed that the drug was "being used extensively by high school children in cigarettes." "Its effect," he told the House committee, "is deadly."[12]

No estimates of how many Americans were using marihuana were ever discussed. No qualified experts were summoned to support the bureau's claim either that children were using marihuana, that marihuana was causing Americans to commit crimes, or that marihuana was "deadly."

What the committee did hear was excerpts from newspapers and

[10]Quoted in D. Musto, *The American Disease* (New Haven: Yale University Press, 1973), p. 227.
[11]*Ibid.*
[12]Hearings before Committee on Ways and Means on H.R. 6385. House of Representatives, 75th Congress. 1st Session, 1937, p. 6.

magazines describing the dangers of the drug: "The leading newspapers of the United States have recognized the seriousness of this problem and many of them have advocated Federal legislation to control the traffic in marihuana."[13] What the committee did not know was that the bureau had supplied many of the gruesome stories upon which the newspapers based their appeal for something to be done.

The other main piece of evidence to be introduced was Eugene Stanley's article "Marihuana as a Developer of Criminals."[14] No reference was made to any of the studies carried out in the Canal Zone which contradicted everything Stanley or Anslinger said about marihuana.

The committee heard from Dr. James Munch, a pharmacologist who had been giving marihuana to dogs. Asked if the drug altered the personality of dogs, the pharmacologist answered with an unqualified "yes. So far as I can tell, not being a dog psychologist."[15]

The Treasury Department's medical witness was none other than Commissioner Harry Anslinger, who offered his own medical opinion of the dangers of marihuana, an opinion that was liberally spiked with a historically inaccurate rendering of the hoary legend of the Assassins. After the Treasury Department presented its case it was time to hear from the other side.

According to the provisions of the bill, industrial uses of the plant were to be protected from interference by defining the term "marihuana" to exclude the mature stalk and its compounds or manufactures. This provision had been included to appease the rope and cordage industry. Seeds, however, had not been excluded from the definition of marihuana, even though there was a recognized industrial use for them in producing oil for the paint and varnish industries. The reason for not excluding marihuana seeds was that they contained minute amounts of the intoxicating substance produced by the plant.

The failure to exclude marihuana seeds from the law brought a cry of protest not only from the paint and varnish makers but also from the birdseed industry, which used millions of pounds of cannabis seed a year as bird food. The birdseed representative appeared almost too late to present his case, explaining that the birdseed industry had only just realized that marihuana was another name for the hemp plant! When asked whether the seeds had the same effect in pigeons as in humans, the birdseed spokesman replied that he had never noticed any special

---

[13] *Ibid.*, p. 30.
[14] E. Stanley, "Marihuana as a Developer of Criminals," *American Journal of Police Science* 2(1931): 252–61.
[15] Hearings, p. 51.

effect. "It has a tendency to bring back the feathers, and improve the birds," he told the committee.[16]

So as not to ruin the birdseed industry, the provisions of the bill were changed. Marihuana seeds would be excluded from the definition of marihuana, provided that they were sterilized, a process that would ensure that they could not be used to grow new plants.

More serious opposition came from the medical profession. Dr. William Woodward, the legislative council for the AMA, challenged the Treasury Department on all fronts:

> We are told that the use of marihuana causes crime. But as yet no one has been produced from the Bureau of Prisons to show the number of persons addicted to marihuana. An informal inquiry shows that the Bureau of Prisons has no information to this point. You have been told that school children are great users of marihuana cigarettes. No one has been summoned from the Children's Bureau to show the nature and extent of the habit among children. Inquiry into the Office of Education, and they certainly should know something of the prevalence of the habit among school children of this country, if there is a prevalent habit, indicates that they had not occasion to investigate it and know nothing of it.[17]

The danger, Woodward insisted, was only in the minds of the Bureau of Narcotics. There was no evidence to believe that marihuana posed any danger to the country. Although he assumed that there must

---

[16]However, an 1895 text on pigeons states: "Hempseed, if sound and good, they are very fond of, and it is very beneficial at times, especially in cold weather, or given as a relish and not as regular food. It is, in fact, a stimulant, and to be so regarded. If a bird appear low-spirited, nothing will cheer it up more than a little good hempseed mixed with some dry raw rice" (quoted in W. M. Levi, *The Pigeon* [Sumter, S.: Levi Publishing Co., 1957] p. 450).

Another text written in 1914 notes: "Hemp, sometimes recommended, is of use only as a pick-me-up in the case of a bird that happens to be out of sorts . . ." (quoted in Levi, *The Pigeon,* 450).

In 1912, Dr. Victor Robinson wrote about cannabis seeds: "Some birds consume them to excess which should lead us to suspect that these seeds tho they cannot intoxicate us, have a narcotic effect on the feathered creatures, making them dream of a happy birdland where there are no gilded cages, and where the men are gunless and the women hatless" (V. Robinson, "An Essay on Hasheesh; Including Observations and Experiments," *Medical Review of Reviews* 18 [1912]: 162).

In 1957, W. M. Levi, who during 1917–8 had been a first lieutenant in charge of the Pigeon Section, U.S. Signal Corps, and president of the Palmetto Pigeon Plant from 1923 to 1956, also referred to the effects of hemp seeds on pigeons: "In addition to the actual physical effect produced upon the bird's body, its feeding has a decided beneficial psychological effect upon the bird's happiness. Pigeons fed sparingly with a little hemp in the middle of the day during the moulting season take a new interest in life which is almost inconceivable" (Levi, *The Pigeon,* p. 499).

[17]Hearings, p. 92.

be some basis to all the furor over marihuana in the press, Woodward asked why the facts upon which these statements had been made had not been introduced as firsthand testimony. Since when, he wanted to know, did press coverage constitute anything more than heresay.

The AMA was not even aware that an antimarihuana law was being prepared by the bureau. "During the past 2 years," he told the committee, "I have visited the Bureau of Narcotics probably 10 or more times. Unfortunately, I had no knowledge that such a bill as this was proposed until after it had been introduced."[18]

Had he been aware of such an event, no doubt Woodward would have been able to call upon expert testimony from witnesses such as Drs. Bromberg and Siler whose studies did not support the bureau's allegations. "We cannot understand yet, Mr. Chairman," Woodward said, "why this bill should have been prepared in secret for 2 years without any intimation even to the profession, that it was being prepared."

The answer, of course, was that the bureau did not want any opposition. By bringing it up without any prior warning, it forced the opposition to prepare a last-minute case.

The AMA, however, objected to the marihuana law not because of any liberal attitude toward the drug or its users (Dr. Morris Fishbein, editor of the *Journal of the American Medical Association*, had sanctioned publication of an article in *Hygeia* which claimed that marihuana was an inciter of sex crimes, murder, and insanity[19]), but for other reasons. Enforcement of the Harrison Act and Prohibition had led to a certain amount of annoyance and outright harassment of physicians. Many doctors felt that these laws were an infringement of their right to treat their patients as they saw fit. Even though the number of prescriptions for cannabis was minimal and the tax was only one dollar an ounce, the AMA remembered the difficulties doctors had faced in connection with other drug laws and therefore it opposed any further infringements of like nature on the medical profession.

At the time Woodward appeared before the committee, the AMA was not one of Congress's favorite institutions. Many of the committee's members were still upset at the AMA's successful fight to block health insurance from being included in the Social Security Act[20] and they were not in any mood to consider further interference from the AMA, regardless of how much merit there was to Woodward's statement. "If you want to advise us on legislation," Woodward was told, "you ought to

[18]*Ibid.*, p. 116.
[19]G. R. McCormack, *"Marihuana,"* Hygeia 15 (1937): 898–9.
[20]Musto, *American Disease*, p. 228.

come here with some constructive proposals, rather than criticism, rather than trying to throw obstacles in the way of something that the Federal Government is trying to do."

Soon after the hearings were over, the bill came to a vote in the House of Representatives. Just before the vote was taken, a short exchange took place showing that Congress was not even aware of what the drug marihuana was, although they were being asked to outlaw its use:

> *Mr. Snell:* What is the bill?
> *Mr. Rayburn:* It has something to do with something that is called marihuana.
> I believe it is a narcotic of some kind.[21]

The House passed the bill and sent it on to the Senate. It was slightly amended by the Senate and sent back to the House which passed it without even a roll call. There was virtually no debate. President Roosevelt's signing of the bill into law merited only a scant three and a half lines in the *New York Times* on August 3, 1937: "President Roosevelt signed today a bill to curb traffic in the narcotic, marihuana, through heavy taxes on transactions."

[21]U.S., Congress, House, *Congressional Record*, 81st Cong., 1st sess., 1937, p. 5575.

Epilogue

In the years that elapsed between the passage of the Marihuana Tax Act and the present, America experienced three major wars, a presidential assassination, the resignation of both a president and a vice-president in disgrace, a Communist witch-hunt, a flight to and landing on the moon, beatniks, hippies, yippies, desegregation, major riots in many of the nation's cities and campuses, domination of family life by television, the generation gap, and a longing to be perpetually young. Keeping pace with all these significant social and political events was a change in the nation's attitudes and behavior concerning marihuana.

Almost immediately after the Marihuana Tax Act became law, the Bureau of Narcotics was forced to reconsider its position on one of the main arguments it had used to secure passage of the law. First in the trial of Ethel "Bunny" Sohl in Newark, New Jersey, in January 1938, and then in the trial of Arthur Friedman in New York City in April of the same year, the defense argued that the murders committed by their clients were the result of their use of marihuana. An expert witness, Dr. James Munch, who had previously testified on behalf of the bureau at the congressional hearings on marihuana, testified again at both trials that marihuana would make people do things they would not otherwise do. The implication was that the accused were not responsible for their actions. The jury accepted the defense in both cases, and instead of asking for the death penalty they recommended life imprisonment.

By contending that marihuana incited its users to violence, Anslinger had unwittingly undermined his own efforts to secure maximum sentences in any and all drug-related trials. He now had no other choice but to revise the bureau's position with regard to marihuana's effects on crime. Instead of claiming that marihuana invariably incited criminal activity, the bureau's new position was that the effects of marihuana were so variable that no general statement could be made as to its effects on criminality.

248

The bureau also had to deal with direct challenges to its promulgations concerning marihuana, the most important of which was a lengthy scientific study which came to be known as the LaGuardia Report. Reacting to sensationalistic newspaper claims that New York's youth was teetering on the brink of an orgy of marihuana-induced crime and sex, Mayor Fiorello LaGuardia asked the cooperation of the New York Academy of Medicine to conduct an investigation of the alleged problem in New York. The academy appointed a distinguished panel of social and medical scientists to perform the first sociological and laboratory studies of marihuana in America. The report, published in 1944, contradicted the bureau's official position on every one of its conclusions, among which were that:

> Marihuana is used extensively in the Borough of Manhattan but the problem is not as acute as it is reported to be in other sections of the United States.
> The distribution and use of marihuana is centered in Harlem.
> The majority of marihuana smokers are Negroes and Latin Americans.
> The practice of smoking marihuana does not lead to addiction in the medical sense of the word.
> The sale and distribution of marihuana is not under the control of any single organized group.
> The use of marihuana does not lead to morphine or heroin or cocaine addiction and no effort is made to create a market for these narcotics by stimulating the practice of marihuana smoking.
> Marihuana is not the determining factor in the commission of major crimes.
> Marihuana smoking is not widespread among school children.
> Juvenile delinquency is not associated with the practice of smoking marihuana.

And finally:

> The publicity concerning the catastrophic effects of marihuana smoking in New York City is unfounded.[1]

The second part of the study involved medical and psychological tests of individuals under the influence of marihuana. Seventy-seven volunteers were studied; seventy-two were prisoners, five were paid subjects; forty-eight were previous marihuana users, twenty-nine had never used marihuana before. Marihuana was administered either in the form of cigarettes or as an extract taken by mouth.

A number of minor transient effects were observed such as euphoria, anxiety, relaxation, nervousness, hunger, thirst, disorientation, loss of motor coordination, impaired learning and memory, and in some

---

[1]La Guardia Commission, *The Marihuana Problem in the City of New York* (Metuchen, New Jersey: Scarecrow Reprint Corp. 1973), p. 24–25.

instances, mild psychotic reactions consisting of "mental confusion and excitement of a delirious nature with periods of laughter and of anxiety." Contrary to the position of the Federal Bureau of Narcotics the committee found that

> Marihuana does not change the basic personality structure of the individual. It lessons inhibition and this brings out what is latent in his thoughts and emotions but it does not evoke responses which would otherwise be totally alien to him. It induces a feeling of self-confidence, but this is expressed in thought rather than in performance.[2]

In essence, the findings of the committee were totally in opposition to the statements issued by the Federal Bureau of Narcotics and newspaper reports from around the country.

The LaGuardia Report was not the only laboratory study of marihuana in the 1940s. The United States Public Health Service also conducted experiments on the effects of the drug. Unlike the LaGuardia study, however, subjects in this study were allowed to smoke as many marihuana cigarettes as they wanted for thirty-nine days. The marihuana was supplied by the Bureau of Narcotics. All six subjects in the experiment were prisoners, all had been previous users of marihuana, and ironically, all had been imprisoned for violation of the Marihuana Tax Act.

While the researchers noted a lessening of inhibition and removal of restraint resulting from marihuana use, "in the majority of cases . . . aggression and belligerency are not commonly seen."[3] The researchers also noted that tolerance to marihuana appeared to have developed during the study but in no instances did they observe physical dependence.

Several other studies were also reported in the 1940s, but these were primarily reports of psychiatric problems allegedly related to marihuana use. For the most part, the patients were nearly always black. One study involved thirty-four black and one white soldiers. In another, the ratio of blacks to whites was twenty to one. At Fort McClellan, Alabama, where the ratio of recruits was seven whites to one black, fifty-five black and five white soldiers were referred for psychiatric service related to marihuana use.

Commenting on the large numbers of black soldiers requiring treatment, Charen and Perelman, the authors of one of these studies stated:

> The preponderance of Negros is due, we believe, to the peculiar need marihuana serves for them. The Negro psychopath or neurotic faces not only inner anxiety resulting from childhood family relationships, but also suffers

---

[2]*Ibid*, p. 218.
[3]*Ibid*, p. 214.

from a feeling of resentment towards the submission which is required by the white stereotypes of Negro behavior. Marihuana, insofar as it removes both anxiety and submission and therefore permits a feeling of adequacy, enables the Negro addict to feel a sense of mastery denied him by his color. The white psychopath or neurotic not faced with a dual problem of personality and environmental frustration finds alcohol or other forms of satisfaction more acceptable.[4]

This view was shared by others as well. Said Drs. E. Marcovitz and H. J. Myers:

It needs to be emphasized that the problem is not the drug but the user of the drug—the addict in relation to himself and his society.[5]

The LaGuardia Report along with these psychiatric studies, and especially medical studies from Mexico, did not go unnoticed on the international scene. During the first meeting of the United Nations Commission on Narcotic Drugs held after World War II in 1946, the commission decided that there was no necessity for appointing a sub-committee to study cannabis. The commission gave as its reasons for this decision, "some medical opinion in the United States [i.e., the LaGuardia Report] and in Mexico had been advanced that marihuana did not offer any real danger, and had little influence on criminal be-haviour. Indeed, the Mexican physicians were of the opinion that its use had no ill effect on the health of the user. The representative for Mexico wondered whether in these circumstances too strict restrictions on the use of this plant, the production of which was in fact prohibited in Mexico, would not result in its replacement by alcohol, which might have worse results."[6]

Anslinger, the American representative "did not share this point of view and quoted a number of concrete examples, proving the relation-ship between the use of marihuana and crime. He considered the recent report of certain United States physicians on the subject to have been extremely dangerous."[7]

Higher Penalties

When the Marihuana Tax Act became law in 1937, it called for imprisonment of up to five years and/or a fine of $2000 as punishment

[4]S. Charen and L. Perelman, "Personality Studies of Marihuana Addicts," *American Journal of Psychiatry*, 102 (1946): 68.

[5]E. Marcovitz and J. J. Myers, "The Marihuana Addict in the Army," *War Medicine*, 6 (1946): 389.

[6]K. Bruun, L. Pan, and I. Rexed, *The Gentlemen's Club* (Chicago: University of Chicago Press, 1975), p. 195.

[7]J. J. Anslinger, "More on Marihuana and Mayor La Guardia's Committee Report," *Journal of the American Medical Association* 128 (1945): 1187.

for breaking each provision of the law. The length of the actual term and fine were left to the discretion of the court. These penalties and sentencing powers remained in force until 1951 when the Boggs Act became the new law of the land.

Passage of the Boggs Act (named after its sponsor, Congressman Hale Boggs) followed on the heels of an alleged upsurge in narcotic usage, especially on the part of the young after 1947. According to Anslinger:

> the present wave of juvenile addiction struck us with hurricane force in 1948 and 1949, and in a short time had two Federal hospitals bursting at the seams.[8]

In Congress, Representative Boggs warned his fellow lawmakers that:

> In the first 6 months of 1946, the average age of addicted persons committed... at Lexington, Ky. was 37½ years.... During the first 6 months of 1950, only 4 years later, the average age dropped to 26.7 years, and 766 patients were under the age of 21.... In New York City alone it has been estimated that 1 out of every 200 teen-agers is now addicted to some type of narcotics.[9]

In Boggs's opinion, the reason for the epidemic rise in drug addiction among the young was the mild sentences being handed out for violation of the country's drug laws, a view solidly endorsed by Commissioner Anslinger.

To meet the threat to America, Boggs called for draconian penalties for those found guilty of violation of the nation's drug laws. At first, Congress was unwilling to adopt such measures. But during the hearings before the Special Senate Committee to Investigate Organized Crime in Interstate Commerce headed by Senator Kefauver, Congress got the impression that organized crime was behind much of the drug traffic in America, and in 1951 it endorsed Boggs's proposals. As a result, conviction for a first drug-related offense called for imprisonment of two to five years. Conviction for a second offense was punishable by a mandatory sentence of not less than five nor more than ten years. Conviction for a third offense carried a penality of ten to twenty years.

While the legislators were primarily concerned with the heroin user, they included marihuana in the Boggs Act because of the belief that marihuana was a "stepping stone" to heroin use. This "stepping stone" theory had become Commissioner Anslinger's new weapon in his fight to keep America safe from the evil he saw in marihuana. Testifying before a committee headed by Boggs, Anslinger explained that

[8] *New York Times,* June 19, 1951.
[9] *Congressional Record,* 97th Congress, 1951, p. 8197.

> Over 50 percent of those young addicts started on marihuana smoking. They started there and graduated to heroin; they took the needle when the thrill of marihuana was gone.[10]

In 1956, some congressmen were of the opinion that even stiffer penalties were needed to meet the challenge of drug abuse. At the Daniel Committee hearing which eventually led to the adoption of the Narcotic Control Act of 1956, Texas Sen. Price Daniel played straight man to Commissioner Anslinger:

> *Daniel:* Now, do I understand it from you that, while we are discussing marijuana, the real danger there is that the use of marijuana leads many people eventually to the use of heroin, and the drugs that do cause them complete addiction, is that true?
>
> *Anslinger:* That is the great problem and our great concern about the use of marijuana, that eventually if used over a long period, it does lead to heroin addiction.[11]

Later on in the question period, Senator Walker resurrected the marihuana-mayhem theme Anslinger had previously discarded in light of its use as a defense ploy. But he couldn't completely renounce the connection:

> *Welker:* Mr. Commissioner, my concluding question with respect to marijuana: Is it or is it not a fact that the marijuana user has been responsible for many of our most sadistic, terrible crimes in this Nation, such as sex slayings, sadistic slayings, and matters of that kind?
>
> *Anslinger:* There have been instances of that, Senator. We have had some rather tragic occurrences by users of marijuana. It does not follow that all crimes can be traced to marijuana. There have been many brutal crimes traced to marijuana. But I would not say that it is the controlling factor in the commission of crimes.
>
> *Welker:* I will grant you that it is not the controlling factor, but is it a fact that your investigation shows that many of the most sadistic, terrible crimes, solved or unsolved, we can trace directly to the marijuana user?
>
> *Anslinger:* You are correct in many cases, Senator Welker.
>
> *Welker:* In other words, it builds up a false sort of feeling on the part of the user and he has no inhibitions against doing anything; am I correct?
>
> *Anslinger:* He is completely irresponsible.[12]

The feeling of the committee with respect to marihuana was summed up by Senator Daniel as he addressed his fellow lawmakers:

> [Marihuana] is a drug which starts most addicts in the use of drugs. Marihuana, in itself a dangerous drug, can lead to some of the worst crimes

---

[10]U.S. Congress, House of Representatives, Committee on Ways and Means Hearings on H.R. 3490, 82nd Congress, 1st Session, 1951, p. 206.

[11]Quoted in R. King, *The Drug Hang Up* (Springfield, Ill.: C. C. Thomas, 1974), p. 90.

[12]*Ibid.*, p. 91.

committed by those who are addicted to the habit. Evidently, its use leads to
the heroin habit and then to the final destruction of the persons addicted.[13]

Convinced that marihuana posed a dual threat to domestic tranquility, Congress included it in the Narcotics Act of 1956 which raised the
mandatory minimum sentence for marihuana possession and also called
for a minimum ten-year prison sentence to anyone selling narcotics,
including marihuana, to a juvenile.

The International Game

By 1948, after his initial setback at the United Nations two years
earlier, Anslinger began urging the U.N. commission to adopt a Single
Convention which would encompass all existing international agreements on drugs, and at the same time he began lobbying for more
stringent international measures against cannabis to bring it under the
guidelines of the proposed Single Convention.

This was Anslinger at his devious best. From past experience, he
knew how to play off international and domestic politics against each
other. First, he used the bureau's "gore" file to persuade U.N. members
of the crimes marihuana was capable of inciting and then he turned
around and used American ratification of an international agreement
against cannabis to buttress the bureau's domestic campaign against the
drug.

By 1954, the U.N. Economic and Social Council was finally persuaded that "there is no justification for the medical use of cannabis
preparations"—a very important victory for Anslinger and other U.N.
supporters of his anticannabis ideas since in essence this pronouncement stripped cannabis of any remaining legitimacy.

In 1961, the United Nations finally adopted the Single Convention,
the terms of which stated that each participating country could "adopt
such measures as may be necessary to prevent misuse of, and illicit
traffic in, the leaves of the cannabis plant."[14]

Anslinger could not have asked for more. However, Congress
waited until 1967 to approve American participation in the convention.
Proof of Anslinger's perspicacity came three years later in the form of the
Comprehensive Drug Abuse Prevention and Control Act. As part of the
law, Congress decreed that in the case of drugs such as cannabis which
had no recognized medical uses, the attorney general was invested with

[13]*Congressional Record*, 102nd Congress, 1956, p. 9015.
[14]U.N. Single Convention on Narcotic Drugs, 1961, Article 28(3).

authority over reclassification since control of such drugs was required by "United States obligations under international treaties."

DISSENT

During the late 1950s and early 1960s, the main users of marihuana were still blacks and Mexican-Americans. Most Americans were either completely unaware of any marihuana problem, or if they were aware, they could not have cared less since it involved minority groups and fringe elements of white society only. But in the middle 1960s, a sudden "epidemic" of marihuana use erupted not in the ghettos of America's cities but in its bastions of higher learning. The new users were not the poor and the uneducated black or Mexican-American, but native-born, middle-class, white college students. By 1969, as many as 70 percent of the students at some colleges had allegedly tried marihuana at least once,[15] and the parents of these students began to worry lest their sons and daughters lose their sanity, become involved in sexual orgies, become wanton murderers, go on to heroin, or wind up in prison. Marihuana seemed to have snuck up on them from behind and crashed into them unexpectedly like a rear-end collision.

A *New York Times* commentator spoke for most Americans when he wrote:

> Nobody cared when it was a ghetto problem. Marijuana—well, it was used by jazz musicians in the lower class, so you didn't care if they got 2-to-20 years. But when a nice, middle-class girl or boy in college gets busted for the same thing, then the whole country sits up and takes notice.[16]

The soaring use of marihuana on college campuses and the ever-present danger that a son or daughter might wind up in prison brought pressure to bear on the nation's lawmakers to reevaluate the marihuana laws, and new fact-finding commissions were appointed.

Even before the rising tide of marihuana had begun to engulf the college campuses, however, there were rumblings of disagreement with the Bureau of Narcotics's position on marihuana.

In 1962, President Kennedy's Ad Hoc Panel on Drug Abuse dismissed the alleged link between marihuana and sexual abuse and criminality as "limited." The dangers claimed for marihuana, it said, were "exaggerated," and it challenged the "long criminal sentences imposed on an occasional user or possessor of the drug" as being in "poor social perspective."[17]

[15]*Time* Sept. 26, 1969.
[16]*New York Times*, Feb. 15, 1970.
[17]Quoted in King, p. 93–94.

In 1963, the President's Advisory Commission on Narcotics and
Drug Abuse was outspoken in its condemnation of contemporary
marihuana policy:

> An offender whose crime is sale of a marijuana reefer is subject to the
> same term of imprisonment as the peddler selling heroin. In most cases the
> marijuana reefer is less harmful than any opiate. For one thing, while
> marijuana may provoke lawless behavior, it does not create physical depen-
> dence. This Commission makes a flat distinction between the two drugs and
> believes that the unlawful sale or possession of marijuana is a less serious
> offense than the unlawful sale or possession of an opiate.[18]

The same criticism of the law lumping marihuana with narcotic
drugs was voiced in 1967 by President Johnson's Commission on Law
Enforcement and Administration of Justice:

> Marijuana is equated in law with the opiates, but the abuse characteristic
> of the two have almost nothing in common. The opiate produces physical
> dependence. Marijuana does not. A withdrawal sickness appears when use
> of the opiates is discontinued. No such symptoms are associated with
> marijuana. The desired dose of opiates tends to increase over time, but this is
> not true of marijuana. Both can lead to psychic dependence, but so can
> almost any substance that alters the state of consciousness.[19]

The Johnson commission also challenged the "stepping stone"
theory:

> There is evidence that a majority of the heroin users who come to the
> attention of public authorities have, in fact, had some prior experience with
> marijuana. But this does not mean that one leads to the other in the sense
> that marijuana has an intrinsic quality that creates a heroin liability. There are
> too many marijuana users who do not graduate to heroin, and too many
> heroin addicts with no known prior marijuana use, to support such a theory.
> Moreover there is no scientific basis for such a theory.[20]

In 1970, one of Anslinger's best weapons in his battle to stifle criticism of the bureau's marihuana policy was dealt a serious blow—
Congress demanded an end to ignorance. In its compromise with President Nixon over general hospital appropriations, Congress demanded
that the Secretary of Health, Education and Welfare issue annual reports
on the health consequences of marihuana along with recommendations
for reassessing the legal status of marihuana.

At the same time, however, Congress adopted the Comprehensive
Drug Abuse Prevention and Control Act. Although the law characterized marihuana as a drug with high addiction liability, potentially
dangerous, and having no recognized medical use in the United States,

[18]Ibid., p. 94.
[19]Ibid., p. 94–95.
[20]Ibid., p. 95.

it did lower federal penalties for first-time marihuana convictions and permitted probation. The act also placed discretion over reclassification of marihuana in the hands of the Attorney General. Finally, the act also called for yet another commission to evaluate marihuana.

Although he had agreed to a fact-finding commission, President Nixon said "this about that":

> As you know, there is a commission that is supposed to make recommendations to me about this subject, and in this instance, however, I have such strong views that I will express them. I am against legalizing marijuana. Even if this commission does recommend that it be legalized, I will not follow that recommendation. . . . I do not believe that legalizing marijuana is in the best interests of our young people and I do not think it's in the best interests of this country.[21]

For its part, the commission recommended legalization and it did not recommend legalization. It suggested that private use and distribution of small amounts of marihuana be legalized whereas public possession be subject to confiscation and forfeiture.

True to his promise, President Nixon rejected these recommendations. But local communities and various states had already begun to take the legalization question into their own hands. In 1971, the college town community of Ann Arbor, Michigan, adopted the unprecedented step of decriminalizing marihuana from a felony prison offense to a misdemeanor, with a maximum sentence of ninety days in jail and/or a $100 fine.

The new law did not go unchallenged. Opponents appealed to the state court that Ann Arbor had no legal authority to enact legislation with was contrary to state law, but the courts ruled against them. The penalty was subsequently dropped to a five-dollar fine which could be paid like a local traffic ticket.

Undeterred, opponents of the law made the marihuana statute an issue in the local elections and they were successful in electing a majority of antimarihuana councilmen. In 1973, Ann Arbor's lenient marihuana laws were rescinded.

Now the pro-marihuana forces went to work. A referendum on the marihuana issue was called for. In 1974, a majority of the electorate voted for the "decriminalization ordinance" and once again marihuana became a five-dollar misdemeanor in Ann Arbor.

Meanwhile, a number of states were enacting new marihuana legislation of their own. In 1973, Oregon became the first state to decriminalize marihuana by changing the penalty for possession from a felony prison sentence to a $100 civil misdemeanor fine. Other states to

[21]*Ibid.*, p. 101.

follow Oregon's lead included Alaska, California, Colorado, Michigan, Nebraska, New York, North Carolina, Ohio, and South Dakota.

Although they have not yet decriminalized marihuana, other states, like New Mexico, Louisiana, Florida, and Illinois, have passed laws making marihuana available for therapeutic purposes such as in the treatment of glaucoma for which marihuana has been found beneficial.

On the federal level, a speech instructor in Washington, D. C., Robert Randall, became the first American since 1937 to be allowed to smoke marihuana legally. Randall suffers from glaucoma. As a result of studies showing marihuana's ability to ameliorate the effects of the disease, a court battle in which the District of Columbia Supreme Court acquitted him for growing marihuana on the unique defense of "necessity" to commit a criminal act to safeguard his health, and dogged persistence in fighting bureaucratic red tape, he was accorded the right to use the drug without fear of punishment.

Although a far step from decriminalization, Randall's case represents a major push in that direction since official recognition that marihuana has therapeutic value undermines one of the bulwarks supporting its illegality as put forth by the Comprehensive Drug Abuse Prevention and Control Act of 1970.

Another significant event on the national level was the formation of the National Organization for the Reform of Marihuana Laws (NORML) in 1970. NORML is a national lobbying group dedicated to persuading the nation's lawmakers that marihuana is a relatively harmless drug and its use should be decriminalized. Its impact on the national level is yet to be determined. Its significance is that it represents a concerted, devoted, and formally organized attempt to change the current marihuana laws.

MARIHUANA TODAY

Beginning in the late 1960s, there has been a virtual inundation of scientific papers published on marihuana. In 1979, I was able to locate over 8000 references dealing with cannabis, most of which were published after 1965.

Whereas many of the social questions about marihuana are no longer being debated—e.g., does marihuana incite criminal behavior? (it doesn't); is marihuana a "stepping stone" to heroin? (it isn't); does marihuana unleash hitherto inhibited sexual passions? (it doesn't)—there is still a considerable controversy about whether marihuana is medically safe. Questions about marihuana's botanical classification are still at matter of debate and there are still many other areas of debate concerning cannabis. In the remaining pages of this book, some of the recent developments in cannabis research and some of the major controversies associated with marihuana use today will be examined.

PREVALENCE

In 1972, the National Commission on Marihuana estimated that about twenty-four million Americans over the age of eleven had tried marihuana, at least eight million were still using it, and about half a million were using it every day. The commission suggested that "marihuana use may be a fad, which if not institutionalized, will recede substantially in time."[22]

During the late 1960s and early 1970s, marihuana became a symbol of the generation gap, of opposition to the Vietnam War, of frustration and anger at efforts to suppress protest. Smoking marihuana represented a direct challenge to the establishment—"We're smoking marihuana—what are you going to do about it?"

By the mid-1970s, marihuana was no longer a symbol or merely a fad—it was commonplace. Current estimates place the number of people who have used it at least once in the United States at over fifty million. At least twelve million are believed to use it on a regular basis and there is no sign that its use is abating. While still illegal in the United States, almost as many people smoke marihuana as drink alcohol, which is legal.

BOTANICAL CLASSIFICATION

Ever since Linnaeus first dubbed the hemp plant *Cannabis sativa*, there has been vigorous debate among botanists as to whether there is only one species of the plant with different varieties, or whether there are in fact several distinct species among which *Cannabis sativa* and *Cannabis indica* were the two clearest examples of the latter argument. In 1924, the Russian botanist Janischewsky championed the polytypic argument and claimed that in addition to *Cannabis sativa* and *Cannabis indica*, there was a third distinct species which he called *Cannabis ruderalis*.

One of the main problems in deciding between the monotypic and polytypic arguments is that the characteristics of the cannabis plant change depending on the conditions under which it is grown. For example, seeds taken from the United States and planted in India will

[22]National Commission on Marihuana and Drug Abuse, *Marihuana: A Signal of Misunderstanding* (Gov't Printing Office: Washington, D.C., 1972), p. 332.

eventually give rise to plants that resemble those that have always been grown in India if the seeds are continually replanted, and vice versa for those taken from India and replanted in the United States. However, despite the genetic plasticity of the seeds, there are still enough subtle differences between the plants to enable botanists to differentiate between the three different species. As stated by R. Schultes, one of the foremost authorities on the botany of cannabis: "critical studies of the literature; examination of material from many areas preserved in several of the world's largest herbaria; preliminary fieldwork in Afghanistan; and a survey of the plantings of cannabis in Mississippi from seed imported from many localities around the world under the auspices of the National Institutes of Health—all have combined to convince us that Cannabis is not monotypic and that the Russian concept that there are several species may be acceptable."[23]

As presently classified, cannabis is included along with the hops plant (*Humulus*) in a distinct family called Cannabaceae, although some botanists still prefer to assign it to the Moraceae family which also includes the mulberry plant to which cannabis was closely tied in ancient China.

The origin of the cannabis plant is generally placed in Central Asia, and from there it is believed to have spread to China, India, Persia, the Arab countries, Europe, Africa, and the Americas.

Instead of being merely a question of academic hair-splitting, the issue of a mono- versus a polytypic species has taken on far-reaching implications in the law courts. The single-species argument was the position taken by the U.S. Congress when it adopted the Marihuana Tax Act in 1937. At that time it outlawed *Cannabis sativa, not* marihuana, believing them to be one and the same. No mention was made of *Cannabis indica* or *Cannabis ruderalis*, since it was assumed that these were different varieties of *Cannabis sativa* rather than different species.

In recent court cases, however, defense lawyers have argued that their clients were caught in possession of *Cannabis indica* or *Cannabis ruderalis*, and that these materials are not legally outlawed since the Marihuana Tax Act specifies *Cannabis sativa* only. Since there are several distinct species of cannabis, they argue, then it must be proved that their clients were in possession of *Cannabis sativa*, and since there is no way of making such a judgment once the plant is chopped into pieces, they have moved for dismissal of any and all charges. Not surprisingly, the prosecution dismisses the polytypic argument and instead argues for the monotypic position.

---

[23]R. E. Schultes, W. M. Klein, T. Plowman, and T. E. Lockwood, "Cannabis: An Example of Taxonomic Neglect," in *Cannabis and Culture*, ed. V. Rubin (The Hague, Netherlands: Mouton), p. 24.

Chemistry

The chemical materials in cannabis which give it its peculiar characteristics are called cannabinoids. Cannabinol, once considered the principal active ingredient in marihuana, was isolated as early as the 1890s. Subsequent tests, however, showed it to be biologically inactive (although recent studies have shown that it may affect the actions of other cannabinoids). In the 1930s, another important cannabinoid, cannabidiol, was isolated, but it too was found devoid of biological activity (although like cannabinol, it may affect the actions of other cannbinoids).

The major psychoactive substance in marihuana was finally isolated and identified in 1964 by two Israeli chemists, Y. Gaoni and R. Mechoulam, as l-delta-9-trans-tetrahydrocannabinol (Δ^9-THC). Subsequently, a number of other cannabinoids have been identified which either exert some biological effects of their own or else modify the effects of Δ^9-THC, among which are Δ^8-THC, cannabicyclol, cannabichromene, cannabigerol, cannabivarol, cannabidivarol, and a long list of similar compounds.

The proportion of these substances in the plant varies according to where it is grown. Cannabis grown in the temperate climates, where its fiber is strong, contains little Δ^9-THC and a relatively high proportion of cannabidiol. On the other hand, in hot climates where the plant is grown for its psychoactive effects, it contains a high proportion of Δ^9-THC and relatively little cannabidiol.

Actually, there are two main systems of nomenclature where the cannabinoids are concerned. The pyran system is the one which refers to the principal psychoactive substance in marihuana as Δ^9-THC, whereas the monoterpenoid system calls this compound Δ^1-THC. The differences result from the way in which the atoms in the tetrahydrocannabinol molecule are numbered.

The amount of tetrahydrocannabinols present in marihuana depends on the particular species (i.e., *Cannabis sativa*, *Cannabis indica*, *Cannabis ruderalis*) and the conditions under which it is raised. Marihuana extract distillate may contain as much as 30 percent Δ^9-THC, but this is a considerably higher percentage than that usually found in marihuana. When marihuana is burned as it is when it is smoked, however, about 50 percent of the Δ^9-THC content may be destroyed.

The identification and quantification of Δ^9-THC in marihuana was an achievement of enormous importance for cannabis research, since it meant that at long last it was possible to compare and contrast the effects of marihuana used in different laboratories and even in different countries. By specifying the Δ^9-THC content present in the marihuana being tested, scientists had the equivalent of a ruler against which they could evaluate the potency of a particular sample of marihuana.

In addition to the cannabinoids, there are a considerable number of noncannabinoid compounds present in cannabis, among which are various alkaloids, terpenes, phenols, flavonoids, and sugars. Whether these materials affect the actions of the cannabinoids in any way is unknown as yet. Whatever their contribution, however, the most important ingredient in marihuana is still Δ^9-THC.

ANALYSIS

A major interest in cannabis research, at least from a forensic standpoint, has been the development of test procedures to identify whether a substance is or is not cannabis.

The two major tests up until very recently have been the Beam and Duquenois tests. In the Beam test, cannabis is mixed with alcohol and potassium hydroxide. If a purple color develops, cannabis is presumed present. The Beam test, however, is more sensitive to some cannabinoids (e.g., cannabidiol and cannabigerol) than others, and the mixture will not turn purple if these cannabinoids are missing. The Duquenois test involves mixing the unknown substance with vanillin, acetaldehyde, alcohol, and hydrochloric acid. If a violet color develops, the test substance is presumed to be cannabis. Although the Duquenois test is more sensitive than the Beam test, it is not as specific—a violet color will also develop in the presence of other substances, e.g., coffee.

Up until recently, these two tests, in conjunction with botanical examination of plant samples, were the methods relied upon by the Federal Bureau of Narcotics and Dangerous Drugs in identifying marihuana.

However, other methods have since been developed which are more sensitive and are able to determine not only if a substance is cannabis, but also which cannabinoids are present, and how much of each cannabinoid is contained in a test substance.

PHARMACOLOGY

The smallest amount of Δ^9-THC in a marihuana cigarette that will produce a "high" is about 5 mg. However, since about 50 percent of this amount will be destroyed in the smoking process, the threshold dose is about 2.5 mg. For a 70-kg man, this would amount to a dose of 0.035 mg/kg. Studies of acute toxicity in animals indicates that the LD_{50}, i.e., the doses that would kill 50 percent of the animals, is 42.5 mg/kg if injected directly into the blood stream and about 106 mg/kg when inhaled in smoke. In other words, a lethal dose of Δ^9-THC is about 5000 times higher than that which produces a "high."

When smoked, the effects of marihuana begin to be felt in about five to fifteen minutes. Maximum effect occurs in about sixty minutes. The parts of the body that receive the highest amount of the drug are those which have the richest blood supply, e.g., the liver, lung, kidney, and spleen. Surprisingly, the brain attains relatively low levels compared with these other organs.

Δ^9-THC is metabolized by the liver to 11-hydroxy-delta-9-tetrahydrocannabinol (11-OH-Δ^9-THC) which also has psychoactive effects. This metabolite is then itself broken down into other metabolites, which are in turn broken down further, and eventually these metabolites are eliminated through the feces and the kidney. About 50 percent of the Δ^9-THC content in the body is eliminated in the form of metabolites in the first twenty-four hours. However, traces of the drug can still be found in the human body as long as eight days later.

Studies in animals have shown that the cannabinoids and/or their metabolites may accumulate in the brain following frequent exposure. The greater the accumulation, the longer it would take for the brain to rid itself of the drug and this could account for reports of flashbacks and memory impairment in longtime users of marihuana.

Tolerance (the phenomenon whereby greater amounts of drug have to be taken to receive the same kind of effect originally experienced) occurs to some of the drug's effects, but not all. In animals, tolerance has been observed in the suppression of aggressiveness in Siamese fighting fish, the loss of the righting reflex in frogs, analgesia in rats, ataxia in dogs, hypothermia, bradycardia, electroencephalographic activity, and brain tissue respiration, just to list a few phenomena. On the other hand, tolerance has not been observed for the drug's tachycardia effect in man.

To account for the claim by many marihuana users that they do not become "high" when they first begin using the drug, some researchers have postulated the concept of "reverse tolerance" whereby sensitivity increases, rather than decreases, following repeated drug usage. However, there is little scientific basis to support such a notion. Instead, it appears that new users have to learn to identify a "high" so that they can recognize it with repeated usage.

Closely related to tolerance is the phenomenon of physical dependence. Physical dependence is evident when a characteristic withdrawal syndrome occurs when chronic drug use is discontinued to certain drugs. Although dependence is always associated with tolerance, the reverse is not necessarily the case—tolerance need not result in drug dependence. The latter seems to be the case for marihuana. Although there are a few reports of marihuana-related withdrawal symptoms consisting of anxiety, restlessness, headache, nausea, sweating, increased pulse rate, and acute abdominal cramps, such experiences are uncommon.

Physical Effects

In 1968, the first "double-blind" study (in which neither the researcher nor the subject knows if marihuana or some inert placebo is being tested at the time) was reported by a group of Harvard scientists. Although the study was sanctioned by the Federal Bureau of Narcotics, the scientists noted that "we do not consider it appropriate to describe here the opposition we encountered from governmental agents and agencies and from university bureaucracies."[24]

Part of the experiment was aimed at comparing the effects of marihuana on previous users with people who had never used the drug before. It took over two months to locate nine volunteers among the Boston college population who qualified for nonuser status!

After a series of experiments comparing users and nonusers, the researchers could detect no adverse effects from smoking marihuana by either group. Marihuana increased heart rate and dilated blood vessels in the eye, but did not affect pupil size, respiratory rate, or blood sugar levels.

On the basis of their findings, the scientists concluded that marihuana was a mild intoxicant and that previous studies in which adverse effects had been found had either used doses of marihuana that were much higher than those commonly used, and/or failed to incorporate proper control procedures which enabled researchers in those studies to confirm any preexisting biases they might have originally had.

In general, most studies have since corroborated these findings. No damaging effects to the body have been found resulting from occasional use of marihuana. Although marihuana produces many changes in the body, these changes rarely have clinical importance. This is not to say, however, that chronic use of marihuana, or regular use of more potent forms of marihuana than that currently available in the United States, may not prove harmful.

Several alarming reports over the last few years have, in fact, pointed to serious potential dangers resulting from chronic marihuana

[24]A. T. Weil, N. E. Zinberg, and J. M. Nelsen, "Clinical and Psychological Effects of Marihuana in Man," *Science*, 162 (1968): 1234.

use. Although most of these reports have been refuted, they are worthy of attention for what they say and for the flaws that have been noted in connection with such studies.

ADVERSE EFFECTS

Chromosomal Damage. In 1974, Dr. Morton Stenchever reported that he had discovered twenty female and twenty-nine male marihuana users who had three times the number of chromosomal breaks more than a group of twenty nonmarihuana users.[25] Among the users with chromosomal damage, twenty-two had used marihuana only once a week or less.

However, Stenchever presented little information about his marihuana users. He had no idea if they had had any chromosomal damage before they had become marihuana users, nor did he know if they were users of any other drugs linked to chromosomal damage.

A subsequent study by other researchers failed to corroborate Stenchever's results.[26] The subjects in this latter study had no chromosomal aberrations before being recruited for the experiment nor were they users of any drugs associated with such damage.

Immunity. Dr. Gabriel Nahas, an outspoken opponent of marihuana usage, reported that T-lymphocytes taken from marihuana smokers and grown in laboratory cultures exhibited depressed cellular immunity responses.[27] Although Nahas's results have been corroborated by other scientists, there have also been failures in attempts to support this finding. At UCLA, researchers challenged the immune systems of chronic marihuana smokers directly, not in a laboratory culture. All reacted with strong immune reactions.[28] Moreover, there is no evidence linking marihuana to susceptibility to colds, infections, or cancer, all of which might be expected if marihuana compromised the body's immune systems.

Lung Damage. Several studies have reported serious lung damage

[25]M. A. Stenchever, T. J. Kunysz, and M. Allen, "Chromosomal Breakage in Users of Marihuana," *American Journal of Obstetrics and Gynecology* 118 (1974): 106–13.

[26]W. W. Nichols, R. C. Miller, W. Heneen, C. Bradt, L. E. Hollister, and S. Kanter, "Cytogenetic Studies on Human Subjects Receiving Marihuana and Delta-9-Tetrahydrocannabinol," *Mutation Research* 26 (1974): 413–7.

[27]G. G. Nahas, N. Suciu-Foca, J. P. Armand, and A. Morishima, "Inhibition of Cellular Mediated Immunity in Marihuana Smokers," *Science* 183 (1974): 419–20.

[28]M. J. Silverstein, and P. J. Lessin, "Normal Skin Test Responses in Chronic Marihuana Users," *Science* 186 (1974): 740–1.

on the part of chronic marihuana smokers.[29] Bronchitis, emphysema, and lesions of lung tissue have been noted in marihuana users, but it is not known if it is the kind of smoke (marihuana) or the amount of smoke (any smoke, e.g., cigarettes) that is responsible for the damage.

Brain Damage. One of the most persistent claims about chronic use of marihuana is that it causes brain damage. In 1971, Dr. A. M. G. Campbell published a report purporting to document such damage.[30] The report concerned air encephalogram measurements in ten marihuana smokers who had been using marihuana daily for three to eleven years. According to their report, the brains of these marihuana users had enlarged cerebral ventricles, suggestive of brain atrophy.

Shortly after its publication, however, the report was criticized for its shortcomings. One researcher noted that "in the 10 cases reported [by Campbell] all 10 men had used LSD—many of them over 20 times—as well as cannabis, and 8 of the 10 had used amphetamines. One subject had a previous history of convulsions, four had significant head injuries, and a number had used sedatives, barbiturates, heroin, or morphine. On the basis of these facts, speculative connection between cannabis use and brain damage is highly suspect."[31]

It might also be suggested that the changes in ventricle size preceded marihuana usage and that these men had resorted to marihuana as one way of coping with whatever symptoms they were experiencing as a result of the changes in their brains.

Psychosis. A venerable claim about marihuana is that it causes insanity. During the nineteenth century, Moreau had experimented with marihuana as a "model psychosis." The Indian Hemp Drugs Commission and several other reports by physicians serving in India also seriously considered marihuana's potential for mental illness. While many of these reports affirmed the possible link between chronic cannabis use and mental illness, the methods and data of the time would not stand up to modern criteria for such studies.

Previously, and even currently, most of the problems associated with cannabis came from non-Western countries where malnutrition, disease, and various social conditions undoubtedly combined to precipitate psychopathology. The use of cannabis by patients in psychiatric institutions does not mean that cannabis precipitates psychoses. It is just

[29]F. S. Tennant, M. Preble, T. J. Pendergast, and P. Ventry, "Medical Manifestations Associated with Hashish," *Journal of the American Medical Association*, 216 (1971): 1965–1969.

[30]A. M. G. Campbell, M. Evans, J. L. G. Thomason, and M. J. Williams, "Cerebral ATrophy in Young Cannabis Smokers," *Lancet* 1 (1971): 1219–24.

[31]E. M. Brecher, "Marihuana: The Health Question," *Consumer Reports*, 40 (1975): 147.

as likely, for instance, that people with psychiatric problems will rely on cannabis to deal with their problems when cannabis is readily available, just as alcohol is often relied on to deal with personal difficulties in this country. And although cannabis may precipitate psychiatric illness in certain individuals, it may not be very unique in this respect.

By far the most common adverse response to marihuana in this country is acute panic. Disorientation, depersonalization, confusion, and dizziness sometimes occur in people not accustomed to the drug or in people who absorb larger doses than they have previously been accustomed to. In such cases, intense panic and anxiety are sometimes experienced as a response to these feelings. In general, these feelings can be calmed through the support and assurance of more experienced users. In any case, they disappear as the drug is eliminated from the body.

Another not uncommon reaction to use of marihuana is acute paranoia. This response, however, is often a reaction to fear of detection by the police.

Several modern-day studies, especially one conducted on chronic ganja users in Jamaica, lend no support to the premise of marihuana-induced insanity.[32] A 1971 report by Drs. Harold Kolansky and William Moore, which appeared in the *Journal of the American Medical Association*, allegedly documenting psychosis in a number of their patients, has been discredited.[33] In one of these cases, the researchers cite the example of a young boy who was seduced by a homosexual who happened to give the boy a marihuana cigarette. According to Kolansky and Moore, the marihuana made him psychotic!

Amotivational Syndrome. Up until very recently, marihuana has been associated with the poor, especially those in certain minority groups like the Chicano and the Negro in America. Since there was (and still is) little incentive to work harder at menial tasks in which these people are often employed, it is not surprising that their work output may have been less than expected. And since a lack of motivation is contrary to the Protestant work ethic, it had to be accounted for. Unless one adopts a racist attitude (which many do) and argues that some races are less capable than others because they are born that way, other explanations must be sought. In the case of marihuana, the fact that it was often associated with the poor and underprivileged in many countries throughout the world made it a convenient scapegoat upon which to blame an apparent lack of motivation on the part of those who used the drug.

[32]V. Rubin, and L. Comitas, *Ganja in Jamaica* (The Hague, Netherlands: Mouton, 1975).
[33]H. Kolansky, and W. Moore, "Effects of Marihuana on Adolescents and Young Adults," *Journal of the American Medical Association* 216 (1971): 486–92.

Recent studies from Jamaica, however, indicate that where marihuana (ganja) is an intrinsic part of everyday life, work output at menial jobs does not suffer. In rural Jamaica, anthropologists report that "rather than hindering, [ganja] permits its users to face, start and carry through the most difficult and distasteful manual labor. . . . workers are motivated to carry out difficult tasks with no decrease in heavy physical exertion, and their perception of increased output is a significant factor in bolstering their motivation to work."[34]

THERAPEUTIC USES

Over its long history, cannabis has been used to treat a multitude of medical problems from toothaches to venereal disease. The many problems for which it has been tried have been documented throughout this book. Adoption of antimarihuana laws throughout the world, however, virtually eliminated any modern efforts to investigate possible therapeutic applications of the drug. Only in recent years has there been a resurgence of research in this area.

Glaucoma. In 1971, during experiments conducted for an altogether different purpose, researchers accidentally discovered that marihuana substantially reduced intraocular pressure.[35] This discovery generated considerable interest on the part of some physicians since they saw a possible use for marihuana in the treatment of glaucoma—the third-leading cause of blindness in America.

Glaucoma is a disorder in which fluid pressure inside the eye increases and ultimately damages the optic nerve, causing blindness. Subsequent studies have borne out marihuana's ability to reduce intraocular pressure among not only glaucoma sufferers, but nonsufferers as well. While marihuana has no curative action in the disorder, it is able to delay further loss of sight through its ability to reduce intraocular pressure. As already noted, marihuana's efficacy in the treatment of glaucoma has been recognized at both the federal and state levels, and many glaucoma sufferers are able to use marihuana legally to treat their disorder.

Cancer Chemotherapy. As if they did not already suffer enough, cancer patients undergoing chemotherapy experience several disconcerting and unpleasant side effects of treatment such as vomiting and nausea. By chance, one such patient happened to use marihuana after receiving chemotherapy and he found that the vomiting he usually experienced was alleviated. He reported this effect to his doctors, and

[34]Rubin and Comitas, *Ganja.*
[35]R. S. Hepler, and I. R. Frank, "Marihuana Smoking and Intraocular Pressure," *Journal of the American Medical Association* 217 (1971): 1392.

subsequent testing at the Harvard Medical School proved so satisfactory that marihuana has become a routine adjunct to cancer chemotherapy at some hospitals.[36]

Asthma. Asthma is a respiratory disorder in which breathing becomes labored due to constriction of the bronchial vessels of the lung. Among marihuana's many actions in the body is dilation of the bronchial vessels, allowing more air to enter the lung. Although there are other drugs which also produce bronchodilation, marihuana's actions turned out to be longer lasting.[37] Recent interest in this potential application for asthma sufferers has seen the development of an aerosal of Δ^9-THC, but only for experimental purposes.

Epilepsy. During the late 1940s, in one of the few studies to be conducted with marihuana, researchers reported a beneficial effect of the drug in the treatment of epilepsy.[38] Five epileptic children were treated. In three cases, the outcome was the same as that seen with traditional drug therapy. In the other two, seizures were almost entirely suppressed for one child and were totally eliminated in the other, although conventional drug therapy had previously proven unsatisfactory. Although this report should have generated considerable interest among the medical profession, it was totally ignored until the 1970s when the anticonvulsant properties of certain cannabinoids (particularly cannabidiol) were rediscovered and are currently receiving clinical testing for possible formal use in the treatment of epilepsy.

Other conditions for which marihuana is currently being evaluated include hypertension, analgesia, and insomnia. Conceivably, marihuana may one again become a familiar drug in the medical drug arsenal.

Summary and Conclusions

Cannabis is undoubtedly one of the world's most remarkable plants. Virtually every part of it has been used and valued at one time or another. Its roots have been boiled to make medicine; its seeds have been eaten as food by both animals and men, been crushed to make

[36]S. E. Sallan, N. E. Zinberg, and E. Frei, "Antiemetic Effects of Delta-9-Tetrahydrocannabinol in Patients Receiving Cancer Chemotherapy," *New England Journal of Medicine* 293 (1975): 795–7.

[37]D. P. Tashkin, B. J. Shapiro, and I. M. Frank, "Acute Effects of Smoked Marihuana and Oral Delta-9-Tetrahydrocannabinol: Mechanisms of Increased Specific Airway Conductance in Asthmatic Subjects," *American Review of Respiratory Diseases* 109 (1974): 420–8.

[38]J. H. Davis, and H. H. Ramsey, "Antiepileptic Action of Marihuana-Active Substances," *Federation Proceedings* 8 (1949): 284–5.

industrial oils, and been thrown onto blazing fires to release the minute intoxicating cannabinoids within; the fibers along its stem have been prized above all other fibers because of their strength and durability; and its resin-laden leaves have been chewed, steeped in boiling water, or smoked as a medicine and an intoxicant.

Cannabis is also remarkable for being able to change its sex—under certain conditions, male plants can turn into females and vice versa. Its hereditary characteristics are also transmutable—plants grown from seeds taken from American plants and grown in India will, within a few generations, resemble plants that have always grown in India more closely than their American relatives, and vice versa for seeds taken from India and grown in America.

It is not without reason that cannabis has been many things to many people.

For most of its history, cannabis has led two lives. In countries such as India and the Middle East, cannabis has been extolled and villified for its resinous exudation; in Russia, Europe, and America, national and private fortunes have been built around its fiber.

Around 1850, East conquered West. Cannabis fiber was replaced by other materials and cannabis resin began appearing in doctors' bags, pharmacies, cafes, and private homes. At first, it was simply a novelty in the West, something to conjure up the mystery and enchantment of far-off countries. Writers and artists, and later musicians, intoxicated themselves with it because they felt it expanded their consciousness and gave them insights unattainable by other means. There was little concern over the use of the drug until the middle classes across Europe and American began to notice that minority groups, immigrants from certain countries, and the unskilled working class (often one and the same) were using the drug. Because these people seemed unmotivated, lazy, prone to criminality, sexual promiscuity, and mental illness, cannabis came to be regarded as a social danger, responsible for these and all other ills characteristic of the lower socioeconomic classes. Whereas these people used marihuana to help them cope with the drudgery of their everyday lives, the middle classes considered that marihuana was responsible for their problems. Each class saw cause and effect in a different perspective.

The middle-class perception of marihuana as evil has persisted over the centuries and has been almost universal until the last fifteen years. Only after the sons and daughters of prominent middle-class parents had been arrested and branded as criminals, and in many cases sentenced to long terms in prison, only after it became apparent that marihuana was no longer a minority-group problem, only after fear and panic about marihuana's alleged dangers began to dissipate in the light of evidence to the contrary from their own sons and daughters, only when the erstwhile marihuana users became the nation's lawmakers—only then did attitudes and laws about marihuana change.

The 12,000-year-long history of cannabis clearly shows that laws against its usage—whether it was hashish in the Arab countries, dagga in Africa, or marihuana in America—have been adopted in response to a perceived threat to society. Since the main users of cannabis drugs were typically poor and from minority groups as well, cannabis was a feared substance, something capable of unleashing the unbridled passions thought to be characteristic of these people. Only when marihuana became commonplace were such beliefs challenged and disregarded.

In the United States, it is fashionable to single out Harry Anslinger as the cunning, ruthless mastermind behind the country's antimarihuana laws. True enough, Anslinger was not above distortion and exploitation of the marihuana issue when it suited his purposes. He felt that the ends justified the means, and for Anslinger, marihuana posed a danger to the nation that had to be suppressed. In Anslinger's mind, drug use, whether narcotics or marihuana, was a criminal act, not a disease. As such, it had to be fought and overcome by any means available.

Had it not been for Anslinger, the United States might not have witnessed as concerted an effort to outlaw marihuana nationally as it did, but there still would probably have been some federal legislation outlawing the drug. Other countries had such laws and did not have any Anslinger-like bureaucrat to muster support for these laws. The combination of the man, the office, and the times fashioned America's policy toward marihuana—other countries adopted antimarihuana laws because they also perceived a threat from marihuana or because they felt obliged to do so as a result of agreement on the international level, to oppose and restrict marihuana usage. One man, whatever the issue, does not single-handedly persuade an entire nation to persecute a group of people or a drug like marihuana.

Whatever marihuana's past, its future will inevitably be that of decriminalization and eventual legalization, subject no doubt to the same regulatory measures as those that apply to alcohol. Whether the United States and the rest of the world faces a real threat to its social and economic stability, to progress, and to morality (however they are defined), as a result of the liberalization of marihuana (and other drugs) is left to the future. If the past is any example, instability, lack of progress, and immorality will or will not occur regardless of whatever happen where marihuana is concerned.

Bibliography

Agehananda Bharati. *The Tantric tradition*. London: Rider & Co., 1965.

Aldrich, M. R. Tantric cannabis use in India. *Journal of Psychedelic Drugs*, 1977, *9*, 227–233.

Aldrich, M. R. A brief legal history of marihuana. Phoenix: Do I Now Foundation, n.d.

Allbutt, R. C. *A system of medicine*. New York: Macmillan, 1900.

Allen, J. L. *The reign of law: A tale of the Kentucky hemp fields*. New York: Macmillan, 1900.

Almanach Prophetique pour 1849. Paris: Aubert and Co., 1849.

American State Papers. Washington, D.C.: Gales and Seaton, 1860.

Andrews, G., & Vinkenoog, S. (Eds.). *The book of grass*. New York: Grove Press, 1967.

Anslinger, H., & Cooper, C. R. Marihuana, assassin of youth. *American Magazine*, 1937, *124*, 18–19, 150–153.

Anslinger, H. J. & Oursler, W. *The murderers. The story of the narcotics gangs*. New York: Farrar, Strauss, 1961.

Armstrong, W. D. & Parascandola, J. American concern over marihuana in the 1930's. *Pharmacy in History*, 1972, *14*, 25–34.

Arnold, D. O. The meaning of the La Guardia report: The effects of marihuana. In J. L. Simmons (Ed.), *Marihuana: Myths and realities*. North Hollywood, Calif.: Brandon House, 1967, 111–135.

Artamonov, M. I. Frozen tombs of the Scythians. *Scientific American*, 1965, *212*, 101–109.

Avalon, A. *Tantra of the great liberation*. New York: Dover, 1972.

Ball, M. V. The effects of haschisch not due to cannabis indica. *Therapeutic Gazette*, 1910, *34*, 777–780.

Ball, M. V. Marihuana—Mexican name for cannabis, also called loco weed in certain parts of Texas. In *Canal Zone papers*. Balboa Heights. Univeristy of Virginia Law Library, Charlottesville, Virginia.

Balzac, H. *Letters to Madame Hanska*. Boston: Little, Brown, 1900.

Barash, L., Stankiewica, H., & Farmilo, R. C. A review of hemp cultivation in Canada. Unpublished manuscript, Addiction Research Foundation, Toronto, Ontario, Canada, 1971.

Beal, S. *Fo-sho-hing-tsan-king*. Oxford: Clarendon Press, 1883.

Becker, H. S. *Outsiders: Studies in the sociology of deviance*. New York: The Free Press, 1963.

Becker, H. S. History, culture and subjective experience: An exploration of the social bases of drug-induced experiences. *Journal of Health and Social Behavior*, 1967, *8*, 163–176.

Bell, J. On the haschish or Cannabis indica. *Boston Medical and Surgical Journal*, 1857, *56*, 209–216.

Belinger, L. Textiles from Gordion. *Bulletin of the Needle and Bobbin Club*, 1962, *46*, 5–20.

Benet, S. Early diffusion and folk uses of hemp. In V. Rubin (Ed.), *Cannabis and culture.* The Hague: Mouton, 1975, 39–49.

Betts, E. M. (Ed.). *Thomas Jefferson's farm book.* Princeton: Princeton University Press, 1953.

Bishop, J. L. *A history of American manufactures.* New York: Augustus M. Kelley, 1966. (Originally published, 1868.)

Blackwood, A. A psychic invasion. In *The tales of Algernon Blackwood.* New York: E. P. Dutton, 1939.

Bloomquist, E. R. *Marihuana.* Beverly Hills, Calif.: Glencoe Press, 1968.

Blum, A. *On the origin of paper.* New York: R. R. Bowker, 1934.

Bogardus, E. S. *The Mexican in the United States.* Berkeley: University of California Press, 1934.

Bonnie, R. J. & Whitebread, C. H. The forbidden fruit and the tree of knowledge: An inquiry into the legal history of American marihuana prohibition. *Virginia Law Review,* 1970, *56,* 971–1023.

Bonnie, R. J. & Whitebread, C. H. *The marihuana conviction.* Charlottesville: University of Virginia Press, 1974

Bouquet, R. J. Cannabis. *Bulletin on Narcotics,* 1950 2, 14–30.

Bowrey, T. *A geographical account of countries round the Bay of Bengal, 1669 to 1679.* Nendeln, Liechtenstein: Kraus Reprint, 1967.

Boyce, S. S. *Hemp.* New York: Orange and Judd, 1900.

Bragman, L. J. The weed of insanity. *Medical Journal and Record,* 1925, *122,* 416–418.

Brand, J. *Observations on the popular antiquities of Great Britain.* London: Henry Bohn, 1848.

Brigham, A. Review of Moreau de Tours, J: "Du hachisch et de l'alienation mentale." *American Journal of Insanity,* 1846, *2,* 275–281.

Bromberg, W. Marihuana: A psychiatric study. *Journal of the American Medical Association,* 1939, *113,* 4–12.

Browne, E. G. A chapter from the history of Cannabis indica. *St. Bartholomew's Hospital Journal,* 1897, *4,* 81–86.

Brunner, T. F. Marihuana in ancient Greece and Rome? The literary evidence. *Bulletin of the History of Medicine,* 1973, *47,* 344–355.

Burke, T. *Limehouse nights.* New York: Robert M. McBride, 1926.

Burton, R. *Anatomy of melancholy.* New York: Vintage, 1977.

Camp. W. A. Antiquity of hemp as an economic plant. *Journal of New York Botanical Gardens,* 1936, *37,* 110–114.

Campbell, J. M. On the religion of hemp. In *Indian Hemp Drugs Commission Report.* Simla, India: 1893–1894, vol. 2, pp. 250–252.

Cannabis indica. *Journal of the Medical Society of New Jersey,* 1938, *35,* 51–52.

Carrier, L. *The beginnings of agriculture in America.* New York: Johnson Reprint Co. 1962.

Carter, T. F. *The invention of paper in China.* New York: Columbia University Press, 1925.

Chang, K. *The archeology of ancient China.* New Haven: Yale University Press, 1968.

Chang, K. C. *Food in Chinese culture.* New Haven: Yale University Press, 1977.

Charen, S. & Perelman, L. Personality studies of marihuana addicts. *American Journal of Psychiatry,* 1946, *102,* 674–682.

Chohoki, K. *[A handy guide to papermaking]* (C. E. Hamilton, Trans.). Berkeley: University of California Press, 1948.

Chopra, I. C., & Chopra, R. N. The present position of hemp drug addiction in India. *Indian Medical Research Memoirs,* 1939, *31,* 1–119.

Christison, A. On the natural history, action, and uses of Indian hemp. *Monthly Journal of Medical Science,* 1851, *13,* 26–45.

Clark, V. S. *A history of manufactures in the United States.* New York: McGraw-Hill, 1929.

Cole, C. W. *Colbert and a century of French mercantilism.* Columbia University Press, 1939.

Coleman, J. W. *Slavery times in Kentucky.* Chapel Hill: University of North Carolina Press, 1940.

Cooper, C. R. *Here's to crime.* Boston: Little, Brown, 1937.

Craven, W. F. *The southern colonies in the seventeenth century.* Baton Rouge: Louisiana State University Press, 1949.

Creighton, C. On indications of the hachish-vice in the Old Testament. *Janus,* 1903, *8,* 241–246, 297–303.

Crosby, A. W. *America, Russia, hemp and Napoleon.* Columbus: Ohio State University Press, 1965.

Culpeper, N. *Complete herbal.* London: Richard Evans, 1813.

Da Orta, G. *Colloquies on the simples and drugs of India.* London: Henry Southern, 1913.

Darmester, J. (Ed.). *The Zend-Avesta.* London: Oxford University Press, 1883.

D'Erlanger, B. H. *The last plague of Egypt.* London: Lovat Dickson & Thompson, 1936.

De Givry, E. G. *Illustrated anthology of sorcery, magic and alchemy.* New York: Causeway Books, 1973.

De Nerval, G. *The women of Cairo, scenes of life in the Orient.* New York: Harcourt and Brace, 1956.

De Pasquale, A. Farmacognosia della "canape indiana." *Estratto dai Lavori dell'Instituto di Farmacognosia dell'Universita di Messina,* 1967, *5,* 24.

De Quincey, T. *Confessions of an Opium Eater.* New York: American Library, 1966.

De Sumichrast, F. C. (Ed.). *The works of Théophile Gautier.* New York: George D. Sproul, 1890.

Dickson, D. T. Bureaucracy and morality: An organizational perspective on a moral crusade. *Social Problems,* 1968, *16,* 143–156.

Dimoff, P. Autour d'un projet de roman de Flaubert: "La Spirale." *Revue d'Histoire Littéraire de la France,* 1948, *48,* 309–335.

Dolan J. P. A note on the use of cannabis sativa in the 17th century. *Journal of the South Carolina Medical Association,* 1971, *67,* 424–427.

Doolittle, J. *Social life of the Chinese.* New York: Harper & Bros., 1865.

Dope cigarette peddling among British musicians. *Melody Maker,* February 22, 1936.

Drake, W. D. *The connoisseur's handbook of marihuana.* San Francisco: Straight Arrow Books, 1971.

Duster, T. *The legislation of morality: Law, drugs, and moral judgment.* New York: The Free Press, 1970.

Du Toit, B. M. Cannabis sativa in Sub-Saharan Africa. *South African Journal of Science,* 1974, *70,* 266–270.

Du Toit, B. M. Dagga: The history and ethnographic setting of Cannabis sativa in southern Africa. In V. Rubin (Ed.), *Cannabis and culture.* The Hague: Mouton, 1975, 81–118.

Du Toit, B. M. Historical factors influencing cannabis use among Indians in South Africa. *Journal of Psychedelic Drugs,* 1977, *9,* 235–246.

Dwarakanath, S. C. Use of opium and cannabis in the traditional systems of medicine in India. *Bulletin on Narcotics,* 1965, *17,* 15–19.

Eaton, C. *A history of the old South.* New York: Macmillan, 1966.

Eaton, V. G. How the opium habit is acquired. *Popular Science Monthly,* 1888, *33,* 663–667.

Eberland, W. *The local cultures of South and East China.* Leiden: E. J. Brill, 1968.

Ebin, D. (Ed.). *The drug experience.* New York: Grove Press, 1965.

Effects of hashish. *Scientific American,* 1869, *21,* 183.

Eliade, M. *Shamanism.* New York: Pantheon Books, 1964.

Emboden, W. A. Ritual use of Cannabis sativa L.: A historical-ethnographic survey. In P. T. Furst, (Ed.), *Flesh of the gods: The ritual use of hallucinogens.* New York: Praeger, 1974.

Fleischhauer, W. The old man of the mountain: The growth of a legend. *Symposium,* 1955, *9,* 79–90.

Fossier, A. E. The marihuana menace. *New Orleans Medical and Surgical Journal,* 1931, *44,* 241–252.

Frank, T. *An economic survey of ancient Rome.* Patterson, N.J.: Pageant Books, 1959.

Frazer, J. G. *Balder the beautiful.* London: MacMillan, 1920.

Frazer, J. G. *The magic art.* London: MacMillan, 1920.

Frazer, J. G. *The scapegoat.* London: MacMillan, 1920.

Gates, P. W. *Agriculture and the Civil War.* New York: Knopf, 1965.

Glatt, M. M. Historical note—hashish and alcohol "scenes" in France and Great Britain 120 years ago. *British Journal of Addictions,* 1969, *64,* 99–108.

Godwin, H. Pollen-analytic evidence for the cultivation of cannabis in England. *Review of Palaeobotany and Paynology,* 1967, *4,* 71–80.

Godwin, H. The ancient cultivation of hemp. *Antiquity,* 1967, *41,* 42–49.

Gomila, F. R., Lambow, M. C. Present status of the marihuana vice in the United States. In R. Walton, (Ed.), *Marihuana.* Philadelphia: J. P. Lippincott, 1938.

Gordon, B. L. *Medicine throughout antiquity.* Philadelphia: T. A. Davis, 1949.

Gowers, H. E. Haschisch hallucinations. *The American Physician,* 1906, *32,* 72–76.

Granet, M. *Chinese civilization.* London: Kegan Paul, Trench, Trubner and Co., 1930.

Gray, J. P. On the use of Cannabis indica in the treatment of insantiy. *American Journal of Insanity,* 1860, *16,* 80–89.

Gray, L. C. *History of agriculture in the southern United States.* Gloucester, Mass.: Peter Smith, 1958.

Greyre, G. *The masters and the slaves.* New York: Knopf, 1968.

Grierson, G. A. On references to the hemp plant occurring in Sanskrit and Hindi literature." In *Indian Hemp Drugs Commission Report.* Simla, India: 1893–1894, vol. 3, pp. 246–249.

Grinspoon, L. *Marihuana reconsidered.* Cambridge, Mass.: Harvard University Press, 1971.

Grover, G. W. *Shadows lifted or sunshine restored on the horizon of human lives: A treatise on the morphine, opium, cocaine, chloral and hashish habit.* Chicago: Stromberg, Allen & Co., 1894.

Guerra, F. Sex and drugs in the 16th century. *British Journal of Addiction,* 1974, *69,* 269–290.

Hamarneh, S. Pharmacy in medieval Islam and the history of drug addiction. *Medical History,* 1972, *16,* 226–237.

Hamilton, H. C. The pharacopoeial requirements for Cannabis sativa. *Journal of the American Pharaceutical Association.* 1912, *1,* 200–203.

Hamilton, H. C. Lescohier, A. W., & Perkins, R. A. The physiological activity of Cannabis sativa. *Journal of the American Pharaceutical Association,* 1913, *2,* 22–30.

Harrison, R. H. *Healing herbs of the Bible.* Leiden: E. J. Brill, 1966.

Hasheesh. *Medical Record,* 1935, *142,* 488.

Hashish. *Once a Week,* 1868, *18,* 350–351.

The hashish. *Chamber's Edinburgh Journal,* 1848, *10,* 341–343.

A hashish-house in New York: The curious adventures of an individual who indulged in a few pipefuls of the narcotic hemp. *Harper's New Monthly Magazine,* 1883, *67,* 944–949.

Hayden, W. *Narrative.* Wilmington, Del.: Afro-American Historical Series, n.d.(Originally published, 1846.)

Hayes, M. H., & Bowery, L. E. Marihuana. *Journal of Criminology,* 1933, *23,* 1086–1098.

Hechtlinger, A. *The great patent medicine era, or without benefit of doctor.* New York: Grosset & Dunlap. 1970.

Helmer, J. *Drugs and minority oppression*. New York: Seabury Press, 1975.

Herndon, G. M. Hemp in colonial Virginia. *Agricultural History*, 1963, *37*, 86–93.

Herndon, G. M. A war inspired industry. *Virginia Magazine of History and Biography*, 1966, *74*, 301–311.

Hill, H. The ganja problem in Singapore. *International Criminal Police Review*, 1968, *23*, 209–213.

Hobby, E. W. *Eastern Uganda*. London: Anthropological Institute of Great Britain, 1902.

Hodgson, M. G. S. *The order of Assassins*. S'Gravenhage: Mouton, 1955.

Hoffman, A. *Unwanted Mexican Americans*. Tucson: University of Arizona Press, 1974.

Hopkins, J. F. *A history of the hemp industry in Kentucky*. Lexington: University of Kentucky Press, 1951.

Howe, J. Early attempts to introduce the cultivation of hemp in eastern British America. Paper presented at the meeting of the New Brunswick Historical Society, 1897.

Hunter, D. *Papermaking through eighteen centuries*. New York: Wm. E. Rudge, 1930.

Increasing menace of marihuana. *Canadian Medical Association Journal*, 1934, *34*, 561.

Indian Hemp Drugs Commission Report (7 vols.). Simla, India: 1893–1894.

James, T. Dagga: A review of fact and fancy. *South African Journal*, 1970, *44*, 575–580.

Jarvis, C. S. The drug smugglers of Egypt. *Cornhill*, 1937, *156*, 588–605.

Julien, M. S. Chirurgie Chinoise—Substance anesthétique employée en Chine, dans le commencement du IIIᵉ siècle de notre ere, pour paralyser momentanement la sensibilité. *Comptes Rendus de l'Académie des Sciences*, 1894, *28*, 195–198.

Junod, H. A. *The life of a South African tribe*. Neuchatel, Switzerland: Attinger Bros., 1912.

Kalant, O. J. Ludlow on cannabis: A modern look at a nineteenth century drug experience. *International Journal of the Addictions*, 1971, *6*, 309–322.

Kalant, O. J. Moreau, hashish and hallucinations. *International Journal of the Addictions*, 1971, *6*, 553–560.

Kalant, O. J. Report of the Indian Hemp Drugs Commission, 1893–1894: A critical review." *International Journal of the Addictions*, 1972, *7*, 77–96.

Kaplant, J. *The marihuana prohibition*. New York: Pocket Books, 1972.

Kemp, P. *The healing ritual*. London: Faber and Faber, 1935.

Keng, H. Economic plants of ancient North China as mentioned in Shih Ching (Book of Poetry), *Economic Botany*, 1974, *28*, 391–410.

Kimmens, A. C. (Ed.). *Tales of hashish*. New York: Wm. Morrow, 1977.

King, F. A. The origin of hemp "the assauger of grief." *East African Medical Journal*, 1953, *30*, 345–347.

King, R. *The drug hang-up*. Springfield, Ill.: Charles C Thomas, 1974.

Kingman, R. The green goddess: A study in dreams, drugs and dementia. *Medical Journal and Record*, 1927, *126*, 470–475.

Kolb, L *Drug addiction*. Springfield, Ill.: Charles C Thomas, 1962.

Kopp, R. Baudelaire et le haschisch, expérience et documentation. *Revue des Sciences Humaines*, 1967, *125*, 467–476.

Kung, C. T. *Archeology in China*. Toronto: University of Toronto Press, 1959.

LaGuardia Committee on Marihuana. *The marihuana problem in the City of New York*. Metuchen, N.J.: Scarecrow Reprint Corp., 1973. (Originally published, 1944.)

Laidler, P. W. Pipes and smoking in South Africa. *Transactions of the Royal Society of South Africa*, 1938, *26*, 1–1.

Laird-Clowes, W. An amateur assassin. *Belgravia*, 1877, *31*, 353–359.

Lane, E. W. *The thousand and one nights*. London: Routledge, 1889.

Lane, F. C. The rope factory and hemp trade in the fifteenth and sixteenth centuries. *Journal of Economic and Business History*, 1932, *4*, 824–840.

Larken, P. M. *An account of the Zande*. Khartoum: McCorquodale & Co., 1926.

Laufer, B., Hambly, W. D. & Linten, R. Tobacco and its uses in Africa. Chicago: Auld Museum of Natural History, 1930.

Leo Africanus. *The history and description of Africa and of the notable things therein.* New York: Burt Franklin, n.d.

Lescarbot, M. *The history of New France.* Toronto: Champlain Society, 1914. (Originally published, 1609.)

Levey, M. Medieval Arabic toxicology. *Transactions of the American Philosophical Society,* 1966, *56,* 5–43.

Lewis, B. The sources for the history of the Syrian Assassins. *Speculum,* 1952, *27,* 475–489.

Li, H. L. An archaeological and historical account of cannabis in China. *Economic Botany,* 1974, *28,* 437–448.

Li, H. L. Origin and use of cannabis in eastern Asia: Linguistic-cultural implications. *Economic Botany,* 1974, *28,* 293–301.

Lipson, E. *The economic history of England.* London: A. C. Black, 1931.

Lucas, A. Some notes on hashish. *Cairo Scientific Journal,* 1911, *5,* 144–159.

Ludlow, F. H. *The hasheesh eater: Being passages from the life of a Pythagorean.* New York: Harper & Bros., 1857.

Lyman, S. M. Strangers in the cities: The Chinese on the urban frontiers. In C. Wallenberg (Ed.), *Ethnic conflict in California history.* Berkeley: University of California Press, 1970.

MacCulloch, J. A. (Ed.). *The mythology of all races.* Boston: Marshall Jones, 1928.

MacDonald, N. Hemp and imperial defence. *Canadian Historical Review,* 1936, *17,* 385–398.

Manorique, S. *Travels of Fray Sebastien Manorique* (1629–1643) E. E. Luard & Fr. H. Hasten (Eds. and trans.). Oxford: Hakluyt Society, 1927.

Marcovitz, E., & Myers, H. J. The marijuana addict in the army. *War Medicine,* 1944, *6,* 389.

Marihuana grown on vacant lots. *Journal of the American Medical Association,* 1935, *105,* 891.

Maurer, D., & Vogel, D. *Narcotics and narcotic addiction.* Springfield, Ill.: Charles C Thomas, 1954.

McCormack, G. R. Marihuana. *Hygeia,* 1937, *15,* 898–899.

McGuigan, H. *Experimental pharmacology.* Philadelphia: Lea & Febiger, 1919.

McKee, S. Report on Manufactures. In S. McKee (Ed.), *Alexander Hamilton's papers on public credit, commerce and finance.* New York: Liberal Arts Press, 1957.

Meisler, S. Federal narcotics czar. *The Nation,* 1960, *190,* 159–162.

The menace of marihuana. *International Medical Digest,* 1937, *77,* 183–187.

Merlin, M. D. *Man and marihuana.* Rutherford, N.J.: Fairleigh Dickinson University Press, 1968.

Mikuriya, T. H. Physical, mental, and moral effects of marihuana: The Indian Hemp Drugs Commission. *International Journal of the Addictions,* 1968, *3,* 253–270.

Mitchell, R. D. Agricultural change and the American revolution. A Virginia case study. *Agricultural History,* 1973, *47,* 119–132.

Moldenke, H. N., & Moldenke, A. L. *Plants of the Bible.* Waltham, Mass.: Chronica Botanica, 1952.

Monroe, J. Canvas, cables, and cordage, made from American and foreign flax and hemp, contrasted. In *Documents, Legislative and Executive, of the Congress of the United States* (vol. 1). Washington D.C.: Gales and Seaton, Co. 1834.

Mookerjee, H. C. India's hemp drug policy under British rule. *Modern Review,* 1948, *84,* 446–454.

Moon, J. B. Sir William Brooke O'Shaughnessy—the foundations of fluid therapy and the Indian telegraph service. *New England Journal of Medicine,* 1967, *276,* 283–284.

Moore, B. *The hemp industry in Kentucky.* Lexington, Ky.: James E. Hughes, 1905.

Moquin, W. (Ed.). *A documentary history of the Mexican Americans.* New York: Praeger, 1971.

Moreau, J. J. *Hashish and mental illness.* New York: Raven Press, 1973.

Morgan, H. W. *Yesterday's addicts.* Norman: University of Oklahoma Press, 1974.

Morley, J. E., & Bensusan, A. D. Dagga: Tribal uses and customs. *Medical Proceedings,* 1971, *17,* 409–412.

Mosk, S. A. Subsidized hemp production in Spanish California. *Agricultural History,* 1939, *13,* 171–175.

Mundy, P. *The travels of Peter Mundy in Europe and Asia. 1608–1667.* Oxford: Hakluyt Society, 1914.

Munroe, J. On the use of American canvas, cables and cordage in the navy. In *Documents, Legislative and Executive of the Congress of the United States* (vol. 2). Washington, D.C.: Gales and Seaton, 1860.

Murphy, E. F. *The black candle.* Toronto: Thomas Allen, 1926.

Musto, D. F. The Marihuana Tax Act of 1937. *Archives of General Psychiatry,* 1972, *26,* 101–108.

Musto, D. F. *The American disease: Origins of narcotic control.* New Haven: Yale University Press, 1973.

Nahas, G. G. *Marihuana—deceptive weed.* New York: Raven Press, 1973.

Nettels, C. P. *The emergence of a national economy.* New York: Holt, Rinehart & Winston, 1962.

Norwich, I. A chapter of early medical Africana. *South African Medical Journal,* 1971, *8,* 501–504.

Nowell, C. E. The old man of the mountain. *Speculum,* 1947, *22,* 497–519.

Osofsky, G. Harlem tragedy: An emerging slum. In J. A. Schwarz (Ed.), *The ordeal of Twentieth century America.* Boston: Houghton Miffin, 1974, 89–111.

Oteri, J. S., & Silvergate, H. A. In the marketplace of free ideas: A look at the passage of the Marihuana Tax Act. In J. L. Simmons (Ed.), *Marihuana: Myths and realities.* North Hollywood, Calif.: Brandon House, 1967, 137–162.

Our home hasheesh crop. *Literary Digest,* 1926, *89,* 64–65.

Parry, A. The menace of marihuana. *American Mercury,* 1935, *36,* 487–490.

Partridge, W. L. Cannabis and cultural groups in a Colombian municipio. In V. Rubin (Ed.), *Cannabis and culture.* The Hague: Mouton, 1975, 147–172.

Paulson, R. (Ed.). *Hogarth's graphic works.* New Haven: Yale University Pres, 1970.

Pelner, L. Long road to Nirvana: Dissertation on marijuana. *New York State Journal of Medicine,* 1967, *67,* 952–956.

Père Ange. *Pharmacopoea Persica.* Paris: 1681.

Pinkerton, J. (Ed.). *A general collection of the best and most interesting voyages and travels in all parts of the world.* London: Longman, Hurst, Ries, Orme, and Brown, 1811.

Pliny, G. C. *Natural History.* London: Loeb Classical Library, 1928.

Plutarch. *Of the names of rivers and mountains, and of such things as are to be found therein.* In *Essays and miscellanies,* London: Simplin, Marshall, Hamilton Kent & Co., n.d. (vol. 5).

Purvis, J. P. *Through Uganda to Mt. Elgon.* London: Fisher Unwin, 1909.

Raven-Hart, R. *Cape of Good Hope.* Cape Town: A. A. Balkewa, 1971.

Reasons, C. E. The addict as a criminal, perpetuation of a legend. *Crime and Delinquency,* 1975, *21,* 19–27.

Reininger, W. Remnants from prehistoric times. In G. Andrews and J. Vinkenoog (Eds.), *The Book of Grass.* New York: Grove Press, 1967.

Reznick, S. P. Marihuana addiction. *Social Work Technique,* 1937, *2,* 173–177.

Rice, T. T. *The Scythians.* New York: Praeger, 1957.

Robertson, M. The poison ship. *Harper's Monthly Magazine,* 1915, *30,* 952–957.

Robinson, V. An essay on hasheesh; including observations and experiments. *Medical Review of Reviews,* 1912, *18,* 159–169, 300–313.

Rohmer, S. *Dope.* New York: McKinlay, Stone and MacKenzie, 1914.

Rosenthal, F. *The herb.* Leiden: E. J. Brill, 1971.

Rowell, E. A. & Rowell, R. *On the trail of marihuana, the weed of madness.* Mountain View, Calif.: Pacific Press, 1939.

Roy, J. C. The soma plant. *Indian Historical Quarterly,* 1939, *15,* 197–207.

Rubin, V. (Ed.). *Cannabis and culture.* The Hague: Mouton, 1975.

Rubin, V., & Comitas, L. *Ganja in Jamaica, a medical anthropological study of chronic marihuana use.* The Hague: Mouton, 1975.

Rudenko, S. I. *Frozen tombs of Siberia.* Berkeley: University of California Press, 1970.

Saulnier, V. L. L'enigme du pantagruelion ou: Du tiers au quart livre. *Études Rabelaisiennes,* 1956, *1,* 48–72.

Schaefer, F. Hemp. *CIBA Review,* 1945, *49,* 1779–1794.

Schafer, E. H. *The golden peaches of Samarkand.* Berkeley: University of California Press, 1963.

Schafer, R. J. *The economic societies in the Spanish world (1763–1821).* Syracuse, N.Y.: Syracuse University Press, 1958.

Schaller, M. The federal prohibition of marihuana. *Journal of Social History,* 1970, 61–73.

Schultes, R. E. Man and marihuana. *Natural History,* 1973, *82,* 59–65.

Schultes, R. E., Klein, W. M., Plowman, T., & Lockwood, T. E. Cannabis: An example of taxonomic neglect. *Botanical Museum Leaflets,* 1974, *23,* 337–367.

Scoville, W. C. *The persecution of Huguenots and French economic development, 1680–1720.* Berkeley: University of California Press, 1960.

Shoenfeld, D. D. The sociological study. In LaGuardia Committee on Marihuana, *The marihuana problem in the City of New York.* Metuchin, N.J.: Scarecrow Reprint Corp., 1973. (Originally published, 1944.)

Sigg, B. W. *Chronic cannabism, fruit of under-development and capitalism.* Unpublished manuscript, Algeria, 1963. [Available from Addiction Research Foundation, Toronto, Canada].

Silvestre de Sacy, M. *Memoir on the dynasty of the Assassins, and on the origin of their name.* Paper presented at a public meeting of the Institute of France, July 1809. In J. von Hammer-Purgstall (Ed.). *The History of the Assassins.* New York: Burt Franklin, 1968.

Simon, C. From opium to hasheesh: Startling facts regarding the narcotic evil and its many ramifications throughout the world. *Scientific American,* 1921, *125A* (Nov. 21), 14–15.

Soueif, M. I. The social psychology of cannabis consumption: Myth, mystery and fact. *Bulletin on Narcotics,* 1972, *24,* 1–10.

Southard, S. L. Cordage made from American and Russian hemp contrasted. In *Documents, Legislative and Executive, of the Congress of the United States* (vol. 3). Washington, D.C.: Gales and Seaton, 1834.

Southard, S. L. Experiments on American water-rotted hemp, and comparison of it with Russian hemp. In *Documents, Legislatives and Executives of the Congress of the United States* (vol. 3). Washington, D.C.: Gales and Seaton, 1860.

Spencer, R. R. Marihuana. *Health Officer,* 1936, *1,* 299–305.

Stanley, H. M. *Through the dark continent.* New York: Harper & Bros., 1879.

Starkie, E. *Baudelaire.* New York: New Directions, 1958.

Stefanis, C., Ballas, C., & Madianou, D. Sociocultural and epidemiological aspects of hashish use in Greece. In V. Rubin (Ed.), *Cannabis and culture.* The Hague: Mouton, 1975, 303–326.

Stock, L. F. *Proceedings and debates of the British Parliaments respecting North America* (vols. 3 & 4). Washington, D. C.: Carnegie Institute of Washington, 1930.

Stow, E. W. *The native races of South Africa.* Cape Town: Juta and Co., 1910.

Talbott, J. H. *A biographical history of medicine: Excerpts and essays on the men and their work.* New York: Grune & Stratton, 1970.

Taylor, B. *A journey to Central Africa: or Life and landscapes from Egypt to the Negro kingdoms of the White Nile.* New York: G. P. Putnam, 1970.

Taylor, N. *Narcotics: Nature's dangerous gifts.* New York: Dell, 1966.

Thisle, J., & Cook, J. P. (Eds.). *Seventeenth century economic documents.* Oxford: Clarendon Press, 1972.

Thompson, G. *Travels and adventures in southern Africa.* Cape Town: Von Riebeeck Society, 1967.

True, R. H., & Klugh, G. F. American-grown cannabis indica. *Proceedings of the American Pharmaceutical Association,* 1909, *57,* 843–847.

Tsien, T. H. *Written on bamboo and silk.* Chicago: University of Chicago Press, 1962.

Tulles, R. P. H. Totemism among the Fang. *Anthropos,* 1912, *1,* 1–87.

Tusser, T. *Five hundred points of good husbandrie.* London: 1580.

Urquhart, D. *The pillars of Hercules; or A narrative of travels in Spain and Morocco in 1848.* New York: Harper & Bros., 1855.

Van der Merwe, N.J. Cannabis smoking in 13th–14th century Ethiopia. In V. Rubin (Ed.). *Cannabis and culture.* The Hague: Mouton, 1975, 77–80.

Van Linschoten, J. *The voyage of John Huyghen Van Linschotin to the East.* New York: Burt Franklin, n.d.

Van Vechten, C. *Peter Whiffle; his life and works.* New York: Knopf, 1925.

Vasquez De Espinosa, A. *Description of the Indies.* Washington, D.C.: Smithsonian Institute Press, 1960. (Originally published, ca. 1620.)

Vedder, H. *Southwest Africa in early times.* New York: Barnes and Noble, 1966.

Veith, I. (Ed.). *The yellow emperor's classic internal medicine.* Baltimore: Williams and Wilkins, 1949.

von Hammer-Purgstall, J. *The history of the Assassins.* New York: Burt Franklin, 1968.

von Wissman, H. *My second journey through Equatorial Africa.* London: Chatto and Windus, 1891.

Walton, J. The dagga pipes of southern Africa. *Research of National Museum,* 1963, *1,* 85–113.

Walton, R. P. *Marihuana.* Philadelphia: J. P. Lippincott, 1938.

Warden, A. J. *The linen trade.* New York: A. M. Kelley, 1968. (Originally published, 1864.)

Wasson, R. G. *Soma, divine mushroom of immortality.* New York: Harcourt Brace Javanovich, 1975.

Waterman, L. *Royal correspondence of the Assyrian Empire.* Ann Arbor: University of Michigan Press, 1930.

Watt, J. M., & Breyer-Brandwijk, M. G. *The medicinal and poisonous plants of southern Africa.* Edinburgh: E. & S. Livingstone, 1932.

Weber, C. M. Mary Warner. *Health Digest,* 1936, *3,* 77–78.

Werner, J. Frankish royal tombs in the cathedrals of Cologne and Saint-Denis. *Antiquity,* 1964, *38,* 201–216.

Wilkinson, P. B. Cannabis indica: An historical and pharmacological study of the drug. *British Journal of Inebriety,* 1929, *27,* 72–81.

Willoughby, W. W. *Opium as an international problem.* Baltimore: Johns Hopkins University Press, 1930.

Wilson, C. *Anglo-Dutch commerce and finance in the eighteenth century.* Cambridge: Cambridge University Press, 1941.

Wolf, W. Uncle Sam fights a new drug menace: Marihuana. *Popular Science Magazine,* 1936, *128,* 14–15, 119–120.

Wollner, J. J., Matchett, J. R., Levine, J., & Valaer, P. Report of the marihuana investigation. *Journal of the American Pharmaceutical Association,* 1938, *27,* 29–36.

Wong, K. C., & Lien-Teh, W. *History of Chinese medicine*. Shanghai: National Quarantine Service, 1936.

Youngs, F. A. *The proclamations of the Tudor queens*. Cambridge: Cambridge University Press, 1976.

Yule, H. (Ed.). *The book of Ser Marco Polo*. New York: Book League of America, 1929.

Zetterstrom, K. Bena Riamba, brothers of the hemp. *Studia Ethnographica Upsaliensia*, 1966, *26*, 151–165.

Zins, H. *England and the Baltic in the Elizabethan era*. Manchester: Manchester University Press, 1972.

Index